The Two-Fold Thought
of Deleuze and Guattari

CRITICAL PERSPECTIVES
A Guilford Series
DOUGLAS KELLNER, Editor
University of Texas at Austin

The Two-Fold Thought of Deleuze and Guattari

Intersections and Animations

CHARLES J. STIVALE

THE GUILFORD PRESS
New York   London

©1998 The Guilford Press
A Division of Guilford Publications, Inc.
72 Spring Street, New York, NY 10012
http://www.guilford.com

Printed in the United States of America

This book is printed on acid-free paper.

Last digit is print number: 9 8 7 6 5 4 3 2 1

Library of Congress Cataloging-in-Publication Data

Stivale, Charles J.
    The two-fold thought of Deleuze and Guattari : intersections and
animations / Charles J. Stivale.
        p.   cm. — (Critical perspectives) (Includes bibliographical
references and index.)
    ISBN 1-57230-325-5 (alk. paper). — ISBN 1-57230-326-3 (pbk. :
alk. paper)
    1. Deleuze, Gilles. 2. Guattari, Felix. 3. Criticism—
History—20th century. I. Title. II. Series. III. Series: Critical
perspectives (New York, N.Y.)
PN94.S75   1998
194—dc21   98-6844
                                                                      CIP

To Michael Giordano,
who enlivens the fold of friendship

PREFACE

> What one says comes from the depths of
> one's ignorance, the depths of one's own
> underdevelopment.
>
> *–Gilles Deleuze to Michel Cressole (1973c)*

> To some extent, one is always at the extreme
> *(pointe)* of one's ignorance, which is exactly
> where one must settle in, at the extreme of
> one's knowledge or one's ignorance, which is
> the same thing, in order to have something to
> say.
>
> *–Gilles Deleuze to Claire Parnet, ABC*
> *(Deleuze and Parnet 1996): "N comme*
> *Neurologie" (N as in Neurology)*

Date: Sun, 05 Nov 95 22:30:37 +0100 [16:30 EST]
To: deleuze-guattari@jefferson.village.virginia.edu
From: Melissa McMahon @xxx.xxx
Subject: Deleuze is dead
Sender: owner-deleuze-guattari@jefferson.village.virginia.edu

Tonight it was announced on French radio that Deleuze has committed
suicide (one report said that he "s'est défenestré" i.e. threw himself out
a window).

End of File

When the message above appeared online as electronic mail, I watched
the subject line flash across my screen, then let the news settle in. I had not
been as jolted by Guattari's death (by natural causes) several years earlier,
in 1992, for that news reached me well after the fact, and then in the form
of clippings mailed to me by a solicitous French friend. In the intervening
years, Internet access became a daily convenience, then a habit (some would
claim a necessity), with the Deleuze–Guattari List serving as an anchor for

online exchanges and for creative connections to ongoing research on the pair's writings. Thus, the news about Deleuze was transmitted to list sub-scribers within minutes of its revelation in France.

Following this post on a Sunday afternoon (in the United States), Sunday evening (in Europe), and Monday morning (in Australia), there ensued several days of crisscrossed transmissions, of grief and disbelief at first, then expressing more typical philosophical speculation and even some (atypical) tasteless parody. More than a month after the an-nouncement and its confirmation in the press, an occasional post or comment prompted new discussion strings on the subject.

In retrospect, I realize that the news of Deleuze's suicide should not have come as such a jolt. After all, had he not commented dryly during the previous year that, given his weakened physical state, "It's a bit like I were already gone"? And had not this impassioned reader of Beckett already found his nearly exact counterpart in the dying Malone who says: "What tedium. And I thought I had it all thought out. If I had the use of my body I would throw it out of the window. But perhaps it is the knowledge of my impotence that emboldens me to that thought. All hands together, I am in chains" (Beckett 1951, 73; 1962, 55–56)? At the time, however, this model and passage were far from my mind.

Among all the messages transmitted during the first week, the following communiqué resonated the most for me:

Date: Tue, 7 Nov 1995 05:40:43 GMT
To: deleuze-guattari@jefferson.village.virginia.edu
From: eric @xxx.xxx
Subject: RE: That old guy that died
Sender: owner-deleuze-guattari@jefferson.village.virginia.edu

Gilles Deleuze wrote some pretty cool stuff. A friend turned me on to ATP [*A Thousand Plateaus*] a couple of years ago and it is changing my life (arguably!) for the active. I know that they wrote that book for someone who had no prior history with philosophy and it's possible, I suppose, that at some point in the future ATP will be the starting reader in some PHIL1A [introductory philosophy] class somewhere, but I don't know if they ever came across anyone who fit that ideal in either of their lifetimes. As someone who fits that ideal, I think it would have been neat to tell Deleuze that "it works" while knocking back some shots.
[signed] eh

End of File

For some reason that I still do not fully comprehend, "eh"'s quick and quirky note reminded me of just how useful the works of French philosopher Gilles Deleuze and counterpsychoanalyst Félix Guattari could be when approached in the manner of "eh"—as a result of being "turned on" by a friend. A number of readers of "eh"'s post have responded to it with annoyance, for its all too casual, American-style tone, or simply for employing the words "cool" and "neat" in any context associated with Deleuze and Guattari. For me, his post evoked a sign of friendship in a rather uncomplicated manner. Indeed, it underscored the gift of their writings that solicit no reciprocal exchange. This rapport of friendship lies, I believe, at the very core of these authors' collaborative engagement, and this core of friendship is fully confirmed by Deleuze both in his manner and in specific statements he makes in *L'Abécédaire de Gilles Deleuze* (Deleuze's ABC Primer), particularly in the section entitled "F comme Fidélité" (L as in Loyalty).

Such a rapport has marked my own encounters with Deleuze and Guattari's works and, beyond them, with the thoughts and writings of many others. Begun in discussion groups and seminars at the University of Illinois, Urbana–Champaign, in the mid to late 1970s, these encounters continued via correspondence and collaboration throughout the 1980s with readers of Deleuze and Guattari worldwide, and have developed in the 1990s at conferences, in group projects, and, most regularly, through electronic mail exchanges, online discussions, and the creation of a global web of links through which works by and on Deleuze and Guattari are made increasingly accessible.

The subject of this book is the writings of these two provocative thinkers and, especially, the diverse ways in which their thought is intertwined and enfolded through their collaboration. This book's ostensible goal is to provide an initial orientation to these collaborative works, especially for readers who have little or no access to the original French texts or to the many commentaries on them. I say "ostensible goal" because I realize just how tendentious any such orientation becomes. That is, by focusing on certain works and specific facets within those works by Deleuze and Guattari, I necessarily exclude much material and discussion that other readers, with a different orientation, might judge of greater import. Let me emphasize at the outset that my own background is in French literary and cultural studies, not in philosophy, economics, or political science (to select but a few other fields from which Deleuze and Guattari draw). Thus, I undertake this study necessarily as a creative expression of my own angle of approach in reading Deleuze and Guattari's works, the "ground" (*fond*) of a critical formation in domains favorable to this reading, given the authors' interest in things French, literary, and cultural. And, drawing upon the sign of friendship like Deleuze and Guattari themselves, but of course in a more modest fashion, my reflection has developed in connection with work that many other readers and interlocutors have elaborated and, indeed, continue to express daily in ongoing interchange.

I hope to contribute to critical discussions of Deleuze and Guattari in two complementary ways: by examining their writings in relation to intersections between the authors' production of concepts, and by developing creative animations of the thought that these intersections suggest to Deleuze and Guattari's readers and interlocutors. I derive these intersections and animations predominantly from Deleuze and Guattari's works written together in productive collaboration from the late 1960s onward. With *Anti-Oedipus,* Vol. 1 of *Capitalism and Schizophrenia* (1972a), *Kafka: Toward a Minor Literature* (1975), *Rhizome: Introduction* (1976), and *A Thousand Plateaus,* Vol. 2 of *Capitalism and Schizophrenia* (1980), they redefined the grounds on which critical thinking might proceed, drawing from and leading into an array of domains and a multiplicity of perspectives, from and to art and cinema, semiotics and technoculture. As is evident from the bibliography, each of these primary texts is now available in translation, and no commentary or gloss can replace direct engagement with them. However, I believe that a prudent orientation to this collaboration might allow readers not only to approach the primary texts more fruitfully, but also to consider possibilities of working with concepts introduced within them. Finally, I hope that this orientation might help readers to approach in a more knowledgeable fashion the works developed individually by each author, particularly the phase of the 1980s that culminated shortly before Guattari's death in 1992 with the publication of their final collaboration, *What Is Philosophy?*

In embarking upon my examination of this collaborative reflection and creation, I offer a word of caution about the way in which I approach the challenging and compelling terminological and conceptual edifice that Deleuze and Guattari produced. This study consists neither of an exercise in parsing which terms might be derived from which author, nor of examining their collaborative works in a vacuum, separate from earlier and later writings. Furthermore, comments that I have received on earlier versions of this study have pertinently addressed questions that I and many others face in discussing Deleuze and Guattari's works. For example, must one read and prepare such analyses "schizoanalytically" or "rhizomatically"— that is, by following certain analytical models proposed in Deleuze and Guattari's works—in order to be "true" to the spirit, if not the letter, of their writings (assuming that one could determine what being "true" might mean here, and as if Deleuze and Guattari would care)? More specific to my own concerns in this study, would the reader be best served by a discontinuous, intermittent, randomly connected style or by an analytical mode bent on "multiplicity" at all costs for discussions of Deleuze–Guattarian concepts? Obviously not, since Deleuze and Guattari themselves do not do so, relying rather on careful argumentation and exposition of examples, however subtly and intricately interwoven. So how does one make their concepts more accessible, particularly in conjunction with particular forms of creative production?

I adopt a reading strategy according to the authors' own method for critical collaboration, their *pensée à deux*, or "two-fold thought" (my free translation of "thought" or "thinking shared by two"). I am inspired in this strategy by Deleuze's own suggestive statement: "One must speak of the *pensée à deux* as nineteenth-century psychiatrists spoke of *la folie à deux* [a shared madness]. But that is quite all right" (Maggiori 1991, 19). Indeed, the "two" of "two-fold" actually produces "*n*-folds" if we understand this collaborative activity as a constant overlap of two particular sensibilities and *savoirs* (modes of knowing). The result of this collaboration has been to produce myriad intricate "folds" (*plis*) of the individual problematics, and simultaneously to provoke new concepts and speculative insights into diverse facets of contemporary existence and creative activity.

In numerous interviews, the authors have commented on their collaborative methods for producing such intersections and inspiring further animations. Notably, they have suggested that one develops an idea as a "state" within oneself through "stutterings, ellipses, contractions and expansions, inarticulate sounds" that are more easily expressed "as two" (*à deux*). By preparing multiple written versions from this original expression, they understand their burgeoning ideas as "function[ing] like an encrustation or a citation within the other's text," thus producing "a writing of variations" (*une écriture de variations*) (Maggiori 1991, 18). Rather than study the collaborative process per se, however, I wish to consider Deleuze and Guattari's works as expressing "thought" that arises from two individual, fluctuating subjectivities. These works seek to produce a dispersed articulation of concepts *intermezzo*, that is, "in-between" the two sites of critical articulation. Yet this "thought" tends constantly beyond the "two-fold," to intersect with other lines of production and creation, hence the "animations" that they inspire.

My study proceeds by enfolding the authors' conceptual intersections articulated by this "two-fold thought" within my own complementary, illustrative "animations," that is, "enlivening" readings (in the French sense of *animer*) derived from these "intersections." Much of the difficulty encountered by readers approaching Deleuze and Guattari stems from the authors' conceptual fecundity which, while anything but systematic, *can* be understood as systemic. That is, the authors do structure their thought following successive systemic models, however multifarious: desiring machines, Bodies without Organs, assemblages, rhizome, plateaus, becomings, the war machine, and so on. These loose conceptual arrays—

described by Deleuze as "a set of split rings [that] you can fit any one of [. . .] into another" (P, 39; N, 25)—allow for a multiplicity of productive, creative effects that the reader, however discerning, might not easily confirm within the dynamic movement of Deleuze–Guattarian prose.

Moreover, readers seemingly "caught" in this burgeoning terminological thicket often become frustrated by the apparent paucity of specific "examples" that might clarify the authors' conceptual trails. Not that Deleuze and Guattari simply theorize in a vacuum: one need only read the opening section of *Anti-Oedipus*, "The Desiring-Machines," for example, to see the specific references with which they bolster their arguments. However, one reaction to Deleuze and Guattari's works that I have noted occasionally is the reluctance, indeed uneasiness, on the part of willing but daunted readers to leap into some decidedly peculiar conceptual terrain. In particular, Deleuze and Guattari's frequent recourse to "difficult" referents—Artaud, Nietzsche, Freud's Schreber, and Proust, to name but a few encountered early in *Anti-Oedipus*—often does not fully satisfy the reader unfamiliar with and/or uninterested in the idiosyncratically French reconceptualization of this cultural baggage. A concerted effort to engage these specific referents would no doubt make the theoretical reflections resonate more productively since, after all, Deleuze and Guattari are writers entitled to draw upon the texts that they deem most appropriate, however diverse and possibly unfamiliar those texts may be to many of their readers. However, to work with the Deleuze–Guattarian terminology while providing some more familiar reference, I choose to develop throughout this study several conceptual "animations." The purpose of these "animations" is to take the Deleuze-Guattarian reflections as a platform for creative understanding of texts of interest to me. I hope thereby to produce a useful orientation for readers interested in developing their own work with and beyond the authors' primary writings.

One means to attempt this is to employ the Deleuzian model of "series" as a guide with and through the focal texts. That is, I consider their works both to draw out and clarify different concepts developed through their "two-fold thought," and to move beyond textual interpretation toward the constitution of a hybrid, analytical "synthesis" in its own right. Constantin V. Boundas has reiterated the importance of making such "serial" connections. He did so quite implicitly by assembling the selections in *The Deleuze Reader* so as to maximize the readers' possibilities of "tracing [a text's] active lines of transformation, stuttering, and flight" (1993b, 22). Moreover, in approaching Deleuze's contributions to a theory of subjectivity, Boundas also extols reading Deleuze "the way he reads others: we must read him according to the series he creates, observe the ways in which these series converge and become compossible, and track down the ways in which they diverge and begin to resonate" (1994, 101;

see also Canning 1994). Pursuing this strategy in my own fashion, I hope to suggest some understandings one might derive from key concepts in Deleuze and Guattari's "intersections" and thus, through productive "animations," how to take seriously the authors' suggestion of employing "theory" as a functional "toolbox" (Foucault 1977, 208; 1994, 2:309).

Having previously published several studies on specific works "read with" Deleuze and Guattari (some presented here in revised form), I am sensitive to the particular challenge in this orientation: on the one hand, of not sacrificing the complexity and subtlety of the authors' "thinking," on the other hand, of providing adequate access to it for interested readers. I am well aware in this regard of an increasing number of worthy predecessors, writing in English and in French, over the past decade whose works would offer readers immense benefit. Among many individual works, one might consult Eric Alliez (1993), Ronald Bogue (1989), Phillip Goodchild (1996b), Jean-Clet Martin (1993), Brian Massumi (1992), and Todd May (1994). Furthermore, different collections of essays—for example, example, *SubStance* 44–45 and 66 (Stivale 1984a, 1991b), Boundas and Olkowski (1994), Patton (1996), *Theory, Culture and Society* 14, no. 2 (Goodchild 1997a), *South Atlantic Quarterly* 96, no. 3 (Buchanan 1997a), and Ansell-Pearson (1997c)—and essays by an array of authors—in the aforementioned collections, and by Braidotti, Buydens, Canning, Cohen, Colombat, Dean and Massumi, De Landa, Goodchild, Griggers, Grosz, Hardt, Holland, Kroker, Perez, Rosenberg, Shaviro, and Zourabichvili, among others who deserve equal mention—constitute important contributions to our general understanding of a complex body of work. They all develop different forms of "animation" related to Deleuzian and Deleuze–Guattarian concepts while undertaking their own, individual extensions of these concepts into new directions and domains.

In "doing publicity" for these many other works, I draw from the friendship and exchange that these studies represent in order to commence intermezzo. That is, like Deleuze and Guattari in their "two-fold thought," I acknowledge undertaking this study as part of an "in-between" zone of ongoing engagement with the reflections of contemporaries both in writing and in the electronic medium. Indeed, as the present decade unfolds, the scholar's isolation in the cubicle or "ivory tower" diminishes increasingly in proportion to interlocutors' connections to daily and global conversations on computer lists and synchronous discussion sites. The efforts of the Spoon Collective and the support of the Institute for Advanced Technology in the Humanities at the University of Virginia, to name but two sources, have notably fostered discussion lists and projects devoted to a number of authors and subjects, including Deleuze and Guattari. Elsewhere, with different sets of links made available through individual and institutional World Wide Web references, different local initiatives reveal the extent of interest and activity in this domain of critical reflection. These initiatives not only constitute a resource for daily conceptual engagement, but also provide vital connections to a community of thinkers from a multitude of countries and backgrounds.

Hence, the gesture that one "normally" makes in a preface such as this—of distinguishing how one's study stands apart from those that have preceded it, and thus of promoting it as a "better read"—seems singularly inappropriate. For in this text I will deliberately forge links with a growing network of *chercheurs*—"seekers" as well as "researchers," and not necessarily solely the institutionally "bound"—in domains that relate as much to Deleuze and Guattari as to an overlapping array of contemporary topics. In this way, I have pursued this study along a path already traced by the focal authors themselves, the path of "friendship" understood as much more than supportive relationships between like-minded colleagues. Following Boundas's insistence on reading Deleuze (and Guattari, I would add) as he/they read others, I understand the "friend" as just such a "series," the "conceptual personae" that all concepts need, according to Deleuze and Guattari at the start of their final collaborative work, *What Is Philosophy?* From this perspective, "friendship" and the generation of concepts are intricately linked as the basis of a "two-fold thought" that leads, in turn, to a generous pedagogy of intersections and animations generated through a productive engagement with these authors' works.

Following the opening chapter in which I situate the "two-fold thought" in terms of Deleuze and Guattari's collaborative prehistory and trace several reading trajectories through Deleuze and Guattari's early writings, I then organize the particular intersections and animations into three sections:

- In Section I, I engage the initial conceptual explosion that Deleuze and Guattari produce in *Anti-Oedipus* and *Kafka: Toward a Minor Literature*, juxtaposing their challenges to psychoanalysis and Marxism with a textual "cluster" around the creation and production of Francis Ford Coppola's *Apocalypse Now*. Then I consider the recent development of interchanges in cyberspace as one approach for comprehending Deleuze and Guattari's provocative conceptual model of the "rhizome."

- In Section II, I extend my understanding of different terms—machines, plateaus, becomings, among others—from different literary and sociocultural perspectives: the "literary seam" that Deleuze and Guattari mine throughout *A Thousand Plateaus* (Chapter 4), an animation of the concept of "becomings" as portrayed in "cyberpunk" fiction (Chapter 5), the expression of a literary "war machine" in a tale by Michel Tournier (Chapter 6), and "spaces of affect" in the "event" of Cajun music and dance practices (Chapter 7).

• In Section III, rather than attempt to "conclude" a study on authors who deliberately situated their works "in-between" beginnings and endings, I move toward "closure" with three "Post-Texts": both the 1985 interview with Guattari, "Pragmatic/Machinic" (Chapter 8), and the "Comments on a Meeting with Gilles Deleuze" (Chapter 9), reveal the generosity, patience, and lively friendship that these men offered to anyone interested in engaging their work and thoughts. Following these "Comments," I take up a well-known quote by Foucault—"perhaps one day, this century will be known as Deleuzian" (1977, 165; 1994, 2:76)—to reflect upon how one might "be Deleuzian" in our era (Chapter 10). As textual referents, I draw from what I consider to be Deleuze and Guattari's "gift of pedagogy" in *What Is Philosophy?* and also from another context particularly dear to them, Carlos Castaneda's "search" for power and knowledge following the teachings of don Juan. I believe that this production of intersections and animations reveals the extent to which Deleuze and Guattari offer us philosophy conceived "other-wise" by allowing us means to conceptualize the complexity of creation and existence in terms of our "actuality."

• In the Appendix I present my translation (with Melissa McMahon) of a previously untranslated article of Deleuze's, "A quoi reconnaît-on le structuralism?" ("How Do We Recognize Structuralism?"), from 1967.

ACKNOWLEDGMENTS

Any attempt to account adequately for the debt I owe to readers of Deleuze and Guattari around the globe will fail miserably, and not only because I would surely miss someone in constructing any list of names. The construction of such lists also has fallen into a strategy of marking territory, with exclusions and inclusions, that runs counter to both the letter and spirit of the work I pursue here. Risking both failure and violation of these principles, I limit my thanks to Douglas Kellner and Peter Wissoker for their patience, encouragement, and understanding during the completion of this project; to Melissa McMahon for her collaboration and invaluable contribution, especially in our translation of Deleuze's structuralism essay (the Appendix); to Fabienne-Sophie Chauderlot, Michael Giordano, Lawrence Grossberg, Doris Y. Kadish, Donna Landry, Charles Leayman, Todd May, Frédéric Pallez, Paul Patton, John Rouse, Greg Seigworth, and David Suchoff for comments on different stages of chapters included here; and to Sydney Lévy and Michel Pierssens, editors of *SubStance*, for their continued support.

I gratefully thank Wayne State University's Office of Research and Sponsored Programs for a subvention in support of the translation appearing in the Appendix, and Wayne State University's Humanities Center for stipends in support of Chapter 7. I am also grateful to the Committee on Grants of Franklin and Marshall College for the research support that made possible the interview with Félix Guattari presented in Chapter 8 and the discussion with Gilles Deleuze offered in Chapter 9.

Given the requirements of producing written work within a global marketplace, I do have accounts to render in the form of specific acknowledgments to editors and presses for permission to republish versions of earlier or current work:

For an earlier version of Chapter 1, David Downing, editor of *Works and Days*, has granted permission to reprint "The Machine at the Heart of Desire: Félix Guattari's Molecular Revolution," *Works and Days* 2 (1984): 63–85.

For earlier versions of Chapters 2, 4, 5, 6, and 10, the University of

Wisconsin Press has granted permission to reprint "Gilles Deleuze and Félix Guattari: Schizoanalysis and Literary Discourse," *SubStance* 29 (1981): 46–57. "The Literary Element in *Mille Plateaux*: The New Cartography of Deleuze and Guattari," *SubStance* 44/45 (1984): 20–34. "Nomad Love and the War Machine: Michel Tournier's *Gilles et Jeanne*," *SubStance* 65 (1991): 44–59. "Introduction: Actuality and Concepts," *SubStance* 66 (1991): 3–9. "Mille/Punks/Cyber/Plateaus: Science Fiction and Deleuzo-Guattarian 'Becomings,' " *SubStance* 66 (1991): 66–84.

For a section of Chapter 3 previously published, Lusitania Press has granted permission to reprint "Cyber/Inter/Mind/Assemblage" in *Being On Line, Net Subjectivity*, ed. Alan Sondheim (1996): 119–125. Also, thanks to Fadi Abou-Rihan, Jon Beasley-Murray, Erik Davis, Mani Haghighi, Nick Land, Karen Ocana, Greg Polly, and Steve Shaviro for use of their posts to the Internet Deleuze–Guattari List. Special thanks to Joan Broadhurst Dixon for the invitation to the Virtual Futures I Conference (1994).

For Chapter 7, Westview Press has granted permission to reprint "Of *Heccéités* and *Ritournelles*: Movement and Affect in the Cajun Dance Arena," in *Articulating the Global and the Local*, eds. Ann Cvetkovich and Douglas Kellner (1997): 129–148. La Lou Music has granted permission to include the text of Beausoleil's "La Valse du Malchanceux."

For Chapter 8, the editor of *PRE/TEXT*, Victor J. Vitanza, has granted permission to reprint "Pragmatic/Machinic: Discussion with Félix Guattari (19 March 1985)," *PRE/TEXT* 14, nos. 3–4 (1993): 215–250. For helping me prepare questions posed to Guattari, I must thank Jack Amarigilio, Serge Bokobza, Rosi Braidotti, Peter Canning, Stanley Gray, Lawrence Grossberg, Alice Jardine, Charles D. Leayman, Vincent Leitch, Stamos Metzidakis, and Paul Patton.

For Chapter 9, the Vaudeville Multimedia Collective has granted permission to reprint "Comments on a Meeting with Gilles Deleuze," *The N(th) Dimension* 1 (1996, WorldWideWeb publication, www.vville.com/artists/semuta/n26.html). http://www.sirius.com/vaudevil/nthdimension/nth.html.

For the Appendix, Hachette Livre has granted permission to translate (with Melissa McMahon) "A quoi reconnaît-on le structuralisme?" by Gilles Deleuze, in *Le XXe siècle: Histoire de la philosophie* 8, ed. François Châtelet (1973): 299–335.

Finally, to Lezlie Hart Stivale, I express my gratitude and love for enduring all the directions to and through which these flows have led.

ABBREVIATIONS

Works by Gilles Deleuze and Félix Guattari

PT   *Psychanalyse et transversalité* (1974)
RM   *La révolution moléculaire* (1977)
Q   *Qu'est-ce que la philosophie?* (1991)
WIP   *What Is Philosophy?* (1994)

Other Works

GJ   *Gilles and Jeanne* (Tournier 1983 [1987])
Hearts   *Hearts of Darkness* (Barr and Hickenlooper 1991)
Notes   *Notes* (Eleanor Coppola 1979)

CONTENTS

III.   Post-Texts

Appendix

1

GILLES DELEUZE AND FÉLIX GUATTARI

SITUATING A "TWO-FOLD THOUGHT"

> It is not by means of an exegetical practice
> that one could hope to keep alive the thought
> of a great thinker who has passed away.
> Rather, such a thought can only be kept alive
> through its renewal, by putting it back into
> action, reopening its questioning, and by
> preserving its distinct uncertainties—with all
> the risks that this entails for those who make
> the attempt.
>
> –Félix Guattari, "Microphysics of Power/Micropolitics
> of Desire" (1986b; Genosko 1996)

Pensée à deux, "two-fold thought": thinking, reflection accomplished between "two" individuals, yet something more than a mere duality. As Deleuze remarked pointedly to Michel Cressole about his work with Guattari, "Since each of us, like anyone else, is already various people, it gets rather crowded" (N, 7; P, 16). It is quite understandable, then, that as they commenced their final collaborative work, *What Is Philosophy?*, Deleuze and Guattari would turn to *l'ami*, the "friend," as a generative concept, but of course, in their own particular way. For they situate the "friend" in terms of "conceptual personae" (*personnages conceptuels*), affirming and yet questioning the signification of "friend" among the Greeks. These authors apparently understood this concept as "a presence that is intrinsic to thought, a condition of possibility of thought itself, a living category, a transcendental lived reality [*un vécu transcendental*]" (WIP, 3; Q, 9). Concluding that "friendship must reconcile the integrity of the essence and the rivalry of claimants," Deleuze and Guattari ask, "Is this

1

not too great a task?" (WIP, 4; Q, 10). For assistance in responding, they turn briefly to Maurice Blanchot, particularly to *L'amitié* (Friendship) and *The Infinite Conversation*. Their reflections affirm a strong tribute to Blanchot as a "rare thinker" to have situated the "friend" within philosophy as "internal to the conditions of thought as such" (WIP, 4). Following Blanchot, Deleuze and Guattari ponder the "conceptual personae" of "weary men," "thinking weary," opening themselves to friendship, linked together through their thought (Blanchot 1969, xx; 1993, xix–xx). In this way, they foreground "a certain distress between friends" as a process that the authors describe curiously, in interrogative form, as one that "converts friendship itself to thought of the concept as distrust and infinite patience?" (WIP, 5; Q, 10).[1]

This notion of a commencement at "the end," with reference to Deleuze and Guattari's final collaborative work, serves several purposes. Throughout this study, I emphasize and pursue the "line" of friendship as a series that cuts across the complex strata of the authors' "two-fold thought." Taken as concept, the "friend" maintains both the "two-ness" of the relationship and the multiplicity of concepts that it produces, under guises too numerous to enumerate (lover, claimant, rival . . .). The "friend" also helps me better to situate the other facet of my translation of *pensée à deux* as "two-fold," the "fold" (*le pli*). While this concept acquires its own resonance later in Deleuze's writings, especially in *Foucault* (1986) and *Le pli* (1988), it is ever present in Deleuze and Guattari's collaboration. That is, the collaboration continually reveals the overlaps of reflection and the production of other concepts that are remarkable characteristics of their work, creating what Blanchot described about writing as a "lacunary interlacing" of the becoming of writing, "multidimensional," a "cloud of intermittences" (1993, 260; 1969, 388–389).[2] Moreover, evoking "the end" at the start raises the fundamental question of "beginning" at all, a problem posed implicitly by Deleuze and Guattari themselves. For their concept to which I referred in the Preface, intermezzo, the "in-between," characterizes the dynamics of any activity, experience, or even feeling, as an ongoing process of creation and of becoming.[3]

By referring yet again to an "in-between" process, I run the risk of hurling the susceptible reader immediately into the deep end of the Deleuze–Guattarian conceptual pool, as it were. I believe, therefore, that some account of the precollaborative phase of the writings of Deleuze and Guattari is warranted despite the apparent methodological inconsistency of such an approach. Recalling my own experience of treading water in that very deep end in the late 1970s, I realize that I too commenced intermezzo, in terms of these authors' individual and collaborative works. It will be useful, then, first to situate a certain number of details with which I only became familiar subsequently regarding Deleuze's and Guattari's activities in the 1950s and 1960s.[4] As I present these individual situations, I will also intersperse several reading "trajectories" into and through Deleuze and Guattari's work. I will briefly outline the trajectory that I pursued in collaboration with different friends, but not necessarily as a recommended course of reading. Rather, I offer it as a way to map a particular conceptual configuration that helped me to gain at least a provisional familiarity with Deleuze's and Guattari's individual projects, as well as a greater appreciation of their collaborative one.

The personal reading trajectory that I outline below led me, in fact, to develop yet another trajectory through a direct confrontation with Guattari's earliest essays. That is, having written two articles on the authors' collaborative works (Stivale 1981, 1984b), I tried to comprehend Guattari's distinctive critical undertaking of radical psychoanalysis and psychotherapeutic practice. While I admit to having undertaken this work at first mainly in order to situate his project in relation to his collaboration with Deleuze, I soon became impressed by the vitality of Guattari's thinking and writing in and of themselves, despite (or perhaps due to) the many challenges posed by his complex writing style. This engagement with his earliest books—*Psychanalyse et transversalité* (1972) and *La révolution moléculaire* (1977a) in particular—resulted in another essay (Stivale 1984c), part of which I provide here in extensively revised form. This overview constitutes an additional, even complementary, reading trajectory that might help the reader situate more fully certain concepts—particularly "machine," "desire," "subject-groups," and "transversality"—within a specifically Guattarian context.

Fortunately, since the late 1970s and early 1980s, a number of scholars have explored the works of Deleuze and Guattari more deeply, with Gilles Deleuze certainly remaining the better known of the two.[5] Besides individual works and essay collections devoted to his writings (see Ansell-Pearson 1997c; Badiou 1997; Broadhurst 1992; Buydens 1990; Colombat 1990; Goodchild 1996a; Hardt 1993; Martin 1993; May 1997; and Zourabichvili 1994, among others), Deleuze participated toward the end of his life in *L'Abécédaire de Gilles Deleuze* (Gilles Deleuze's ABC Primer), filmed in 1988 and broadcast every two weeks from late fall 1994 into 1995 on Europe's Arte channel. These discussions between Deleuze and Claire Parnet, organized according to a thematic, alphabetized order ("A as in Animal" to "Z as in Zigzag"), gave the viewing public the possibility to become more familiar with a philosophical thought related to everyday life.[6] I refer the interested reader to these many works for more nuanced examinations of the diverse facets in Deleuze's individual work and the "image of thought" in which he was keenly interested throughout his career. Drawing from this *Abécédaire*, I provide a third trajectory to conclude this chapter by considering the importance of the "encounter" (*rencontre*) for Deleuze's conception of the "image of thought" as well as certain facets of this "encounter" in Deleuze and Guattari's writings of the late 1960s. As we shall see, these forms of "thought" implicate and encompass action, creation, and in short, philosophy, as these authors will formulate it in their collaborative writings to the end of their lives.

SITUATIONS 1: DELEUZE[7]

One writer who has considered Deleuze's impact on his own life and work is Michel Tournier. In the section entitled "The Mythic Dimension" of his intellectual autobiography *The Wind Spirit* (*Le vent paraclet*), Tournier reminisces about his association with Gilles Deleuze at the Lycée Carnot in the early 1940s: "All of the tired philosophy of the curriculum passed through him and emerged unrecognizable, but rejuvenated, with a fresh, undigested, bitter taste of newness that we weaker, lazier minds found disconcerting and repulsive." Tournier recounts that Deleuze "set the tone of the group" of like-minded *lycéens,* that "it was he who sustained our ardor," and concludes: "Anyone who has never known such a feverish need to delve deeply, to think systematically and use one's mind to the full, who has never experienced such a frenzied passion for the absolute, will I fear never know quite what thinking means" (1988, 128; 1977, 155–156).

Tournier also reflects on their studies in philosophy, their fate, as future philosophy teachers, to "become guardians of those twelve citadels of granite named for their 'placental' progenitors: Plato, Aristotle, Thomas, Descartes, Malebranche, Spinoza, Leibniz, Berkeley, Kant, Fichte, Schelling, and Hegel" (1988, 129; 1977, 158). Tournier indicates that he and his contemporaries responded by "rop[ing] science and religion together with humanism and the clammy 'inner life' and [pitching] them all into the flames." Yet this was no nihilistic, dispassionate endeavor; to the contrary, he notes, "We were intoxicated with the absolute and with the power of intelligence. Physicists had discovered that matter is made of energy, an idea to which we subscribed with the proviso that the energy of which matter is composed is mental in nature" (1988, 130–131; 1977, 158–159). Tournier then recounts how, in this heady atmosphere, "in fall 1943 a meteor of a book fell onto our desks: Jean-Paul Sartre's *Being and Nothingness*." After the initial exultation of "seeing a philosophy born before our very eyes" (1988, 131; 1977, 159–160), Sartre floored them in 1945 with his claims that "existentialism is a humanism": "Our master had gone and fished up that worn-out old duffer Humanism," says Tournier, "still stinking with sweat and 'inner-life,' from the trash heap where we had left him" (1988, 132; 1977, 160). While Tournier admits the "juvenile excess in our condemnation"—"a liquidation of the father by overgrown adolescents afflicted with the awareness that they owed him everything"—he also understands their response as containing a "grain of truth," for Sartre was suffering "from an excess of moral scruple . . . [and was] a Marxist who was never able to give up the secret ambition of becoming a saint" (1988, 133; 1977, 161–162).[8]

I cite these passages as much for what Tournier says about Deleuze as for the manner in which they worked and thought together, in the movement of minds, in a quasi-mystical union (at least by Tournier's account) that some might recognize as "friendship." I also wish to evoke the atmosphere from which Deleuze emerged, "relatively unscathed" at the *agrégation* (Tournier 1988, 134; 1977, 162), and to explain the use of the term "situations" in dividing this introductory chapter. For much of the work in French philosophy undertaken from the late 1940s onward developed under the shadow and weight of Sartrean doctrine and authority, in response to which the fashion arose among young philosophers to "appear to despise Sartre" (Althusser 1992, 323; 1993, 329). Although somewhat younger than Deleuze, Foucault described to Madeleine Chapsal—for *La Quinzaine littéraire* (16 May 1966) upon the publication of *Les mots et les choses*—what the Sartrean legacy meant for his "generation of people who were not yet twenty during the war": while "we felt that Sartre's generation was indeed courageous and generous, with its passion for life, politics, and existence, we discovered something else, another passion: the passion of the concept and of what I will call 'system.' " In contrast to Sartre's search for all-encompassing "meaning," Foucault pointed to "Lévi-Strauss for societies and Lacan for the unconscious [as having] shown us that meaning was probably only a kind of surface effect, a shimmering foam, and that it was the system that traverses us deeply, that was there before us, that sustains us in time and space." Defining "system" as "an aggregate of relations that are maintained and transformed independently of the things they connect," Foucault insisted that, contrary to Sartrean "freedom," "we think within an anonymous and constraining thought that is one with an era and a language." Thus, concluded Foucault, "the current task of philosophy and of all the theoretical disciplines that I have indicated to you is to reveal this thought preceding thought, this system preceding any system, the basis upon which our 'free' thought emerges and flickers for a brief moment" (1994, 1:514–515).[9]

In contrast to Tournier's reverential description, Deleuze's own definition of his project in the early years, as presented in his 1973 letter to Michel Cressole, is both more revealing and more amusing:

> I belong to a generation, one of the last generations, that was more or less bludgeoned to death with the history of philosophy. The history of philosophy plays a patently repressive role in philosophy. . . . Many members of my generation never broke free of this; others did, by inventing their own particular methods and new rules, a new approach. I myself "did" history of philosophy for a long time, read books on this or that author. But I compensated in various ways. (N, 5–6; P, 14)[10]

Deleuze's "Lettre à Michel Cressole" (1973c), originally appended to Cressole's 1973 study of Deleuze's work, responds to Cressole's polemical accusations, expressed in an earlier letter. There, Cressole reproaches Deleuze for his alleged status as "Grand Sorcerer" of philosophy on the Vincennes campus, a role that supposedly blocked Deleuze off from further production and even trapped him into silence (Cressole 1973, 103–104). Refusing to "admit" anything in the face of what he judged to be Cressole's police "surveillance" tactics, Deleuze recapitulates his own understanding of this work, particularly the survival strategies he adopted:

> I suppose the main way I coped with it at the time was to see the history of philosophy as a sort of buggery [*enculage*] or (it comes to the same thing) immaculate conception. I saw myself as taking an author from behind, and giving him a child that would be his own offspring, yet monstrous. It was really important for it to be his own child, because the author had to actually say all I had him saying. But the child was bound to be monstrous too because it resulted from all sorts of shifting, slipping, dislocations, and hidden emissions that I really enjoyed. (N, 6; P, 14–15)

Deleuze pursues this image by providing specific examples of his "doing" history of philosophy: he refers first to his work on Bergson (1966 [1988]), an author erroneously ridiculed, says Deleuze, since his detractors clearly "don't know enough of history," particularly of "how much hatred Bergson managed to stir up in the French university system at the outset, and how much he became the focus for all sorts of crazy and unconventional people [*fous et marginaux*], right across the social spectrum" (N, 6; P, 15). Deleuze then states that his work on Nietzsche (1962 [1983]; 1965) "extricated me from all this" since, rather than allowing one to inseminate him, it is Nietzsche "who gets up to all sorts of things behind your back." Through Nietzsche, Deleuze opened himself to "the multiplicities everywhere within [individuals], the intensities running through them," that is, a depersonalization "opposite [that] effected by the history of philosophy; it's a depersonalization through love, rather than subjection" (N, 6–7; P, 16).[11]

Following Deleuze's chronology, we can see this "opening" and "depersonalization" then leading him "along these meandering lines" to undertake two conjoined projects, *Différence et répétition* (1968b [1994]) and *Logique du sens* (1969 [1990]). While still heavily laden with many "academic elements," according to Deleuze "they're an attempt to jolt, to set in motion something inside me, to treat writing as a flow, not a code" (N, 7; P, 16).[12] In this regard, Deleuze expresses to Cressole his regret at the latter's failure to develop his one "beautiful, even rather marvelous passage" in which Cressole explains how he read and made his own use of *Anti-Oedipus*.[13] Deleuze calls this quite exquisitely

> [an] intensive way of reading, in contact with what's outside the book, as a flow meeting other flows, one machine among others, as a series of experiments for each reader in the midst of events that have nothing to do with books, as tearing the book into pieces, getting it to interact with other things, absolutely anything, ... [this] is reading with love [*une manière amoureuse*]. (N, 8–9; P, 18)

These different "ways" of reading require of us an effort to understand Deleuze's project as simultaneously making his texts "monstrous" and yet doing so through "loving" depersonalization. I believe that this admittedly confusing formulation informs the "two-fold thought" in fundamental ways. For not only does the creative thought process entail modes of "thinking otherwise," as an Outside thought, perhaps monstrous in its daring, or even its simplicity. This process also situates the "person" along, or in relation to, the "line Outside," "something more distant than any external world. But it's also something closer than any inner world" (N, 110; P, 150). Deleuze considers this to be no easy process, but one of "manag[ing] to fold the line and establish an endurable zone in which to install ourselves, confront things, take hold, breathe—in short, think. Bending the line so we manage to live upon it, with it: a matter of life and death" (N, 111; P, 151). This process is thus simultaneously "loving" in the potential it offers for overlapping an-other's thought, and menacing in the risks that this very process entails, a process informing the animations that I develop in the subsequent chapters of this study.

TRAJECTORIES 1: BECOMING(S) POSTSTRUCTURAL

Recalling the years in the late 1970s and early 1980s during which I became familiar with the works of Deleuze and Guattari, with the help of my friends, I must conclude that this period was a truly wonderful time to be both in French studies and "in" theories that would eventually contribute to "cultural studies." In 1975, I entered the PhD program in French at the University of Illinois, Urbana–Champaign, after two years of MA and *maîtrise* study in Paris. I had received superb training in language, French culture, and traditional literary analysis at the Sorbonne, but had spent my days in France almost totally oblivious to the intellectual debates and crucial contemporary works with which I would later become familiar. At Urbana–Champaign, I was fortunate to meet professors and fellow graduate students who were able to provide me with much needed assistance to pursue a comprehensive orientation, first, to the linguistic and literary studies that constituted "structuralist poetics," and then to the works of the 1970s that subverted the "heroic" confidence of structuralist analysis.[14]

The trajectory for my study of Deleuze and Guattari received its initial impulsion from an article by Michel Pierssens entitled "L'appareil sériel" (1973; The serial apparatus) that I encountered in 1975–1976. His essay begins with this canny insight:

> When Gilles Deleuze directs himself toward literature, he always does so in order to call it as a witness, never addressing it as an object. For him, literature does not exist for its literarity, but for what unforeseen revelations or simple testimony it might bring to domains that by rights escape it—philosophy, psychoanalysis. . . . On this level, what counts is not writing, as an abstract universal or as general procedure and model of the work of forms as inscription. What counts, rather, is the literary work [*oeuvre*] itself as locus of a precise and crazy operation, a machination, a departure point [*mise en route*] of sense. (1973, 265)

In Pierssens's concise presentation, I was exposed for the first time to the ways in which the text worked as a generative, sense-making apparatus through the textual network that he associated with "series," "singularities," and "intensities." Moreover, Pierssens insisted that this was not just any "sense," but one that "operates [*marche*] and traces, that intervenes in return within the edifice controlling the reading activity in which it [sense] is produced" (1973, 265). Pierssens's essay also had the distinct merit of providing an "animation" of a literary text with which I was thoroughly familiar, Stendhal's *Le rouge et le noir*. While I immediately seized upon the study for my work on Stendhal, I ultimately found this essay to be less valuable for that specific literary analysis than for Pierssens's tantalizing theoretical juxtaposition of terms from *Différence et répétition* and *Logique du sens* within an original analytical framework.

Above all, the footnotes and references initiated my trajectory into Deleuze's texts: while I had little success at all comprehending *Différence et répétition*, there was something compelling about *Logique du sens* that I simply could not escape. I was particularly drawn to Deleuze's elaboration of "sense" in terms of the interplay of "series." For I was able to situate his concept of "structure"—"a natural excess of the signifying series and a natural lack of the signified series" (LSEng, 49; LSFr, 64)—within the fairly recognizable coordinates of "structuralism" with which I was then occupied in my studies. Yet what I found even more appealing was Deleuze's insistence that, beyond the "minimal conditions for a structure" (i.e., two heterogeneous series), their convergence toward a "paradoxical element" was also a factor in the structural operation—an element that "belongs to no series; or rather, it belongs to both series at once and never ceases to circulate throughout them" (LSEng, 50–51; LSFr, 65–66). This formulation of "structure" seemed to admit not only of an at least provisional specification of "sense" (within and between the interplay of the "series" themselves), but also the possibility of its constant displacement and productive force (through the circulation of the "paradoxical element"). As I would discover later in "A quoi reconnaît-on le structuralisme?" (1973b), Deleuze actually had developed in his writings of the late 1960s an astoundingly idiosyncratic and original conceptualization of both "structure" and "structuralism" to which he associated a number of contemporary theorists.[15]

While still trying to come to terms to some degree with Deleuze's concept of "series," I proceeded on to another text, *L'Anti-OEdipe,* that seemed to completely undo everything that I thought I had understood from *Logique du sens.* Once within the orbit, as it were, of *L'Anti-OEdipe,* I juxtaposed additional essays that brought their own forms of clarity and difficulty, for example, Deleuze's response to Michel Cressole, "I Have Nothing to Admit" (Deleuze 1973c; republished as "Lettre à un critique sévère" [Letter to a Harsh Critic] in Deleuze 1990 [1995]), and Guattari's essay on "micropolitics of desire" (1974b), both translated in the *Semiotext(e) "Anti-Oedipus"* issue (1977). Furthermore, while still adjusting to the jolt from *L'Anti-OEdipe,* I acquired three more works, two books by Deleuze and Guattari—their *Kafka: Pour une littérature mineure* (1975) and *Rhizome: Introduction* (1976)—and one by Deleuze and Claire Parnet, *Dialogues* (1977). I thus found myself trying to situate four phases of their work: Deleuze's philosophical inquiries into "sense" and "structure" alongside Guattari's reflections on the "(micro)politics of desire" in conjunction with the diverse and unfolding facets of the authors' first, second, and third collaborative works. Clearly, such a muddle is not an approach that I would recommend at all today, but frankly, back then, who knew? And what else could one do? The challenge was and remains to arrive at some understanding of the individual works while also establishing a clear picture of the developmental articulation between them.

Fortunately for those of us seeking a dialogue via seminars and working groups with non-Francophone colleagues in other fields, the numerous translations that became available by the late 1970s made such cross-disciplinary engagement increasingly possible. Notably, the translation *Anti-Oedipus* first appeared in 1977, and that same year *Semiotext(e)* published a special issue on *Anti-Oedipus* containing texts translated from French (by Deleuze and Guattari [1973b, 1973c], Artaud [1976, 1977], Lyotard [1972], Donzelot [1972], and Hocquenghem [1977]) and original essays in English (Dyer and Brinkley [1977], Lotringer [1977a, 1977b], Rajchman [1977]). Thus, the reading group constituted by Lawrence Grossberg with graduate students and faculty in 1978–1980 helped us come to terms with a number of the crucial texts challenging us at the time.[16] Despite the aforementioned textual and critical muddle in which I found myself (or, at least, now see myself then), I was able to bring to the group a certain comparative linguistic perspective that clarified some of the texts read in translation (e.g., by Lacan and Foucault). As for Deleuze and Guattari's works, I liken my experience of discussions and readings from *Anti-Oedipus* to running repeatedly into a brick wall until I finally noticed a crack in the wall, that is, until we began to make some tentative connections. Of course, we were not entirely able to situate this work within the specific sociohistorical and psychotherapeutic conjuncture that inspired Deleuze and Guattari to collaborate in its creation.[17] But gradually, through much exchange of ideas and frustrations, we were able to situate more precisely a few key terms and to establish at least a provisional understanding of the authors' strategies and goals.

One concept proposed by Deleuze and Guattari in *Anti-Oedipus* that posed particular problems for us was the "body without organs" (aka BwO). I have noticed over the past two decades that the "body without organs" has remained perplexing to most readers and discussants of this work. For example, the first moderator of the online Deleuze–Guattari List, the late Michael Current, generated a productive debate on the topic in spring–summer 1994, and list participants have returned to this topic intermittently ever since. Echoing Erik Davis's query from the Deleuze–Guattari List (April 1994), "What does the 'BwO' do for you?," I have wondered from the start what I do for or on it, and when, and how? Although I develop this concept more extensively in Chapter 2 in conjunction with the *Apocalypse Now* textual "cluster," I want to focus briefly on the concept here a means of situating my initial engagement with Deleuze and Guattari and of indicating some other terms usually associated with this concept.

Although a definition of the body without organs is tricky given its various transformations throughout Deleuze and Guattari's works, I can suggest the following: for every social interaction or situation, a highly complex and collective overlapping of expression of desire is in play, the elements of which are at once dispersed and highly dynamic. Just as this dynamic energy propels desire's expression and production, so too does a counterforce, the body without organs, arrest this movement provision-ally, yet also propel this productive energy further. The body without organs functions, therefore, as a key component for conceptualizing at once desiring and social production. But Deleuze and Guattari also present it in relation to two other components (AOEng, 8–16; AOFr, 14–22), as follows:

- The body without organs functions as an Immobile Motor vis-à-vis the Working Parts and the Adjacent Part. These components each have additional corresponding traits:
  - Their "machinic form": The "motor" constitutes a Miraculating "machinic form" in relation to the Paranoid form of "desiring-machines" and the Celibate form of the adjacent part, the subject;
  - Their "energy form": Besides the "machinic" form, each compo-nent evinces an "energy form," the "motor" 's Numen in relation to the desiring-machines's Libido and the subject's Voluptas;
  - Their interlinked "syntheses": The body without organs functions concurrently as the disjunctive synthesis of recording, between the con-nective synthesis of partial objects and productive flows and the conjunc-tive synthesis of *consommation* (both consumption and consummation) through intensities and becomings. Thus the pervasive force of desire (at once psychic and social) is "machined" by the overarching system of the vital progression's three syntheses: the connective coupling of machines one to another; the disjunctive process of recording and inscription of these machines in relations of difference to one another; and the recon-ciliation or conjunction of the opposition between the desiring-machines and the body without organs, setting the process in motion again and thereby producing a discernible, yet decentered subject on (or near) the recording surface (AOEng, 16–18; AOFr, 22–24).[18]

However mystifying this outline may be (not merely due to its all-too-brief form here), my presentation serves, at least, to provide a sample of the challenging terminology that greeted Parisians in 1972 and, in translation, critics and theorists in other countries during the following decades. I have grappled over the years with developing and retaining some anchoring references to the body without organs as a way to elaborate its complex progression more succinctly. I wish to outline briefly three such series of bodies without organs. Each of these series depends on where and how I could envisage connections of the body without organs to different plateaus, or conceptual domains.

The first series I borrow from Deleuze and Guattari and develop more thoroughly in the context of *Anti-Oedipus* in the next chapter. Proust maintains an important status for the authors in their attempt to distinguish between molar (or global) images and more molecular flows.[19] Pursuing this distinction within Proust's fiction as it elaborates the functioning of connective, disjunctive, and conjunctive syntheses, Deleuze and Guattari see these movements as interlinked in a forward progression. This movement of syntheses detaches subjectivity from the expressive flow and yet also creates and connects the detached subjectivity back into the narrative through the recursive flow of Time. Could Proust's seven-volume work be as aptly entitled *A la recherche du corps sans organes* (In search of the body without organs) as a complement to *In Search of Lost Time*? Not time in some simplistic conceptualization, but perhaps through the constant interchange between *Aeon*, a time of duration, and *Chronos*, a time of unfolding? The concept of body without organs has helped me understand Proust's texts and their volatile imagery as evoking the subject-less "subject(ivity)" around which the novels revolve and evolve.

I develop another series with reference to Carlos Castaneda's books about don Juan's teachings (Castaneda 1972, 1974) in which the BwO takes on many forms. One form is the ever-disconcerting "plane" into which Carlos kept finding himself cast through his life experimentations as prescribed by don Juan's wisdom and practice. Recounted through a gradual process of a subject's "becomings," all of these "tales" depict the slow methodological "destratification" of the anthropologist, once locked inexorably into his disciplinary procedures and would-be objectivity. In relation to the "territory" of the subject, Castaneda's tales portray a constant and progressive "deterritorialization," away from the fixed parameters of a hierarchized, logical rationality (or molar perspective), toward something much more fluid, molecular, fleeting, toward a "line of flight" (see the dénouement of Casteneda's *Tales of Power* [1974], 294–295). For don Juan never doubted the importance and seriousness of the disjunctive forces in play that jolt Carlos repeatedly out of his striated, hierarchized existence. On the way toward "knowledge," each experience/experimentation propels Carlos ever forward in his own "becomings," yet consistently decentered from the fixed identity that constitutes whom he thinks he is, at times "becoming animal," at others "becoming vegetal," and still others "becoming imperceptible." Inherent to the concept of the BwO in *Anti-Oedipus*, these "becomings" receive full and explicit treatment in *A Thousand Plateaus* (see Plateaus 6 and 10).

But what of the political importance of the body without organs, that is, how it might function in relation to institutions and subject(ivities)? For the examples I have selected in this anchoring series to be fully satisfying, more extensive development would be required. Nonetheless, I have tried to conceptualize the molar striation of institutions in terms of "governing bodies" with and without their "organs," for example, some professional "bodies" (such as the Modern Language Association, or MLA), and even "academia" more generally and amorphously. One goal in developing professional, scholarly, and pedagogically productive dialogue and teaching is to facilitate possibilities for creative flows and then to see where these might take students and interlocutors in the course of mutual exchange, learning, and teaching. Yet, try as one might to open up possible lines of exchange and even conceptual breakthroughs along "lines of flight" away from the hierachizing, striating confines of institutions, these "bodies" proliferate "organs" and thus "reterritorialize" many of our efforts and energies through diverse forms of "capture" and limitation. In the MLA (and its regional offshoots such as Midwest MLA, etc.), one readily discerns and contends with diverse mechanisms for self-governance and thus for surveillance and control of scholarly and political action and debate, for supporting and regulating the market economy of the professorate, for regularizing research standards, and for "channeling" (or reterritorializing) critical exchange and expression into highly constructed forums.[20] As for academic institutions, many efforts promoting progressive pedagogy have been thwarted time and again by the array of "organs" and "bodies" that cordon off and reterritorialize creative impulses and intellectual life according to the "imperatives" of enrollment-driven budgets and the publication cycle necessary for professional advancement (still hierarchically) and to retain academic employment.[21]

As I hope is now clear from this brief elaboration of one concept introduced in *Anti-Oedipus,* the work that we began in the 1970s has required both continued reflection and considerable negotiation as Deleuze and Guattari have pursued their collaborative project. For example, besides the new perspectives on the body without organs that they develop in *A Thousand Plateaus,* they introduce in *Kafka . . .* the concept of a "minor literature"—one that stands in contrast and resistance to a "major," dominant literature—and then proceed in *A Thousand Plateaus* to theorize the "minor" as a "becoming minoritarian" with both linguistic and sociopolitical ramifications (ATP, 291–294; MP, 356–360).[22] They also develop the concept of "rhizome," first in a short work (Deleuze and Guattari 1976), then as the introduction to *A Thousand Plateaus,* as a framework for their multiplanar interdisciplinary theorization of multiplicity. And throughout this work, Deleuze and Guattari do not abandon the concept of the body without organs. Indeed, Deleuze provides an extremely useful summary statement of the concept's importance in private notes he composed in the late 1970s (i.e., during work on *A Thousand Plateaus*) in response to Michel Foucault's first volume of *The History of Sexuality* (1976):

> For me, desire . . . implies the constitution of a field of immanence or a "body without organs," which is only defined by zones of intensity,

thresholds, gradients, flux. This body is as biological as it is collective and political. . . . It varies (the body without organs of feudalism is not the same as that of capitalism). If I call it body without organs, it is because it is opposed to all the strata of organization, that of the organism, but just as much the organizations of power. (Deleuze 1994, electronic text)

Once *A Thousand Plateaus* appeared, my own work took yet another turn as I slowly have come to terms with this massive volume since 1980. At the same time, the publication of selected essays by Guattari in translation, *Molecular Revolution* (1984), presented an opportunity for me to define more clearly the specificity of his critical project, particularly his early writing. Hence my reading trajectory brought me forward both within the complex and progressive elaboration of the Deleuze–Guattarian collaborative enterprise and toward a dual consideration (that still continues) of specific works by Deleuze and by Guattari. It is to a consideration of the latter that I turn now.

SITUATIONS 2: GUATTARI [23]

In 1972, when the Parisian intellectual scene was jolted by the publication of *L'Anti-OEdipe*, Vol. 1 of *Capitalisme et schizophrénie*, Guattari was already prominent both in leftist French political circles and in the psychoanalytic arena, though in lockstep neither with orthodox Freudian practice nor with the reigning Lacanian alternative to orthodoxy.[24] Indeed, Deleuze recalled quite clearly the importance of this friendship and collaboration of nearly twenty-five years in the following terms: "And then there was my meeting with Félix Guattari. . . . " (N, 7; P, 16). Deleuze described him as "a man of the group, of bands or tribes, and yet he is a man alone, a desert populated by all these groups and all his friends, all his becomings" (DEng, 16; DFr, 23). Deleuze discussed the importance of this collaboration for his work in a number of texts, and all of them suggest the significant connections that Guattari was able to provoke in Deleuze's creative process and, of course, vice versa.[25]

Guattari has discussed in a number of interviews his activities and the circumstances under which he and Deleuze came to work together. Of the "disparate paths" of his own early political and clinical practice, Guattari explains the awkwardness of being a militant "Marxist inspired by Trotsky," a "Freudo-Lacanian" in his psychotherapeutic work, and philosophically inclined to be "Sartrean," "all of [which] did not flow together very well" (Genosko 1996, 121).[26] Thus, under the tutelage of François Tosquelles, Guattari began to develop an original analytic path in which he "sought to make discernible a domain that was neither that of institutional therapy, nor institutional pedagogy, nor of the struggle for social emancipation, but which invoked an analytic method that could traverse these multiple fields (from which came the theme 'transversal-ity')" (Genosko 1996, 121). This approach would allow Guattari to go beyond the limits of specific problems of mental illness, and to relate this method more broadly to "the relations of the individual to the collectivity, the environment, economic relations, aesthetic productions, etc." (Genosko 1996, 122). However, since the approach did relate to psycho-therapy, Guattari found that it allowed "the disengagement of analysis from the personological and familialist frameworks to give an account of assemblages of enunciation of another sort" (Genosko 1996, 122). And it was from this "decentering" of the analytical problematics that he devel-oped with Deleuze new perspectives on "the function of pre-personal subjectivity—prior to the totalities of the person and the individual—and supra-personal, that is, concerning phenomena of the group, social phe-nomena" (Genosko 1996, 122).

Prior to and during May 1968, Guattari admitted to feeling "like I was riding a powerful wave, connecting all kinds of vectors of collective intelligence." Afterward, however, the early promise became more am-biguous: "I was hoping that a collective development could be pursued, but instead a sort of prohibition against thinking set in" (1986a, 84–85; 1995, 28–30). So Guattari qualifies his meeting with Deleuze as nothing short of a "miracle," one that acquired unforeseen dimensions when Deleuze himself proposed their direct and intimate collaboration: "Only the two of us. It was a frenzy of work that I hadn't imagined was possible until then." Guattari explains the initial project with Deleuze in 1969 as simply one of "discuss[ing] things together, [of] do[ing] things together" which, for Guattari, meant "throwing Deleuze into the stew [of the post-May 1968 turmoil]" (1986a, 81–82; 1995, 28). In retrospect, Guattari saw quite clearly the impact of this collaboration on his own work:

> [This was] both a careful and scholarly enterprise, and a radical and systematic demolition of Lacanism and all my previous references; clari-fying concepts that I'd been "experimenting with" in various fields, but couldn't reach their full extension because they were too attached to their origins. . . . The philosophical shoring up was above all a long term project with Deleuze, which gave my earlier attempts at theorizing an entirely new energy. (1986a, 85–86; 1995, 30–31)[27]

Moreover, throughout his career, Guattari never ceased linking political activity to his theoretical reformulations, yet also never lost sight of creativity as the basis for all human activity and expression. One can judge from his writings the extent to which he was profoundly engaged in philosophical and artistic reflections, albeit of a different sort than in Deleuze's project.[28] One text in which these concerns emerge is "Créativité et folie" (Creativity and madness), a discussion published in 1984 between Guattari and his colleague and mentor Jean Oury, the founder of the La Borde Clinic.[29] As Guattari says therein, all discussion of the terms "creativity" and "madness" in an institutional context "must be considered within an aesthetic frame of reference" (1984, 34). Both Guattari and Oury understand the importance of performance as an event that can become "the keystone of an aesthetic assemblage" [*agencement esthétique*], whether in art or in psychotherapy (1984, 35–36). This performative aspect of the event extends to thinking itself, and in any development of "interpretation," says Guattari, "the creative process cannot be framed in too rigid a manner without stopping, without blocking it off" (1984, 38). Guattari posits several examples of what he sees as the crucial importance of "questions of assemblage [*agencement*], of threshold, of consistency, that facilitate the passage from one site to another," in theater, in music, as well as in the psychotherapeutic context. And to emphasize this intersection, Guattari asks, perhaps only somewhat jokingly, "What types of music do we produce here [at La Borde] in supposed spaces of institutional psychotherapy? Have we become new music schools, new conservatories?" (1984, 46). These assemblages of creativity and "madness" constitute a powerful approach for producing "crystals of singularity," for causing them to "engender unforeseeable becomings," and to "contract more or less monstrous marriages" (1984, 47). This reflection clearly echoes and folds back into Deleuze's own conception of making philosophy "monstrous" (N, 6; P, 14–15).

TRAJECTORIES 2: THE MACHINE AT THE HEART OF DESIRE

As Guattari has suggested on numerous occasions, his work emerges from two overlapping sites: on the one hand, a clinical practice at La Borde Clinic and different forms of analytic practice that deliberately emphasized sociocultural and artistic investments; on the other hand, an array of political engagements that sought to make available sociocultural and creative enunciations to the widest assemblage imaginable of collective agents. Unfortunately, much of Guattari's early writing and interviews have, until recently, been unavailable in translation. For example, the earliest collection of translated essays concerning Guattari's political and psychiatric activities, *Molecular Revolution: Psychiatry and Politics* (1984), not only soon went out of print, but was also unsatisfactory from several perspectives.[30] It is within Guattari's first collection of essays, *Psychanalyse et transversalité* (Psychoanalysis and transversality) that we can situate the developing Deleuze–Guattarian "two-fold thought," since Deleuze's Preface to the collection, "Trois problèmes de groupe" (1972, 1977 ["Three Group-Problems"]), suggests the developing intersection of their thought.

Deleuze introduces Guattari as someone interested much less in the "unity of an Ego [*Moi*]," than in dissolving this *Ego* by seeking new forms of group subjectivity. Indeed, says Deleuze,

> Guattari embodies in the most natural way the two aspects of an anti-Ego: on the one hand, like a catatonic pebble, a blind and hardened body penetrated by death the instant he takes off his glasses; on the other hand, a body blazing with a thousand fires, swarming with multiple lives whenever he gazes, acts, laughs, thinks, or attacks. (Deleuze 1972, i; 1977, 99; translation modified)

Deleuze sums up these dual facets as portraying the "schizophrenic powers" of the psychoanalyst and militant doubly named "Pierre and Félix" (1972, i). His subsequent review of three sorts of "group-problems," related at once to psychotherapy and political action, constitutes a brief summary of the problematics that inform Guattari's work and writings between 1955 and 1968. Particularly astute is Deleuze's final summary of the problematics addressed by Guattari:

> It is here [in the conflict between institutional psychotherapy, the antipsychiatric movement à la R. D. Laing, and "community" psychiatry (*psychiatrie de secteur*) with its neighborhood grids] that Guattari raises his particular problematics on the nature of care-giver/cared-for groups potentially able to form subject-groups, i.e. able to make the institution the object of a veritable creation in which madness and revolution, without becoming indistinguishable, echo precisely this aspect of their difference within the singular positions of a desiring subjectivity. (1972, xi; 1977, 108; translation modified)

This perspective will also contribute to their own collaboration, particularly Guattari's conception of psychotherapy and political militancy as a "desire-machine, that is, a war- and analysis-machine [*machine de désir, c'est-à-dire de guerre et d'analyse*]" (1972, xi; 1977, 108).

From essays written early in Guattari's career, it is clear that his psychotherapeutic concept of "transversality"—of the nature of the "group" within the psychiatric institution—constituted a critique of the Freudian and Lacanian dependence on totalizing, referential myths (Oedipus, the great Other, and the unconscious structured as language) for rearticulation and interpretation of all subjective histories. In "Introduction à la thérapie institutionnelle" (1962–1963, in PT, 32–51; Introduction to institutional psychotherapy) and "Le transfert" (1964, in PT, 52–58;

"Transference," in Genosko 1996, 61–68), Guattari describes an "effect of subjectivity" by which a subject affirms himself/herself through language on the plane of groups, thereby constituting a "subjective unity of the group" on the social plane (PT, 43). Since the ailing subject is "a citizen first, and individual afterwards" (PT, 45), to effect a cure the subject must shift from his or her exterior, subjugated group association (e.g., a factory, a club) to an institutional subject group constantly interpreting its own position.

Furthermore, Guattari's essay "La transversalité" (1964, in PT 72–85; "Transversality," MR, 11–23) sows seeds of concepts later elaborated in *Anti-Oedipus,* for he does not merely develop the institutional problematic posited in the earlier essays, but constitutes an initial sketch of the approach that will become "schizoanalysis." On the one hand, Guattari rejects outright the Freudian portrayal of the source of neurotic anxieties in the "castration complex," an "internal danger," according to Freud, "that lays the ground for the external" such that anxiety would precede repression (MR, 12; PT, 73). On the other hand, he affirms that the object of institutional therapeutics "is to try to change the data accepted by the super-ego into a new kind of acceptance of 'initiative,' rendering pointless the blind social demand for a particular kind of castrating procedure to the exclusion of anything else" (MR, 13–14; PT, 73–74). Opposing what he considers a Freudian "signifying logic," Guattari thus foregrounds the social realm as the source from which both illness and cure derive. The cure is produced, says Guattari, through institutional therapeutics that subvert the dominant "logic"—an essentialism in which castration and punishment form the basis of "social reality." These therapeutics thus would permit precise, "transversal" relationships to be constructed, thereby freeing patients to recognize the social determination of anxiety.

Another insight that Guattari brings to this analytical framework of "transversality" is the distinction between "subject-groups" and "subjugated groups." He defines their opposition, respectively, as "that of a subjectivity whose work is to speak, and a subjectivity which is lost to view in the otherness of society" (MR, 14; PT, 76).[31] Guattari affirms the importance of developing within group analysis something akin to a "group transference" (MR, 17; PT, 78–79), one that must not be fixed, that is, territorialized, but that instead must be a "transversality in a group." Such a concept is opposed to "(a) verticality, as described in the organogramme of a pyramidal structure (leaders, assistants, etc.); [and to] (b) horizontality, as it exists in the disturbed wards of a hospital, or, even more, in the senile wards; in other words, a state of affairs in which things and people fit in as best they can with the situation in which they find themselves" (MR, 17; PT, 79).

Guattari describes this new concept in terms of a "coefficient of transversality," comparing it to the "adjustable blinkers" worn by horses that allow them the visual range from total blindness to full vision:

> In a hospital, the "coefficient of transversality" is the degree of blindness of each of the people present. However, I would suggest that the official adjusting of all the blinkers, and the overt communication that results from it, depends almost automatically on what happens at the level of the medical superintendent, the nursing superintendent, the financial administrator and so on. Hence all movement is from the summit to the base. There may, of course, be some "pressure from the base," but it never usually manages to make any change in the overall structure of blindness. Any modification must be in terms of a structural redefinition of each person's role, and a reorientation of the whole institution. So long as people remain fixated on themselves, they never see anything but themselves. (MR, 18; PT, 80)

Seeking to undo the vertical and horizontal relations so prevalent in institutions, "transversality" would be achieved in hospitals "when there is a maximum of communication among different levels and, above all, in different meanings. . . . Only if there is a certain degree of transversality will it be possible—though only for a time, since all this is subject to continual re-thinking—to set going an analytic process giving individuals a real hope of using the group as a mirror" (MR, 18, 20; PT, 80, 82). Since this approach explicitly questions power relations while it suggests therapeutic aims, the concomitant political and psychoanalytical implications are evident, as Guattari concludes:

> It is my hypothesis that there is nothing inevitable about the bureaucratic self-mutilation of a subject group, or its unconscious resort to mechanisms that militate against its potential transversality. They depend, from the first, on an acceptance of the risk—which accompanies the emergence of any phenomenon of real meaning—of having to confront irrationality, death, and the otherness of the other. (MR, 23; PT, 85)[32]

Guattari subsequently extends this work on "transversality" to emphasize its importance for the study of "group subjectivity." For example, in "Réflexions pour des philosophes à propos de la psychothérapie institutionnelle" (1966, in PT, 86–97; Reflections for philosophers on institutional psychotherapy), Guattari refers to the alterity of the subject enunciated by Rimbaud's "je est un autre" (I is an other). Rather than remaining a subject, this "other" is "a signifying machine that predetermines what will have to be good or bad for me and my peers in one or another area of consumption" (telle ou telle aire potentielle de consommation) (PT, 93). He calls for new philosophical research that would determine "concepts likely to found a field of reference responding, on the one hand, to the demands of the objective sciences and, on the other hand, to the demands of 'techniques' of concrete human existence" (PT, 95). This call resonates with the subsequent work he would undertake both with Deleuze and in his own writing.

TRAJECTORIES 3: A "TWO-FOLD THOUGHT"

In some ways, one can understand what I call the "two-fold thought" as the progressive engagement, intersection, and overlapping of philosophical *rencontres,* or "encounters," to which Deleuze refers throughout his career as a way of exploring the "image of thought" in its diverse forms. In fact, it is no exaggeration to insist upon "thought" as a fundamental concept in Deleuze's project, as he did himself in the Preface to the English translation of *Différence et répétition*:

> Finally, in this book it seemed to me that the powers of difference and repetition could be reached only by putting into question the traditional image of thought. . . . A new image of thought—or rather, a liberation of thought from those images which imprison it: this is what I had already sought to discover in Proust. Here, however, in *Difference and Repetition,* this search is autonomous and it becomes the condition for the discovery of these two concepts. It is therefore the third chapter which now seems to me the most necessary and the most concrete, and which serves to introduce subsequent books up to and including the research undertaken with Guattari where we invoked a vegetal model of thought: the rhizome in opposition to the tree, a rhizome-thought instead of an arborescent thought. (DREng, xvi–xvii)

Indeed, the 1971 edition of *Proust et les signes* contains a new concluding chapter bearing the same title as Chapter 3 of *Difference and Repetition,* "The Image of Thought," and not surprisingly, the argument and language of each are similar, although more elaborate in the latter work. Just as Deleuze does for philosophy, Proust in his major cycle of novels "sets up an image of thought in opposition to that of . . . what is most essential in a classical philosophy of the rationalist type: the presuppositions of this philosophy." Among these are "the mind as the good will of thinking" (PSEng, 159; PSFr, 186), that is, that "thinking is the natural exercise of a faculty, and that this faculty is possessed of a good nature and a good will" (DREng, 132; DRFr, 173). Rather than being based on friendship, however, philosophy,

> like friendship, is ignorant of the dark regions in which are elaborated effective forces which act on thought, the determinations which force us

to think; a friend is not enough for us to approach the truth. . . . As a matter of fact, the truth is not revealed, it is betrayed; it is not communicated, it is interpreted; it is not willed, it is involuntary. (PSEng, 160; PSFr, 187)

Hence the importance in Proust's final volume, *Le temps retrouvé* (Time Regained), of the leitmotif of "the word force: impressions which force us to look, encounters which force us to interpret, expressions which force us to think" (PSEng, 161; PSFr, 188). Hence the importance in *Difference and Repetition* of that which forces us to think, "an object not of recognition but of a fundamental encounter," the primary characteristic of which "is that it can only be sensed," the second, that it "moves the soul, 'perplexes' it—in other words, forces it to pose a problem" (DREng, 139–140; DRFr, 182–183). While one can observe different aspects of this "fundamental encounter" in each collaborative work by Deleuze and Guattari, I propose here a third "trajectory" that juxtaposes Deleuze and Guattari's "encounter" in the latter's essay "Machine et structure" (1969, in PT, 240–248; "Machine and Structure," MR, 111–119) with comments made by Deleuze twenty years later in his interviews with Claire Parnet.

Guattari's "Machine and Structure" functions as an important transitional essay in his early career that clearly indicates the encounter of his thought with Deleuze's. Deleuze had prepared a preface to *Psychanalyse et transversalité* in which he indicates the particular importance of this essay and of Guattari's "D'un signe à l'autre" (1966, in PT, 131–150; From one sign to the other) for the development of the machinic functions (PT, xi).[33] Guattari starts this essay by distinguishing "structure" from "machine" in an attempt to "identify the peculiar positions of subjectivity in relation to events and to history" (MR, 111; PT, 240). In turn, he derives this distinction from what he considers to be the complementary categories of "series" and "singularity" introduced by Deleuze in *Logique du sens*. In an initial terminological footnote, Guattari suggests the categories he derives from Deleuze's work: "Structure, in the sense in which I am using it here, would relate to the generality characterized by a position of exchange or substitution of particularities, whereas the machine would relate to the order of repetition ('as a conduct and as a point of view concern[ing] non-exchangeable and non-substitutable singularities' [DREng, 1; DRFr, 7])" (MR, 111; PT, 240). Of Deleuze's three minimum general conditions that determine structure, Guattari associates the first two with his own conception of the term: "(1) There must be at least two heterogeneous series, one of which is defined as the signifier and the other as the signified; (2) Each of these series is made up of terms that exist only through their relationship with one another" (LSEng, 50–51; LSFr, 66). As for the third condition, that "two heterogeneous series converge toward a paradoxical element, which is their 'differentiator,' "

Guattari relates this exclusively to the order of the "machine" (MR, 111; PT, 240).

This model is crucial for Guattari and also points to the burgeoning "encounter" of the two authors that I outlined briefly above in the second "situation." For Guattari, "structure" positions its elements, including the subject or agent of action, in an all-encompassing "system of references." This system consists of two heterogeneous series that relate each element to the others and thereby enclose the ego-centered subject as but one of many other enclosed elements. In contrast, the "machine" is not such a structural representation, but a particular kind of "event." That is, like Deleuze's concept of "singularity," the machine is a point of convergence for the heterogeneous series to which the subject or agent of action remains remote, as the "the unconscious subject" that exists "on the same side as the machine, or better, alongside the machine" (MR, 111–112; PT, 241). This distinction leads Guattari to examine the fundamental alienation under capitalism that characterizes the individual's relation to the machine. The result of the alienated relationship is that "this residual human activity is no more than an adjacent and partial procedure that accompanies the subjective procedure produced by the order of the machine" (MR, 113; PT, 242). In this way, "the machine has passed into the heart of desire," that is, human activity constitutes nothing more than "residual work" or the machine's psychic "imprint" on the individual's imaginary world.[34]

Given the emphasis that Deleuze places on "series" and "structure" in *Logique du sens* (and in "How Do We Recognize Structuralism?"; see Appendix), we can see clearly how Guattari's and Deleuze's thought established significant links: "The machine, as a repetition of the particular, is a mode—perhaps the only possible mode—of univocal representation of the various forms of subjectivity in the order of generality of the individual or the collective plane" (MR, 114; PT, 243). Guattari's lines of reflection, therefore, lay the groundwork for an important facet of the ongoing collaborative work, and he extends his insights further toward the political domain that both authors would consider crucial for defining "schizoanalysis." Guattari suggests that, as desire's "focaliz[ation] in the totality of structure," this machine process might well emerge differently, as "a new weapon, a new production technique, a new set of religious dogmas, or such major new discoveries as the Indies, relativity, or the moon." However, to counter this process, "a structural anti-production develops until it reaches its own saturation point," and the revolutionary breakthrough, to survive, would then be forced to develop yet "another discontinuous area of anti-production that tends to re-absorb the intolerable subjective breach" (MR, 117; PT, 246).

This process corresponds to the ternary terminology that Deleuze and Guattari subsequently develop to describe both the vital progression of displaced subjectivity and the importance of territoriality. That is, following the emergence of new productions of "territorialization," the resultant effects of "deterritorialization" or antiproduction lead to a reabsorption, or "reterritorialization." In turn, this process of provisional closure requires yet another breakthrough, starting the ternary process all over again, and Guattari here addresses difficulties in organizing revolutionary action. Specifically, he consider the problems in "setting up an institutional machine whose distinctive features would be a theory and practice that ensured its not having to depend on the various social structures—above all, the State structure" (MR, 118; PT, 246–247). What would be required for such a "machine" of institutional subversion to function independently of social or State structures, Guattari argues, is that it "demonstrate proper subjective potential and, at every stage of the struggle, should make sure that it is fortified against any attempt to 'structuralize' that potential" (MR, 118–119; PT, 247). This revolutionary framework articulates the interlocking psychic and political planes, the planes of desire and of the socius, that Guattari and Deleuze will extend as "schizoanalysis" in *Anti-Oedipus*.

In anticipating this seminal first collaborative work by Deleuze and Guattari, I have attempted here to show the bases upon which the authors moved from individual research into the "encounter" of their collective enterprise. For Deleuze, this process consisted of exploring the diverse facets of "sense" in terms of its different "series" and then "singularities," elaborated particularly in *Logique du sens*. He then developed these in terms of "syntheses" that constitute the machinic and energetic production of desire developed henceforth in the authors' collaborative works. Meanwhile Guattari had already undertaken both a critique of Lacanian psychoanalysis (while still fully engaged in his own analysis with Lacan) and a reconceptualization of semiotic production along lines that conjoined social and psychic processes, quite evident in his early writings.

This mode of "encounter" constitutes a constant reference point in Deleuze's reflections, particularly in the extended series of interviews with Parnet that were filmed in 1988 and televised seven years later. In "C as in Culture," Deleuze expresses his fundamental belief in *rencontres* between people as well as between an individual and a work of art or a philosophical work. Furthermore, the kind of philosophical creation he valued most was one that result in "getting out or beyond" philosophy (*d'en sortir*). He points to his work on Leibniz and "the fold" that resulted in Deleuze's extraordinary epistolary "encounters" with members of an association of letter-folders and with surfers, both groups recognizing their own supposedly nonphilosophical activities in what Deleuze described in his work. According to Deleuze, like the surfers, "we never stop inserting ourselves in the folds of nature, the most mobile folds of waves, living in the folds of waves" ("C as in Culture"). This "getting out or beyond" philosophy corresponds to a kind of transversal jump, intersections with other modes of thought and experience, what he calls "percepts" and "affects" in art, music, and literature. For, throughout *L'Abécédaire*, Deleuze insists that all great philosophers and writers—from Nietzsche and Spinoza to T. E. Lawrence and Antonin Artaud—engaged philosophy as a mode of "becoming" that exceeds the strength of those experiencing it, causing them to "see" as visionaries ("I as in Idea").

With this trajectory, I have attempted to suggest some forms of "encounter" that the "image of thought" encompasses, a subject to which I return in the final chapter. The "two-fold thought" that we engage along with Deleuze and Guattari is one of action and opening outward, of involuntary revelations and adventures, of sliding toward possibly barbaric formulations, unheard-of juxtapositions of concepts, monstrous couplings. In linking the "two-fold thought" to different Deleuze–Guattarian terms—"nomad thought" (Deleuze 1973a), "Outside thinking" (Foucault 1966b), "rhizomatics" and "pragmatics" (ATP, 15–17; MP, 24–26)—we develop actively, with and through these authors, this wrenching process of displacement, intersections, and animations. Whether in the domains of philosophy, psychotherapy, or sociopolitical action, the "image of thought" remains for Deleuze and Guattari a constant concern throughout their distinct, yet conjoined careers, and becomes the basis for answering the "final" and fundamental question, *What Is Philosophy?*, posed in the title of their last collaborative work.

I

FROM SCHIZOANALYSIS TO RHIZOMATICS

2 APOCALYPSE . . . WHEN?

1972/1979, ONE OR SEVERAL WILLARDS?

> KURTZ: What did they tell you?
> WILLARD: They told me you had gone totally insane and that your methods were unsound.
> KURTZ: Are my methods unsound?
> WILLARD: I don't see any method at all, sir.
>
> —Apocalypse Now *(1979)*

In this chapter, I approach *Anti-Oedipus* from the perspective of the "machinic" syntheses that Deleuze and Guattari propose as constituting the psychosocial dynamic propelled by desire. To do so, I consider two related facets of their initial collaborative project, the elusive concept inherent to these syntheses known as the "body without organs," and the broader approach that the authors propose called "schizoanalysis." As a way of better understanding these syntheses and their production, I provide a "conceptual travelogue" of sorts, juxtaposing Francis Ford Coppola's *Apocalypse Now* (1979) to other textual material relating the ordeal of this film's production, to Eleanor Coppola's *Notes* (1979), and to the recent documentary on the making of *Apocalypse Now, Hearts of Darkness* (1991). Specific facets within Coppola's adaptation and the twice-told tale of the film's production allow me to re-view the conceptual journey "upstream" that occurs in *Anti-Oedipus*—the machinic syntheses (defined in AO, Chap. 1), the analyses and critique of Freud and Marx (AO, Chaps. 2 and 3), and the Introduction to "schizoanalysis" with which this perplexing and suggestive endeavor "ends" (AO, Chap. 4). Through this juxtaposition of textual and cinematic enunciations within the sociopolitical foci of imperial (post)-colonial contexts, I explore the conceptual tracks that are constitutive of Deleuze and Guattari's "schizoanalytic" approach. I conclude the chapter by linking this initial collaborative project to the authors' second book, *Kafka: Toward a Minor Literature,* and particularly to their move toward a mode of production, indeed a mode of thinking, that they call "rhizomatics."

When venturing into Chapter 1 of *Anti-Oedipus* for the first time, I experienced what many readers have mentioned to me since, a sensation of disorientation and even a sort of violation from the opening phrases: "Ca fonctionne partout, tantôt sans arrêt, tantôt discontinu. Ca respire, ça chauffe, ça mange. Ca chie, ça baise. Quelle erreur d'avoir dit le ça. Partout ce sont des machines. . . . " (AOFr, 7; "It is at work everywhere, functioning smoothly at times, at other times in fits and starts. It breathes, it heats, it eats. It shits and fucks. What a mistake to have ever said the id. Everywhere it is machines" [AOEng, 1]). Like Butch and Sundance (in the 1969 movie *Butch Cassidy and the Sundance Kid*) exhausted from days of pursuit by relentless trackers, one is tempted to react by asking, "Who are those guys!?" For the Parisian intelligentsia of the early 1970s, this book implicitly evoked what Stendhal's narrator in *Le rouge et le noir* considered politics to be for the novel, a pistol shot in the opera. With its critique of the appropriation of power in psychoanalytic and social discourse and practices, *L'Anti-OEdipe* was a *pavé* in several senses (a paving stone and a hefty tome), hurled onto the scene as a grating, radical, and complex dissent from the mixed chorus of Lacanian and Marxist debates.[1]

Slowly working my way through each chapter with invaluable help from friends, I encountered what Foucault called, in his Preface to the English translation of *Anti-Oedipus,* its "traps" (*pièges*), that is, its humor, "so many invitations to allow oneself to be driven away, to take leave of the text slamming the door behind you" (AOEng, xiv; Foucault 1994, 3:136). Indeed, I eventually realized that this disconcerting and disorderly book merits being read in a disconcerting and disorderly manner, from the back forward, or from the middle outward, or as Brian Massumi suggested in regard to *A Thousand Plateaus,* like a record, skipping from cut to cut as each chapter/concept attracts or repels you (Massumi 1987, xiii–xiv). It was the volume's proposed "schizoanalysis" of psychoanalytic and social domains in Chapter 4 that eventually revealed for me more clearly than its polemical opening shots how this particular assemblage of concepts might be effectively deployed. I have since come to understand better how the authors' "two-fold thought" was initially articulated in this work, and particularly how its ostensible "end," Chapter 4, is "assembled" (*s'agence*) in relation to the preceding chapters, through myriad folds of different conceptual strata.

It is also more evident to me now how the volume in its entirety constitutes but the opening round in the authors' collaborative engagement with contemporary psychoanalytic and sociocultural critique. Chapter 1, even with its opening, elliptical slap in the face, still expresses succinctly the overlapping schizoanalytic "units" elaborated later. The extended analyses in Chapters 2 and 3 each treat a major domain challenged by schizoanalysis: the Freudian problematic, particularly as it relates to subject formation (Chap. 2), and the Marxian problematic (Chap. 3), particularly in terms of the constitution of a "socius" and its complex relations to capital and to subjectivity. Then, in Chapter 4, the "Introduction to Schizoanalysis" is a manifesto that provides less a "program" than a vision of possibilities for reflection and action, but a vision already developed in various ways in the earlier chapters. Sporadic skirmishes among Deleuze–Guattarians about which work is "more revolutionary" or "reactionary," the *Anti-Oedipus* or *A Thousand Plateaus,* seem quite specious. For each work articulates particular perspectives from precise sociocultural moments, but also lays the groundwork for different forms of engagement, as well as for theoretical and conceptual speculation. Whereas *A Thousand Plateaus* may retreat from the dogmatic edge of absolute "deterritorialization" supposedly extolled in *Anti-Oedipus,* the latter has its own limited, even reductive, positions that the authors nuance subsequently—for example, the different sets of binaries such as the molar/molecular and subject-/subjugated groups.[2]

Michel Foucault maintains in the Preface to the English translation that

> it would be a mistake to read *Anti-Oedipus* as the new theoretical reference . . . [but] as an "art," in the sense that one speaks of "erotic art," for example . . . An analysis . . . [that] yields answers to concrete questions . . . : how does one introduce desire into thought, into discourse, into action? How can and must desire deploy its forces within the political domain and grow more intense in the process of overturning the established order? (AOEng, xii; Foucault 1994, 3:133–135)

When I first began to write about *Anti-Oedipus,* I sought to locate its analytical deployment through the ways that both literary and critical discourses might constitute "desiring machines." I wanted to ascertain the extent to which such "machinic desire" might make possible breakthroughs in textual constraints, allowing literary works to function, however minimally, as "revolutionary" investments of desire capable of exploding the fundamental structures of capitalist society (Stivale 1981).[3] I considered this approach to be all the more appropriate since, in this first volume as well as in their subsequent works, Deleuze and Guattari developed schizoanalysis in terms of literary discourse, through analyses of specific authors such as Proust and Kafka, as well as through analysis of exemplary "cases" in support of their more general theoretical arguments. To these literary elements, I now juxtapose a particular cinematic, autobiographical, confessional, and documentary discursive nexus: to Francis Ford Coppola's *Apocalypse Now* (1979) as one link (freely derived from Conrad's *Heart of Darkness*), I conjoin two other "texts," Eleanor Coppola's personal narrative of the film's production, *Notes* (1979), and the more recent documentary of this same production, *Hearts of Darkness* (Barr and Hickenlooper 1991).

These juxtapositions serve several purposes: first, they help me to animate *Anti-Oedipus* as a travelogue of sorts, a conceptual journey "upstream" through the deployment of different concepts: desiring machines, the syntheses and their production, the "body without organs" and its relation to subjectivity, elaboration of a universal history, and a new "method" called "schizoanalysis." Second, these juxtapositions facilitate an understanding of the multiple confrontations of creativity and madness that contribute to Deleuze and Guattari's own mode of "animating" concepts in *Anti-Oedipus,* their sometimes difficult evocation of literary works. Third, these juxtapositions provide ample ground for developing the particular cinematic and discursive nexus upon which I have chosen to focus and for drawing upon different critical paths traced around and through the conceptual assemblage of "apocalypse."

A brief word here about this chapter's title that mimics the title of Plateau 2, "1914: One or Several Wolves?", in *A Thousand Plateaus*. At the start of Plateau 10 ("1730: Becoming-Intense, Becoming-Animal, Becoming-Imperceptible . . . "), Deleuze and Guattari briefly recall the scenario of the film *Willard* (1971), in which the eponymous protagonist betrays his rat companion Ben and is forced to undergo a hideous death, like so many before him in the film, at the "mercy" of the rat pack. One purpose of this plateau's opening section—subtitled "Memories of a Moviegoer"—is to provide a succinct example summing up diverse territorializing processes that determine, for Deleuze and Guattari, a possible "becoming-animal" of humans. For viewers of Coppola's *Apocalypse Now,* the name "Willard" evokes a different sort of protagonist, one who passes through his own set of "becomings" (as did his counterpart Marlow in Conrad's *Heart of Darkness*), affecting not only Willard himself, but those around him. These "becomings" unfold "in-between," in relationship to other "machinic" assemblages—notably, the "war machine" that sends Willard on his mission, "for [his] sins"—and to other processes of "becomings"—

most evidently, those of the rogue Colonel Kurtz whom Willard is ordered to kill. Yet, like linking rings or Venn diagrams, these "assemblages" and "becomings" enfold and overlap others, at once narrative, familial, and capitalist, through the different manifestations of "production" from the heart of which the film emerges.

TERRITORIES

To offer a general overview of Deleuze and Guattari's earliest expression of the "two-fold thought,"[4] I originally followed a particular path, or "series," in the schizoanalytic project along several phases: how Deleuze and Guattari define the tasks of schizoanalysis proposed in *Anti-Oedipus,* how they extend their critique of the psychic and social regimes with the support of literary discourse, and how they elaborate a literary schizoanalysis in *Kafka: Toward a Minor Literature.* To begin, let us consider the following question posed by George Stambolian to Félix Guattari: "What, then, is the basic difference between schizoanalysis and psychoanalysis?" Guattari's reply precisely distinguishes these modes of analysis:

> Psychoanalysis transforms and deforms the unconscious by forcing it to pass through the grid of its system of inscription and representation. For psychoanalysis, the unconscious is always already there, genetically programmed, structured, and finalized on objectives of conformity to social norms. For schizoanalysis, it's a question of constructing an unconscious, not only with phrases but with all possible semiotic means, and not only with individuals or relations between individuals, but also with groups, with physiological and perceptual systems, with machines, struggles, and arrangements of every nature. There's no question here of transfer, interpretation, or delegation of power to a specialist. (Guattari 1979b, 59; Genosko 1996, 206)

We can see here Guattari's preoccupation with psychotherapeutic practice, already enunciated in his articles of the 1960s (e.g., in "The Transfer" ["Le transfert," PT, 52–58] and "Transversality" ["La transversalité," PT, 72–85]). For these distinctions—between structure and construction, between individual relations and group assemblages—constitute a focal point addressed in *Anti-Oedipus*: "Psychoanalysis, with its Oedipal stubbornness, . . . settles on the imaginary and structural representatives of reterritorialization [exemplified by the neurotic on the couch] while schizoanalysis follows the machinic indices of deterritorialization" (AOEng, 316; AOFr, 378). The authors thus contrast two systems: on the one hand, what they judge to be a system of reduc-

tions in analytic theory and practice, "the reduction of desiring production to a system of so-called unconscious representations, . . . the
reduction of the factories of the unconscious to a piece of theater,
Oedipus or *Hamlet*; the reduction of the social investments of libido to
domestic investments, and the projection of desire back onto domestic coordinates, Oedipus again" (1972b, 50; N, 17; P, 29). This is, of
course, a hierarchizing system of structures that closes off libidinal
flows, reterritorializing and repressing them within this system's categories. On the other hand, this system is opposed by "a materialist
psychiatry . . . that brings production into desire, on the one hand,
and desire into production on the other." The result is to "set against
this fascism positive lines of flight because these lines open up desire,
desire's machines, and the organization of a social field of desire"
(1972b, 50–51; N, 17–19; P, 30–32). For the anti-Oedipal viewpoint
holds, counter to traditional and most "second generation" Freudians,
that the unconscious is neither figurative, "since its *figural* is abstract,
the figure-schiz," nor is it structural or symbolic, since "its reality is
that of the Real in its very production, in its very inorganization," nor
is it representative, "but solely machinic, and productive" (AOEng,
311; AOFr, 371).

From this fundamental tenet derives the destructive task of schizoanalysis, "a whole scouring of the unconscious, a complete curettage. Destroy
Oedipus, the illusion of the ego, the puppet of the superego, guilt, the
law, castration" (AOEng, 311; AOFr, 371). However, the positive tasks of
schizoanalysis must be undertaken at the same time as the destructive
task. The first positive task consists of "discovering in a subject the nature,
the formation, or the functioning of *his* or *her* desiring-machines, independently of any interpretations" (AOEng, 322; AOFr, 385; translation
modified). Their project develops these tasks in *Anti-Oedipus* in terms of
a stark contrast:

> If the essential aspect of the destructive task is to undo the Oedipal trap
> of repression properly speaking, and all its dependencies . . . , the essential
> aspect of the first positive task is to ensure the machinic conversion of
> primal repression, there too in an adapted variable manner. (AOEng, 339;
> AOFr, 406)

To these two tasks of schizoanalysis, one destructive, the other positive,
the authors link a concurrent second positive task whereby schizoanalysis
schizophrenizes (rather than neuroticizes as does psychoanalysis) the
investments of the unconscious desire of the social field by making use
"only of indices—the machinic indices—in order to discern, at the level of

groups or of individuals, the libidinal investments of the social field" (AOEng, 350; AOFr, 419).[5]

* * *

As a way of evoking from the start Francis Ford Coppola's simultaneously creative and destructive undertaking in *Apocalypse Now,* the documentarists Barr and Hickenlooper open their reconstruction of the film's production with excerpts from Coppola's press conference at the 1979 Cannes Film Festival. Coppola's ponderous statement extends the already prevalent "myth" of madness, self-destruction, and existential interrogation as operative creative and artistic principles of this film. Coppola declares, with a simultaneous French translation punctuating each phrase,

> My film is not a movie, my film is not about Vietnam, it is Vietnam, it's what it was really like. It's crazy, and the way we made it is very much like the way the Americans were in Vietnam, in the jungle. There were too many of us, we had access to too many . . . too much money, too much equipment, and little by little, we went insane. (*Hearts*)[6]

Were one to rely solely on the documentary's self-serving portrayal, both the production and the narrative of *Apocalypse Now* would provide a dual animation of different elements of *Anti-Oedipus,* an animation that I will develop in due course. Fortunately, we have access to other documents and narratives regarding both the film's production and Willard's tale in *Apocalypse Now* that help subvert the mythic elements underlying a certain reading/viewing of this film.

For readers who might be unfamiliar with Coppola's film, a brief summary is in order. Like Joseph Conrad's *Heart of Darkness, Apocalypse Now* is recounted by means of a framed narration (through voiceover in the film). These images and the narration present the mission of Ben Willard (the film's freely adapted counterpart of Conrad's Charlie Marlow) to find a rogue colonel, Walter Kurtz, and to terminate his command—a mission that does not and will never officially exist, according to Willard's superiors. During transport upriver on a patrol boat (a PBR) with a four-man crew, Willard studies classified dossiers on Kurtz and muses on all he learns with growing fascination regarding his adversary's achievements. Meanwhile, Willard and the crew pass through successive encounters with American forces and Vietcong resistance until the remaining survivors arrive at the Kurtz compound in Cambodia. How and why Willard completes his mission are subjects for scrutiny in the following pages.[7]

I wish to explore complementary facets of Willard's tale and Coppola's myth. For, as we shall see, Colonel Kurtz's apparent desire and (narrated) "becomings" that so tempt Willard during his journey relate directly to the dream of merging with the flows of a warrior band in a nomadic military operation supposedly beyond the limited "logic" of the U.S. government's war machine. However, through Willard's disembodied (and retrospective) narration, Coppola's Kurtz still seeks dual validation: on the one hand, in his own text (a lengthy manuscript viewed ever so briefly in the film); on the other hand, within the family scenario through a concern for his son's recollection of the father's acts, indeed for their re-presentation to the son in his manuscript. Willard thus reconstitutes the simultaneous roles of confessor (for Kurtz) and confessee (to the implied narratee, the viewer). He also accepts the roles of paid assassin— what Kurtz contemptuously describes as being "an errand boy sent by grocery clerks to collect a bill"—and delivery boy of Kurtz's manuscript, that Willard clutches as he returns to the boat in the final scenes—by then having completed his mission.

As for the production itself, at work in *Apocalypse Now* is the "war machine" 's extended (and extenuated) capitalist venture that develops on a number of planes. During the film's lengthy production, the "war machine" emerged briefly in the late 1960s, that is, during Coppola's first attempt to produce the film, through the U.S. Army's refusal to cooperate with the director's ambition to film in Vietnam. Later, this machine is depicted more emphatically through Ferdinand Marcos's somewhat sporadic military support of the film's production. These conjoined incursions, military and cinematic, are set against the backdrop of Coppola's own financial struggle to retain total control over his project while negotiating with Hollywood moguls who grew increasingly nervous about the seemingly never-ending project.[8] And we cannot forget that Coppola was hardly the only filmmaker or his backers the only studio involved in exploiting the Vietnam War for dual cinematic and commercial ends.[9] Finally, the intersection of military and cinematic machines is also inextricably imbricated in the familial machine as all-encompassing end and starting points of the different tales recounted, by Willard as well as by Coppola. However, the latter tale is further re-presented more acutely and painfully in Eleanor Coppola's *Notes* (1979), begun during the location shooting of *Apocalypse Now* (1976–1977) and then developed during the film's editing process in California (1977–1978). These starkly frank and revealing personal reflections were then strategically selected and heavily edited for inclusion as voiceover narration in the Barr and Hickenlooper documentary with which the Coppolas willingly cooperated. The diverse elements of the film's narrative—at once Willard's, the film crew's, and the Coppolas'—provide rich textual details for animating concepts proposed in *Anti-Oedipus.*

DETERRITORIALIZING

The functional tasks of schizoanalysis, presented in Chapter 4 of *Anti-Oedipus,* constitute the schizoanalyst's essential guidelines based on the outline of the operation of machinic components' in Chapter 1, entitled "Desiring-Machines." As I indicated in the previous chapter, these elements of the vital psychosocial progression constitute Deleuze and Guattari's attempt to treat the regimes of desiring and social production in terms of a radically new paradigm: machinic production. We may establish the conjuncture between this progression's components—machinic and energetic—and art, literature in particular, through the syntheses of this progression's unfolding. For Deleuze and Guattari, "The work of art is itself a desiring machine. The artist stores up his treasure so as to create an immediate explosion, and that is why, to his way of thinking, destructions can never take place as rapidly as they ought to" (AOEng, 32; AOFr, 39). Furthermore, Deleuze and Guattari refer to Engels who demonstrated, they maintain, "already apropos of Balzac, how an author is great because he cannot prevent himself from tracing flows and causing them to circulate, flows . . . that necessarily nourish a revolutionary machine on the horizon" (AOEng, 133; AOFr, 158). Here again, the authors seek to release lines of flight, defining "style, or rather the absence of style—asyntactic, agrammatical" as "the moment when language is no longer defined by what it says, even less by what makes it a signifying thing, but by what causes it to move, to flow, and to explode—desire." Hence, they maintain that "literature is like schizophrenia: a process and not a goal, a production and not an expression" (AOEng, 133; AOFr, 158–159).

As I suggested in Chapter 1, this pervasive force of desire is "machined" by the overarching system of the vital progression's three syntheses: the connective synthesis of production, the disjunctive synthesis of recording, and the conjunctive synthesis of consumption–consummation. We may briefly define these syntheses as follows: the *connective synthesis* is the coupling of machines one to another, resulting in the production of partial objects and of the ceaseless flow of desire. The *disjunctive synthesis* results from these connections as machines attach, record, or inscribe themselves in grids or chains onto the "body without organs," halting the process momentarily as so many points of disjunction in relations of difference to one another. The *conjunctive synthesis* is brought about by the reconciliation or conjunction of the opposition between the desiring-machines and the "body without organs." This conjunction sets the process in motion again, producing a discernible subject on (or near) the recording surface. Yet this subject is a peculiar one,

> with no fixed identity, wandering about over the body without organs, but always remaining peripheral to the desiring-machines, being defined by the share of the product it takes for itself, garnering here, there, and everywhere a reward in the form of a becoming or an avatar, being born of the states that it consumes and being reborn with each new state. (AOEng, 16; AOFr, 22–23)

Let us consider more closely the key term, "body without organs," that confronts readers most forcefully in *Anti-Oedipus* and then, with subsequent modifications and elaboration, in *A Thousand Plateaus*. Already, in "Machine and Structure" (discussed above, Chap. 1), Guattari argues that a force of "anti-production" stymies the individual subjectivity both from realizing human desires and from achieving social engagement. Beneath the "machinic couplings" elaborated in *Anti-Oedipus* is what Artaud describes as the "body alone [that] needs no organ" (AOEng, 9; AOFr, 15), and this terminological derivation from Artaud is crucial. For, from the start of its adaptation in *Anti-Oedipus,* the body without organs (BwO) is understood with artistic implications, as an art of life, as it were, that has social as well as subjective ramifications. The BwO is "an enormous undifferentiated object," when "a producing/product identity . . . stops dead for a moment, [when] everything freezes in place—and then the whole process will begin all over again" (AOEng, 7; AOFr, 13). The painting by Richard Lindner serving as frontispiece to *Anti-Oedipus* offers visual representation of desiring production: "a huge, pudgy, bloated boy working one of his little desiring-machines, after having hooked it up to a vast technical social machine" (AOEng, 7; AOFr, 13). But just as "desiring-machines make us an organism," it is "at the very heart of this production, within the very production of this production, [that] the body suffers from being organized in this way, from not having some other sort of organization, or no organization at all" (AOEng, 8; AOFr, 14).

Enter Antonin Artaud who, by dint of his own illness and sufferings, "one day find[s] himself with no shape or form whatsoever." He discerns how the BwO resists organ-machines, how it "resist[s] linked, connected, and interrupted flows [by setting] up a counterflow of amorphous, undifferentiated fluid": gasps and cries as "sheer unarticulated blocks of sound" to resist "articulated phonetic units" in desiring-production (AOEng, 9; AOFr, 15). As for social production, capital is the BwO of "the capitalist being," producing "surplus values, just as the body without organs reproduces itself, puts forth shoots, and branches out to the farthest corners of the universe . . . Machines and agents cling so closely to capital that their very functioning appears to be miraculated by it" (AOEng, 10–11; AOFr, 16–17). Thus functions the imbrication of "attraction-machine" and "repulsion-machine," of "paranoiac machine" succeeded by a "miraculating-machine": "The body without organs, the unproductive, the unconsumable, serves as a surface for the recording of the entire process of production of desire, so that desiring-machines seem to emanate from it" (AOEng, 11; AOFr, 17).

In Chapter 4, Deleuze and Guattari nuance these distinctions. While the body without organs is "produced in the first passive synthesis of connection," it has a dual potential "to neutralize—or on the contrary, put into motion—the two activities, the two heads of desire." When produced "as the amorphous fluid of antiproduction," it can "repel the organs-objects"; when "produced as the support that appropriates for itself the flow production," it can attract the organs-objects. In neither case, Deleuze and Guattari argue, does the body without organs oppose the organs-objects, for the body without organs and organs-partial objects "are opposed conjointly to the organism." In this way, the authors maintain that the body without organs is "in fact produced as a whole, but a whole alongside the parts—a whole that does not unify or totalize them, but that is added to them, like a new, really distinct part" (AOEng, 326; AOFr, 384).

Far from being reconstituted, then, as a form of connection as in desiring-production (under the connective synthesis or coupling), a law of distribution comes into play for the recording process:

> No matter what two organs are involved, the way in which they are attached to the body without organs must be such that all the disjunctive syntheses between the two amount to the same on the slippery surface. . . . The schizophrenic "either . . . or . . . or" refers to the system of possible permutations between differences that always amount to the same as they shift and slide about. (AOEng, 12; AOFr, 18)

Deleuze and Guattari offer some examples. They mention Samuel Beckett's *Malone*, "the schizophrenic . . . [who] inscribes on his own body the litany of disjunctions," the disjunctive synthesis of recording coming "to overlap the connective synthesis of production." They discuss the delirium of Freud's Schreber, who employs disjunctions "to divide himself up into parts." They note the cross-examination to which the schizophrenic is constantly subjected, in the manner of Beckett's *Molloy* (AOEng, 12–14; AOFr, 18–20). And returning yet again to Artaud, who scrambles all codes with his own system of coordinates, Deleuze and Guattari oppose the "specifically ternary and triangular schema such as Oedipus" to the schizophrenic alternate "recording code," arguing: "The full body without organs is produced as antiproduction, that is to say, it intervenes within the process as such for the sole purpose of rejecting any attempt to impose on it any sort of triangulation implying that it was produced by the parents" (AOEng, 15; AOFr, 21).

Yet the BwO is not the end of the process, for "a genuine reconciliation of [desiring-machines and BwO, of paranoiac machine and miraculating-machine, of attraction and repulsion] can take place only on the level of a new machine, functioning as 'the return of the repressed' " (AOEng, 17; AOFr, 23). Deleuze and Guattari borrow (from Michel Carrouges 1954) "the term 'celibate machine' to designate this machine that succeeds the paranoiac machine and the miraculating-machine." With this term, they describe the production of the subject "as a mere residuum alongside the desiring-machines" via the conjunctive synthesis of consummation (AOEng, 17–18; AOFr, 24). And in this new machine, it is "the *subject* that is missing in desire, or desire that lacks a fixed subject. . . . Between the act of producing and the product, something becomes detached, thus giving the vagabond, nomad subject a residuum. The objective being of desire is the Real in and of itself" (AOEng, 26–27; AOFr, 34).[10]

Deleuze and Guattari insist, though, that the parallel they establish between desiring-machines and technical social machines is, on the one hand, "merely a distinction of régime. . . . Except for this difference in régime, they are the same machines, as group fantasies clearly prove." On the other hand, the parallel is "in no way meant as an exhaustive description of the relationship between the two systems of production." Pointing to art as a domain in which group fantasies are created and employ "desiring-production to short-circuit social production," Deleuze and Guattari foreshadow their later development of "rhizomatics": "Desiring-machines . . . continually break down as they run, and in fact run only when they are not functioning properly: the product is always an offshoot of production, implanting itself upon it like a graft, and at the same time the parts of the machine are the fuel that makes it run" (AOEng, 31; AOFr, 38–39). From the perspective of couplings, breakdowns, and conjunctions of machinic desire and production, the superimposed narratives of *Apocalypse Now* provide a means to understand ways in which a creative enterprise may progress through stops and starts while being explicitly inscribed within the capitalist machine.

*   *   *

"A producing/product identity . . . [that] stops dead for a moment, [when] everything freezes in place—and then the whole process will begin all over again" (AOEng, 7; AOFr, 13)—were it not for the chronological impossibility, this description of the body without organs would seem to refer both to the production of *Apocalypse Now* and to certain aspects of the tales, Conrad's and Coppola et al.'s. For these tales converge in the machinic breakdown, momentary halts, and reengagement of the machine all over again, with successive slippages and breakthroughs in both narrative and production. The intersection of the creative impulse and affective and corporeal responses becomes all the more evident if one traces a particular series, a sequence of events that might constitute a process of machinic syntheses. To wit:

- Willard waits in his hotel room, literally deterritorialized, far from the jungle where "Charlie" gets stronger ("Charlie doesn't get a lot of R & R") while Willard, in the "shit" of Saigon, is growing soft, thinking himself toward and through madness while drinking himself senseless. Through this room and this "thought," the viewer enters the narrative that converges on different hearts of darkness and light in the film's production.
- In this scene, Martin Sheen as Willard dances drunkenly before a mirror, and Francis Ford Coppola enters into Sheen's "personal territory, a man alone in his most private moment" (*Notes,* 87), as he films the actor. Eleanor Coppola provides insight about the source of this scene:

> In Francis's dream, he had Marty go to the mirror and look at himself, admire his mouth, etc., and when he turned around, Francis could see that Marty had suddenly turned into Willard. (*Notes,* 85)

As the documentary *Hearts of Darkness* reveals, Coppola pushed Sheen forward into this "dream" as if seeking the actor's breaking point as the most productive locus of creation. After Sheen/Willard cut his hand while punching his image in the mirror, Sheen refuses to let Coppola interrupt the filming: "I wanted to have this out right here and now," says Sheen retrospectively; "it had to do with facing my own worst enemy, myself; I was in a chaotic spiritual state" (*Hearts*). There follows in *Hearts of Darkness* an insert of Sheen/Willard (in the *Apocalypse Now* hotel scene) gripping his bleeding fist, lying on the floor, sobbing "My heart is broken," words not heard in *Apocalypse Now*—the viewer sees Willard/Sheen crying, but his words have been edited. Eleanor Coppola observes: "[Sheen] had gotten to the place where some part of him and Willard merged" (*Notes,* 86), and an unnamed crew member maintains, "Francis did a dangerous and terrible thing. He assumed the role of a psychiatrist and did a kind of brainwashing on a man who was much too sensitive. He put Martin in a place and didn't bring him back" (Vallely 1979, 46). As Sheen recalls, "I pretended I couldn't remember a lot of the things I'd done that night, and actually, I remembered it all" (*Hearts*).

• The process of coupling organs-objects on an amorphous BwO lurches forward: Sheen responds to this "direction" by internalizing this memory through his role, as Sam Bottoms (who played Lance in the film) later recalls, referring to Sheen's March 1, 1977, heart attack:

> When you ask Marty to examine his darker nature, it meant closing himself down a lot, and becoming very inward in order to find the killer who could carry out the task and terminate Kurtz. I think Willard was definitely responsible for Marty's breakdown. (*Hearts*)

Less publicly reported was Sheen's nervous breakdown that Sheen re-counted dramatically in 1979: "I completely fell apart. My spirit was exposed. I cried and cried. I turned completely gray—my eyes, my beard—all gray. I was in intensive care" (Vallely 1979: 48). He returned to the set after six weeks, following a recuperation that was at once necessary (for completing the film, of course, but also, from Sheen's perspective, for restoring his own self-esteem and ensuring his survival) and even upsetting (for the production): "Francis put his ear on Marty's chest to check him out. He said he looked too good. The shot . . . [is] in the briefing scene where Marty is supposed to be really hung over and dissipated-looking" (*Notes*, 185). For Sheen, a nomad subject, a residuum in terms of the lumbering creative machine, this recuperation was part of his personal struggle, through his inner turmoil, his collapse, and then return:

> I knew I would never come back until I accepted full and total responsi-bility for what had happened to me. No one put a gun to my head and forced me to be there. I was there because I had a big ego and wanted to be in a Coppola film. (Vallely 1979, 48)

> I just knew if I wanted to live, I could live. . . . It was my choice, and if I wanted to die, that was my choice too. (*Hearts*)

The process of creative syntheses—production, recording, consump-tion–consummation—is propelled by Coppola's pursuit of a deliberately provocative approach to the film, exemplified in the Willard/Sheen opening scene. In the retrospective interviews for *Hearts of Darkness,* Coppola claimed that he had never cared for the ending provided in John Milius's original script. The finale was to have consisted of a final gun battle pitting the Vietcong against Willard, Kurtz, and his men, at the end of which Kurtz opens fire on their rescue helicopter, exclaiming, "I fought too hard for this land" (*Hearts*). Instead, Coppola chose "to take [Milius's] script and mate it with [Conrad's] *Heart of Darkness* and [with] whatever happened to me in the jungle" (*Hearts*). The documentarists here insert the voiceover of Eleanor Coppola reading from *Notes*:

> More and more it seems like there are parallels between the character of Kurtz and Francis. There is the exhilaration of power in the face of losing everything, like the excitement of war when one kills and takes the chance of being killed. Francis has taken the biggest risk possible in the way he is making this film. (*Hearts*)

Edited from the documentary is the final sentence of this entry: "He is feeling the power of being the creator/director and the fear of completely failing" (*Notes*, 27). Already these dual facets, of power and failure, of production and breakdown, were enunciated by Coppola in a taped conversation he had with Hollywood producers who (Coppola claimed) had leaked news of Sheen's heart attack to the trade press: "If Marty dies," says Coppola, "I want to hear that everything is OK, until I say that Marty is dead" (*Hearts*).

These poles—of omnipotence and impotence, of creative genius and abysmal failure—recur as motifs throughout *Notes* and *Hearts of Darkness* and serve to define the creative and affective "territory" on which and through which these syntheses unfold. Coppola fears having no completed script, and he expresses his growing uncertainties about his film's ending, his ambivalence about the value of his project, and indeed about his entire career. Natural phenomena impinge upon this process, most dramatically the typhoon that wipes out the initial set in the Philippines (in May 1976). Coppola manifests abrupt mood swings, shifting from depression to exhilaration, that traverse not only his days and nights, but the entire set—for example, the shift from "electricity in the air" and a "circus mood" to discomfort and toil while shooting the Do Lung Bridge scene (*Notes*, 89–96). This mix of affect and creativity—indeed, affect qua creativity— produces distinct displacements of boundaries, veritable deterritorializations, for all involved:

> It seems like almost everyone on the production is going through some personal transition, a "journey" in their life. Everyone who has come out here to the Philippines seems to be going through something that is affecting them profoundly, changing their perspective about the world or themselves, while the same thing is supposedly happening to Willard in the course of the film. Something is definitely happening to me and to Francis. (*Notes*, 108)

Following part of this quote, delivered via Eleanor Coppola's voiceover in *Hearts of Darkness*, the documentary sequence segues to two participants/observers of the production, Sam Bottoms (who says simply,

"We were just bad, we were bad boys" in reference to drug use during filming), and Frederic Forrest (who played Chef in the film). Commenting on the "utterly mad" environment on the set, "like you were in a dream," Forrest describes his jungle scene with Sheen in which Willard and Chef are startled by a tiger:

> For me that was the essence of the whole film, the look in that tiger's eyes, the madness like it didn't matter what you wanted, there was no reality any more. . . . If the tiger wanted it, you were his. (*Hearts*)

A voiceover from the film follows in the documentary, with Willard repeating Chef's hysterical statement, "Never get out of the boat, absolutely, goddamned right, unless you were going all the way" (*Hearts/Apocalypse Now*).

Despite this plea to maintain fixed, secure territorial boundaries, no such guarantees are possible within the inexorable movement of syntheses. The ceaseless flows of desire, whether creative or capitalist, proceed through diverse couplings (i.e., intersections of desiring, productive force in situ) toward equally diverse moments of "freez[ing] in place," when a "body suffers" from disorienting forms of organization. Yet from each point of arrest emerges a subsequent "distribution," a "new machine" pressing forward within the process of production, at once a graft on the production and a component that provides further impetus for its progress. The production of *Apocalypse Now* reveals certain parallels with the syntheses deployed by Deleuze and Guattari: Sheen sinking into his "self" qua "becoming Willard," the other actors coping with this Willard-becoming and undergoing their own processes of confrontation, the bodily breakdowns that ensue (whether caused by drugs, depression, or physical impairment), Coppola's self-interrogation and affective oscillations, the continuing reemergence of new creative assemblages, with subsequent limits reached and reterritorializations imposed. Deleuze and Guattari suggest a means for understanding this process:

> How does delirium begin? Perhaps the cinema is able to capture the movement of madness, precisely because it is not analytical and regressive, but explores a global field of coexistence . . . [showing] that every delirium is first of all the investment of a field that is social, economic, political, cultural, racial and racist, pedagogical, and religious. (AOEng, 274; AOFr, 325–326)

As for as Kurtz's tale as recounted by Willard, this narration takes us toward complementary facets of these syntheses.

SYNTHESES

The machinic processes that animate Deleuze and Guattari's examination of psychoanalysis and familialism in Chapter 2 emerge throughout *Anti-Oedipus* in particular instances of literary discourse. The connective synthesis of production, for example, seems evident in Proust's *A la recherche du temps perdu*. Deleuze and Guattari describe the impact of this synthesis on them as readers struck

> by the fact that all the parts are produced as asymmetrical sections, paths that suddenly come to an end, hermetically sealed boxes, noncommuni-cating vessels, watertight compartments, in which there are gaps between things that are contiguous. . . . It is a schizoid work par excellence: it is almost as though the author's guilt, his confession of guilt are merely a sort of joke. . . . This is why in Proust's work, the apparent theme of guilt is tightly interwoven with a completely different theme totally contradict-ing it; the plantlike innocence that results from the total compartmentali-zation of the sexes, both in Charlus's encounters and in Albertine's slumber, where flowers blossom in profusion and the utter innocence of madness is revealed, whether it be the patent madness of Charlus or the supposed madness of Albertine. (AOEng, 42–43; AOFr, 51)

In discussing the legitimate use of the connective synthesis, Deleuze and Guattari affirm that critical interpretations of the contradictory themes in Proust, for example, homosexual guilt and the innocence of flowers, have either diagnosed them as indicative of a "dominant depressive nature and a sado-masochistic guilt," or have declared them irreducible, or have attempted to resolve the contradictions, to show that they are merely apparent. "In truth," say Deleuze and Guattari, "there are never contradic-tions, apparent or real, but only degrees of humor" (AOEng, 68; AOFr, 81). In fact, the narrator of *A la recherche* . . . is initially surrounded, they argue, by blurred nebulae, "*molar* or connective formations comprising singular-ities distributed haphazardly." Series emerge, and "persons figure in these series, under strange laws of lack, absence, asymmetry, exclusion, non-communication, vice, and guilt. Next, everything becomes blurred again, . . . but this time in a *molecular* or pure multiplicity," as the narrator connects with this "immense flow that each partial object produces and cuts again, reproduces and cuts at the same time" (AOEng, 69; AOFr, 81). The passage in which Albertine receives the first kiss illustrates for Deleuze and Guattari that "more than vice, says Proust, it is madness and its innocence that disturb us. If schizophrenia is the universal, the great artist is indeed the one who scales the schizophrenic wall and reaches the land of the unknown, where he no longer belongs to any time, to any milieu, to any school" (AOEng, 69; AOFr, 82).[11]

For the disjunctive and conjunctive syntheses, Deleuze and Guattari refer to works by an array of authors. The disjunctive synthesis emerges clearly in the works of Klossowski and Beckett (AOEng, 76–77; AOFr, 91–92),[12] while the conjunctive synthesis emerges in the works of diverse Anglo-American writers:

> From Thomas Hardy, from D. H. Lawrence to Malcolm Lowry, from Henry Miller to Allen Ginsberg and Jack Kerouac, men who know how to leave, to scramble the codes, to cause flows to circulate, to traverse the desert of the body without organs. They overcome a limit, they shatter a wall, the capitalist barrier. And of course they fail to complete the process, they never cease failing to do so. (AOEng, 132–133; AOFr, 158)

Deleuze and Guattari argue that this synthesis is especially resonant in the works of Artaud and Kafka:

> Artaud puts it well: all writing is so much pig shit—that is to say, any literature that takes itself as an end or sets ends for itself, instead of being a process that "ploughs the crap of being and its language," transports the weak, the aphasiacs, the illiterate. . . . The only literature is that which places an explosive device in its package, fabricating a counterfeit currency, causing the superego and its form of expression to explode, as well as the market value of its form of content. (AOEng, 134; AOFr, 160)

This nomadic and polyvocal use of the conjunctive synthesis is opposed to a segregative and familialist use. For Deleuze and Guattari, Artaud's schizophrenia constitutes him as the fulfillment of literature: "From the depths of his suffering and his glory, he has the right to denounce what society makes of the psychotic in the process of decoding the flows of desire ([as in] *Van Gogh, the Man Suicided by Society*), but also what it makes of literature when it opposes literature to psychosis in the name of a neurotic or perverse recoding ([as does] Lewis Carroll, or the coward of belles-lettres)" (AOEng, 135; AOFr, 160).[13]

The works of Artaud reveal a crucial focal point in schizoanalysis, for which "reading a text is never a scholarly exercise in search of what is signified, still less a highly textual exercise in search of a signifier, . . . [but instead] a productive use of the literary machine, a montage of desiring machines, a schizoid exercise that extracts from the text its revolutionary forces" (AOEng, 106; AOFr, 125–126). Deleuze and Guattari contrast André Breton to Artaud in order to exemplify the Oedipalizing literary force that

> deploys a form of superego proper to it, even more noxious than the nonwritten superego. Oedipus is in fact literary before being psychoana-

lytic. There will always be a Breton against Artaud, a Goethe against Lenz, a Schiller against Hölderlin, in order to superegoize literature and tell us: Careful, go no further! . . . The Oedipal form of literature is its commodity form. (AOEng, 134; AOFr, 159)

Deleuze and Guattari so posit an important construct of schizoanalysis, to which they return in Chapter 4 in their "Introduction," the two poles between which the types of libidinal investment pass. On the one hand, the molar pole is characterized by "paranoiac, signifying, structured lines of integration," by perverse reterritorializations of flows, and by reactionary or fascist social investments; on the other hand, the molecular pole is characterized by "schizophrenic, machinic, dispersed lines of escape," by schizophrenic deterritorializations, and by revolutionary social investments (AOEng, 340; AOFr, 406–407).[14] Drawing upon Guattari's early writing (see Chap. 1 above), the authors argue that to the paranoiac molar pole belongs the subjugated group "with Oedipus and castration forming the imaginary structure under which [its] members . . . are induced to live or fantasize individually their membership in the group" (AOEng, 64; AOFr, 75). They oppose this group to the subject-group, the schizo-revolutionary group that "follows the *lines of escape* of desire; breaches the wall and causes flows to move; . . . proceeding in an inverse fashion from that of the other pole: I am not your kind, I belong eternally to the inferior race, I am a beast, a black" (AOEng, 277; AOFr, 329).[15]

Deleuze and Guattari warn that these groups are constantly shifting, a subject-group threatened by subjugation, or a subjugated group forced to the revolutionary pole (AOEng, 64; AOFr, 75). The example they present is that of the surrealist group, "with its fantastic subjugation, its narcissism, and its superego," opposed to the loner functioning "as a flow-schiz, as a subject-group, through a break with the subjugated group from which he excludes himself or is excluded: Artaud-the-schizo" (AOEng, 349; AOFr, 418–419). On this schizo-revolutionary pole, they maintain that artistic value emerges "in terms of the decoded and deterritorialized flows that [art] causes to circulate beneath a signifier reduced to silence, beneath the conditions of identity of the parameters, across a structure reduced to impotence" (AOEng, 370; AOFr, 444). Art accedes in this way "to its authentic modernity," they conclude, "the pure process that fulfills itself, and that never ceases to reach fulfillment as it proceeds—art as 'experimentation' " (AOEng, 370–371; AOFr, 445).

* * *

Yet another quote from *Anti-Oedipus* could very well apply to *Apocalypse Now*: "A huge, pudgy bloated boy, working one of his little desiring-machines, after having hooked it up to a vast technical social machine"

(AOEng, 7; AOFr, 13). These images apply both to the production and to the tale, but particularly to the production, since the pudgy, bloated boy seems to multiply, to be dual, and to mirror itself as others in the Kurtz/Brando/Coppola conjunction/disjunction. Coppola seems particularly susceptible to these shifting sites of subjectivity. According to Eleanor Coppola's *Notes*, at times during the filming Coppola identified with Willard: "When [Sheen] was close to death, ... he [Coppola] was as near death as he has ever experienced. He said he could see reality receding down a dark tunnel, and he was totally scared that he couldn't get back" (166). However, faced with Brando during the production, Coppola had to cope with a quite bloated pudgy "other" and "same." The appearance of the overweight Brando was just part of Coppola's "ultimate nightmare" (*Notes*, 120), for not only was Brando sensitive about his weight, he had never read *Heart of Darkness*, and he was totally unprepared to follow a script (see *Notes*, 108–110; *Hearts*). One result of these circumstances was an apparent breakdown of the production since Brando required Coppola to orient him with lengthy discussions, leaving the crew entirely without work for days on end. Yet through this clash of machines and bodies and their subsequent breakdowns came the creative response: Coppola's decision to film Brando's scenes as extensive improvisations by the actor.

In order to follow this complex movement of subjectivities and creation, we must distinguish at least three conjoined processes at work: the Brando/Kurtz connection (through Brando's interpretation of the role and direction by Coppola), the Coppola/Kurtz disjunction (the director-producer's attempt to come to grips with his "own" hearts of darkness, depicted in *Notes* and the documentary, as well as in various interviews), and the Willard/Kurtz conjunction (the narrative reconstitution of Kurtz as a body without organs upon which the inscription of both the sociocultural dynamics and the narrator's desire develops during the trip upriver).

1. Brando/Kurtz

In *Hearts of Darkness*, Coppola says of the Kurtz role: "I wanted a character of a monumental nature who is struggling with the extremities of his soul, and is struggling with them on such a level that you're in awe of it [while he] is destroyed by them" (*Hearts*). Coppola had first conceived of Kurtz as "a Gauguin figure, with mangoes and babies, a guy who'd really gone all the way," but "Marlon wouldn't go for it" (Marcus 1979, 54). Brando's idea was to play Kurtz as a displaced Daniel Berrigan, dressed in Viet Cong (VC) clothes, so that his interpretation "would be all about the guilt [Kurtz] felt at what we'd done," an approach that Coppola opposed. If we rely on Eleanor Coppola's *Notes*, it was Brando himself who determined the direction that the film's final segment would take, moving his interpretation toward a Kurtz who was "a mythical figure, a theater personage," combined with Coppola's own vision of Conrad's novel and his response to Brando's physical condition (*Notes*, 109–110, 137). Their compromise was the improvisation, with the added touch of Brando shaving his head, providing Coppola with "that terrible face" (Marcus 1979, 54).[16] While this "compromise" actually was the director's only choice, it allowed him to make the most efficient use of the short time he had with Brando on the set: Coppola directed how the "scene should go," asking questions off camera, and Brando responded in stream-of-consciousness fashion. Different reactions to Coppola's depiction of Kurtz have been quite negative,[17] and some of the outtakes from the improvisations, presented in *Hearts of Darkness*, are quite hilarious. For example, during one improvisational reflection, Brando pauses dramatically in midsentence to announce that he has swallowed a bug, and at the end of another rumination he walks ponderously toward a dramatically lit doorway and solemnly announces, "I can't think of any more dialogue." Nonetheless, the Brando/Kurtz connection opens a refreshing and productive play of desire and creativity that permits Coppola to add a distinct and original texture to the final segment of the film.

2. Coppola/Kurtz

One might even be tempted to argue that through this improvisation process, Coppola works implicitly within the "destructive task of schizoanalysis":

> Successively undoing the representative territorialities and reterritorializations through which a subject passes his individual history . . . to a point where the process cannot extricate itself, continue on, and reach fulfillment, except insofar as it is capable of creating—what exactly?—a new land. (AOEng, 318; AOFr, 379–380)

It is disturbing, then, but almost predictable, that what I call the Coppola/Kurtz disjunction works in a nearly opposite fashion. That is, in terms of Coppola's inherent ambivalence, between omnipotence and impotence, the filmmaker seems to be working to resolve his artistic and personal difficulties (often hard to distinguish). Indeed, Marsha Kinder attributes Coppola's "retention of Kurtz's obsession with power [to] his own 'irresistible fascination' with this dimension of the story, which applied to his own experience of making the film" (1979–1980, 71), that is, to his own need to master his diverse insecurities, at once financial, creative, and familial. However, as regards the narrative development of

Kurtz, Coppola seems entirely subjugated to the fixed parameters of his directorial craft, falling back on ready-made props. This subjugation runs expressly counter to his desire to enter into some nonsubjugated creative process in order to make "an unusual, surrealist movie" (Marcus 1979, 55). Coppola's own words reveal more eloquently than any commentator's remarks how the "solution" he adopts for the narrative dilemma of the Kurtz/Willard encounter—recourse to the mythology of the Fire King, borrowed from James Frazer's *The Golden Bough*—fits entirely within a fundamentally limited mythological framework.[18]

Greil Marcus surprises Coppola in their interview by contradicting the director's view of having created a movie that might extend the action into "a different reality." For Marcus, the emergence of such a "reality" is something that could have overwhelmed Willard—notably, the temptation to take over Kurtz's compound after killing him—but is finally a recourse that Willard rejects. To Marcus's argument, Coppola reveals his own sense of the ending:

MARCUS: If [Willard] had not [rejected that choice], then he, and maybe we, would have been swallowed by the extended realities you're talking about. But he rejects that. That seemed very clear. Is that not what you meant?

COPPOLA: No ... When I finally got there, the best I could come up with was this: I've got this guy who's gone up the river, he's gonna go kill this other guy who's been the head of all this. Life and death. ... [A friend mentioned the myth of] the Fisher King—I went and got [*The Golden Bough*], and I said, of course, that's what I want. That's what was meant by the animal sacrifices.... At this point [Willard is in Kurtz's compound], he is listening to Brando, and Brando asks him to do something for him: to go back home, and tell his son certain things, takes his notes, and say that he wasn't what the army is gonna make him out to be, and to, ah, incidentally—kill him.

MARCUS: Kurtz is consciously participating in the myth of the Golden Bough; he's prepared that role for Willard, for him to take his place.

COPPOLA: He wants Willard to kill him. So Willard thinks about this: he says, "Everyone wanted him dead. The army ... and ultimately even the jungle; that's where he took his orders from, anyway." The notion is that Willard is moved to do it, to go once more into that primitive state, to go and kill.... As he comes out [from killing Kurtz], he flirts with the notion of being king, but something ... does not lure him. He starts to go away, and then the moment when he flirted with being king is superimposed. And that's the moment when we use "the horror, the horror." (Marcus 1979, 55)[19]

Marcus sees quite well the potential with which Coppola worked in developing Kurtz's character. But he also points out that, all dreamlike cinematography and special effects aside, the dream quality was subsumed by Coppola's need to work within the mythological dimension. Thus, despite his vision of producing a fully surrealist representation of Vietnam—and to achieve thereby a creative and affective process less subjugated to directorial norms—Coppola finally accedes to a fully formed and quite circumscribed device to end his film.

However, I am less interested in this much analyzed recourse to a mythological framework than in what it entails for a story and a production that rely so intensely on a purported process of "going insane." For Coppola's recourse situates his work clearly within the psychoanalytical framework that Deleuze and Guattari vehemently oppose in *Anti-Oedipus,* particularly with Coppola's appeal to Kurtz's request that Willard speak to his son. Deleuze and Guattari say something quite appropriate for this context:

> Psychoanalysis undoes [myth and tragedy] as objective representations, and discovers in them the figures of a subjective universal libido; but it reanimates them, and promotes them as subjective representations that extend the mythic and tragic contents to infinity. Psychoanalysis does treat myth and tragedy, but it treats them *as* the dreams and the fantasies of private man, *Homo familia.* . . . What acts as an objective and public element—the Earth, the Despot—is now taken up again, but as the expression of a subjective and private reterritorialization: Oedipus is the fallen despot—banished, deterritorialized—but a reterritorialization is engineered, using the Oedipus complex conceived of as the daddy-mommy-me of today's everyman. (AOEng, 304; AOFr, 362)

For the sake of (or for lack of) an ending, Coppola resituates all of Kurtz's deterritorializing and lines of flight—all of his "[un]sound methods," all of what Nick Land calls Kurtz's "implement[ation of] schizoanalysis, lapsing into shadow, becoming imperceptible" (1995, 203)—within the neat parameters of privatized myth and tragedy, *Homo familia,* a term to which I will return below.

3. Willard/Kurtz

As we have seen, Coppola reflected at great length upon the Willard/Kurtz conjunction, as have numerous critics to whom I have previously referred. However, Coppola's engagement with this pair corresponds both to affective parameters (identifying with one and then with the other at different moments of the production) and to artistic needs (notably, his difficulties with determining an ending). The intersti-ces of the action episodes in *Apocalypse Now* (described below, under "Reterritorializations") are filled by the dual exercise, at once hermeneutic and confessional, to which Willard delivers himself in his study of the Kurtz dossier. This "exercise" is presented to the viewer through voiceover narration scripted in large measure by Michael Herr, author of *Dispatches* (1968), who "determined the [narration's] tone, the hipster voice Willard is given," according to Coppola (Marcus 1979, 53–54).[20]

This narration serves a strictly narrative function, of course: it provides Willard's running commentary on the collective experience, of the PBR crew and of Vietnam—for example, about Kilgore, about the Viet Cong (aka "Charlie"), about the hypocrisy of military violence following the incident in which the PBR crew massacres the Vietnamese occupants of a sampan. However, the Kurtz/Willard conjunction also constitutes the means through which Willard-as-narrator prepares himself for the mission by reconstituting Kurtz as a body without organs based on a textual corpus to which he has been given privileged access. The constant, almost mantralike return to Kurtz throughout Willard's preparation places this personage at the center of the film because he is juxtaposed to each action episode. I wish to follow this process in some detail because the film's five hermeneutic and confessional segments (with a prelude, an interlude, and the final "practice" session in Kurtz's compound) allow us to see the complex reconstitution of subjectivities: on the one hand, a textual body (the documents and photos of Kurtz) assembled and dispersed, first through Willard's progressive reflections on this material, then in the "practice" session during which Kurtz as body with organs undoes Wil-lard's careful preparations; on the other hand, the cinematic "body" (the film itself) shifting from images that move toward a creative disruption of narrative expectations, then into final reassemblage around mythical, familial, and patriarchal parameters:

Prelude: The Nha Trang I Corps Briefing

Following Willard's forced awakening at the hands of soldiers at his Saigon hotel, his arrival at the Nha Trang I Corps command post is accompanied by Willard's ponderous voiceover narration about receiv-ing a "real choice mission . . . for my sins," about going to the "worst place in the world," about the river winding "like a circuit cable plugged straight into Kurtz." The voiceover then presents a very odd, but telling statement:

> It was no accident that I got to be the caretaker of Colonel Walter E. Kurtz's memory, any more than being back in Saigon was an accident.

There is no way of telling his story without telling my own, and if his story
is really a confession, then so is mine.

This retrospective narrator, like Conrad's Marlow, serves to create
time shifts, but not merely as "counterpoint between Willard's continuous
journey toward Kurtz and the violently disjunctive scenes of war" (Lindroth 1983, 117). Both Saigon and Willard's caretaker role apparently are
"no accident" because, having undergone some process of transformation
in the journey through time and space to find Kurtz, Willard seems
convinced of a predestined mission that the "retelling" through voiceover
might fulfill. In a sense, the viewer/analyst is being set up to collaborate
in the narrator/analysand's circular journey, toward his eventual return
to the Saigon "shit." Yet this collaboration inscribes the viewer—perhaps
inevitably—within a subjugated position that corresponds entirely to the
paternal logic of *Homo familia*.

In light of this key voiceover statement, the briefing unfolds within
a paternalistic scenario, playing out as revelation of embarrassing family
secrets. The mission's spokesman is a dutiful "son" (Harrison Ford,
addressed as "Lucas" by the General), clearly uncomfortable as he coughs
his way through the details of the mission. The General (G. D. Spradlin),
as moralizing father figure and *Homo familia*, provides the necessary
analytic spin on Kurtz's acts: he is a soldier transformed from an
outstanding "man of wit and humor" into a criminal on the lam with his
worshipping native army. The General diagnoses Kurtz's activities conveniently as those of a man gone "obviously insane." And then there is the
hungry "uncle," Jerry, nearly anonymous except for his piercing gaze and
his love of roast beef and Marlboros.[21] His only line, summarizing the
mission directive, along with the proffered cigarette, have since entered
into cinema history: "Terminate . . . with extreme prejudice." The scene
ends with the establishment of an unspoken alliance through the silent
crisscrossing gazes—Jerry's, Willard's, and the General's—and Willard has
apparently been successfully inscribed within the fixed parameters that
define Kurtz's subjectivity as criminal and insane. Then the camera
displaces Willard's gaze through a slow pan toward the window and the
white light of Vietnam.

Study Session 1

Each of Willard's self-briefing episodes on the PBR boat mixes images of
photos and documents with Willard's voiceover commentary and his
musings, usually juxtaposed with events on the boat and the river. Hence,
the result of the first documentary encounter is at once his bewilderment
and awe. On the one hand, through the voiceover, Willard offers harsh

thumbnail sketches of each crew member: Chef from New Orleans, Lance from the beaches south of L.A., Mr. Clean from the South Bronx, and Phillips the Chief (no origin) in whose boat Willard is merely an uninvited guest.[22] Refusing Willard's proffered cigarette ("[I] Don't smoke"), the Chief ominously recalls having pulled a "Special Ops up the Nung River"—as the viewer learns, precisely where the crew is headed, beyond Do Lung Bridge. However, this tool of the "war machine," the PBR and its crew, has now been diverted by military logic itself toward a particular deterritorialization, with Willard functioning as the nomadic, residual subject (outside the "family"), yet also the hidden despot whose paranoia and power will soon dominate everyone.

On the other hand, the seemingly incidental details of the crew's description foreground Willard's first "study session," unfolding in conjunction with the crew's antics: Mr. Clean dancing to "Satisfaction," Lance surfing behind the boat, and the Chief stretching out lazily, in the only repose this character will have. Noting that he "heard [Kurtz's] voice on the tape [during the Nha Trang briefing], and it really put a hook in me," Willard cannot "connect up that voice with this man" represented in the file. For him, Kurtz's exemplary career took a startling turn after his first tour in Vietnam, after his report to the Joint Chiefs was "restricted," and after he was admitted to and then completed Airborn Training at age thirty-eight: "Why the fuck would he do that?" asks Willard, musing on the PBR, in contrast to the postmission Willard whose full (yet reterritorialized) understanding and acceptance of Kurtz qualifies him for the "caretaker" role.

Study Session 2

Following both the AirCav sequence with Kilgore as errant master of the military "machine" and the stroll of Willard and Chef in search of mangoes, only to find a tiger, Willard takes Chef's frenzied cry—"Never get off the fuckin' boat!"—as a warning against doing what Kurtz did: he left the boat, "split from the whole fuckin' program." Reading at night by flashlight, Willard tries to discover why Kurtz would cast away certain promotion in order to join the Green Berets and return to Vietnam with Special Forces. The documentation that Willard manipulates—notes, application forms, Kurtz's diploma, photos of Kurtz's wife and son—offers evidence of Kurtz's progressive deterritorialization within and by means of the military apparatus. This study helps authenticate Willard's conclusions: "The more I read and began to understand, the more I admired him. . . . A tough motherfucker. . . . He could have gone for general, but he went for himself instead." Additional documents on Kurtz's unauthorized Operation Archangel of October 1967 show that Kurtz had gauged the capitalist axiomatics quite cannily: producing attractive copy for the press—not to mention actually producing strategic results—far outstripped any mere hierarchical dictates issued by a military command structure that Kurtz held in contempt.

Study Session 3

The Hau Phat USO episode provides a segue to this "study session" since Willard links the utterly absurd spectacle, and debacle, of Playboy models dancing in the jungle to Kurtz wanting to "put a weed up Command's ass," the ineffective "four-star clowns who were going to end up giving the whole circus away."[23] Reading details of Kurtz's extremely effective operation—his order to assassinate four ARVN (South Vietnamese) allies and the resultant disappearance of enemy activity in Kurtz's sector—lays the ground for Willard's inner conflict, the clash of territories and subjectivities. Through a flashback overlay of Willard's face with images from the Nha Trang briefing, the double voiceover creates something like a duel between the official, paternal/military interpretation and Willard's own growing appreciation of Kurtz's process of deterritorialization. First, the General's voice and gestures (". . . he joined Special Forces, and after that his [methods became unsound]") intersects with Willard's reflection, "The Army tried one last time to bring him back into the fold." Then, the subordinate Lucas's voice and gestures ("his Montagnard army treat him like a god and follow every order, however ridiculous") precede Willard's satisfied comment, "He kept going . . . he kept winning. . . . He was gone. . . . The VC knew his name, and they were scared of him." Throughout this session, Willard not only handles the usual evidential documents, but he also follows the course of Kurtz's skirmishes with the VC by tracing and circling locations on a map, as if needing confirmation of Kurtz's affective deterritorialization by means of fixed territorial markers.

Study Session 4

Willard's brief but important conversation with the Chief reveals to the latter the goal of Willard's mission, and they strike a bargain: to cut the PBR crew loose once they take Willard close to his destination. The "study session" that follows consists solely of a voiceover in which Willard recites the text of Kurtz's letter to his son juxtaposed with aerial shots of the PBR moving upriver and with various tell-tale signs of combat. Besides these jarring images, external visually to Willard's *tête-à-texte*, the intensity of this session is translated with close-ups on Willard's face—indeed, the opening shot consists of his left eye filling the entire screen. He thus takes on and absorbs the crucial text in which Kurtz's words via Willard's voice, and not those of "official" documents, justify assassinating the ARVN officials and offer a "philosophy" of action:

> In a war, there are many moments for compassion and tender action. There are many moments for ruthless action. What is often called ruthless may in many circumstances be only clarity, seeing clearly what there is to be done and doing it, directly, quickly, awake, looking at it. . . . I am unconcerned. I am beyond their timid, lying morality, and so I am beyond caring. You have all my faith. Your loving father.

The final image of this session is of a grainy black-and-white photo askew on the screen to which Willard returns again and again. The photo contains only the silhouette of a large form, seemingly a round head and shoulders, profiled in a square doorway, "catching the light only dimly, as if [Kurtz] barely remains in the phenomenal world at all—a ghostly presence that outlines the abstract form of his doom as the embodied core of darkness" (Stewart 1981, 461).

Interlude: The Sampan Massacre

The close connection between the introspective "study sessions" and the narrative unfolding is nowhere more evident than in the massacre of the sampan occupants by the PBR crew, a scene that originated in the actors' desire "to do a My Lai Massacre" (Sam Bottoms in *Hearts*). Clearly, the Chief's main motivation for this "regular check" is to show Willard and the crew who really is in charge, he himself, not Willard. When massacre ensues, the Chief attempts to extend his command authority to the nurturing role of transporting the wounded Vietnamese woman for medical aid, but he is thwarted. Willard resolves the command question— to use Kurtz's words from the letter to his son—"clearly and quickly" by executing her with his handgun, telling the Chief, "I told you not to stop. . . . Now let's go." With Willard squatting down on the PBR deck, the film slowly fades to black and stays that way for a full fifteen to thirty seconds—"like a wound in narrative" (Stewart 1981, 462)—before the soundtrack and a very dim image of the boat at dusk return.

This darkness, after a pivotal scene of murder as compassion, ruthlessness as clarity, is the heart of the film. Willard's comment through voiceover—"These boys were never going to look at me the same way again, but I felt like I knew one or two things about Kurtz that weren't in the dossier"—suggests just how close to Kurtz Willard has come, or may have always been. For Willard's own "clarity" of action is what he has come to read, or wants to read, in the deterritorializing narrative that he assembles during his "study sessions." At this point, Coppola seems quite ready to achieve his goal of creating and expressing a different and "extended reality," particularly as the next scene depicts the continuous deterritorialization of flows—mud, rain, gunfire, bodies, screams in the night—at the Do Lung Bridge.

Study Session 5

Besides displaying yet again the absurd futility of combat, especially as background spectacle for Lance's acid trip, the pause at the bridge offers a last chance for mail delivery to the crew, providing Willard with a communiqué, and thus initiating his fifth and final "study session." Willard learns that a Captain Richard Colby, photo attached, preceded him on an identical mission and, although presumed dead, wrote a letter to his wife that was intercepted by the authorities. With a snapshot of his home taped to the top of the page, the scrawled letter reads:

> SELL THE HOUSE
> SELL THE CAR
> SELL THE KIDS
> FIND SOMEONE ELSE
> FORGET IT! I'M NEVER COMING ~~HOME~~ BACK
> FORGET IT!!!

That "HOME" is crossed out and is replaced with "BACK" seems a curious detail for a man cutting loose from all attachments in order to join forces with Kurtz. But the importance of Willard's final session may well be lost as the film speeds into high gear, first, with the firefight in which Mr. Clean is killed, then with the Chief's death by a spear on which he tries to impale Willard, who must break the Chief's neck. This sequence of death and disarray is almost the echo of Willard's own dismay at what he reads in Colby's photo, tale, and text. The reconstitution of subjectivities (his own and Kurtz's) and the deterritorialization that he has been experiencing through the process of textual assemblage encounter the nightmare of what he fears most, his own doubt, yet also a mirror of his own life. Indeed, Colby's peculiar scrawled message seems to echo Willard's own certainty, expressed earlier, that home "just didn't exist anymore."

Hands-On: The Kurtz Compound

Foreboding, fear, and then anticipation all mix as Willard, Chef, and Lance approach the compound where the truly "hands-on session" occurs between Kurtz and Willard, who seems to make little use of the knowledge he has gleaned from his study of the Colonel. Rather than sending the surviving crew members back before they reach the compound, as he had earlier promised, Willard seems to abandon them to their particular flows: Lance to his continued immersion into complete deterritorialization, thereby securing his eventual survival; Chef to the specific task of calling in the air strike within the territorial confines "on the boat," thus probably signing his death warrant. Unlike these polar opposites, Willard remains in the floating state of anticipation and wonderment, with his subjectivity located somewhere between that of remaining a willing captive or becoming a dutiful son. During his recuperation following the initial capture and torture, he observes Kurtz, and is allowed to examine his uniform, his medals, and his books. Yet Willard simply has no sense—meaning or direction—of what he should or will do, and even of what "the generals back in Nha Trang" would want him to do, or what Kurtz's "people back home" would want him to do if *they* could see what Willard sees. The viewer, having witnessed so many scenes involving Willard's careful study of evidence regarding Kurtz during the trip upriver, might well be baffled by Willard's doubt and indecision now that he has reached his destination. But the viewer should understand Willard's predicament: the appeal of deterritorialized flows documented in the study materials may have clashed with the living example of Colby—portrayed upon Willard's arrival as the paterfamilias of a small, nomadic jungle tribe. His presence reveals to Willard all too starkly where these flows might actually lead. Indeed, Kurtz as *Homo familia* has replicated an extended family himself, as the photojournalist (Dennis Hopper) reminds Willard: "Out here, we're all his children."

Furthermore, the Kurtz myth clashes with Kurtz's own becomings. Kurtz makes a lengthy statement to Willard about his epiphany—"like I was shot with a diamond bullet right through my forehead"—at the VC's response to the inoculation of children by the Special Force troops: they cut off and piled up the inoculated arms. This revelation led Kurtz to the conclusion that implicitly echoes the letter to his son: "You have to have men who are moral and, at the same time, are able to utilize their primordial instincts to kill without feeling, without passion, without judgment." Coming as this statement does at "the end"—the end of the river, the end of Kurtz's itinerary—we can see that Kurtz now does fear judgment, that he is no longer beyond the "timid, lying morality" of his judges, no longer "beyond caring." Between the logic of the military "machine"—the judgment and "stench of lies" of the "grocery clerks" back in Nha Trang, Saigon, and Washington—and the family drama—anxiety about his legacy in the memory of his son—Kurtz finally accedes to the overcoding of the familial, endorsing Willard's mission and thereby sanctioning his aquatic rebirth and survival as caretaker.

However, the more obvious Kurtz successor, the former Captain Colby, is already present and integrated into the "warrior–poet" life-style. For Coppola, one radical "solution" to the problem of the ending would be incompatible with respecting Kurtz's overwhelming concern for his legacy, and for his narrative's transmission—if Colby were to challenge Willard on the steps following Kurtz's assassination, defeat him, and replace Kurtz as someone not invested in a "caretaker" mission on behalf of the fallen idol. In fact, Coppola had considered a much larger role for Colby, evidenced by his decision to cast Scott Glen, a promising actor in the late 1970s and not a mere extra, to play Colby. Moreover, in an earlier draft of the script (dated 3 December 1975), Coppola presents Willard and Colby in the PBR alone with the body of Kurtz, returning down river, after a final gun battle in the compound against attacking North Vietnamese forces.[24]

Clearly, this approach was no longer acceptable to Coppola, locked as he was into the attractively familiar coordinates of mythology and the implicit family drama that he imposed on the final sequence and ending. Coppola's recourse to the myth of the Fire King ultimately triangulates the narrative within the "daddy-mommy-me" coordinates. Regarding the film's finale, I part company with Nick Land's otherwise superb analysis:

> Evening at the end of the river: . . . You have a 28-centimetre serrated combat knife in your left hand. The Willard skin is coming away in ragged scraps, exposing something beyond masculinity, beyond humanity, beyond life. Patches of mottled technoderm woven with electronics are emerging. Daddy and mummy means nothing anymore. You scrape away your face and step into the dark. . . . (Land 1995, 203–204)

To the contrary, daddy and mummy mean a great deal, indeed, they are of utmost importance both to the tale and to the production of *Apocalypse Now*. Quite pertinent in this regard is the way that each phase of the trip upriver corresponds not only to the specific steps of Willard's reconstruction of Kurtz's tale, but also to Coppola's "journey" to produce *Apocalypse Now*. In this light, Deleuze and Guattari's presentation of three phases of the socius and capital illuminate these conjunctions more clearly.

RETERRITORIALIZATIONS

The long development of a "universal history" in Chapter 3 of *Anti-Oedipus* ostensibly moves Deleuze and Guattari away from the frontal attack on

Freudian orthodoxy (and even on a certain Lacanian perspective) and toward a lucid sociopolitical, ethnological, and economic analysis. Several authors have already provided quite thorough examinations and critiques of the three phases that Deleuze and Guattari propose.[25] I see my task, then, as engaging these phases—the primitive territorial machine, the despotic barbarian machine, and the capitalist machine—for a narrative purpose that will first entail some summary and then animation of the Deleuze–Guattarian concepts in light of *Apocalypse Now*.

I begin by following the lead of Nick Land, ever the effective "mediator," who sees *Anti-Oedipus* as "an anticipatively assembled inducer for the replay of geohistory in hypermedia, a social-systemic fast feed-forward through machinic delirium" (1995, 191). Pursuing the traces of this "universal history" with a vengeance, Land likens the primitive territorial production to "the Kurtz-process [that] masks itself in wolf-pelts of regression, returning to the repressed, discovering a lost truth, excavating the fossils of monsters" (1995, 193). Land continues:

> [This process] codes by deterritorializing; unfixing by hunter-gathering, according to a cold or metastatic cultural code that equilibrates on a (Bateson) "plateau." Earth begins its migration-in-place towards the globe. (1995, 193)

At this point in history, societies are not yet ruled by the modern privatization of organs. In the primitive territorial machine, exchange is secondary to "the task that sums up all the others: marking bodies, which are the earth's products ... [by] tattooing, excising, incising, carving, scarifying, mutilating, encircling, and initiating" (AOEng, 144; AOFr, 169). Here, on the primitive socius, social relations are defined predominantly by kinship, by alliance, and by filiation, the last of which Deleuze and Guattari compare to "two forms of a primitive capital: fixed capital or filiative stock, and circulating capital or mobile blocks of debts" (AOEng, 146; AOFr, 172).[26]

To this process of coding corresponds a distinct mode of territorial representation, one based on a fluid bodily graphism, "a geo-graphism, a geography ... oral [formations] precisely because they possess a graphic system that is independent of the voice, ... but connected to it, coordinated ... and multidimensional" (AOEng, 188; AOFr, 222–223). This duality of savage inscription—voice audition and hand graphics—is complemented and completed by a third element, "eye-pain," constituting a libidinal economy of territorial representation:

> A voice that speaks or intones, a sign marked in bare flesh, an eye that extracts enjoyment from the pain. . . . A magic triangle. Everything in this

system is active, acted upon, or reacted to: the action of the voice of
alliance, the passion of the body of filiation, the reaction of the eye
evaluating the declension of the two. (AOEng, 189–190; AOFr, 224)

This primitive inscription machine entails, then, primitive, "open mobile
and finite blocks of debt: this extraordinary composite of the speaking
voice, the marked body, and the enjoying eye" (AOEng, 190; AOFr, 224).

Against this primitive assemblage a different kind of coding exerts itself
in the form of despotism, "an ulterior zone, a heart of darkness," says Land,
"introduc[ing] an organizing principle that comes from elsewhere—from
'above'—a deterritorialized simplicity or supersoma overcoding the aborigi-
nal body as created flesh" (1995, 196). This "despotic machine or the
barbarian socius," as Deleuze and Guattari call it, supplants the primitive
formation such that "the full body as socius has ceased to be the earth, it
has become the body of the despot, the despot himself or his god" (AOEng,
193–194; AOFr, 228–230). With this new alliance system and direct filiation
between despot and deity comes an overcoding that destroys the primitive
system of filiation and alliance and imposes a State apparatus. This "pseudo
territoriality is the product of an effective deterritorialization that substitutes abstract signs for the signs of the earth," creating an earth as State-
owned property, confirming the primitive machine's "dread of decoded
flows . . . [flows] that might escape the State monopoly, with its tight
restrictions and its plugging of flows" (AOEng, 196–197; AOFr, 232–233).
And the system of "barbarian or imperial representation" now takes on a
more familiar cast; the subordination of the voice to a graphism becomes a
writing, flattens out into meanings, under the imperialism of the signifier,
"the signifier as the repressing representation, and the new displaced
represented that it induces, the famous metaphors and metonymy—all of
that constitutes the overcoding and deterritorialized despotic machine"
(AOEng, 209; AOFr, 247).[27]

Deleuze and Guattari here evoke Antonin Artaud's *Héliogabale* as a
text that best sketches the flows determining the "entire history of
primitive coding, of despotic overcoding, and of the decoding of private
man turn[ing] on these movements of flows: . . . the graphic flux goes
from the flood of sperm in the tyrant's cradle, to the wave of shit in his
sewer tomb" (AOEng, 211; AOFr, 250). Kafka's "In the Penal Colony"
also indicates, say Deleuze and Guattari, the means by which the State
apparatus defines the imperial barbarian law, with its "paranoiac-schizoid
trait of the law (metonymy)," partitioning off nontotalized parts; and the
"maniacal depressive trait (metaphor)," the law's self-sufficiency and
inscrutability (AOEng, 212; AOFr, 251). And through the order of the
law—for example, the invention of vengeance, the incitement of *ressenti-
ment*—eventually comes Oedipus. The "Oedipal cell" completes "its migration

. . . finally becom[ing] the representative of desire itself. . . . Hence desire, having completed its migration, will have to experience this extreme affliction of being turned against itself" (AOEng, 216-217; AOFr, 255–257).

Nick Land can help us move quickly into the third phase, the triumph of capitalism: "By the time global history comes up on the screen, commoditization has berserked history, reorganizing society into a disorganizing apparatus that melts ritual and laws into axiomatic rules" (1995, 199). Capitalism knows no exterior limit, but instead finds its continuity "in this unity of the schiz and the flow," that is, "an interior limit that is capital itself and that it does not encounter, but reproduces by always displacing it" (AOEng, 230-231; AOFr, 273-274). Decoding of flows ensues, but also always reterritorializing them through an axiomatic, says Bogue, with "all social relations emanating from capital as their quasi-cause":

> Put simply, the capitalist machine takes an abstract flow of labour (deterritorialized workers) and an abstract flow of capital (deterritorialized money) and conjoins the two flows in various relations (the set of abstract rules for the conjunction of flows comprising an axiomatic). . . . Worker and capitalist (and all variations thereof) are functions of capital, mere points of the becoming-concrete of abstract quantities. (Bogue 1989, 101)

And what about representation in this new formation? Again, Nick Land expresses this quite succinctly: "If money is libidinized on the 'model' of excrement, it is not because it conserves or reactivates an infantile fixation, but because it escapes stable investment. . . . The privatization of the anus [AOEng, 143; AOFr, 168] is the social permission to destroy value, meaning and progress. Cyberspace psychosis takes over" (1995, 200). Beyond the Saussurean linguistics of the signifier comes "a linguistics of flows"—notably, Louis Hjelmslev's linguistics which, for Deleuze and Guattari, "implies the concerted destruction of the signifier, and constitutes a decoded theory of language about which one can also say—an ambiguous tribute—that it is the only linguistics adapted to the nature of *both* the capitalist *and* the schizophrenic flows" (AOEng, 243; AOFr, 289).[28] Here they praise Lyotard's *Discours, figure* (1971) for showing how "the figural" works on and against the signifier's coding. Think of writing, for example, that conceives of language and letters "as breaks, as shattered partial objects . . . constitut[ing] asignifying signs that deliver themselves to the order of desire: rushes of breath and cries" (AOEng, 243; AOFr, 289). Or think of the plastic arts (e.g., Paul Klee), or dreams: "These constellations are like flows that imply the breaks effected by points, just as points imply the fluxion of the material they cause to flow or leak: the sole unity without identity is that of the flux-schiz or the break-flow . . . desire, which carries us to the gates of schizophrenia as a process" (AOEng, 244; AOFr, 290).[29]

Yet, in the capitalist State, "the hour of Oedipus draws nigh" by dint of a "privatization of the public: the whole world unfolds right at home," giving private persons a special role, "of *application*, and no longer implication, in a code" (AOEng, 251; AOFr, 299). This State "is produced by the conjunction of the decoded or deterritorialized flows . . . [while] capitalism merely ensures the regulation of the axiomatic," of which capitalism is the axiomatic's offspring (AOEng, 252; AOFr, 300). Under capitalism, and contrary to certain readings of history, Deleuze and Guattari argue, the State does not arbitrate between social classes, and as a result "the bourgeois field of immanence . . . institutes an unrivaled slavery, an unprecedented subjugation: there are no longer even any masters, but only slaves commanding other slaves" (AOEng, 254; AOFr, 302). Modern societies are thus locked into a bipolar oscillation:

> Born of decoding and deterritorialization, on the ruins of the despotic machine, these societies are caught between the Urstaat that they would like to resuscitate as an overcoding and reterritorializing unity, and the unfettered flows that carry them toward an absolute threshold. . . . They vacillate between two poles: the paranoiac despotic sign, the sign-signifier of the despot that they try to revive as a unit of code; and the sign-figure of the schizo as a unit of decoded flux, as schiz, a point-sign or flow-break. (AOEng, 260; AOFr, 309–310)

Hence the family's function as "an open praxis," "the subaggregate to which the whole of the social field is applied" (AOEng, 262–265; AOFr, 313–315). We are colonized by Oedipus: the daddy-mommy-me, "the personal and private territoriality that corresponds to all of capitalism's efforts at social reterritorialization" (AOEng, 266; AOFr, 317). And the tale of Oedipus under capitalism links to the Hellenist tale, "the mother as the simulacrum of territoriality, and the father as the simulacrum of the despotic Law," both products of capitalism as "locus of retention and resonance of all social determinations." We seem to hear the Doors as soundtrack to *Anti-Oedipus*: "Yes, I desired my mother and wanted to kill my father; a single subject of enunciation—Oedipus—for all the capitalist statements, and between the two, the leveling cleavage of castration" (AOEng, 269–270; AOFr, 321).

And yet, in this history of Oedipus as universal of desire, add Deleuze and Guattari, there is one condition "not met by Freud: that Oedipus is capable, at least at a certain point, of conducting its autocritique," that is, Oedipus has the capacity "to overturn the theater of representation into the order of desiring production: this is the whole task of schizoanalysis" (AOEng, 271; AOFr, 323–324). Or in a different register:

> You are on a voyage to the end of the river, into jungle-screened horror. The ivory trade is just cover. Commerce is like that. It allows things to disappear while remaining formally integrated. It is a line of flight, a war. Kurtz is deterritorializing security into Meltdown, the ultimate Pod nightmare. No surprise that command control want him dead. They transmit a terminator machine into Cambodia, jacking it into a river that winds through the war like a main circuit cable, and plugs straight into Kurtz. (Land 1995, 202)

* * *

Despite the brilliance of his cinematic vision and technique in this film, Coppola turns away from the deterritorializations that we can glimpse in certain scenes, a retreat that is not terribly surprising, but is disconcerting given the promotional myth of "insanity" touted for the production of the film. Yet, the work of the viewer/reader—indeed, our "work" just in living—is not removed from this resistance to deterritorialization. For Deleuze and Guattari, the schizoanalytic creation of "a new land" implies that

> we must go back by way of the old lands, study their nature, their density; we must seek to discover how the machinic indices are grouped on each of these lands that permit going beyond them. How can we reconquer the process each time, constantly resuming the journey on these lands—Oedipal familial lands of neurosis, artificial lands of perversion, clinical lands of psychosis? (AOEng, 318; AOFr, 380)

It is by now a commonplace that Coppola sought to reverse the course of time, to offer "the history of Vietnam in reverse" (Coppola, speaking in *Hearts*), in depicting the movement of the PBR crew as it moved closer to the Kurtz compound.[30] The source of this vision, Conrad's narrative in *Heart of Darkness,* is emphasized throughout the film *Hearts of Darkness* through the documentary's use of Orson Welles reading from this novel as dramatic voiceover: "Going up that river was like traveling back to the earliest beginnings of the world, when vegetation rioted on the earth and the big trees were kings . . . " (*Hearts*; Conrad 1910, 102). However, as Herman Rapaport points out quite pertinently, the French expression "comment se faire un corps sans organes?" (how can one make oneself a body without organs?) may be strategically "reinterpreted as, how is one to produce a corps without organs, a military corps like an 'I Corps'? How does the 'unit' disarticulate, dematerialize, frag?" Rapaport sees this to be both a military and a geographical question, "for I am thinking of the corps as corpse of Vietnam, of the thousand plateaus which Deleuze and Guattari pass over" (1984, 137). The geographic as well as the military specificity of this "corps" is important for tracing the upriver trajectory in *Apocalypse Now*, from the capitalist de-/reterritorializing axiomatic into the despotic regime and onward toward the primitive:

- *Willard on R & R.* Entirely out of place in the "shit" of Saigon—excremental culture overwhelms and repulses the warrior/assassin who can never go "home" except to return to the jungle—Willard at once completely decoded vis-à-vis capitalism's axiomatic and yet the perfect cog in the capitalist war machine, awaiting a mission, to be set in motion;
- *At Nha Trang Mission Control.* The discrete charm of the "grocery clerks"—between business and beef, talk of "methods," "murder," "the dark side," "gone insane," "beyond the pale"—recordings of Kurtz's voice: "what do you call it when the assassins accuse the assassin?"—the assertion of the axiomatic's reterritorializing force, to align the warrior/assassin Willard alongside the terminal diagnosis, at least provisionally;
- *Kilgore's AirCav Operations.* Production command (Coppola's "TV crew"), war as performance—death cards, "lets Charlie know who did this"—Kilgore's "weird light": Wagner "scares the hell out of the slopes . . . my boys love it"—heavy ordnance but "fantastic peak" at Charlie's point: "Charlie don't surf!"—the warrior/lord of the capitalist axiomatic, "If I say it's safe to surf this beach, it's safe to surf this beach!"—Willard's assessment of "Napalm in the morning": "If that's how Kilgore fought the war, I began to wonder what they really had against Kurtz. It wasn't just insanity and murder. There was enough of that to go around for everyone";
- *The French Plantation* (omitted from the film, but cut scenes are shown in *Hearts of Darkness*). "A place that's like a dream . . . fog machines . . . real machine guns . . . French people, from Hong Kong or from France . . . white wine served ice cold . . . I want the French to say, 'My God, how do they do that?' " (Coppola in *Hearts*): production excess constructs the colonialist enclave—the post-Kilgore crew collides with the pre-Kilgore, bourgeois territorializing machine: "dinner with a family of ghosts . . . floating loose in history without a country"—Willard's naive question: "Why don't you go back home to France?" elicits responses with Oedipal and patriarchal resonance, from "the French": "This is our home . . . it belongs to us, it keeps our family together, we fight for that, while you Americans are fighting for the biggest nothing in history"; and from Coppola: "[retrospectively] I was angry at the French sequence [for budgetary reasons], I cut it out out of that . . . [on location] Everyone forget that we even shot it; no longer does it exist" (*Hearts*);
- *Willard, Chef, and the Tiger.* In search of mangoes, a saucier's dream brushes against the predatory real: "Never get off the fuckin' boat";

- *Hau Phat USO Show.* The final gasp of the capitalist axiomatic, Playmates dancing where rules no longer apply—Willard "ordering" fuel, the quartermaster dealing dope, the soldiers crossing the moat, everyone now taking the "show" into their own hands—Vietnamese gaze from beyond the fence, the last barrier before despotic paranoia: "Charlie didn't get much USO, he was dug in too deep or moving too fast . . . he had only two ways home, death or victory";
- *The "Sampan Off the Port Bow."* The Chief's "routine check" transformed into a free fire zone over "a fuckin' puppy"—the despot's bullet rules, Willard takes charge, musing bitterly: "Cut 'em in half with a machine gun, then give 'em a bandaid. . . . It was a lie, and the more I saw of them, the more I hated lies";
- *Do Lung Bridge.* The last outpost, "the asshole of the world"—search for command where the Roach rules: "Hey soldier, do you know who's in command here?" The Roach: "Yeh . . ."—despotic lines redrawn daily, "what we coded by day, they de-coded by night" (Rapaport 1984, 137), beyond which "was only Kurtz";
- *Upriver, between the Despot and the Primitive.* Mail call and "incoming" for Clean—the Chief takes the native's pointed message in the back—Willard in command, but only of the painted, dancing Lance, and Chef who signs on for the mission, but only "on the boat!";
- *At Kurtz's Compound.* "Come on in, it's been approved!"—the warrior/assassin meets the "poet-warrior" and his heads, "Sometimes he goes too far. . . . He'd be the first to admit it"—slow death, end of river: Willard joins the compound, between the primitive bodily inscription and despotic paranoia—Chef's head leaves the boat, an organ without body on Willard's lap—to go out like a soldier, standing up: the sacrifice and "the horror"—Almighty Almighty: Willard returns downriver, but where? To the codes and lies he knows so well? Or to complete the mission to Kurtz's son: "If you understand me, Willard, you will do this for me"?

As Willard admits in the reflections that immediately follow Kurtz's request, "They were going to make me a major for this, and I wasn't even in their fuckin' army anymore." We can surmise, then, that fulfilling the filial duty prevails, and that his statement at the start of the tale—"Everyone gets everything they want"—was apocryphal since his ultimate mission finally provides him with direction and purpose, and reconstitutes the familiar process of Oedipalization, the son triangulated within predictable parameters. An obvious parallel emerges, both in Eleanor Coppola's *Notes* and in the documentary *Hearts of Darkness,* between the tale of *Apocalypse Now* and its production and postproduction. I need hardly dwell on the fact that in its very inception and completion, the film was a capitalist exploitation of resources and labor throughout its entire production.

These facts have been amply documented and critiqued following the release of *Hearts of Darkness* (see Sussman 1992; Worthy 1992). Even upon the film's release, Dempsey stated quite succinctly:

> In spite of his genuine artistic goals, [Coppola] got caught up in the same wheeler-dealer's recklessness—pyramiding a top-heavy, complex, multi-million dollar set of interlocking deals and schedules on to the quicksand of a fuzzy, unshaped screenplay—which the crass hacks in the international film industry, cold-assed businessmen who feel nothing but contempt for artists, continually get involved in. (1979–1980, 7–8)

Many images from the film's production shown in *Hearts of Darkness* reveal its lavish and gratuitous expense, most evident in Coppola's grandiose plans for the French plantation scene. This excess is confirmed innocently in *Notes* only a month after shooting began (8 April 1976) at Coppola's birthday party for three hundred guests, with a cake "six feet by eight feet . . . made of twelve sheet cakes iced together." Eleanor Coppola records the following reaction: "I could hear two GI extras talking. They were standing on a bench behind me. One said, 'Wow, this is the most decadence I've ever seen' " (*Notes*, 11).

Moreover, listening to Coppola's various business negotiations recorded in the documentary, one cannot place him above or beyond the cold-assed suits in Hollywood—indeed, Coppola seems to revel in negotiating and to exult in the power, even because of (not despite) pressing so close to the edge of his own limits.[31] What is stunning throughout Eleanor Coppola's *Notes*, however, is almost how perfectly the family and the capitalist reterritorializing axiomatic overlap. With the entire family—director, wife, and three children—present on location for most of the filming in 1976, Eleanor Coppola comments early on about her discomfort at having a laundry maid, "a human washing machine . . . and dishwasher." As she soon learns from a neighbor, the maid "was glad to have a job with a nice family. . . . She earns, in pesos, about $55 a month plus room and board. Here a major appliance costs more" (*Notes*, 13). Indeed, in August 1976, Eleanor Coppola defines herself in terms of a specific hierarchy while attempting to sum up an understanding of her personal struggle:

> I am the mother of these children, the wife of the director of this multimillion-dollar production, and I hadn't given a thought to my family this morning. . . . Riding along in the car, I began going through my wife/mother versus artist argument in my head for about the five hundredth time. Both sides have this perfectly reasonable position; neither gives in. (*Notes*, 96–97)

During this sojourn, the family members constantly collide with (while enjoying) their power and privilege as consumers/exploiters in different social encounters (see *Notes,* 21–25, 180–182). This should hardly surprise Eleanor Coppola: for example, her husband displays their excesses quite publicly, in the film's production as well as in all the social activity that the production stimulates for cast, crew, and companions. Moreover, she also recognizes that "money, power and family" are the themes with which her husband had been struggling for years in the *Godfather* films (*Notes,* 26). What is clear from *Notes,* and indeed quite poignant, is Francis Coppola's struggle to "create new lands" in his art, attempting to balance and negotiate realization of an artistic vision with the constant demands of doing financial battle with the Hollywood machine. This struggle is complicated and rendered all the more desperate, at least from the wife's perspective in *Notes,* as Coppola assumes increasing personal liability for his film's financing due to the very excesses that the movie production and the artistic process seem to impose.

Much less evident is the way in which Eleanor Coppola's own ordeal with this production and its postproduction are subsequently occulted, no doubt—judging from the selected use of her oral text (from *Notes*) and the footage in *Hearts of Darkness* that she herself shot during the film on-location phase—with her willing participation. Indeed, a significant textual gap exists between the pain that she endures and reports fully in *Notes* and the historical re-vision presented in the documentary. Like the tale of *Apocalypse Now,* this affective, emotional journey follows a geographical movement across different territories, and territorialities:

• A first phase extends from the start of production well into the summer of 1977, with two lengthy stays on different locations in the Philippines (March to June 1976, July to December 1976) broken only by a brief return home to Napa Valley, California, in June. After the winter of 1977 spent in Napa Valley and San Francisco, she makes a third (and final) trip to the Philippines locations after Sheen's heart attack and her husband's own nervous breakdown there.

• A second phase, of anger and resentment, overlaps with the first: once resettled into her Napa Valley home, Eleanor Coppola experiences months of growing artistic (for Francis Coppola) and marital (for them both) crisis, culminating in the "great kick in the gut," her husband's revelation in late September/early October 1977 that he is in love with another woman (*Notes,* 192–196).

• The third phase (set in California) is her "awakening," which involves reassessing her existence and returning to "old lands" in order to strike out for "the new." She depicts this process as painful, tentative, but quite genuine, despite her evident position of privilege that allows her the freedom and luxury for such explorations. This process leads eventually, perhaps inevitably, to accommodation, reterritorialization within the security of the family homestead, with *Homo familia.*

In this light, the use of selected excerpts from *Notes* in the documentary vividly demonstrates the power of the capitalist reterritorializing axiomatic. Eleanor Coppola's voiceover recitation of precisely selected excerpts from this very personal work serves only to provide sequential movement, filler, and "mood" pieces for the primary tale of her husband's production. Gone from the documentary is the forthright critique of the production strategies, telexed by Eleanor Coppola in February 1977 from California to Coppola and to key members of his crew:

> I would tell him what no one else was willing to say, that he was setting up his own Vietnam with his supply lines of wine and steaks and air conditioners. Creating the very situation he went there to expose. That with his staff of hundreds of people carrying out his every request, he was turning into Kurtz—going too far.
>
> I called him an asshole. . . . I got back an avalanche of anger. Francis felt completely betrayed. (*Notes,* 159)

Gone is any hint of Eleanor Coppola's emotional upheaval, her "rigid thinking" and "belief system about marriage" finally "cracked wide open," her "change from feeling loss and pain, to feeling exhilarated about building something new" (*Notes,* 228). Gone is her admission and acceptance that "the man I love, my husband, the father of my children, the visionary artist, the affectionate family man, the passionate and tender lover, also can lie, betray and be cruel to people he loves" (*Notes,* 253). Given Eleanor Coppola's anxiety early in the shooting (August 1976) about producing a subjective documentary with her own personal view— "maybe no one would be interested in it and feel cheated" (*Notes,* 83)—it is not surprising that the decision was made for her in *Hearts of Darkness.* This appropriation and reterritorialization of *Notes* renders the final words of her written account all the more disturbing for all the "new land" that was lost from view:

> I find myself continually looking to see if this phase of our lives is over. When it's past, I probably won't know it, won't see it until later, in the distance behind me. (*Notes,* 266)

TOWARD RHIZOMATICS

Following the publication of *Anti-Oedipus,* the schizoanalytic reflection on the relation of literary discourse to desire and power continued in various interviews with Deleuze and Guattari, and also in the "Balance Sheet Program for Desiring Machines" (written in 1973b) that they appended to an augmented edition of their initial collaboration.[32] It was not until the publication of *Kafka: Pour une littérature mineure* (1975) that the authors advanced their joint exploration to reveal the possibilities of an extended literary schizoanalysis. To George Stambolian's query, "Why this method to analyze and to comprehend literature?," Guattari answered, "It's not a question of method or doctrine. . . . The book [*Kafka*] is a schizoanalysis of our relation to Kafka's work, but also of the period of Vienna in 1920 and of a certain bureaucratic eros which crystallized in that period, and which fascinated Kafka" (1979b, 60; Genosko 1996, 207). We can approach this literary schizoanalysis briefly by examining its realization of the destructive and twin positive tasks of schizoanalysis, but we must remain aware, however, of the simultaneity of these processes.

Deleuze and Guattari undertake the destructive task by asserting that Kafka escapes the universal Oedipalization through his enlargement of Oedipus, of the name of the father to absurd proportions in the "Letter to the Father," thereby unblocking the Oedipal impasse: "Deterritorializing Oedipus into the world instead of reterritorializing everything in Oedipus and the family" (KEng, 10; KFr, 19). This destructive task constitutes a given work as what Deleuze and Guattari call, in their subtitle, a "minor literature," where a "minor writer" (e.g., Kafka) uses a "major" language (German) in such a way as to create a disruptive, revolutionary "minor" tongue at the very heart of a "major" literature.

The characteristics or tasks of a "minor literature" (Chap. 3) are, first, the deterritorialization of the language (e.g., Kafka's strange use of a German language of Prague origin); second, plugging the individual element found in major literatures into the political-immediate (e.g., the familial triangle connected to commercial, economic, bureaucratic, or juridical triangles, which determine the familial triangle's values); and third, rendering literature as the "people's business" through the collective arrangement of literary enunciation, whereby literature

> produces an active solidarity in spite of skepticism; and if the writer is in the margins or completely outside his or her fragile community, this situation allows the writer all the more the possibility to express another possible community and to forge the means for another consciousness and another sensibility. (KEng, 17; KFr, 31–32)

This de-Oedipalization reveals the close link between the destructive task and the two positive tasks: corresponding to the first task (the machinic conversion of the text), Deleuze and Guattari present the "Kafka machine" with all of its components: the machinic assemblage of Kafka's novels which functions through the proliferation of numerous series (Chap. 6), connectors (Chap. 7), and blocks and intensities (Chap. 8). And all of these flows, these connections and disjunctions within the textual machine, are elements of the immanent "states of desire" (KEng, 7; KFr, 15):

> These two coexistent states of desire are two states of the law. On the one hand, there is the paranoiac transcendental law that never stops agitating a finite segment and making it into a completed object, crystallizing all over the place. On the other hand, there is the immanent schizo-law that functions like justice, an antilaw, a "procedure" that will dismantle all the assemblages of the paranoiac law. Because, once again, this is what it is all about—the discovery of assemblages of immanence and their dismantling. (KEng, 59; KFr, 108–109)

Since writing's double function—"to translate everything into assemblages and to dismantle the assemblages" (KEng, 47; KFr, 86)—is put into practice in Kafka's works, it is through this dismantling that the "Kafka machine" connects with the second positive task, the schizophrenization of investments of unconscious desire in the social field. Not only does a minor literature deterritorialize language, it also plugs the individual into the "political-immediate" and collectively assembles enunciations. Deleuze and Guattari refer to the French used by Artaud and Céline (until *Guignol's Band*), as well as to Kafka's German, to evoke the revolutionary effect of the major languages used in minor literature:

> To make use of the polylingualism of one's own language, to make a minor or intensive use of it, to oppose the oppressed quality of this language to its oppressive quality, to find points of nonculture and underdevelopment, linguistic Third World zones by which a language can escape, an animal enters into things, an assemblage comes into play. (KEng, 26–27; KFr, 49)

In Kafka's work, this process of deterritorialization emerges in the "bachelor machine," or "line of flight," the "secret" of which is "his production of intensive quantities. . . . He produces this production of intensive quantities directly on the social body, in the social field itself." This solitary agent is not so much an individual subject but, like the community to which it belongs, is rather a general function of the collective arrangements to which it is connected. Deleuze and Guattari conclude: "Production of intensive quantities in the social body, proliferation and precipitation of series, polyvalent and collective connections brought about by the bachelor agent—there is no other definition possible for a minor literature" (KEng, 71; KFr, 128–130).[33]

This political, collective assemblage of elements on the social body leads our inquiry to the second "moment" of the schizoanalytic project. Guattari has explained that everything that is written is linked to a political position with two fundamental axes:

> Everything that's written in refusing the connection with the referent, with reality, implies a politics of individuation of the subject and of the object, of a turning of writing on itself, and by that puts itself in the service of all hierarchies, of all centralized systems of power, of what Gilles Deleuze and I call "arborescences," the regime of unifiable multiplicities. The second axis, in opposition to arborescences, is that of the "rhizome," the regime of pure multiplicities, . . . the pattern of . . . breaks in reality, in the social field, and in the field of economic, cosmic and other flows. (1979b, 65; Genosko 1996, 210–211)

This "rhizomatic" regime provides the new model posited in the short volume entitled *Rhizome: Introduction* (1976) and revised for the introductory "plateau" of *A Thousand Plateaus*. The definition of "rhizome" evokes once again the ideal circumstances that did not prevail either in the tale or in the production of *Apocalypse Now*: opposed to centered, hierarchized systems, the rhizome is

> an acentered, nonhierarchical, nonsignifying system without a General and without an organizing memory or central automaton, defined solely by a circulation of states. What is at question in the rhizome is a relation to sexuality—but also to the animal, the vegetal, the world, politics, the book, things natural and artificial—that is totally different from the arborescent relation: all manner of "becomings." (ATP, 21; MP, 32)

As these "becomings" can only be examined, Deleuze and Guattari argue, through the machinic assemblages of desire and collective assemblages of enunciation, I will continue my exploration/animation of connections and becomings in the domain of cyberspace fluxes, jumps, and interchange.

3
THE RHIZOMATICS
OF CYBERSPACE

> The mode of interaction that this [cyberspace]
> milieu fosters—congeries of personae whose
> greatest commonality is a single physical
> substrate in which they are loosely grounded,
> collective structures whose informing
> epistemology is multiplicity and
> reinvention—makes transformation as reflexive
> as it is transitive, and it is one of the "schizo"
> modes that Gilles Deleuze and Félix Guattari
> describe.
>
> –*Allucquère Roseanne Stone, "Virtual Systems" (1992)*

In this chapter, I address the questions of multiplicity, intersections, and animations through examination of the important Deleuze–Guattarian concept "rhizome," a concept which
they employ in the introductory "plateau" of *A Thousand
Plateaus*, "Introduction: Rhizome," but had actually introduced
separately four years earlier (Deleuze and Guattari 1976). With
the "rhizome" concept, Deleuze and Guattari link the two
volumes of *Capitalism and Schizophrenia*, thereby positing the
multiplicity of sociocultural and creative dynamics other than
in binary terms. The "rhizome" constitutes a model of continuing offshoots, taproot systems that travel horizontally and
laterally, constantly producing affective relations/becomings
that themselves contribute to the dynamic multiplicity of creation and existence. By developing and extending what I call
"the rhizomatics of cyberspace," I attempt to animate the

potential of this crucial concept in terms of the technological metaphor for online communication in virtual spaces of research, discussion, and real-time interactions.

INTERMEZZO

The context for this chapter is the continuing dialogue between Deleuze–Guattarians and this dialogue's intersections within online and conference exchanges. This chapter is based on ongoing discussions that have taken place for four years on the Deleuze–Guattari List (henceforth abbreviated D&G List) and on an earlier version of these reflections prepared for the initial "Virtual Futures" conference held at the University of Warwick, May 1994, in England. I continue this study where I "logged on" to my own rhizomatic connections with Deleuze and Guattari nearly twenty years ago, taking creative license out of necessity (and pleasure) for our subject:

> It is transmitting everywhere, at times without let-up, at other times discontinuously. It displaces, it heats up, it devours. It eliminates, it copulates. What a mistake to have ever masculinized this "it"; it is multiply engendered, and engendering. Everywhere it is machines, and not at all metaphorically: machines servicing machines, with their couplings and connections. An organ-machine is plugged into a source-machine, node-to-node, one emitting a flow, the other cutting it off, yet relaying and emitting again. . . . In this way, we all become *bricoleurs,* each of us with his and her little machines; an organ-machine sits on my lap, *ça chauffe,* for an energy-machine from which it gains strength, *ça mange,* and it transmits its bits, always flows and cuts, through myriad lines. If the President Schreber has sunbeams flowing from his ass, Vice President Gore would like little informational segments popping one by one from his, all under legislative sanction and surveillance. *Anus solaire, anus informatique.* And rest assured that *ça marche,* it works; both the President Schreber and Vice President Gore feel something, produce something, and can even explain the process theoretically. Something is produced: machine effects, and not metaphors. (See AOEng, 1–2; AOFr, 7)

This is, of course, my attempt at once to evoke and to adapt the opening paragraph of *Anti-Oedipus,* eighteen lines of text that compelled me, and still compels me, to reformulate notions of interconnectivity, both human and human–computer. This adaptation helps me to pursue Deleuze and Guattari's "two-fold thought" in terms of a folded interconnectivity to which their earliest works attest. This process of interconnectivity continues well into their later works: for example, in "Introduction: Rhizome," Deleuze and Guattari begin by affirming that "the two of us wrote *Anti-Oedipus* together. Since each of us was several, there was already quite a crowd." This "methodology" is one I follow too: "Here we have made use of everything that came within range, what was closest as well as farthest away" (ATP, 3; MP, 9).

In considering the "rhizomatics of cyberspace," I understand the conjunction of these two terms as indicating a folded synchronicity that provides an effective way to explore both, in all their heterogeneity and multiplicity.[1] Although the term "cyberspace" would seem to be familiar enough to require no explanation, one of its original formulations, as a "consensual hallucination" (Gibson 1984, 51), evokes the human–computer interface as an assemblage with flows, connections, and ruptures. As Michael Benedikt insists, however, this word "gives a name to a new stage, a new and irresistible development in the elaboration of human culture and business under the sign of technology" (1991, 1). Nick Land provides a more exuberant, if overly cautionary, conceptualization of this new stage: "The terminal social signal blotted out by technofuck buzz from desiring-machines. So much positive feedback fast-forward that speed converges with itself on the event horizon of an artificial time-extinction" (1993a, 481–482).[2]

The concept of "rhizome" is, of course, fundamental in the works of Deleuze and Guattari, as Deleuze himself emphasizes in the (1990) Letter-Preface to Jean-Clet Martin's study of his works: "You understand quite well the essential importance for me that the notion of multiplicities holds. . . . 'Rhizome' is the best word to designate [such multiplicity]" (1993, 8). Thus, as in "cyberspace," described by Benedikt in Deleuze–Guattarian fashion—"Its horizons recede in every direction; it breathes larger, it complexifies, it embraces and involves" (1991, 2)—so too "rhizomatics" extend the multiplicity of sociocultural and creative dynamics not in binary terms, but in terms of continuing offshoots, continually producing affective relations and all manner of becomings that themselves contribute to the dynamic multiplicity of creativity. Linking these together, Erik Davis wonders (on the D&G List):

> Where is the immanence of the Net? Where is it produced? Is it only achieved when we ourselves undergo a becoming-digital (scary thought)? Sometimes it all seems so reflective to me, so much control over what I say, who I communicate with, where I go, while all the time the Net itself is totally insane, absolute rhizome, a total "concept" that draws up the conceptual plane of immanence into a nest of infinite speeds. (D&G List, 7 April 1994)

Juxtaposing and merging these terms is but one mode of approach to make their inherent connectivity more immediate and even useful. Were an online linkup to a synchronous Internet site possible within a

written publication, such an experiment—even with the best of connections—would be little more than an opportunity for the reader to peer
over the typist/author's shoulder, as it were, with hopes that "something
rhizomatic" might occur, on the page or online. Indeed, the relationship
that I explore here may already be so self-evident in the late 1990s that
little more elaboration is required. However, here as throughout my own
work on assemblages within particular plateaus, I am guided by Deleuze's
succinct response to Cressole: "One speaks [and writes, I would add] from
the depth of what one does not know, from the depth of one's own
sous-développement à soi [underdevelopment to or within oneself]" (N, 7; P,
16). Although the rhizomatic hyperconnectivity may seem self-evident, a
spate of online discussions on an array of lists, as well as several
conferences at the University of Warwick on the theme "Virtual Futures,"
have suggested direct links to this "underdevelopment" as interlocutors
and conferees attempt to nudge forward a multiplicity, to assemble it
within the unknown depths of a "virtuality." As Nick Land argues,
"Machinic desire is the operation of the virtual; implementing itself in the
actual, revirtualizing itself, and producing reality in a circuit" (1993a, 474).
This theme for "event-scenes" reaches, then, into an actual present as well
as toward virtual futures, and demands that "we" take account, however
incompletely, of this multiplicity that affects us all "in the middle, between
things, interbeing, *intermezzo*" (ATP, 25; MP, 36).

For "rhizomatics" might also be understood in relation to this
"between" that appears, among other places, at the conclusion of Plateau
1 of *A Thousand Plateaus*: "Between things does not designate a localizable
relation going from one thing to the other and back again, but a
perpendicular direction, a transversal movement that sweeps one and the
other away, a stream without beginning or end that undermines its banks
and picks up speed in the middle" (ATP, 25; MP, 37). This image develops
the concept of "becomings" that, through the "rhizome," implicate novel
relations "to sexuality . . . to the animal, the vegetal, the world, politics,
the book, things natural and artificial" (ATP, 21; MP, 32), for example,
the "rhizomatics" of/in "cyberspace." For the perpendicular direction is
that distinct pull of connectivity (you, me online), interconnectivity (you-
and-me, linked online, whether synchronously or asynchronously), and the
hyperconnectivity of transversal connections between sites, databases, and
interlocutors in a "conjunctive synthesis" (to employ a term from *Anti-
Oedipus*), beyond a simple bipolar link, sweeping us along in the information stream.

One thing that has struck me about the opening and closing paragraphs of "Introduction: Rhizome" is the authors' preoccupation with "the
book" (*A Thousand Plateaus* itself as well as *le livre* more generally), a
preoccupation that prompts me to ask (and begin to answer) a question

that relates to inter- and hyperconnectivity: How do Deleuze and Guattari "commence," in this case a book such as *A Thousand Plateaus,* truly intermezzo, in the middle? One obvious answer is that *A Thousand Plateaus* is the second volume of *Capitalism and Schizophrenia,* and as such continues the discussion intermezzo from one volume to the next. We can also understand the opening of "Rhizome" as joining other discussions in progress, most notably the *Dialogues* between Deleuze and Claire Parnet that mutate into a "two-fold thought" similar to the process Deleuze and Guattari are at that very moment (in the mid-1970s) in the process of developing as well. Deleuze concludes his introductory remarks to *Dialogues* in the English translation by describing quite clearly the "in-between" of the "dialogues": "What mattered was not the points—Félix, Claire Parnet, me and many others, who functioned as temporary, transitory and evanescent points of subjectivation—but the collection of bifurcating, divergent and muddled lines which constituted this book as a multiplicity and which passed between the points, carrying them along without ever going from the one to the other" (DEng, ix). Jumping these remarks transversally to the "opening" (which is but a continuation) in "Introduction: Rhizome," we now focus on paragraphs that propose a radically new "intertextuality," with the term "text" understood in the broadest imaginable senses and the "intertextual" extended quite naturally to the hypertextual connection of "rhizomatics" to "schizoanalysis" that this opening plateau constitutes.

ASSEMBLAGE

I dwell on this apparent paradox of "beginning intermezzo" as a way not only to illustrate the "rhizomatic" process generally, but also to describe my own task as undertaking an active assemblage, *agencement,* a term about which Deleuze and Guattari are unequivocal: "We are no more familiar with scientificity than we are with ideology; all we know are assemblages" (ATP, 22; MP, 33). For this machinic process continues to produce even in this site, and consists of what Deleuze and Guattari themselves note with the following query raised midway through "Introduction: Rhizome": "What takes place in a book composed instead of plateaus that communicate with one another across microfissures, as in a brain?" (ATP, 22; MP, 33). Their immediate response is oblique and transversal, offering yet another definition of "plateau" as "any multiplicity connected to other multiplicities by superficial underground stems in such a way as to form or extend a rhizome" (ATP, 22; MP, 33). Erik Davis aligns these jumps with "writing such a book now, here on the Internet. . . . Though we are nestled in a certain cubbyhole (Ah! Here it is, etc.), we have not entered into the special interiority of the book, because the space is already linked to another outside, already proliferated. If not, it's boring—where do I go from here? What, no links? It's a dead end" (D&G List, 22 March 1994).

My own assemblage of voices, lines, and links is but one partial attempt to contribute to the broader exploration that is the "event-scene" of ongoing dialogues. The particular angle of approach that seems most productive is that of the online functioning of contemporary machinic and textual "becomings." The assemblage of "lines" that I produce and that you will read arise themselves from the complex rhizomatic operation of other lines responding to each other, of gleanings both from online "strings" (subject groupings) and "posts" (notably to the D&G List and to other lists) and from offline writings that I employ as no less immanent and pertinent intersections. These links and lines serve as what Deleuze calls *intercesseurs*, or "mediators": "Whether they're real or imaginary, animate or inanimate, you have to form your mediators. It's a series. If you're not in some series, even a completely imaginary one, you're lost" (N, 125; P, 170–171).

Through the work of mediators as "point-relays" in a series, this assemblage propels me onward toward other links within "Introduction: Rhizome." The six "principles," as Deleuze and Guattari grandly call them, are well known for readers of *A Thousand Plateaus*: (1, 2) *connection and heterogeneity*, "any point of a rhizome can be connected to anything other, and must be" (ATP, 7; MP, 13); (3) *multiplicity*, "puppet strings . . . tied not to the supposed will of an artist or puppeteer but to a multiplicity of nerve fibers, which form another puppet in other dimensions connected to the first" (ATP, 8; MP, 15); (4) *asignifiying rupture*, the tendency for lines "broken, shattered at a given spot . . . [to] start up again on one of its old lines, or on new lines," deterritorialized or reterritorialized depending on the level of stratification, on the circulation of intensities (ATP, 9–10; MP, 16–17); (5, 6) *cartography and decalcomania*, that is, "a map that must be constructed, produced" (ATP, 21; MP, 32), "oriented toward an experimentation with the real," "open and connectable in all of its dimensions," passing through "multiple entryways" and not simply returning "back 'to the same,' " and pertaining to "performance" and not to some "alleged 'competence' " (ATP, 12–13; MP, 19–21).

The development of computer networking "in cyberspace"—through connection to online virtual spaces for research, discussion and interactions (e.g., on bulletin boards, chat sites, multiuser domains [MUDs], and Web links)—fills the "mediator" function, thereby connecting cybernetic technology and narrative expression within the assemblage of "rhizomatics." As Deleuze pointed out, it was through "the collection of bifurcating, divergent and muddled lines" between the "points" (Guattari, Claire Parnet, and others) that the question, "What is it to write?" became clearer: "These are lines which would respond to each other, like the subterranean shoots of a rhizome" (DEng, x). I find my own "series" wherever they "c[o]me within range," the closest being gleanings from academic texts and journals at hand, the farthest only keystrokes away. This linked rapprochement of far/near translates the "machinic desire" globally across time–space reduced to pixels and bits and packets, points in time–space, and even points between life–death: from Mairi (in Australia), to Michael (in Iowa), on to Erik (then in New York), and even to lurking Warwickians; at another, from Greg (in Pennsylvania), to Karen (in Montreal), on to Stephen (in Melbourne), and then to Melissa (in Paris/Sydney).[3] Erik Davis would (and did) respond:

> And how do I feel when I'm reading such a book—how am "I" rewritten? I feel like a navigator in a rich fog. I am an assemblage of partial maps, rules of thumb (this may lead to this, etc.), the passion of my own vector. As the cliché goes, I surf. Horizontal, a vector, not "left or right"—and up and down is just the swelling of a [w]ave. I feel up when I get a sense of overseeing a realm of knowledge—that old view from the holy hill. But immediately, I'm swamped by a swell, and the peak I was just on has become a valley, a deep trough of unknowing. I'm terrified; I move. (D&G List, 22 March 1994)

Although Deleuze and Guattari kept their own names "out of habit, purely out of habit" when undertaking A Thousand Plateaus, they say that their purpose in this "two-fold thought" was "to make ourselves unrecognizable in turn. To render imperceptible, not ourselves, but what makes us act, feel, and think. . . . To reach, not the point where one no longer says I, but the point where it is no longer of any importance whether one says I" (ATP, 3; MP, 9). On this passage from identity based on proper name to imperceptibility, one contributor suggested, "When I think of what writing is for me, it's this 'I' that's always moving beyond its own horizon, that won't even think about the 'it's own.' . . . I guess you might call this a kind of secret conversation" (D&G List, 10 April 1994).

I pick up this "string" where it "began intermezzo" for me, following another Deleuze conference (held at Trent University in May 1992), and then through several years of intermittent correspondence with participants at that event. Along a particular series, a name appearing on my screen developed as one "line of flight or rupture" or "circle of convergence" (ATP, 22; MP, 33): from a "Mr. J. E. Broadhurst," a transmission of calls first arrived (in 1993) for a volume on "Cyberotix" and for a conference on "Virtual Futures." My response prompted a series of transmissions over several months from a mutated entity identified as "Ms. J. E. Broadhurst," on subjects as tantalizing as "More Cyberotix" and as succinct as "Money!!!" In more oblique fashion than direct email—via the D&G List—came the roster of announced conference participants, creating further interconnectivity to "point-signs" assembled in constellations of names as exotically familiar as De Landa, Porush, Cadigan, and Bey. Bifurcations spread here, and further becomings as well: to texts published far and wide by these nominally identified subjects; to transmission breakdown and even to the immediacy of voice communication with the mutant J. E.; to the heightened activity of the D&G List on the "rhizome" string (spring 1994) as well as on concurrent plateaus; and to MUD discussions generating uploads and downloads on this and related Net topics.

And then. . . . And then . . . comes the echo of revelation from Deleuze's words to Cressole:

> It's a strange business, speaking for yourself, in your own name, because it doesn't at all come with seeing yourself as an ego or a person or a subject. Individuals find a real name for themselves, rather, only through the harshest exercise of depersonalization, by opening themselves up to the multiplicities everywhere within them, to the intensities running through them. (N, 6; P, 15–16)

In the diverse sites of enunciation through time and spaces in which this text has developed, it has been through the depths (or heights) of this *sous-développement à soi* (one's/my own underdevelopment) that one/I quite (im)properly become(s), for example, an aggregate of "liberated singularities, words, names, fingernails, things, animals, little events: quite the reverse of a celebrity" (N, 7; P, 15–16). Hence, like Deleuze undertaking *Différence et répétition* and *Logique du sens,* there is something that I try "to jolt, to set in motion, something inside me, to treat writing as a flow, not a code," as an appropriate method for assembling, even conjuring our "virtual futures."

INTO THE BwO ZONE

How? By "ma[king] use of everything that came within range" (ATP, 3), by "an intensive way of reading, in contact with what's outside the book, as a flow, meeting other flows, one machine among others" (N, 8–9; P, 18–19), by employing the name as "the direct awareness of such intensive multiplicity" (N, 7; P, 15), thus by reading intensively as "a loving process" (N, 9; P, 18; my translation). Within cyberspace, whether on asynchronous lists, within the virtual spaces of various Internet/sites, or in the hypertextual links afforded by Web connections, this "loving process" evolves through what Brenda Laurel, while discussing "virtual reality" (VR), calls "our passionate response to VR [that] mirrors the nature of the medium itself": "By inviting the body and the senses into our dance with our tools, [VR] has extended the landscape of interaction to new technologies of pleasure, emotion, and passion" (Laurel 1991, 213). N. Katherine Hayles has speculated on the "seductions of cyberspace," and finds dangers as well as possibilities therein, recalling the double-edged pursuit of bifurcations and destratification that Manuel De Landa describes as being "poised on the edge of chaos" (Davis 1992, 48). According to Hayles, "VR invites a hierarchy to be set up between [actual and virtual objects], the vectors . . . privileging computer construct over physical body," a process to which "contribute other technologies of body commodification" (1993a, 182).

The "rhizomatic" connection to Hayles's reflections comes through her positing VR as "a Body Zone, constructed not only through economic and geopolitical spaces but also through perceptual processing and neurological networks" (1993a, 184). This new form of "embodiment"— that Hayles explores elsewhere as "flickering signifiers" (1992, 164–166; 1993b, 76)–mutates in and as a body-without-organs zone, a BwO zone as it were, "endospaces of the body as well as the cyberspaces of virtual reality," connected, says Hayles, "by more than the technology that unites internal perception to external computer. They are also articulated together through their social construction as areas newly available for colonization" (1993a, 185). Borrowing from Bukatman (1993), Hayles pushes this "terminal identity" forward, positing "the simultaneous estrangement of the self from itself and its reconstitution as Other" as a newly cybernetically diffuse subjectivity that constitutes "a second mirror stage, the Mirror of the Cyborg" (1993a, 186).

However, she rewrites "Lacanian psycholinguistics as cyberlinguistics," providing reinscriptions that replace, for example, the "absence/presence" dyad with randomness/pattern; the "play of signifiers" and the "floating signifier," respectively, with "random access memory" and "virtual memory"; and the categories of the imaginary and the symbolic with the physical and the virtual (1993a, 186–187). Here the "terminal identity" mutates into the BwO zone, as embodied conscious subject and merges with a destabilizing puppet object "behind the screen," but that can also "be seen as the originary point for sensations." By serving as "a wedge to destabilize presuppositions about self and Other" (1993a, 187), Hayles argues, this ambiguity and disorientation inherent to the BwO zone can produce a "positive seduction of cyberspace":

> The puppet then stands for the release of spontaneity and alterity within the feedback loops that connect the subject with the world, as well as with

those aspects of sentience that the self cannot recognize as originating from within itself. At this point, the puppet has the potential to become more than a puppet, representing instead a zone of interaction that opens the subject to the exhilarating realization of Otherness valued as such. (1993a, 188)

I follow Hayles's argument in such detail to pursue and negotiate a "line" absent earlier in this assemblage, the caution expressed, for example, by Penley and Ross, who note their "war[iness], on the one hand, of the disempowering habit of demonizing technology as a satanic mill of domination, and wear[iness], on the other hand, of postmodernist celebrations of the technological sublime" (1991b, xii). Just as Hayles carefully treads this "line" intermezzo, Penley and Ross insist that "technoculture, as we conceive it, is located as much in the work of everyday fantasy and actions as at the level of corporate or military decision making" (1991b, xii–xiii). Yet the BwO zone implicates a "long process," according to Deleuze and Guattari, at once "a dreary parade of sucked-dry, catatonicized, vitrified, sewn-up bodies" and the body without organs that is "full of gaiety, ecstasy, [and] dance" (ATP, 150; MP, 187). If, in working with/through this Zone of the "rhizomatic" that perplexes/excites/propels us forward, one happens to deploy a term/concept "inappropriately" or "unproductively" (whatever those terms might connote), so what? One works, nonetheless, and moves along that line until/as it connects with yet another, so many "bifurcations" that move the "rhizome" forward. Yet, De Landa points out with reference to Plateau 6 that,

as [Deleuze and Guattari] say, the key word here is not wisdom, but caution. You don't know what happens at bifurcations. You have absolutely no control. The smallest fluctuation can make things go wrong. The predictive power of humans and technology is nil near bifurcations. All you can do is approach carefully. (Davis 1992, 48)

However, Deleuze and Guattari argue that even "these impasses must always be resituated on the map, thereby opening them up to possible lines of flight" (ATP, 14; MP, 22).

One will often be forced to take dead ends to work with signifying powers and subjective affections, to find a foothold in formations that are Oedipal or paranoid or even worse, rigidified territorialities that open the way for other transformational operations. (ATP, 14–15; MP, 23)

And in a 1989 *Libération* interview, they reiterate:

It's precisely their power as a system that brings out what's good or bad, what is or isn't new, what is or isn't alive in a group of concepts. Nothing's good in itself, it all depends on careful systematic use. In *A Thousand Plateaus,* we're trying to say you can never guarantee a good outcome (it's not enough just to have a smooth space, for example, to overcome striations and coercion, or a body without organs to overcome organizations). (N, 32; P, 49)

Such is the double-edged experimentation of the BwO zone,

an *a priori* synthesis by which something will necessarily be produced in a given mode (but what it will be is not known) and an infinite analysis by which what is produced on the BwO is already part of that body's production, is already included in the body, is already on it (but at the price of an infinity of passages, divisions, and secondary productions). (ATP, 152; MP, 188–189)

Stagnation and the dangers of blockages are always possible. But "to block, to be blocked, is that not still an intensity?," Deleuze and Guattari ask, and then continue: "In each case, we must define what comes to pass and what does not pass, what causes passage and prevents it" (ATP, 152; MP, 189).

"SPAM, SPOOF, LAG, AND LURKING"

On LambdaMOO (a synchronous multiuser dimension, or MUD), an acquaintance (whose self-designated, neutral gender is known as "Spivak") described the discourses of cyberspace with a delightful formulation: "A gentle chiming in [my] ear brings a message from L***: E pages, 'Spam, spoof, lag, and lurking . . . the four big aesthetic values negatively expressed on MOO-dom' " (see Marvin 1995). Because each of these "values" poses the threat of possible "blockages," I want to explore these as potential modes of experimentation in the BwO zone. As forms of play, spoofing and spamming are complementary, though distinct, practices: "spoofing" contradicts a tenet of online "Netiquette" according to which all statements require attribution to a "proper name" so that everyone involved in a computer-generated exchange knows the source of a transmission. Without such attribution, not only is any response other than the expression of surprise or exasperation impossible, but a definite sense of paranoia can set in—explicitly, in the form of "Who said that?" and implicitly in the form "What might s/he/it say/do next?" Spam, on the other hand, is a form of transmission that has been likened to electronic junk mail and that gradually has developed an automatic association with a negative "value" (see Flynn 1994; Godwin 1994). On multiuser sites, while decried in like manner, spam can be a transmission that assumes what Jakobson (1960) called the "phatic" function of language, that is, designating the presence of Net discourse itself, usually playfully, but sometimes in ways that may be irritating, offensive, and even sexually harassing, depending on the sensibilities of the spam recipient (see Stivale 1996b). With both spoofing and spamming, blockages can occur to the extent that synchronous discussion can be interrupted, even seriously so depending on the persistence, and degree of aggression, of the "spoofer" or "spammer." But regular users of synchronous Net sites quickly become accustomed to several conversation strings appearing on-screen at once, so that in some ways "spoofs" and "spams" become the "background" noise around which real discussion takes place, as at a crowded cocktail party. In fact, "spams" and "spoofs" can achieve the status of a counterdiscourse on synchronous sites without which the very environment of exchange would take on a rather dry, lifeless tone.

While these two "values" employ the Net for unattributed or apparently "unproductive" enunciation, the opposite occurs when someone logs on (synchronously) or receives posts from mailing lists (asynchronously) and then only witnesses or reads—"lurks" in Internet slang—in the (virtual) background, never responding or contributing to online discussion. Here no extension of the "rhizome" is possible, at least online; what occurs "in real life" for the "lurker" may be entirely different. However, when all the subscribers started to "lurk," real gaps did occur on one "string" on the D&G List. In response to this lull, Erik Davis employed exhortation and cajoling:

> Come on, when you read a Deleuze post, don't you have that little itch at the end? That sense of some tendril being thrust from the screen through your eyes, your brain, down the nerves to your fingers hovering over that "reply" function? Extend the rhizome! Don't "create" it if you're too sleepy, but let the pingpong ball keep bouncing! (D&G List, 6 April 1994)

I took a different spin, introducing a statement by Deleuze that speaks directly to the questions of silences:

> So it's not a problem of getting people to express themselves but of providing little gaps of solitude and silence in which they might eventually find something to say. Repressive forces don't stop people from expressing themselves, but rather force them to express themselves. What a relief to have nothing to say, the right to say nothing, because only then is there a chance of framing the rare, and ever rarer, thing that might be worth saying. (N, 129; P, 177)

As for the fourth so-called value, lag, Net surfers have become wearily accustomed to this nemesis of swift exchange of data during moments of the twenty-four-hour cycle when transmission speed slows down due (among other causes) to heavy user load. If I want to be sure to connect with European participants in the synchronous sites, for example, the early morning hours in the United States are usually prime Net time for low lag. However, as the day progresses, and as users in different time zones log on, transmission speed is increasingly impeded. Depending on one's server and site, logon itself can be impeded in relation to current user load. When one is in synchronous communication with another person online, lag creates awkward gaps in discussion, and thus contributes to the necessarily mediated slowness of exchange. Yet intensities can still continue to pass, even if the question of speed and slowness, movement and rest becomes all too literal in lagged cyberspace. As Kurtz/Brando mutters in *Apocalypse Now*, "You must make a friend of horror," and so too one learns to "move within" lag, to take advantage of the slowness in order to emit, for example, a series of commands for reviewing posts (to internal bulletin boards on MUDs), and then wait for their transmission to appear, eventually, on screen. Depending on one's "real-life" mode of Net connection, one can certainly multitask, toggling to other windows while waiting out the lag. For the World Wide Web, "lag" poses increasing delays because the downloading of text is accompanied by the often lengthy process of loading images, thereby clogging jumps from one hypertext link to another. While faster processors and more effective browsers can alleviate some of these problems, recent "crises" of access (the AOL difficulties come to mind) suggest that cybernauts will move ceaselessly from threshold to threshold as one form of blockage is relieved, only to be replaced by yet another.

FLAME HOLES

"Flaming," yet another well-known form of potential blockage, came under scrutiny in several ways on the D&G List. On bulletin boards and in newsgroups of all sorts, the fragility of computer-mediated communication becomes all too apparent when some degree of "intensity" within an exchange triggers what is known as a "flame war" (see Dery 1994; Harris 1994). On the D&G List, the quality of discussion (and concomitantly, the low "flame" quotient) has been fairly exceptional. Even so, a participant's earnest, yet misinterpreted, assertions can incite querulous responses, to which other interlocutors inevitably add their remarks, and to which the corrected correspondent then retorts quite defensively, perhaps thereby insulting one previous respondent, and so on (see Millard 1995, 1997). While this is now a banal tale on Listservs and internal MUD lists, even these sparks flying and flowing result at times in one being bolstered "directly on a line of flight enabling one to blow apart strata, cut roots, and make new connections" (ATP, 15; MP, 23). For this very "blockage" of the rhizome resulted on the D&G List in a further exchange about flaming as "rhizomatics of cyberspace":

- Greg Polly wondered if "flame wars [might exist] as the monster black holes of the Internet," and referred to Massumi's *User's Guide* (1992, 125) to describe some motivations and (re)actions of Net surfers: "People sign up in clubs of like-minded to rehearse their own subjection to the club . . . or different quasi-causes enter the same netgroup and battle it out. But when that happens—despite the potentially fertile field of differences—the result is not recombination but further territorializing." He concluded: "And the scary thing that the flame war reveals is how easily one or two fascist adversarial types can hold an entire net hostage, can proscribe any other kind of language game, and can even draw other people into their agon" (D&G List, 8 April, 1994).

- My own quick (and not very well-thought-through) response to Polly included the comment that he seemed to equate Net surfing with the asynchronous sites (bulletin boards, newsgroups) on which "flaming" quite frequently occurs, to which Polly responded, "Not such a metaphysical claim, just that this was my greenhorn experience. And that the ubiquity of flame war was at odds with the utopian discourse one sometimes hears about the Internet" (D&G List, 9 April 1994). I ended my post: "I spend most of my time on synchronous sites (e.g., PMC-MOO); that is not to imply, however, that they are any less 'flamed' . . . actually, it can get quite rough-and-tumble, but extremely rhizomatically so. Black holes? [I wondered, and then profoundly pronounced] Dunno, gotta ponder that" (D&G List, 8 April 1994).

- Polly offered further clarifications the next day: "To my mind a flame war can't be rhizomatic by definition: when I call it a black hole, I'm referring to its power to stop rhizome and lines of flight and institute a dreary polemical becoming-same." He developed this idea further in terms of the Deleuze–Guattarian concept "faciality" (discussed in *A Thousand Plateaus*):

> Far from a rhizomatic combination or jazzing off an enemy position, . . . flaming centers on a personalist mode of vengeance that exploits the subjected form of seeing-yourself-in-the-other's-gaze, the pain and humiliation which that mode of subjectivity entails. Flaming does not involve conceptual improvization or jazzing or riffing but [instead] the constant attempt to reframe the quotations of another so that the "self" inscribed by that post will, by virtue of the reframing, be humiliated before the gaze of others. Subjectivity is ruthlessly kept within the circuit of those eye-beams. (D&G List, 9 April 1994)

- My own response, expressed here (and there as well, since I posted an earlier version of this chapter to the list for purposes of creating new "bifurcations" of this discourse) is, first, that the utopian discourse about the Net is highly overblown, as attested by several essays available at the time of this discussion string and an array of others published since.[4] This very discussion about "flaming" suggests how the rhizome is not necessarily blocked within a "flame" hole. Of course, such impasses might well occur within the BwO zone, and not only in the ways Polly details. More and more, institutions can (and do) intervene, as in the University of Texas at Dallas case where an aggressive bulletin-board user was denied access to his local server when his perceived "flaming" to one list resulted in complaints by other users who disagreed with his positions and modes of expression there (Wilson 1993).[5] But jumping out of the impasse and extending the rhizome can also occur: our continuing "string" on "rhizomatics" and "flaming" was/is proof of that truth, and not simply of the genre "I'm more rhizomatic than thou."

- Following up our posts with his own reflections on the "black holes," Erik Davis agreed with Polly: "I have nothing against withering critiques per se. It's the personalism, the egos, the faces involved that I object to. . . . We should feel the dispute pervade the space in a flash, like a flash of lightning that clears the ground. It's when we grip our swords tightly that the game prolongs." And his riff folds back toward the possibilities of "becoming-imperceptible": "What if we could remember no one's name . . . think of the faces it would dissolve! Am 'I' Michael now, or Stivale, or MBOON, or a woman who's holding on tight to her sword and who cannot even remember her name? There would just be the bouncing ball, the mad dash down the valley, functions and styles commingling and not solidifying into 'spurious ghosts.' " And he concludes, "If I have nothing to protect, nothing to admit, then even the [flaming] phil-lit [philosophy–literature] major poster's digs against Michael for being a 'nonacademic' will slide off me. It becomes a slippery rock that I avoid as me and my pack plummet forward—Look out, black hole ahead! In that sense, maybe I can love the list the more I forget all your names" (D&G List, 9 April 1994).

- Greg Polly responded to me:

> I think I'll dissent from [Stivale's] conclusion about flames and the rhizome. . . . I don't feel convinced that the recent skirmish here on this Net demonstrated that flaming can be subsumed and included by rhizomatics. It seems to me that, on the contrary, what happened was a kind of group decision not to enter into the kind of desire that flaming represents, not to "bring the General in us out," as D&G say in "Rhizome," a decision to stay on the schizo lines and avoid getting pulled onto the

paranoid ones. There's a difference between saying that recent events here demonstrated that flaming can be rhizomatic too, and saying that we luckily *avoided* its rhizome-stopping possibilities, a difference between saying that the rhizome can go on *in* a flame hole and saying that we can preserve the ability to jump out of one or even avoid one before we've entered. (D&G List, 17 April 1994)

- My (not so) quick take in response:

"Unlike psychoanalysis, [or] psychoanalytic competence [say D&G], . . . schizoanalysis rejects any idea of pretraced destiny, whatever name is given to it" (ATP, 13; MP, 20): it appears that Greg makes just such a "pretraced destiny" of the rhizomatic process when it comes into the gravitational pull, as it were, of a flame hole. Indeed, rhizomes can be obstructed, arborified, and then "it's all over, no desire stirs" (ATP, 14; MP, 22), but in a flame war, is *every* outlet necessarily blocked? I think my *différend* with Greg on this point is a matter of perspective: whereas he sees the flame hole necessarily as a blockage out of which lines cannot emerge short of group decisions that enact a resistant, schizzy counter-flame (Go to warp speed, take us outta here, Scotty!), I see the flame as a kind of "tracing" that one can plug "back into the map, connect[ing] the roots or trees back up with the rhizome" (ATP, 14; MP, 22). The rhizome's multientry "essence" (ATP, 14; MP, 22) suggests this: "Accounting and bureaucracy proceed by tracings," as do "flame wars," tracings of the paranoid pole, of the rigid position, staking out the territory, striating the List/discussion time–space; "they can begin to burgeon nonetheless, throwing out rhizome stems, as in a Kafka novel" (ATP, 15; MP, 23): why would the flame hole be the exceptional site within which no stems could emerge? "The coordinates are determined not by theoretical analyses implying universals but by a pragmatics composing multiplicities or aggregates of intensity" (ATP, 15; MP, 23). How? "An intensive trait starts working for itself, a hallucinatory perception, synesthesia, perverse muta-tion, or play of images shakes loose, challenging the hegemony of the signifer" (ATP, 15; MP, 23). Might this "shaking loose," this "challenge," be the immanent "group decision" to which Greg refers? Perhaps the nub of our *différend* (which may not be one) lies in ourselves asserting too strictly a dualism, flame hole/rhizomatic stem, for "there are knots of arborescence in rhizomes, and rhizomatic offshoots in roots . . . despotic formations of immanence and channelization specific to rhizomes, just as there are anarchic deformations in the transcendent system of trees, aeriel roots, and subterranean stems" (ATP, 20; MP, 30–31).

I find myself pressing forward, waking up each morning to move into and along a plateau, "technonarcissism," as D&G call it, "RHI-ZOMATICS = POP ANALYSIS, even if the people have other things to do besides read it, even if the blocks of academic culture or pseudos-cientificity in it are still too painful or ponderous" (ATP, 22–24; MP,

33–35). Attempting to see things in the middle, I try to understand, for example, "black holes" in terms of movements of subjectification and deterritorialization, of passion and consciousness (see ATP, 133, 167–168; MP, 166, 205–206): in cyberspace, in MOO-spaces, "The face constructs the wall that the signifier needs in order to bounce off of; it constitutes the wall of the signifier, the frame or screen. The face digs the hole that subjectification needs in order to break through; it constitutes the black hole of subjectivity as consciousness or passion, the camera, the third eye. Or should we say things differently?" (ATP, 168; MP, 206). Always in flux, intermezzo. . . . How about this, further along: "Instead of opening up the deterritorialized assemblage onto something else, [the machine] may produce an effect of closure, as if the aggregate had fallen into and continues to spin in a kind of black hole. . . . The machine then produces 'individual' group effects spinning in circles," for example, the effect of capture produced in a flame war. "The black hole is a machine effect in assemblages and has a complex relation to other effects. It may be necessary for the release of innovative processes that they *first* fall into a catastrophic black hole: stases of inhibition are associated with the release of crossroads behavior. On the other hand, when black holes resonate together or inhibitions conjugate and echo each other, instead of opening onto consistency, we see a closure of the assemblage, as though it were deterritorialized in the void." (ATP, 333–334; MP, 411–412; my emphasis)

• As for an alternative, Erik Davis's response to Polly's posting queries the potential differences on synchronous multiuser sites known as MOOs, and enlivens the possibilities of spam, spoofs, and other online activities:

> The conversations flow past your eye into nothingness, you riff and jam off of puns and unintentioned allusions as much as points. In fact, points become the rocks that you leap from as you plunge down unknown paths—rocks that you know you cannot "stand on" because you have too much momentum going, you and your pack, and if you let the points' gravity rule over your own momentum, you'll eat shit. Not that the point isn't solid, useful, coherent. It's just that you often only "get it" once it's gone, under your feet, back there. (D&G List, 9 April 1994)

I re-present this "string" extensively because these shifts, jumps, and shoots on the BwO zone suggest, as do Deleuze and Guattari, that "the failure of the plan(e) is part of the plan(e) itself: The plan(e) is infinite, you can start it in a thousand different ways; you will always find something that comes too late or too early, forcing you to recompose all of your relations of speed and slowness, all of your affects, and to rearrange the overall assemblage. An infinite undertaking" (ATP, 259; MP, 316).

CAUTION, NOT WISDOM

This last citation might well serve as yet another epigraph to my own undertaking here, for in preparing this assemblage, I find it continually intersected by new lines that keep the "rhizome" open, in flux, but that produce "bifurcations," online and offline, making me wonder constantly how and if the BwO zone could be (re)presented or (re)produced through such a linear discourse. And I also wonder about the sites of reception of this discourse. A question in this regard was well formulated on the D&G List (by an anonymous participant, identified only as a "chrestomathy of subconscious yearnings"): "How do we decide with Deleuze, or if we want, with rhizomes, what can and cannot be said about them? Can we ask what might seem to be basic questions, such as 'How do we think rhizomatically?' or even 'How can we think rhizomatically?'—or do we just leap to the evident assumption that we do think in this way?" (D&G List, 7 April 1994).

Someone who seems to share these concerns is Deleuze himself, particularly regarding the "rhizomatics" of "cyberspace," for he has taken pains to express his wariness, in an entirely nonrhapsodic way. In a discussion with Toni Negri entitled "Control and Becoming," Deleuze distinguishes between the "disciplinary societies" closely examined by Foucault, societies that we have already "left behind," and contemporary "societies of 'control' " to which corresponds a particular machinic regime, "cybernetics and computers." Deleuze notes:

> But machines don't explain anything, you have to analyze the collective apparatuses [assemblages] of which machines are just one component. Compared with the approaching forms of ceaseless control in open sites, we may come to see the harshest confinement as part of a wonderful happy past. (N, 175; P, 237)

Furthermore, he maintains that "the quest for 'universals of communication' ought to make us shudder" (N, 175; P, 237). He develops a facet of this idea in "Postscript on Control Societies," and (briefly) in *What Is Philosophy?* In these modern societies, "the key thing is no longer a signature or a number, but a code [*un chiffre*]," that is, a "password" that replaces the "order-word" (*mot d'ordre*) of the disciplinary societies: "The digital language of control is made of codes indicating whether access to some information should be allowed or denied" (N, 180; P, 242). The former dichotomy between individuals and masses is replaced by "*dividuals*," on the one hand, and by "samples, data, markets or 'banks,' " on the other. "Disciplinary man produced energy in discrete amounts, while control man undulates, moving among a continuous range of different orbits. *Surfing* has taken over from all the old *sports*" (N, 180; P, 244).[6]

While Deleuze recognizes that some new forms of resistance, such as software piracy and deliberately spreading computer viruses, have already emerged, he doubts that these and other forms of "transversal" resistance would be available to minorities for their own expression: "Maybe speech and communication have been corrupted. They're thoroughly permeated by money—and not by accident but by their very nature" (N, 175; P, 238). And he insists quite starkly:

> We don't have to stray into science fiction to find a control mechanism that can fix the position of any element at any given moment—an animal in a game reserve, a man in a business (electronic tagging). Félix Guattari has imagined a town where anyone can leave their flat, their street, their neighborhood, using their (dividual) electronic card that opens this or that barrier; but the card may also be rejected on a particular day, or between certain times of day; it doesn't depend on the barrier but on the computer that is making sure everyone is in a permissible place and effecting a universal modulation. (N, 181–182; P, 246)

To this stern, apocalyptic, or perhaps *only* pragmatic reflection, Deleuze offers equally grim alternatives: on the level of nascent "control mechanisms," he warns that "we ought to establish [their] sociotechnological principles . . . and describe in these terms what is already taking the place of the disciplinary sites of confinement that everyone says are breaking down." Prison regimes, educational regimes, hospital regimes, corporate regimes—all reveal "the widespread progressive introduction of a new system of domination" (N, 182; P, 246–247). In terms of the regime of communication, Deleuze told Negri that "we've got to hijack speech. Creating has always been something different from communicating. The key thing may be to create vacuoles of non communication, circuit breakers, so we can elude control" (N, 175; P, 238). Yet he concludes that discussion with Negri on a slightly less ponderous note:

> If you believe in the world you precipitate events, however inconspicuous, that elude control, you engender new space–times, however small their surface or volume. It's what you call *pietas*. Our ability to resist control, or our submission to it, has to be assessed at the level of our every move. We need both creativity *and* a people. (N, 176; P, 239).[7]

The inspiration for such "inconspicuous events" are indeed part of "virtual futures." Do they consist in extending the rhizome? How does one "hijack speech" and create "circuit-breakers" capable of escaping control? To answer these questions within the Deleuze–Guattarian assemblages, one might look closely at their final work together, *What Is Philosophy?*, and particularly at Guattari's proposal in *Chaosmose* for a generalized ecology, or an "ecosophy" (see also Guattari 1989b). Within this "ecosophy" would be an "ecology of the virtual" that would have as its goal "not simply [to] attempt to preserve the endangered species of cultural life but equally to engender conditions for the creation and the development of unprecedented formations of subjectivity that have never been seen and never felt" (Guattari 1992, 127–128; 1995, 91). These would be "virtuality machines," "blocks of mutant percepts and affects, half-object half-subject," characterized by "limitless interfaces which secrete interiority and exteriority and constitute themselves at the root of every system of discursivity" (1992, 128–129; 1995, 92).[8] And referring to Maturana and Varela, Guattari proposes the "autopoetic machine" and their notion of "autopoeisis" as "the auto-reproductive capacity of a structure or eco-system [that] could be usefully enlarged to include social machines, economic machines and even the incorporal machines of language, theory and aesthetic creation" (1992, 130). In any case, Guattari concludes:

> All [these assemblages] impl[y] the idea of a necessary creative practice and even an ontological pragmatics. It is being's new way of being [*nouvelles façons d'être de l'être*] that rhythms, forms, colors and intensities of dance create. Nothing happens of itself. Everything is continually begun again starting from zero, at the point of chaosmic emergence. (1992, 131; 1995, 95; translation modified)

CAUTION, REDUX

As I mentioned at the start of this chapter, I develop here an essay originally prepared for the first Warwick "Virtual Futures" conference, held in May 1994.[9] This development has occurred over several years, following online discussions on an array of topics on the D&G List, including several on the aforementioned question of "caution" (see ATP, 160; MP, 198–199, and Chapter 4 below). The debate's substance can be stated simply: Deleuze and Guattari's counsel concerning "caution" in *A Thousand Plateaus* (particularly regarding seeking to deterritorialize) is/is not a disappointing retreat from the more radical, "schizoanalytical" tasks proposed in *Anti-Oedipus*. I evoke this debate here because it provides an interesting bridge between *Anti-Oedipus* and *A Thousand Plateaus*, especially since the "caution" position has tended to be associated with "later" Deleuze–Guattari.

To some extent, this issue has been at the heart of a continuing debate regarding Deleuze and Guattari's works that informed, and continues to inform, various approaches to their study. Not only did my own commentary on the 1994 "Virtual Futures" conference give rise to some exchanges on the D&G List, but at the start of 1995, the question of "caution" arose again on the list in response to Nick Land's essay, "Making It with Death" (1993b). I wish to give the reader a sense of some positions in these debates. Rather than attempt to approximate (and quite possibly distort) these positions through summary, I complete this chapter with the "rhizomatic" trails that moved back and forth from the "rl" (real-life) conference into "cyberspace" discussions.

During the weeks following the 1994 Warwick conference, some reference to an American versus Warwickian "split" was made on the D&G List, to which I responded briefly. Shortly thereafter, I provided the following account of the conference to the D&G List:

> Various real-life tasks have occupied my time since early May such that I've been unable to seize upon the momentum that the splendid University of Warwick conference created in order to provide a report of it to this list. As my previous short post referring to the conference indicated, it was at once productive and fraught with tensions, as much from local sources as from the usual collision of modes of conceptualization.

I here provided the conference schedule of plenary and parallel sessions that culminated in the final session on Sunday, May 6, with Nick Land's presentation of a talk with the announced title "Meltdown." I continued my online commentary:

> References have been made on the list (Michael Current relaying a comment by Joan Broadhurst, to which I responded) that the conference broke down into an American/Warwickian divide. As I have stated, this view misrepresents the unfolding of the conference, not to mention the numerous non-Warwick persons in attendance as well as the dissonance among Warwickians themselves. What the view represents is the cleavage that I perceived from my arrival in Coventry, and I'll repeat myself from an earlier post to the list: "What I did discover, and learn from immensely, was the fascinating preference among *some* folks I met in Warwick toward *Anti-Oedipus* as Ur-text of D&G, mainly since it is perceived to express an unrelenting political position of schizoanalysis. Whereas *A Thousand Plateaus,* and many other D&G pieces/interviews since, express a *pragmatics* and sets of distinctions that extol *caution.* This split, between a politics of deterritorialization without limits and a more cautious view toward the consequences of such a no-holds-barred politics, constituted the crux, I believe, of the *différend* [characterized as American/Warwickian]."
>
> Many of the tensions that built up through the conference seemed to arise from numerous sites: the outright hostility of those Warwickians who, for whatever reason (philosophical, professional, personal, and combinations thereof), had absolutely no sympathy/patience/use for such an event as a "Virtual Futures" conference; a nostalgia among some

present for the "good old days" when theorizing could proceed without consideration of practical consequences, and within this strain of thought emerged an even more peculiar "becoming-same," to the point that one's personal habits (e.g., nonsmoking, in my case) might be called into question as some sort of failure to engage in "necessary" deterritorialization; reflections on different aspects of thought related to virtual futures (not only D&G–oriented) some of which translated as *caution* if not outright skepticism toward an uncritical acceptance of the benefits of "technoculture."

Given my own interests, the papers of Benjamin Macias on virtual communities and Samantha Holland on the cyborg films (especially her form of presentation: she prepared an excellent video in which selected film clips screened behind her reading *in* the video) were quite valuable. Also, all of the plenaries, Stelarc's in particular, opened my mind's eyes to new possibilities on virtual futures. However, the momentum to which I've referred built up to Nick Land's "Meltdown" talk, and this moment was in some ways a culmination and a summing up of much that had preceded. Here is a sample, from the abstract provided to all participants:

> "Modernity races through intensive half-lives: 1500, 1756, 1884, 1948, 1980, 1996, 2004, 2008, 2010, 2011. . . . Closing upon Terrestrial Meltdown Singularity, and triggering terminal political crisis across the planet. Reverse transcription subverts genomic (ROM) command structures, and tradition-based authority dissipates in artificial space. Having climbed the negentropy curve from industrial thermocontrol to the brink of soft technocataclysm, power panics and condenses the Human Security System. Looming green-black schizoshapes begin to come up on the screen.
>
> "Cyberian invasion deploys the future as a weapon, camouflaged in history as global technocapital convergence. Disintegrating social reality skids into cyberpunk, and you find yourself reformatted in Globewar-5. Meltdown virus is infiltrating from tomorrow, cooking protection in bottom-up intelligentsia, and hacking through the ICE-fortresses of SF (security futurism) to spring feral connectionist-AI emergence from anthropomorphizing Asimov-ROM. It's a mess: trashed meat all over the place, and China-syndrome running away from control. Wintermute is getting vicious. Then VIRTUAL FUTURES happens, and things really turn horrific. . . . "

What is one to make of this "vision"? David Porush asked Land, Where is the pleasure coming from in this projection of "meltdown"? Is it the pleasure of the horror? Stelarc's series of queries were even more pointed: wasn't Land positing a kind of technophobia? Land claimed that, on the contrary, it was not him making such a postulate, but that it is inherent to the top-down hierarchy from which meltdown inevitably proceeds. Stelarc objected that he doesn't buy into the discourse of technofear, and that while Land implied a lot of intention on the part of top-down repression, Land's own "bottom-up" intention is to disrupt the top-down through some disabling strategy aimed at the Human Security System, but also carrying on as if some autonomous, intelligent, decentered, self-regulating network were in place now. To Land's response that the nanospasm plateau is not impossible, that the planet is constructed into a kind of nano-playdough, Stelarc expressed doubts that these forces would congeal so simplistically. Stelarc sees the body as accelerating and also being invaded while interfacing with digital systems and data spaces, in some ways enhancing what it means to be human. Land responded that he was simply attempting to designate boundaries that are being set up by security systems.

The next phase of the discussion occurred with Manuel De Landa juxtaposing *Anti-Oedipus* to *A Thousand Plateaus*. He argued that whereas the former preached "let's destratify like crazy," the latter reflected an aging, even a sort of courtesy: if we want to transform this world into something a little less homogeneous, our resistance has to become more pragmatic, and not destratify too fast lest the strata fall on us harder than ever, that is, avoid a careless destratification/acceleration that might provoke restratification with a vengeance. Here, Land vociferously contested the subject positions and intentionality that De Landa was attributing to *Anti-Oedipus/A Thousand Plateaus,* that is, Deleuze and Guattari as constituted subjects vs. (what I'll call) a desubjectified, destratified understanding of these works as "texts," not necessarily attributable to subject-specific intentionalities.

The *différend* heated up at this point with Land questioning De Landa's use of the very term "we" as a stratified "readout" to enunciate his position (i.e., De Landa maintained that our bodies act upon strata through our subjectivity for an empirically objective duration, and while we can deterritorialize/destratify while we are upon them by all kinds of means, these means do not occur solely devoid of subjectivity). Stephen Pfohl interjected that it was not only problematic for Land to use the term "posthuman," but was philosophically irresponsible to discuss these problematics solely in terms of the destratification of flows. Ivan Benjamin asked Land where was his irony, and suggested that in dealing with the future, we're dealing also with it through the now, and not just through flows; that Land's position runs the risk of (a) failing to deal with the now at all, and (b) letting technofear read out of context be employed against any work in the now at all, even on the flow. To Land's retort that Benjamin's response was bizarrely overdefensive given the terrain, and that we have strategies now to employ our tools at hand, Benjamin asked that Land provide an example of such tools at hand, so that we could deploy them. Here, Land fell (dramatically) silent. Stelarc suggested, however, that some alternate strategies might be found, for example, in work by artists to subvert stratified modes of perception.

David Porush continued in the preceding vein: he said that Land unleashed a lot of pleasure in his "meltdown," self-marginalizing subversive text, but also apocalypse: that the text urges and embraces the apocalypse at the same time as it warns against it. Porush said that such pleasure might turn quickly to other things, and that there is something irresponsible in unleashing this apocalyptic view as a form of pleasure. Land said he had a lack of sympathy with responsibility as a concept, that it constitutes a crushing form of stratification. He asked, further, at the end of the day, does being responsible really put you on the side of the angels? We're so sedimented with years of responsibility, but this is merely a way to hang onto a sense of control, which itself is a part of the problem, not part of the solution. Diane Beddoes asked if Land's use of the term "subject" implied such an autonomous sense of subjectivity that his use displaced the term in history. To Land's disagreement with her formulation, Beddoes suggested that he needs to provide a better story than simply to tell us to deterritorialize/destratify.

All this is obviously a reconstruction of the final discussion, totally without the context (a) of the days that led up to it and (b) of the actual talk that Nick Land presented. However, the cyberorgasmic/apocalyptic edge that several discussants pointed to emerged in a number of talks and in a form of discourse, prevalent among one part of the Warwick group, that seemed/seems to equate destratifying/deterritorializing merely with a discursive strategy that provides no practical means of developing new lines of flight. (D&G List, 28 May 1994)

To this summary, Nick Land subsequently responded with a message entitled "Trashing Security":

Charles has finally dragged me out of lurker space. His summary of my session at Virtual Futures seems fairly accurate given the circumstances (rant, mayhem, and heat from all sides) but I'd like to take the question of tactics a bit further in the hope that this list might be interested in prolonging the question. Politics (i.e., pod security, actual or virtual police activity) isn't the issue. Microwar against power is. Whilst I can understand that compared to the motor-mouth aggression preceding my response to the "So what do we do?" question, "Dramatic silence" is not a wholly misleading description; I did finally suggest that catalytic microactivity modeled on a-life is the broad schema for cyberian insurrectionary operations. Bottom-up or self-organizing processes clearly cannot have an overall grand strategy or master plan, and this—combined with the fact that microtactics tend to be technically intricate, highly illegal, and locally sensitive—accounted for my sluggishness in suggesting how they might be accelerated (D&G are not exactly forthcoming on the matter themselves).

If there is anything corresponding to a "Warwickian" D&G it inclines toward the assemblage of machines (involving textual components) oriented to the dismantling of (top-down insular) institutions. The dissociation of all conceptions of "action" organized by linear,

Neo-Christian, heroic-moral, soul-mythologies is a key element in such processes. Universities are an example of inert state-apparatuses which are obviously fucked in the fairly short term, and the drift of collective intelligence into efficient decentred communicative networks has a massively important role to play in kicking them down the slope, but isn't there a concern that the polite vaguely scholarly chat that characterizes much Net talk merely reproduces the docile Oedipalized crap it could be cooking in schizophrenia? Why not swap soft-weaponry/tactical diagrams and reports about trying it out (whilst trying not to get arrested)?
Death to the Human Security System.
—K-423 (30 May 1994).

As online discussions often do, this discussion string quickly moved on to other subjects. Then, in early 1995, another set of interlocutors addressed Land's essay, "Making It with Death" (1993b), and raised and extended this same subject. Melissa McMahon's query whether anyone would be interested in discussing the "death drive" prompted Jonathan Beasley-Murray to recommend Land's essay, initially providing a brief excerpt and commentary: "Land disparages what he sees as the shift between an embrace of this death drive in *Anti-Oedipus* and too much caution in *A Thousand Plateaus*. Aden—you're out there too, I bet—didn't you have some ideas on this as a misreading of *Anti-Oedipus*?" (D&G List, 4 January 1995). There followed several posts (from Melissa McMahon, Karen Ocana, Mani Haghighi, and Fadi Abou-Rihan):

• Referring to a quote from Land that Beasley-Murray provided ("The death drive is Freud's beautiful account of how creativity occurs without the least effort, how life is propelled into its extravagances by the blindest and simplest of tendencies, how desire is no more problematic than a river's search for the sea" [1993b, 74–75]), McMahon suggests that "in D&R Deleuze actually criticises the aspect of Freud's account which characterises the death drive as a kind of blind will to rejoin the inorganic—it may be that this is just one of the death drive's 'faces' ('the repetition that condemns, the repetition that saves . . .')."
• In a post entitled "Making It with Death and Libidinal Materialism," Karen Ocana criticizes Land's essay on a number of grounds: for omitting mention of any feminist materialists with whom she seems to share common ground; for his unproblematically flowing view of matter which, Ocana argues, is "rife with conflict," but "not the same conflict, the same struggle, the same effort as the Protestant work ethic which you probably imbibed as a kid, Nick. It's got to do with, how shall I put it? polyvirality—the multiplicity of forces, forces in combat. This is not just a social phenomenon. It ain't the petty conflict of Viennese nursery pap,

or Artaud's daddy-mommy, it's an impersonal kind of struggle"; and what Ocana sees as "Land's championing of a Spinoza who knows nothing of caution." Says Ocana:

> [Spinoza's motto] is CAUTION. . . . Desire, Spinoza's life-unto-death force, is not opposed to caution. However, it's not the caution of common sense, it's the caution of passion, of the half-second, our animal instinct, passion *tout court* . . . caution may come effortlessly to animals—material beings— but this does not wipe out the effort. Caution is a built-in motor or body or brainpart. It's part of the functioning of animal machines: call it the instinct of self-preservation. This instinct does not preserve the ego, it preserves the life of the animal, the animal-assemblage. Life does not equal ego, nor does life equal death. (D&G List, 12 January 1995)

• Mani Haghighi is even more critical, particularly regarding the question of caution:

> [Land] seems to think that D&G are selling out in *A Thousand Plateaus* by introducing Black Holes as cautionary stop signs on the line-of-flight superhighway. And in the most irritating and posturing way he basically calls them chicken. "It is no exaggeration to suggest that a theory of a 'black-hole effect' or 'too-sudden destratification' [ATP, 503; MP, 628] threatens to cripple and domesticate the entire massive achievement of Deleuze and Guattari" [Land 1993b, 73]. His reasons for this are many, but they all read the notion of Black Holes as repressive blockages that are somehow in the way of this fabulous, effortless flow of matter and desire toward some kind of a glorified death.

Haghighi usefully cites Deleuze and Guattari (e.g., ATP, 334; MP, 412) to argue that rather than denoting fear, "Black Holes often seem to be a necessary stage of a process, something you have to face in order to be capable of escape." He also takes issue with Land's "attempt to deny the fact that Nazism is a paranoid molecular flow-toward-death," and concludes with: "All I'm saying is, caution is not repressive, it's strategic" (D&G List, 15 January 1995).

• Nick Land responded at this point:

> I agree with almost all the criticisms made of "Making It with Death" [MIWD], especially those laid out in Karen's first post. If I was to diagnose the essay as a pathological symptom, it would be to see it as a burnt-out Protestant reaction formation to occidental monotheism, and thus hopelessly crude about war, caution, difficulty (labour I still have problems with). A large influx of midperiod (no pun intended) Irigaray and darkside (anti-Confucian) Chinese philosophy was definitely needed, and the garbage about German idealism was a complete waste of everybody's time.

On the plus side, I would just say that the title is fucking brilliant and the usage of a National Socialist spectre to prop up the very psychosocial control systems that gave rise to the phenomenon in the first place—frenzied reaction to deterritorialization/ethnocultural meltdown—is in need of vicious critique. It also seems to me that Mani goes too far in emphasizing the "fluidity" of the S.S.—phobic authoritarianism is surely constrained when it comes to runaway molecularization (not that I want to sustain a line as simplistic as the millerean Theweleit/MIWD knockdown). (D&G List, 15 January 1995)[10]

- Part of Haghighi's reply to Land reads:

The need for the vicious critique is duly felt. But I'm not sure what you mean by my emphasizing the "fluidity" of the S.S. I never did such a thing. . . . I was trying to disagree with what you say toward the end: "Does anyone really think that Nazism is like letting go? Thewelcit's studies of Nazi body posture should be sufficient to disabuse one of such an absurdity" [Land, 1993b]. I just don't think that the fluidity of Nazism is necessarily linked to the Nazi body posture. (To be honest, I think what is really absurd is making this link.) But on the up side, I think you are suddenly too down on your piece. The more I read it, the more interesting it becomes. A very good sign. (D&G List, 15 January 1995)

- Fadi Abou-Rihan responded to this string that same day:

I keep thinking here of (Deleuze's reading of) the Nietzschean active forces and the overman in the *Genealogy*, both of which make the rule of caution in *A Thousand Plateaus* very problematic. . . . If desire simply *is*, if it does not operate along the lines of utility, efficiency, and lack, then it can signal its own death since caution and pre-caution are predicated on a rationality or common sense eschewed by desiring-production. This is not a question of nihilistic self-destruction, but one of risks and chances. I don't necessarily want to say that the introduction of the rule of caution into *A Thousand Plateaus* is a sign of *Anti-Oedipus*'s domestication during the winter years of the seventies; and I don't want to accuse D&G of puritanism when they invoke the BwO [Body without Organs] of the masochist or the drug user in *A Thousand Plateaus* as a warning against the carelessness of desire. . . . But I do think it is more than slightly hypocritical on their part to insist on a caution that would have suffocated many of their sources and inspirations (Nietzsche, May '68, Schreber, Masoch, Artaud, etc.). (D&G List, 15 January 1995)

Abou-Rihan posits a triadic schema for understanding this "rule of caution,"[11] and then concludes: "If caution persists within this schema, it does not lie on the side of the molecular entirely, and it cannot erase that abyss either. The game of molecularity carries with it its own stakes and risks; they are not external molar traps or internal ineptitudes either" (D&G List, 15 January 1995).

- Later that day, Haghighi responds to Abou-Rihan's post:

> OK, the problem is becoming clearer to me. I never thought of caution as some kind of an external force that comes in and sanitises desire or the death drive. I always thought of it as a formal predicate of desire itself (am I allowed to say things like this?). It seems to me that from this perspective we can avoid the caution/risk dialectic. If desire is intentional (and I have never been able to quite grasp the arguments to the contrary), then caution will have to be as pre-individual and pre-commonsensical as desire. . . .
>   If I'm right, then the paranoid–fascist self-annihilation would be the result of the suppression of a caution that is proper to desire, and deforming desire in the process (rather than allowing a self-destruction that is proper to desire to take its course in spite of an external, suppressive force.) . . . Finally, I think Fadi's triadic schema is very acute, but I still don't understand this insistence to speak of caution as somehow external to the schema. Why isn't caution on the part of the molecular? Sure, it doesn't erase the abyss, nor does it necessarily crush the state at every turn, but why would that make a difference? (D&G List, 15 January 1995)

- Nick Land returns again on this point: "The most concentrated *A Thousand Plateaus* remarks on caution are to be found in the BwO plateau. The suggestion that it should be thought [of] as immanent to desire (as an empirical condition for the tolerance of risk) is very helpful—it is the Chinese way to think—and makes the translation as 'prudence' deeply inappropriate. Caution as a tactics for the prolongation of adventure?" (D&G List, 16 January 1995).

I re-present this string to indicate the complexity of the *Anti-Oedipus* versus *A Thousand Plateaus* debate (see Chapter 2 above, note 2). In my own query to this string at the time, I reposted the 1994 summary of the Warwick conference, as well as Land's reply (see above), and then asked: "I still remain interested in knowing what, despite possible burnout, Nick Land now understands as the divergence and/or the convergence of D&G's positions re the [Body-without-Organs] between *Anti-Oedipus* and *A Thousand Plateaus,* and how we might explain these to readers [on the D&G List], recent as well as 'seasoned' (understood as temporal or culinary terms, as you wish)" (D&G List, 22 January 1995).

From time to time, variations on this discussion arise. For example, in late 1996 and early 1997, the D&G List because the forum for a heated debate on "hard" versus "soft" approaches to Deleuze and Guattari, though considerably hampered by lack of any agreement on these terms. From Down Under, in print, Meaghan Morris noted that the English-language reception of their work "has stressed the harsh tone of the more polemical parts of *Anti-Oedipus*" and privileged the "war machine" concept in *A Thousand Plateaus*. She concludes: "A relentlessly monogeneric rendering of 'Deleuze and Guattari' as the theoretical equivalent of a Nick Cave [and the Bad Seeds] murder ballad does a great disservice to a body of work that is immensely varied in its humours and tones and most formidable for the gaiety with which it launches into adventures of reading, writing, and thinking" (1996, 384–385). Such treatment of *Anti-Oedipus* has, of course, not escaped the notice of its authors. To the question, "Is it not the case that the history of that desiring machine [in *Anti-Oedipus*] is firmly rooted in that system [. . . whereby desire defines itself within the actual system and only appears as something problematic, related in one way or another to the breaking down of that system]?" Guattari responded unequivocally:

> For the most part, the intellectuals in question have not read, or do not want to understand, what was said in the post-68 period. Our conception of desire was completely contrary to some ode to spontaneity or a eulogy to some unruly liberation. It was precisely in order to underline the artificial, "constructivist" nature of desire that we defined it as "machinic," which is to say, articulated with the most actual, the most "urgent" machinic types. (Genosko 1996, 128)

While these debates have yet to reach any satisfactory "conclusion" from any perspective—indeed, it is questionable even if any resolution really is a goal—they also provide insight into the spatiotemporal, global instantaneity that can occur in such exchanges, between Sydney (McMahon), Montreal (Ocana), Guelph (Haghighi), Toronto (Abou-Rihan), Warwick (Land), Durham, NC (Beasley-Murray), and Detroit (Stivale). In any case, I (self-)impose a "circuit breaker" in order to leave these strings where I commenced, *dans le milieu, intermezzo*, with the Deleuze–Guattarian caution, not wisdom, as translated by an *intercesseur/*mediator named De Landa:

> All you can do is approach carefully because the last thing you want to do is get swallowed up by a chaotic attractor that's too huge in phase space. As Deleuze says, "Always keep a piece of fresh land with you at all times." Always keep a little spot where you can go back to sleep after a day of destratification. Always keep a small piece of territory, otherwise you'll go nuts. (Davis 1992, 48)

II MACHINES, PLATEAUS, BECOMINGS

4 NEW CARTOGRAPHIES OF THE LITERARY

FROM *KAFKA* TO *A THOUSAND PLATEAUS*

> You know what your trouble is? . . . You're the
> kind who *always reads the handbook.*
> Anything people build, any kind of
> technology, it's going to have some specific
> purpose. It's for doing something that
> somebody already understands. But if it's new
> technology, it'll open areas nobody's ever
> thought of before. You read the manual, man,
> and you won't play around with it, not the
> same way. And you get all funny when
> somebody else uses it to do something you
> never thought of.
>
> *–William Gibson, "The Winter Market"*
> (*in* Burning Chrome *1986a*)

In this chapter, I consider the "two-fold thought" through the literary "seam" in *A Thousand Plateaus.* I focus on how literature, books, and writing operate in terms of what Deleuze and Guattari call "cartography" and "stratification" by animating these concepts in relation to the textual productions by Quentin Tarantino in *Reservoir Dogs.*

While we have already considered the important role of the literary in *Anti-Oedipus,* it was not until the subsequent analysis in *Kafka: Toward a Minor Literature* that Deleuze and Guattari systematically addressed the works of a single author in light of "machinic" concepts.[1] As I indicated at the end of Chapter 2, the purpose of this critical work seems double:

103

on the one hand, Deleuze and Guattari continue their anti-Oedipal polemic, this time against various literary and psychoanalytic interpretations of Kafka's works; and on the other hand, the authors seek to move beyond the schizoanalytic terms suggested in *Anti-Oedipus,* to situate the machinic functioning in the organic as well. Thus they posit "minor" literature's existence vis-à-vis the "great" or "major" literatures, thereby extending their view of literature as locus of desire and of the real. Deleuze and Guattari also advance their terminology in another important direction: the molecules of the expression-machine function as rhizomes (Kafka's letters; KEng, 29–34; KFr, 53–62); as "animal-becomings" and lines of flight (Kafka's short stories; KEng, 34–38; KFr, 63–69); and finally as machinic assemblages (Kafka's novels; KEng, 38–42; KFr, 69–73).

While *Kafka* . . . represents a limited example of the next step of the schizoanalytic project, "to see how, effectively, simultaneously, the various tasks of schizoanalysis proceed" (AOEng, 382; AOFr, 458), a year later appeared a slim volume curiously entitled *Rhizome: Introduction* that became, in slightly revised form, the opening chapter of *A Thousand Plateaus.* As we saw in Chapter 3, the system called "rhizome" is the production of the multiple occurring "not by always adding a higher dimension, but rather in the simplest of ways, by dint of sobriety, with the number of dimensions one already has available, always $n - 1$ (the only way the one belongs to the multiple: always subtracted)" (ATP, 6; MP, 13). Deleuze and Guattari develop six principal characteristics of a "rhizome," and then they refer to Gregory Bateson's *Steps to an Ecology of Mind* to introduce a key term: "A plateau is always in the middle, not at the beginning or the end. A rhizome is made of plateaus. Gregory Bateson uses the word 'plateau' to designate something very special: a continuous, self-vibrating region of intensities whose development avoids any orientation toward a culmination point or external end" (ATP, 21–22; MP, 32). Deleuze and Guattari define "plateau" as "any multiplicity connected to other multiplicities by superficial underground stems in such a way as to form or extend a rhizome" (ATP, 22; MP, 33). Since "to attain the multiple, one must have a method that effectively constructs it," Deleuze and Guattari eschew typographical, lexical, or syntactic creations like "mimetic procedures used to disseminate or disperse a unity that is retained in a different dimension for an image-book." Such a recourse is necessary, they argue, "only when [such creations] no longer belong to the form of expression of a hidden unity, becoming themselves dimensions of the multiplicity under consideration" (ATP, 22; MP, 33). Instead they promote using words "that in turn function for us as plateaus. RHIZOMATICS = SCHIZOANALYSIS = STRATOANALYSIS = PRAGMATICS = MICROPOLITICS," all of which are at once concepts and "lines, which is to say, number systems attached to a particular dimension of the multiplicities" (ATP, 22; MP, 33).

This concentrated statement reveals the strategic options that Deleuze and Guattari propose for deploying the rhizomatic project: each of the terms serves as a mode of approach to produce assemblages, strata, molecular chains, lines of flight or rupture, circles of convergence which themselves constitute diverse plateaus that usually overlap at various points of the assemblage. In order to extend my considerations of the literary "seam" in conjunction with the Deleuze–Guattarian conceptual trails in *A Thousand Plateaus,* I will now examine some "stitches" along the seam, that is, possibilities for textual production that emerge in two complementary "texts" by Quentin Tarantino, *Reservoir Dogs* as film (1991) and as screenplay (1994).[2]

RHIZOMATICS, STRATIFICATION, AND CARTOGRAPHY

Although Deleuze and Guattari distance themselves quite strongly from any association with the so-called postmodern condition, their work before and since *Capitalism and Schizophrenia* has at the very least participated in the much broader "project" that Jean-François Lyotard defined as the postmodern's search "for new presentations—not to take pleasure in them, but to better produce the feeling that there is something unpresentable" (1986, [1992, 15]).[3] Deleuze and Guattari's work translates this "project" to the extent that they attempt to think through and with the multiplicity of the "unpresentable" and to offer reconstructive strategies that envisage multi- and extradisciplinary connections and subversions. Rather than to reconstitute a homogeneous totality, their goal has been to map very real connections within the complexity of disjunctions and conjunctions between divergent domains, accomplished as we have seen already through the paradoxical strategy of reading/writing intermezzo, in-between, and in the "milieu" (*dans le milieu*) of diverse domains.

From the rhizomatic perspective, the book has neither subject nor object. Instead, it is constituted only by lines of articulation (segmentarity, strata, territorialities), on the one hand, and by lines of flight (movements of deterritorialization and destratification), on the other. For Deleuze and Guattari, these lines and their measurable speeds constitute a machine assemblage oriented toward "the strata, which doubtless make it a kind of organism, or signifying totality, or a determination attributable to a subject." But the book as machinic assemblage has another side, facing "a *body without organs,* which is continually dismantling the organism, causing asignifying particles or pure intensities to pass or circulate, and attributing to itself subjects that it leaves with nothing more than a name as the trace of an intensity" (ATP, 4; MP, 10). Deleuze and Guattari here refer to

"Kleist and a mad war machine, Kafka and a fantastic bureaucratic machine" as examples of the book as assemblage, "in connection with other assemblages and in relation to other bodies without organs," existing only "through the outside and on the outside" (ATP, 4; MP, 10). Furthermore, they point to Kleist's invention of writing as "Open rings," as "a broken chain of affects and variable speeds, with accelerations and transformations, always in a relation with the outside," texts thus opposing the "classical and romantic book constituted by the interiority of a substance or subject" and constituting "the war machine-book against the State apparatus-book" (ATP, 9; MP, 16).

Deleuze and Guattari establish an opposition between the rhizome-book and two other kinds of book: first, the *livre-racine* or "root-book," "the One that becomes two" of the arborified and dichotomized, classical book; and second, the book of modernity based on the root with clustered stems:

> This time, the principal root has aborted, or its tip has been destroyed; an immediate, indefinite multiplicity of secondary roots grafts onto it and undergoes a flourishing development. This time, natural reality is what aborts the principal root, but the root's unity subsists, as past or yet-to-come, as possible. . . . The world has become chaos, but the book remains the image of the world, radicle-chaosmos instead of root-cosmos. (ATP, 5–6; MP, 12–13)

Opposed to these kinds of book is the extreme proliferation of the multiple, of the rhizome. This multiplicity is produced through "sobriety" as writing "at $n-1$ dimensions" consists of subtracting or peeling away, as it were, the layers of subjectivity and representation in the process of constructing the break-flows of the assemblage. The rhizome-text is the "ideal" of a book which, as we have seen, Deleuze and Guattari liken to Kleist's texts. But, Deleuze and Guattari would agree that the texts that one generally encounters, texts with narrative structure, grammar, or logic, are those that Roland Barthes, in a different yet complementary context, calls "incompletely plural, texts whose plural is more or less parsimonious" (Barthes 1970, 12; 1974, 6). Thus, the concept of "rhizome" provides a strategy for constructing the multiple while attempting thereby to negotiate the textual space between the parsimonious plural and the ideal rhizome-text, a strategy of "stratification."[4]

An example of this negotiation emerges in the very first scene of Tarantino's *Reservoir Dogs* in which the dynamic (or with Barthes, "writerly") relationship between filmmaker/author and viewer/reader develops to an extreme degree. This dynamic effect is all the more evident if one compares the screen version of this scene to its representation in the screenplay (Tarantino 1994, 3–12), in which each character's dialogue is quite understandably assigned to a fixed name. On the screen, the opening scene (set in Uncle Bob's restaurant, according to the screenplay) is disconcerting in the appearance both of its banal location and of the interlocutors themselves. Nearly all are dressed in identical suits and ties, like a team of door-to-door salesmen preparing for work, who seem to be assembled for a pep talk given by a balding paterfamilias figure, dressed more casually. This scene seems completely out-of-synch with the nervous banter, and the interlocutors' evident lack of sympathy, or indeed even familiarity, with one another. The viewer/reader is required, therefore, to (re)write the scene at "$n - 1$ dimensions," stripping away possibilities and improbabilities that emerge from this opening display of raw subjectivity in the most quotidian of settings, through the break-flows of shifting filmic and interpersonal points of view. Only at one point in the scene does the alert viewer hear the sole alias that one interlocutor uses to identify another, when "Mr. Pink" refuses to contribute to the tip. Disconcerting in its improbability, this name is yet another incitement to constitute possibilities, adding while also subtracting from them, in a labor of "stratification" that provides a context for comprehension, for "reading" through active viewing, or (re)"writing."[5]

However, in order to oppose writing in the name of a "unitary State apparatus," Deleuze and Guattari also opt for the strategy of "nomadology," pointing to American writing as a truly special case in this regard. Although examples abound that reveal tree-domination and the search for roots (e.g., Kerouac seeking his ancestors), they claim that "everything important that has happened or is happening takes the route of the American rhizome: the beatniks, the underground, bands and gangs, successive lateral shoots in immediate connection with an outside." The European conception of the book—"the search for arborescence and the return to the Old World"—is thus opposed to the American conception: "There is the rhizomatic West, with its Indians without ancestry, its ever-receding limit, its shifting and displaced frontiers. . . . America reversed the directions: it put its Orient in the West, as if it were precisely in America that the earth came full circle; its West is the edge of the East" (ATP, 19; MP, 29). Referring to Leslie Fiedler's *The Return of the Vanishing American* (1968) to point out geography's role in American literature, Deleuze and Guattari assert that the search for an "American code" intersects with other searches:

> In the East, there was the search for a specifically American code and for a recoding with Europe (Henry James, Eliot, Pound, etc.); in the South, there was the overcoding of the slave system, with its ruin and the ruin of the plantations during the Civil War (Faulkner, Caldwell); from the North

came capitalist decoding (Dos Passos, Dreiser); the West, however, played
the role of a line of flight combining travel, hallucination, madness, the
Indians, perceptive and mental experimentation, the shifting of frontiers,
the rhizome (Ken Kesey and his "fog machine"; the beat generation, etc.).
(ATP, 520n18; MP, 29)

And in reference to F. Scott Fitzgerald's specification of geographical
directions in his works, they conclude that "every great American author
creates a cartography, even in his or her style; in contrast to what is done
in Europe, each makes a map that is directly connected to the real social
movements crossing America" (ATP, 520n18; MP, 29).[6]

The necessity of mapmaking exists not only as an underlying principle of the rhizomatic system, but also as an essential element for understanding the role of writing which, Deleuze and Guattari proclaim,
"should be quantified": "The book itself is a little machine; what is the
relation (also measurable) of this literary machine to a war machine, love
machine, revolutionary machine, etc.—and an *abstract machine* that sweeps
them along?" (ATP, 4; MP, 10). The entire terminology that Deleuze and
Guattari introduce in the schizoanalytic project—"multiplicities, lines,
strata and segmentarities, lines of flight and intensities, machinic assemblages and their various types, bodies without organs and their construction and selection, the plane of consistency, and in each case the units of
measure"—serves not only to "constitute a quantification of writing, but . . .
[to] define writing as always the measure of something else. Writing has
nothing to do with signifying. It has to do with surveying, mapping, even
realms that are yet to come" (ATP, 4–5; MP, 10–11). This role of
mapmaking—the measurable relationship between the literary machine
and other specific machines, as well as the abstract machine—provides
both a particular angle from which one can approach the literary enterprise of *A Thousand Plateaus* and a textual strategy, a mapmaking in itself,
in order to examine the role of writing as the functioning of the literary
machine.

Let us observe, first, that while the emphasis of each "plateau" in *A
Thousand Plateaus* is generally on a particular domain, Deleuze and Guattari
develop a strategy through which they progressively insert references to
different domains within each plateau, thus demonstrating the continuous
internal functioning of various regimes of signs and multiplicities.[7] For
example, "the Pragmatic," elaborated in Plateaus 4 and 5 (respectively, on
"Postulates of Linguistics" and "Several Regimes of Signs"), returns
throughout the subsequent plateaus as a fundamental concern of schizoanalysis. More significantly for our present interests, the literary domain serves
as the principal focus in two plateaus (6 and 8, respectively, "November 28,
1947: How Do You Make Yourself a Body without Organs?" and "1874:

Three Novellas, or 'What Happened?' ") and helps to actualize these lines and their concepts from one plateau to another. Furthermore, since this variation corresponds to what Deleuze and Guattari indicate as "the nature of Assemblages," I propose to approach the literary element in *A Thousand Plateaus* along the two axes of mapmaking:

> On a first, horizontal axis, an assemblage comprises two segments, one of content, the other of expression. On the one hand it is a *machinic assemblage* of bodies, of actions and passions, an intermingling of bodies reacting to one another; on the other hand it is a *collective assemblage of enunciation*, of acts and statements, of incorporeal transformations attributed to bodies. Then on a vertical axis, the assemblage has both *territorial sides*, or reterritorialized sides, which stabilize it, and *cutting edges of deterritorialization*, which carry it away. (ATP, 88–89; MP, 112)

THE HORIZONTAL AXIS

On this axis, the literary element serves an exemplary function, of revealing more clearly the abstract concepts suggested by the rhizomatic process. The machinic assemblage of actions and passions develops in direction relation to transformation unfolding, say Deleuze and Guattari, as collective assemblages of enunciation. Let us explore these facets of the horizontal axis in turn:

1. *Machinic assemblages.* Deleuze and Guattari envisage this mapmaking process along a first segment of "content," of intermingling "bodies, actions and passion," for example, in *Reservoir Dogs,* the sociocultural coding, the film's genre overcoding, and the hierarchical relations between characters that gradually emerge. Of all the texts chosen to exemplify this axis, the works of Kafka and Proust appear most often in *A Thousand Plateaus.* Returning frequently to the Kafka-machinic assemblage, notable for its mix of bureaucracy with other bodies, Deleuze and Guattari argue: "In Kafka, it is impossible to separate the erection of a great paranoid bureaucratic machine from the installation of little schizo machines of becoming-dog or becoming-beetle" (ATP, 34; MP, 48). They contrast "passional" love and its double, the domestic squabble (a "*cogito* for two, a war *cogito*"), to "the consciousness-related double of pure thought, the couple of the legislating subject" that develops a "bureaucratic relation and a new form of persecution." Here, "the *cogito* itself becomes an 'office squabble,' a bureaucratic love delusion [whereby] a new form of bureaucracy replaces or conjugates with the old imperial bureaucracy." In this direction, they conclude, "Kafka goes the farthest,"

citing the subjectifications of Sortini and Sordini in *The Castle* (ATP, 132; MP, 165).[8]

As for Proust, his works help to distinguish molar masses (or packs) from molecular multiplicities:

> A pack of freckles on a face, a pack of boys speaking through the voice of a woman, a clutch of girls in Charlus's voice, a horde of wolves in somebody's throat, a multiplicity of anuses in the anus, mouth, or eye one is intent upon. We each go through so many bodies in each other. Albertine is slowly extracted from a group of girls with its own number, organization, code, and hierarchy; and not only is this group or restricted mass suffused by an unconscious, but Albertine has her own multiplicities that the narrator, once he has isolated her, discovers on her body and in her lies—until the end of their love returns her to the indiscernible. (ATP, 35–36; MP, 49)

Later, three moments in the story of Swann–Odette, from *Swann's Way,* reveal the resonance between the face, a landscape, painting, and music: Odette's face, cheeks, eyes as black holes, are linked to Swann's aestheticism, his need for associations (to a landscape, to a fragment of painting). Then this face speeds toward the "single black hole" of Swann's Passion, pulling along all the associations as "Swann's jealousy, querulous delusion and erotomania develop." Finally, the face is "undone," disaggregated "into autonomous aesthetic traits," as art reveals to Swann that the Passion is over, and art recovers its independence (ATP, 185–186; MP, 228–229).

Furthermore, Deleuze and Guattari later oppose what they call an "immanent plane of consistency" of variable speeds to a transcendent organizational plane. They first emphasize how Proust distinguishes a group of girls from a lone girl through their "relations of speeds and slownesses": "A girl is late on account of her speed: she did too many things, crossed too many spaces in relation to the relative time of the person waiting for her. Thus her apparent slowness is transformed into the breakneck speed of our waiting" (ATP, 271; MP, 332). Then, this opposition of planes helps Deleuze and Guattari distinguish the different positions of Swann in relation to those occupied by the narrator in *Remembrance of Things Past*: different planes of jealousy (Odette, Albertine) and of perception of music (Vinteuil's phrase) (ATP, 271–272; MP, 332–333). Hence the further connection to the body of music that furnishes another mix of machinic assemblages, such that "territorial motifs form *rhythmic faces or characters*, and territorial counter-points form *melodic landscapes*. . . . For Swann, the art lover, Vinteuil's little phrase often acts as a placard associated with the Bois de Boulogne and the face and character of Odette: as if it reassured Swann that the Bois de

Boulogne was indeed his territory, and Odette his possession" (ATP, 318–319; MP, 391–392.)[9]

2. *Collective assemblages of enunciation.* At the other end of the same axis, the segment of expression unfolds as a mode of transformation, of "becomings." For example, Deleuze and Guattari argue that "style"—"the procedure of a continuous variation"—"unavoidably produces a language within a language." Referring to "an arbitrary list of authors we are fond of" (Kafka, Beckett, Ghérasim Luca, Jean-Luc Godard), they argue that these authors' styles owe much to their bilingual situation: "Kafka, the Czechoslovakian Jew writing in German; Beckett, the Irishman writing in English and French; Luca, originally from Romania; Godard and his will to be Swiss. . . . The essential thing is that each of these authors has his own procedure of variation, his own widened chromaticism, his own mad production of speeds and intervals" (ATP, 97–98; MP, 123–124). They appeal again to Proust as they conclude:

> It was Proust who said that "masterpieces are written in a kind of foreign language." That is the same as stammering, making language stammer rather than stammering in speech. To be a foreigner, but in one's own tongue, not only when speaking a language other than one's own. . . . That is when style becomes a language. That is when language becomes intensive, a pure continuum of values and intensities. (ATP, 98; MP, 124–125)[10]

What other stylistic traits might produce this procedure of "continuous variation"? In *Reservoir Dogs,* the formal element that provides the greatest source of resistance to linear progression—and thereby the element that constantly contributes to the dynamic film viewer/film reader exchange—is the fractured temporal jumps with which Tarantino constructs his film. This strategy in itself constitutes in some ways a film "foreign language," since it defies the easy "syntax" of the action-heist film, and (dis)plays by other rules. Even more pronounced are the different styles qua "foreign languages" that emerge in various dialogues between interlocutors throughout the film: the most overwhelming, of course, is the discourse of the crime milieu that all the characters seem to share. Yet the scenes between detectives Holdaway and Freddy (aka Mr. Orange) in the diner and on the rooftop provide Holdaway with an opportunity to help Freddy "rehearse" for his "interview" and undercover role as a member of the heist team. Then, in the scenes in the bar with the heist organizers, Joe Cava, Nice Guy Eddie Cava, and Mr. White, and in the false flashback to his "performance" in the rest room, Freddy's role-play gives ample proof of the necessity to have "learned" the walk and the talk. That Freddy succeeds in impressing Joe and his cronies is clear at the end of his fabricated tale of having kept his cool while transporting marijuana and being confronted by a trained police German shepherd in a rest room where Los Angeles sheriffs are exchanging gossip: "That's how you do it, kid," says Joe. "You knew how to handle that situation. You shit your pants, and then you just dive in and swim" (Tarantino 1994, 78).

What is crucial in this scene is that in recounting an entirely fictional encounter so convincingly, so fluently, Freddy demonstrates a mastery of the language and bodily nuances—a veritable communicative competence—that fools the master criminals, further bolstering their confidence in this new member of the team. In terms of the "continuous variation" on the horizontal axis, these languages within a language help constitute a collective assemblage of enunciation binding the criminals together within shifting modes of incorporeal (and with gory regularity, corporeal) transformation. That this collective assemblage is truly a matter of life and death becomes apparent in the final scenes of the film. For the same four characters that were in the bar—the Cavas, Mr. White, and Freddy—are driven apart precisely by this collective quest for enunciative "authenticity," the spoken tongue that sounds either "false" or "true." Mr. White's mistaken faith in Freddy/Mr. Orange's bona fides pits him against his former allies, the Cavas father and son, who heed the "false accent" they perceive in Freddy's explanation. This disagreement impels them all to perform the film's penultimate shoot-out in the dénouement.

Deleuze and Guattari describe the intersection of the literary within other conceptual assemblages: the abstract machine of "faciality" (*visagéité*) operates as a means to open up lines of flight, for example, in Chrétien de Troyes's *Perceval,* Cervantes's *Don Quixote,* and Beckett's *Malloy* and *The Unnameable* (ATP, 173–174; MP, 212–213). In this plateau on "faciality," they again contrast the Anglo-American novel with the French novel which, they claim, "is profoundly pessimistic and idealistic," whereas "from Hardy to Lawrence, from Melville to Miller, the same cry rings out: Go across, get out, break through, make a beeline, don't get stuck on a point [*faire la ligne et pas le point*]" (ATP, 186; MP, 228). Deleuze and Guattari also develop the cartographic problem of three types of lines that they study in detail in Plateau 8: a supple line of primitive segmentarity, a hard line of the State apparatus, and a line or lines of flight of the war machine (ATP, 222; MP, 271). They insist, however:

> We cannot say that one of these three lines is bad and another good, by nature and necessarily. The study of the dangers of each line is the object of pragmatics or schizoanalysis, to the extent that it undertakes not to represent, interpret, or symbolize, but only to make maps and draw lines, marking their mixtures as well as their distinctions. (ATP, 227; MP, 277)

Furthermore, through Nietzsche's Zarathustra and Carlos Castaneda's don Juan, Deleuze and Guattari postulate four dangers: "first, Fear, then Clarity, and then Power, and finally the great Disgust, the longing to kill and to die, the Passion for abolition" (ATP, 227; MP, 277). They then evoke the works of different authors in support of these "dangers": Blanchot on Fear, Castaneda on Clarity and Power, Fitzgerald and Kleist on Disgust, the line of death, concluding by evoking Klaus Mann's novel *Mephisto* and analyses by Jean-Pierre Faye (1972) and Paul Virilio (1975) to reflect on distinctions between and proximities of fascism and totalitarianism (ATP, 227–231; MP, 277–283).

The great well of creativity and the lines of flight in diverse forms of writing are, if not the main subject, then at least an important secondary motif in Plateau 10, on the concept of "becomings." Among other conjunctions of the literary and "becomings," Deleuze and Guattari refer to certain authors in order to discuss collective assemblages of enunciation regarding the nexus of concepts "becoming-intense" (child, woman), "becoming-animal," "becoming-imperceptible," and particularly in relation to the concept of "haecceity."[11] They consider another mode of "becoming" in Plateau 11 on the "refrain" (*ritournelle*), gauging the "becoming-cosmic" of the artist and the poet, whose role is so crucial that Deleuze and Guattari cite Virilio's (1975) terse question, "To dwell as a poet or as an assassin?" Whereas the assassin blocks assemblages and causes peoples to slide ever further into a black hole, the poet "lets loose molecular populations in hopes that this will sow the seeds of, or even engender, the people to come, that these populations will pass into a people to come, open a cosmos" (ATP, 345; MP, 427). Arguing the relation of artist to people has been transformed, they maintain:

> Never has the artist been more in need of a people, while stating most firmly that the people is lacking—the people is what is most lacking. We are not referring to popular or populist artists. Mallarmé said that the Book needed a people. Kafka said that literature is the affair of the people. Klee said that the people is essential, *yet lacking*. . . . The people and the earth must be like the vectors of a cosmos that carries them off; then the cosmos itself will be art. From depopulation, make a cosmic people; from deterritorialization, a cosmic earth—that is the wish of the artisan–artist, here, there, locally. (ATP, 346; MP, 427).[12]

While it would be difficult to argue that "people to come" are engendered in *Reservoir Dogs*, the proliferation of diverse modes of "becoming" therein results in a constant destabilization of the loci of enunciation. For, within the reading/(re)writing process in which the viewer is forcibly engaged, no credible and privileged site of enunciation emerges on which to base a stable understanding of any of the film's events. Opposed to Mr. White and his forceful, principled emphasis on following the plan and saving the wounded Mr. Orange are both the opportunist Mr. Pink and the "kill crazy" Mr. Blonde, who laconically explains that he shoots up the bank because "I don't like alarms" (Tarantino 1994, 60). The film's dialogues function as verbal duels, escalating and descending in intensity, with continual misunderstandings and disagreements resulting in near shoot-outs, as the different codes or "lines" weave in and out of each other, shifting back in time through flashbacks that provide more "relief," understood as both background information and diversion from the intensity of the post-heist debacle.

Deleuze and Guattari provide a powerful description of the cartographic intersection of the horizontal and vertical axes at work in Kafka's fiction:

> On the one hand, the ship-machine, the hotel-machine, the circus-machine, the castle-machine, the court-machine, each with its own intermingled pieces, gears, processes, and bodies, contained in one another or bursting out of containment (see the head bursting through the roof). On the other hand, the regime of signs or of enunciation: each regime with its incorporeal transformations, acts, death sentences and judgments, proceedings, "law." It is obvious that statements do not represent machines: the Stoker's discourse does not describe stoking as a body; it has its own form, and a development without resemblance. Yet it is attributed to bodies, to the whole ship as a body. A discourse of submission to order-words; a discourse of discussion, claims, accusation, and defense. On the second axis, what is compared or combined of the two aspects, what always inserts one into the other, are the sequenced or conjugated degrees of deterritorialization, and the operations of reterritorialization that stabilize the aggregate at a given moment. K., the K.-function, designates the line of flight or deterritorialization that carries away all of the assemblages, but also undergoes all kinds of reterritorializations and redundancies—redundancies of childhood, village-life, love, bureaucracy, etc. (ATP, 88–89; MP, 112)[13]

THE VERTICAL AXIS

On the vertical axis of the assemblage, from the territorial/reterritorialized side to the points of deterritorialization, the function of the literary is demonstrative. That is, beyond the exemplary function explored above, certain literary cases are chosen to demonstrate the operation of the rhizomatic oscillation between territoriality and deterritorialization. Plateau 8 ("1874: Three Novellas, or 'What Happened?' ") is the sole plateau that is explicitly "literary." Here Deleuze and Guattari develop the literary stratification within three short stories: Henry James's "In the Cage," F. Scott Fitzgerald's "The Crack Up" (1956), and Pierrette Fleutiaux's "Story of the Abyss and the Telescope" (1976). Seeking to reveal the essential rhizomatic lines that trace the map of writing and beyond, Deleuze and Guattari deploy three types of lines within each novella, lines that correspond to three forms of territoriality:

1. The line of rigid segmentarity, or molar line, exists for each of us, "on which everything seems calculable and foreseen, the beginning and end of a segment, the passage from one segment to another" (ATP, 195; MP, 239). This line consists both of "molar aggregates segmented (States, institutions, classes)" and of "people as elements of an aggregate" such that no loss of identity can escape control at any moment: "Conjugality. A whole interplay of well-determined, well-planned territories. We have a future but no becoming [*On a un avenir, mais pas de devenir*]" (ATP, 195; MP, 239, translation modified). In James's story "In the Cage," the woman telegraph operator's life is segmented precisely by her daily activity, by the customers and their social classes (which affect how they make use of the telegraph), and by the segments of proximity (the neighboring grocery) and feeling (the fiancé's plans for the future).

For Fitzgerald's "The Crack Up," Deleuze and Guattari initially locate a type of line that, like life itself, "is always drawn into an increasingly rigid and desiccated segmentarity" (ATP, 198; MP, 242). This process may consist of "sudden blows" seemingly coming from outside—"depression, loss of wealth, fatigue and growing old, alcoholism, the failure of conjugality, the rise of the cinema, the advent of fascism and Stalinism, and the loss of success and talent—at the very moment Fitzgerald would find his genius" (ATP, 198; MP, 242). Thus, this line of rigid segmentarity is one that develops by "bringing masses into play, even if it was supple to begin with" (ATP, 198; MP, 243).

In Fleutiaux's novella, "Story of the Abyss and the Telescope," such a line is located as one kind of lookout, the "near-seers" who operate with a simple spyglass and sometimes with "the terrible Ray Telescope," a cutting laser ray that overcodes everything: "It acts on flesh and blood, but itself is nothing but pure geometry, as a State affair, and the near-seers' physics in the service of that machine." Thus, this first form "effectively draw[s] a line; not a line of writing but a line of rigid segmentarity along which everyone will be judged and rectified according to his or her contours, individual or collective" (ATP, 200–201; MP, 245).

2. The line of supple segmentation, or molecular line, emerges in James's story via the telegraph itself, "a supple flow, marked by *quanta*

that are like so many little segmentations-in-progress grasped at the moment of their birth, as on a moonbeam, or on an intensive scale" (ATP, 195; MP, 239). The passionate complicity that develops between the telegraph operator and an unknown customer parallels the determined relationship with her fiancé, two politics (macro- and micro-):

> Two very different types of relations: intrinsic relations of *couples* involving well-determined aggregates or elements (social classes, men and women, this or that particular person), and less localizable relations that are always external to themselves and instead concern flows and particles eluding those classes, sexes, and persons. (ATP, 196; MP, 240)

Here occurs the molecularized "quanta of deterritorialization," an ungraspable matter of "something that has already happened."

In "The Crack Up," this movement of molecularization appears as subtle, supple microruptures, all the more disturbing for their subtlety: this segmentation differs from the rigid segmentarity by its rhizomatic, not its arborescent, nature. Deleuze and Guattari offer the example of the aging process:

> If there is aging on this [supple] line, it is not of the same kind: when you age on this line you do not feel it on the other [rigid] line, you don't notice it on the other line until after "it" has already happened on this [supple] line . . . [when] you reach a degree, a quantum, an intensity beyond which you cannot go. (ATP, 198; MP, 243)

As Fitzgerald presents it, "the second kind [of breakage] happens almost without your knowing it but is realized suddenly indeed" (1956, 69), or in Deleuze and Guattari's terms, "molecular changes, redistributions of desire . . . micro-politics" (ATP, 198–199; MP, 243).

The microsegmentation emerges in Fleutiaux's novella through the activities of the "far-seers" whose vision does not overcode, but rather perceives "tiny movements that have not reached the edge, lines or vibrations that start to form long before they are outlined shapes" (ATP, 201; MP, 245). While this second line "is inseparable from the anonymous segmentation that produces it," the far-seers "can divine the future, but always in the form of a becoming of something that has already happened in a molecular matter; unfindable particles" (ATP, 201; MP, 246). Deleuze and Guattari compare this second line to biology—to "molecular lines that intersect each other within the large-scale cells and between their breaks"— and to society, as "rigid segments and overcutting segments are crosscut underneath by segmentations of another nature." But in Fleutiaux's novella, the supple segmentation is a subject both of politics and of perception, "for perception always goes hand in hand with semiotics, practice, politics, theory" (ATP, 201; MP, 246).

3. The lines of flight, of deterritorialization, or abstract lines are reached by the telegraph operator of "In the Cage" when she can go no further, with "vibrations traversing us [that] may be aggravated beyond our endurance" (ATP, 197; MP, 241). Nothing happened between the operator and the customer, each will go his and her own way, yet everything changed for the operator: she reached a line that "no longer tolerates segments; rather, it is like an exploding of the two segmentary series" (ATP, 197; MP, 241). Her secret became "the form of something whose matter was molecularized, imperceptible, unassignable," and then, on the third line, becomes a pure abstract line:

> To become imperceptible oneself, to have dismantled love in order to become capable of loving. To have dismantled one's self in order finally to be alone and meet the true double at the other end of the line. A clandestine passenger on a motionless voyage. To become like everybody else; but this, precisely, is a becoming only for one who knows how to be nobody, to no longer be anybody. (ATP, 197; MP, 241–242)

In "The Crack Up," the third line is one of rupture, "a clean break," the explosion of the other two. Deleuze and Guattari maintain that through his narrator, "Fitzgerald contrasts rupture with structural pseudo-breaks in so-called signifying chains," yet also draws a distinction from "more supple, more subterranean links or stems" (ATP, 199; MP, 243). The narrator continues:

> The famous "Escape" or "run away from it all" is an excursion in a trap even if the trap includes the South Seas, which are only for those who want to paint them or sail them. A clean break is something you cannot come back from; that is irretrievable because it makes the past cease to exist. (1956, 81)

In other words, Fitzgerald suggests a progressive movement toward absolute deterritorialization: "One is no more than an abstract line, like an arrow crossing the void. Absolute deterritorialization. One has become like everybody/the whole world [tout le monde], but in a way that nobody can become like everybody/the whole world. One has painted the world on oneself, not oneself on the world" (ATP, 199–200; MP, 244, translation modified).

In Fleutiaux's novella, the third line appears only through the ambiguity of the "far-seers" and their privileged position "beyond" the vision of the "near-seers," who nonetheless possess the dreaded "Cutting Telescope" and to whom the "far-seers" must finally answer. Thus, on the supple, molecular line, there is hesitation between two courses, and one day "a 'far-seer' will abandon his or her segment and start walking across a narrow overpass above the dark abyss, will break his or her telescope and depart on a line of flight to meet a blind Double approaching from the other side" (ATP, 202; MP, 247).

This movement of "stratification"—the fluctuation of characters, themes, and discourse between molar and molecular planes into the line of flight and rupture—recalls Deleuze's positing of "serial" oscillation in *Logic of Sense* and surely extends and enriches Deleuze and Guattari's progression of "syntheses" in *Anti-Oedipus*. In *Reservoir Dogs*, this fluctuation occurs intermittently through the processes of molecular segmentation, and in particular is the production of localized, "singular" points of "flight" or rupture glimpsed briefly in different interlocutors' discourse and behavior. Witness the seemingly preposterous roughhousing between Vic Vega (Mr. Blonde) and Eddie Cava in Joe's office. All semblance of tough-guy posturing, of defense and distance, is dropped as the two grown men wrestle on the floor, in a purely physical groping, until Joe yells, "Okay, okay, enough, enough! Playtime's over! You wanna roll around on the floor, do it in Eddie's office, not mine!" (Tarantino 1994, 50). Then, disheveled and wary, yet still excited, they engage in an increasingly racially and sexually charged exchange of homoerotic aggression, until Joe again sternly returns them to the subject at hand (Vic's parole problem). On the level of the narrative movement, this apparently silly example offers a glimpse of the momentary opening of a "line of flight" within the hierarchized relations between serious, tough men. Despite this fleeting moment, however, the slide toward flight is quickly reterritorialized, within a paternalistic, even Oedipal framework, as Sharon Willis notes: " 'Race' becomes a kind of switchpoint here, lying at the center of a knot that condenses oedipal rivalry with homoerotophobic attraction–repulsion" (1993–1994, 54).

This scene, says Willis, provides "a delirious account" of Mr. Blonde/Vic's desocialization, preparing the viewer for a truly intense moment of cinematic "flight" in the following scene. After the departure of Mr. White and Mr. Pink with Nice Guy Eddie from the warehouse, the "kill crazy" Vic/Mr. Blonde is left as the sole captor to continue interrogating the detective who has been taken hostage. He turns the interrogation toward torture, "not to get information, but because torturing a cop amuses me." Proceeding rhythmically, slowly, to the radio music, he jokes and dances before slicing off the detective's ear with a razor, then douses him with gasoline, and prepares to light a match. Throughout *Reservoir Dogs*, the body functions as a site of inscription for the "voices," "codes," lines of stratification that crisscross the text, and "flows" in all senses of the term (witness the growing pool of Mr. Orange's blood). In this scene, however, the (dis)play of symbolic rules of the set genre collapse. Here, a personage exceeds the rules, deterritorializes the tale, collapses the paradigm. For Tarantino, this imploding mix of dark comedy and visual pain is quite deliberate, intended to force the viewer to "have to think about why you were laughing" (Hopper and Tarantino 1994, 17).[14] Then, as the match flickers, the reterritorializing force of the symbolic asserts itself: the bleeding Mr. Orange, given up for dead, empties his gun into Mr. Blonde, saving the suffering, bound detective, and unraveling the "enigma" that runs through the film for the characters—Was the heist a set-up or not?—by revealing his true loyalty, for the fellow detective who had not given him up, even under torture.

Deleuze and Guattari describe this line as "an exploding of the two segmentary series" when a character somehow has "broken through the wall, . . . attained a kind of absolute deterritorialization" (ATP, 197; MP, 241). This line must be actively invented and traced, they argue, as "an affair of cartography," of the existential as well as of textual "lines [that] compose us, as they compose our map" (ATP, 203; MP, 248). For Deleuze and Guattari maintain that this process of active assemblage, of "schizoanalysis," applies as easily to "a life, a work of literature or art, or a society, depending on which system of coordinates is chosen" (ATP, 203–204; MP, 249). This circulation of molar, molecular, and deterritorialized lines is inscribed on an abstract plane of consistency that Deleuze and Guattari also call the "body without organs," the pure surface of intensity on which the lines and points of an assemblage are constructed. Adapting Paul Patton's reflection to the development of textuality, I understand this plane or "body without organs" as serving both as "the point of departure, or precondition for any subsequent function of desire, and as a possible end result of a (disastrous) process of desire." "Either way," Patton concludes, "the body without organs is in some sense the pure matter, the imperceptible and unattainable substance, of which desire is composed" (1981, 44).

We would be mistaken, however, to conceive of this textual deterritorialization, or "line of flight," as an end point, especially in terms of the classical text. The incessant movement of stratification slides toward rupture only to draw back from a too final or absolute deterritorializing oscillation. In *Reservoir Dogs,* this operation is visible in the moments following the film's almost formulaic penultimate "shoot-out": having protected Mr. Orange throughout the ordeal, Mr. White challenges the certainty of both Joe and Eddie that Orange is an undercover cop with his gun, pointing it at Joe and stating coldly, "Joe, if you kill that man, you die next." As Joe shoots Orange, White shoots and kills Joe, Eddie shoots White, and White returns fire, bringing Eddie down. Having backed away during the exchange of shots, Mr. Pink now makes a hasty exit with the bag of diamonds, but the sound of sirens blaring outside the warehouse, immediately followed by background shouts and gunfire, suggest his abrupt capture. Meanwhile, White crawls to comfort the dying Orange who sobs, "I'm a cop. I'm sorry, I'm so sorry." In the screenplay, White continues "stroking Orange's brow" as he "lifts his .45 and places the barrel between Mr. Orange's eyes" (Tarantino 1994, 109). Through Harvey Keitel's interpretation, however, the confession adds to White's moans, and despite the police order to drop the gun, the close-up on White's face, not the gun, shows viewers the twisted mouth in pain as he pulls the trigger. The final fusillade results in "Mr. White [being] blown out of the frame, leaving it empty." What was he thinking? What was the "text thinking" with the empty frame? Mr. White will not "do a little time" as he said to comfort Mr. Orange; he has been blown out of time, blown out of the story, and the "text" remains suspended on the last image, not a smile, as Tarantino had written (1994, 109), but raw pain.

For Deleuze and Guattari, this "stratification" clearly is not limited simply to literary analysis since "lines of writing conjugate with other lines, life lines, lines of luck or misfortune, lines productive of the variation of the line of writing itself, lines that are *between the lines* of writing" (ATP, 194; MP, 238).[15] These are lines by which we and our daily "maps" are crisscrossed and traced, lines that language must follow: "The signifier arises at the most rigidified level of one of the lines, and the subject is spawned at the lowest level" (ATP, 203; MP, 237). Moreover, the lines are "inscribed on a Body without Organs, upon which everything is drawn and flees, which is itself an abstract line with neither imaginary figures nor symbolic functions: the real of the BwO" (ATP, 203; MP, 249).

In Plateau 6, Deleuze and Guattari confront the "practice, set of practices," of the body without organs under the title "How to Make (of/for) Oneself a Body without Organs."[16] For the authors, asking "What is the BwO?" is almost absurd since "you're already on it, scurrying like a vermin, groping like a blind person, or running like a lunatic. . . . On it we sleep, live our waking lives, fight—fight and are fought—seek our place, experience untold happiness and fabulous defeats; on it we penetrate and are penetrated; on it we love" (ATP, 150; MP, 186). Beyond the traits defined in *Anti-Oedipus,* Deleuze and Guattari now develop more elaborate distinctions:

- between types of bodies without organs (genres, substantial attributes) including the hypochondriac body, the paranoid body, schizo and drugged bodies, and the masochist body (ATP, 150; MP, 186);
- between two phases of the body without organs, one for its

fabrication, the other for making intensities pass and circulate on it (ATP, 152–153; MP, 188–190); and

- between an individual body without organs and an aggregate of bodies without organs (ATP, 153–154; MP, 190–191).

They posit this "uninterrupted continuum" as "a fusional multiplicity that effectively goes beyond any opposition between the one and the multiple," and then conclude: "The BwO is the *field of immanence* of desire, the *plane of consistency* specific to desire (with desire defined as a process of production without reference to any exterior agency, whether it be a lack that hollows it out or a pleasure that fills it)" (ATP, 154; MP, 191). And they sum up their discussion so far as follows:

> We distinguish between: (1) BwO's, which are different types, genuses, or substantial attributes. For example, the Cold of the drugged BwO, the Pain of the masochist BwO. Each has its degree 0 as its principle of production [*remissio*]. (2) What happens on each type of BwO, in other words, the modes, the intensities that are produced, the waves that pass [*latitudo*]. (3) The potential totality of all BwO's, the plane of consistency [*Omnitudo*, sometimes called the BwO]. (ATP, 157–158; MP, 195)

The literary element again serves well to exemplify these three aspects of the body without organs. Deleuze and Guattari evoke Artaud's essay, *To Have Done with the Judgment of God* and Burroughs's *Naked Lunch* as illustrating types and phases of the bodies without organs and call Spinoza's *Ethics* "the great book of the BwO" (ATP, 153; MP, 190). It is the region of continuous intensity, or "plateaus" of which the body without organs is constituted, that occurs in Artaud's *Héliogabale* and *The Tarahumaras*. In these works, Artaud express "the multiplicity of fusion, fusionability as infinite zero, the plane of consistency, Matter where no gods go; principles as forces, essences, substances, elements, remissions, productions; manners of being or modalities as produced intensities, vibrations, breaths, Numbers" (ATP, 158; MP, 196). These works by Artaud also address "the difficulty of reaching this world of crowned Anarchy if you go no farther than the organs ... and if you stay locked into the organism, or into a stratum that blocks the flows and anchors us in this, our world" (ATP, 158; MP, 196). Enter Artaud for whom the system of God's judgment "is precisely the operation of He who makes an organism ... because He cannot bear the BwO" (ATP, 158–159; MP, 197). Hence the organism is but one of three great strata that bind us the most directly, with the others being *signifiance* and subjectification—"the surface of the organism, the angle of signifiance and interpretation, and the point of subjectification or subjection" (ATP, 159; MP, 197). To these strata, the body without organs opposes "disarticulation (or *n* articulations) as the property of the plane of consistency, experimentation as the operation on that plane, . . . and nomadism as the movement" (ATP, 160; MP, 197–198).

Therein lie the great tension and movement along the vertical axis between stratification (in organisms, *signifiance*, and subjectification) and destratification (by disarticulation, experimentation, and nomadism). As I indicated in Chapter 3, this tension is a crucial source of criticism by readers who would embrace an ideal of absolute deterritorialization that Deleuze and Guattari supposedly articulated in *Anti-Oedipus*. In *A Thousand Plateaus,* that "tearing the conscious away from the subject in order to make it a means of exploration, tearing the unconscious away from signifiance and interpretation in order to make it a veritable production: this is assuredly no more or less difficult than tearing the body away from the organism. Caution is the art common to all three" (ATP, 160; MP, 198). They therefore counsel:

> You have to keep enough of the organism for it to reform each dawn; and you have to keep small supplies of signifiance and subjectification, if only to turn them against their own systems when the circumstances demand it, when things, persons, even situations, force you to; and you have to keep small rations of subjectivity in sufficient quantity to enable you to respond to the dominant reality. Mimic the strata. (ATP, 160; MP, 198–199)

And they insist unequivocally: "You don't reach the BwO, and its plane of consistency, by wildly destratifying." For this leads only to "those emptied and dreary bodies" who empty themselves rather than seeking means to dismantle patiently and momentarily "the organization of the organs we call the organism" (ATP, 160–161; MP, 199).[17]

For Deleuze and Guattari, Carlos Castaneda's description of experimentation in *Tales of Power* (1974) provides an example of such a process: first, to find a "place," then to find "allies," then gradually to renounce interpretation. In this way, one "construct[s] flow by flow and segment by segment lines of experimentation, becoming-animal, becoming-molecular, etc." In other words, Castaneda makes (of/for) himself (*se fait*) a body without organs, which is "necessarily a Place, necessarily a Plane, necessarily a Collectivity (assembling elements, things, plants, animals, tools, people, powers, and fragments of all these)" (ATP, 161; MP, 199–200). If Deleuze and Guattari insist so fervently on this description of the steps of disarticulation/deterritorialization, it is to avoid the dangers of the restratification/reterritorialization of organisms, signifiance, or subjects onto "cancerous" BwOs like "money (inflation), but also BwO of the State, army, factory, city, Party, etc." (ATP, 163; MP, 201–202).

Just as Artaud attempted to distinguish the cancerous BwO from the full BwO in *To Have Done with the Judgment of God* and especially in his *Letter to Hitler* (where he threatens to unleash a flow against Hitler onto "a map that was not just a map of geography" [ATP, 162–163; MP, 202]), Deleuze and Guattari in their cartography seek to delimit territories and then to deterritorialize, to discern strata and then destratify, to define articulations and then disarticulate. Their use of the literary element is the crucial strategy of rhizomatics, (de)stratifications, and cartography: to reveal the nature of the intensities traced on a plane of consistency, on the BwO defined diversely: as "the egg [or] the milieu of pure intensity"; as "a childhood block, a becoming, the opposite of a childhood memory"; as "the distribution of intensive principles of organs, with their positive indefinite articles, within a collective or multiplicity, inside an assemblage, and according to machinic connections operating on a BwO" (ATP, 164–165; MP, 202–203). Such are the stakes of cartography:

> The identity of effects, the continuity of genera, the totality of all BwO's, can be obtained on the plane of consistency only by means of an abstract machine capable of covering and even creating it, by assemblages capable of plugging into desire, of effectively taking charge of desires, of assuring their continuous connections and transversal tie-ins. (ATP, 166; MP, 204)

In the following two chapters, I consider how these strategies of cartography and (de)stratification might be animated in terms of two other concepts, "becomings" and "the war machine," with analyses of different narrative forms, respectively, cyberpunk fiction (Chapter 5) and a short tale by Michel Tournier, *Gilles and Jeanne* (Chapter 6).

5 MILLE/PUNKS/ CYBER/PLATEAUS

BECOMINGS-*X*

> The hazards of being multiple sometimes
> overwhelm even the most rigorous Brain
> Police Training.
>
> –*Pat Cadigan*, Fools *(1992)*

In this chapter, I explore aspects of the manifold concept of "becomings." To do so, I consider how their facets "fold" and "unfold" within the science fiction literary "seam" known as "cyberpunk." I approach selected novels of this subgenre (particularly narrative "clusters" by William Gibson, John Shirley, and Rudy Rucker) not only to consider the interest as well as the limitations of their various discursive and narrative strategies, but also to produce a more effective animation that might elucidate through these strategies in Deleuze and Guattari's conceptual "assemblage."

A few years ago, I had an opportunity to perceive myself as what Donna Haraway has called "a condensed image of both imagination and material reality," aka a "cyborg" (Haraway 1990; 1991b, 150) when I became the object of the following exchange regarding my status as borrower and researcher on a new university campus. Unable to borrow a book because my identification card had not yet been properly entered into the library system, "I" became the focus of two librarians' concern. The first asked the second, "Why can't I find this book charged out?" The second asked in reply, "Did you create him?" After amoment, the first responded, "Yes, but his code is unknown." The second concluded, "Well, you need to modify him." Needless to say, having received numerous identification numbers, logon names, and passwords as a result of the explosion of online sites of exchange, I have been "modified" many times since. However, the exchange at the library desk has served for me as a nexus or point-sign, providing impetus to reflect on possible rapprochements between recent fictional and theoretical speculation on cybernetics and its impact on material aspects of daily life. Such reflection has seemed almost "natural" from the Deleuze–Guattarian perspective, given their interest in positing relations between desire and psychic and socioeconomic life as "machinic assemblages" (*agencements machiniques*) to which human activity responds and conforms.

When I initially undertook and published this essay (Stivale 1991c), I understood Haraway and Deleuze–Guattari to share, at the very least and in their own ways, an attempt to take "seriously the imagery of cyborgs as other than enemies" (Haraway 1990; 1991b, 180). However, just as "caution, not wisdom" seems to be a key expression for understanding Deleuze and Guattari's interest in liberating flows of desire, so too their discomfort with the transformation of humans into "dividuals" under "control societies" suggests that if it is not an enemy, the "cyborg" might well be an additional "machinic assemblage" to regard with caution.[1] Hence, when Haraway suggests concerning cyborgs that "there is a myth system waiting to become a political language to ground one way of looking at science and technology and challenging the informatics of domination—in order to act potently" (1990; 1991a, 181), we should recall Deleuze and Guattari's caveat that tales, rather than myths and rites, best describe "becomings." That is, rather than explain "blocks of becoming by a correspondence between two relations" à la Lévi-Strauss, Deleuze and Guattari suggest: "Alongside the two models, sacrifice and series, totem institution and structure, there is still room for something else, something more secret, more subterranean: *the sorcerer* and becomings" as expressed in tales (ATP, 237; MP, 290–291). In this chapter, I propose to examine several narrative manifestations of "sorcerers' tales" within that subgenre of science fiction (SF) known as "cyberpunk" as an initial exploration of "becomings," a key concept of the Deleuze–Guattarian "two-fold thought."[2]

That this cyberpunk subgenre is now inactive—at least in its original conceptualization as a mode of speculative fiction—received seemingly irrefutable proof with *Time*'s cover article on "Cyberpunk!" in early 1993 (Elmer-Dewitt 1993).[3] Despite some cogent dissenting views on this topic, however, the impact of cyberpunk remains quite significant, and not only with the global expansion of the Internet and the World Wide Web and the romanticization of "cyberpunk" style.[4] As I prepare this chapter in 1998 by revising an essay begun nearly a decade ago, I find myself consulting a broad range of essays on "the cyber-" written during the past six years, well after the supposed demise of cyberpunk. For example, a recent (and wonderful) issue of *Body and Society* (November 1995), "Cyberspace/Cyberbodies/Cyberpunk: Cultures of Technological Embodiment," contains no less than fourteen essays, plus an introduction by issue editors Mike Featherstone and Roger Burrows (1995). And, perusing a promotional mailing from the *Body and Society* publisher, Sage, I find not only that this issue has been published in volume form (Featherstone and Burrows 1996), but that its announcement is situated on the same page as two related collections of essays, *Cultures of Internet* (Shields 1996) and *Cybersociety* (S. Jones 1995). Thus, besides considering recent developments in studies of "the cyber-," I utilize this genre as a discursive vehicle for introducing some terminological distinctions available, but often hard to activate, in *A Thousand Plateaus*.[5]

I start by situating the Deleuze–Guattarian analysis in relation to the "informatics of domination" that Haraway describes as constituted by

> fundamental changes in the nature of class, race, and gender in an emerging system of world order analogous in its novelty and scope to that created by industrial capitalism, . . . a movement from an organic, industrial society to a polymorphous, information system. (1990; 1991b, 161)

The dichotomy that Haraway draws of the "scary new networks" of these "informatics" now seems a bit limited in our current globally "webbed" information society, in light of the control strategies that have developed in the 1990s, "formulated in terms of rates, costs of constraints, degrees of freedom," and operating through the "privileged pathology . . . [of] stress—communications breakdown" (1990; 1991b, 161–163). These strategies are nonetheless facets of the territorialization that Deleuze and Guattari see as both inimical to, and yet part and parcel of, "becomings." Following Hakim Bey's (1985) emphasis on "psychic nomadism" for realizing the "coming-into-being" of the "TAZ" (Temporary Autonomous Zone), we must maintain an awareness of the hierarchical aspect of "the Net," and of diverse and competing possibilities. Bey describes these as possibilities, on the one hand, for "the alternate horizontal open structure of info-exchange, the non-hierarchic network," of what Bey calls "the Web," and on the other hand, for "clandestine illegal and rebellious use of the Web, including actual data-piracy and other forms of leeching off the Net itself," or what Bey calls "the counter-Net" (1985/1991, 108).[6] By evoking these possibilities, I hope to link the "rhizomatics" I discussed in Chapter 3 to the further animation of concepts via cyberpunk fiction.

MILLE/PUNKS

Cyberpunk novels share a dystopic vision of society that involves varying degrees and kinds of systems' collapse and argue implicitly against the outmoded Gernsbackian idea of a utopian future.[7] Yet, this envisioned society is also engaged in the expansion of human intelligence within "a realm where the computer hacker and the rocker overlap, a cultural Petri dish where writhing gene lines splice" (Sterling 1986, xiii). A focal constant is the fundamentally pervasive proliferation of cybernetic technologies, from the microscopic level of body parts and implants of "wetware" to galactic movement of information into space, and even far beyond the immediate galaxy.[8] At the "core" of this proliferation is a rhizomelike web of cybernetic exchanges and flows or the "consensual hallucination" of "cyberspace," variously called "the Grid" (Shirley 1985), "the Net" (Sterling 1988b/1989), or "the Matrix" (Gibson 1984; 1989, 60–61). These exchanges and flows of information properly constitute a "collective assemblage" moving beyond subject-positions toward a type "that carries or brings out the event insofar as it is unformed and incapable of being effectuated by persons" (ATP, 265; MP, 324). Yet this "consensual hallucination" is created in all of these tales by means of characters who function both as agents and as peripheral elements of this web, all propelled into various modes of "becoming" by dint of their resistance to those agents who would usurp the web for the sole ends of an "informatics of domination," be it socioeconomic, biotechnological, or cybertechnological.

The "machinic assemblages" that Deleuze and Guattari discuss are elements of a vast process of "becoming" that "produces nothing other than itself," that lacks "a subject distinct from itself," that has "no term, since its term in turn exists only as taken up in another becoming of which it is the subject, and which coexists, forms a block, with the first" (ATP, 238; MP, 291). As is evident from the complex interactions of humans and cyborgs in cyberpunk tales, becoming "concerns alliance" rather than filiation, a form of evolution between heterogeneous forms that Deleuze and Guattari dub "involution"—not to make a regression, but "to form a block that runs its own line 'between' the terms in play and beneath assignable relations" (ATP, 238–239; MP, 292). Always involving "a pack, a band, a population, a peopling, in short, a multiplicity" (ATP, 239; MP, 292), becoming produces an "affect," especially in writing. Deleuze and Guattari describe this as "the effectuation of a power of the pack that throws the self into upheaval and makes it reel," an "involution calling us toward unheard-of becomings" (ATP, 240; MP, 293–294), toward "contagion" and "unnatural participations" as the means of establishing these assemblages (ATP, 240–241; MP, 294).

Yet the becomings of these packs are also nourished by the principle that "wherever there is multiplicity, you will also find an exceptional individual" (ATP, 243; MP, 298), an "Anomalous" figure constituted by "a phenomenon of bordering" (ATP, 245; MP, 300). This borderline situation of the "Anomalous" figure accounts for the possibility of its belonging to the pack (e.g., of cyborgs and/or of the interface with cyberspace) and yet also of maintaining a peripheral position "such that it is impossible to tell if the anomalous is still in the band, already outside the band, or at the shifting boundary of the band" (ATP, 245; MP, 300). Not surprisingly, one privileged expression of the different modes of becoming, argue Deleuze and Guattari, is science fiction, having evolved "from animal, vegetable, and mineral becomings to becomings of bacteria, viruses, molecules, and things imperceptible" (ATP, 248; MP, 304).[9]

To extend this admittedly abstract delineation of the concept of "becoming," let us consider several examples drawn from three cyberpunk narrative "clusters": Rudy Rucker's *Software, Wetware,* and *Freeware* trilogy; John Shirley's "A Song Called Youth" trilogy (*Eclipse, Eclipse Penumbra,* and *Eclipse Corona*); and William Gibson's "Sprawl" trilogy (*Neuromancer, Count Zero,* and *Mona Lisa Overdrive*). Besides constituting an unmistakably representative group from a subgenre that has been belittled and scorned,[10] this sample provides clear, yet varied examples of modes both of "becoming" and of the "informatics of domination." All these tales present sociopolitical turmoil in which cybertechnologies play a crucial role, but each varies in the extent to which the political framework and struggles are immediately recognizable from the contemporary "mode of information" (Poster 1989, 1990). As John Shirley notes, "Cyberpunk for me is both a protest and a celebration. Gibson and [Bruce] Sterling were already doing the celebration. . . . I went the next step and looked at the dark side more" (1989b, 91). In Shirley's trilogy, the rise of a fascist multinational/corporate security force, the SA, occurs in a global atmosphere in which armed, but nonnuclear, conflict between the East and the West blocs is at its peak, creating the circumstances for the proliferation of xenophobic and nationalistic policies as well as armed opposition to them by a ragtag band of "anomalous" warriors, the New Resistance. Not only do these opposing groups employ technologically updated, yet relatively conventional assault weapons, the success of their domination or resistance relies on access to circuits of information available only through sophisticated manipulation of "the Grid," both on Earth and on the floating space colony known as "FirStep."

While William Gibson's trilogy is equally global and galactic, its politics are considerably more obscure: in his fictional world the corporate "informatics of domination" replace the national in a vast brokerage of software, hardware, and wetware (cybernetically enhanced bodily implants), and, most importantly, in exploitation of the individual skills necessary for their manipulation. Operating variously in the postindustrial "Sprawl" of the Boston–Atlanta–Metropolitan Axis (or BAMA), in other urban zones in Japan, in California, and in Great Britain, and in the space resort of the Freeside Archipelago, the "resistance" in Gibson's novels is mercenary rather than political. Moreover, its tools are entirely cyber-based, consisting of techniques employed by the "cowboy"—a sophisticated "hacker"—for entering the information "matrix," or "cyberspace," for deploying alternate programs in order to penetrate ICE ("intrusion countermeasures electronics," lethal antitampering devices) that surround vast corporate and private databanks. The ostensible purpose of these strategies is to run cyberscams whose goals may or may not include financial gain, or even survival.

Finally, Rucker's trilogy is the most speculative: besides employing highly transformed versions of Florida, Louisville, and southern California as his settings, he situates the principal locus of conflict on Moonbase settlements colonized by liberated rebel cyborgs, the Boppers. He also defines the "political" conflict as a "biopolitics" of domination. This consists of a struggle among cyborgs for the right to proliferate and reformat into new software and hardware configurations, and to develop their implant "wetware" in order to advance a program of miscegenation aimed at creating an entirely new race on Earth whose name, the "Meatbopper," suggests the convergence of the organic and the cyber-netic. Moreover, as the third volume develops, these liberated cyborg forms are caught in a conflict quite familiar to our own era, the dynamics of technoscientific development for profit versus the possibility of creating new forms for the advancement of knowledge and freedom—in this case, the very freedom of those cyberlifeforms that are created by technos-cience.

This example suggests one obvious way in which "becomings" func-tion as a key plot element in these novels, an extension, in fact, of Rucker's own work in developing "cellular automata," "a type of artificial life rather than artificial intelligence" (1989a, 75–76). In *Software,* the biopolitical infiltration is limited to retrieving and storing a human's cerebral matrix, then downloading it into new cyborg forms. One of these forms has his "origin" as the human cyberneticist Cobb Anderson, but necessarily mutates toward creating a new religious cult in order to attract "followers" susceptible to such re-creation. Just as his human form was instrumental in the invention and then liberation of the original Boppers, this "anoma-lous" character exists as part of a "collective assemblage" in relation to the "mainframe" megacyborg that oversees his operation. When the religious cult plot is finally aborted through hardware vulnerability, the saga continues in *Wetware.* Now the Moon-based Boppers unleash a contagious, procreative "machinic assemblage" named Manchile. The offspring of this fertilizing machine seek not only to increase the numbers of their Meatbopper race, but to overcome the inhibitive programming that guides the activities of Earth-bound cyborgs strictly according to the prime Asimov "laws of robotics": to serve and preserve humans first (Asimov 1956). And as the title of the most recent installment suggests, in *Freeware* this offspring has proliferated to such an extent that Rucker has to provide an elaborate genealogy of characters for the three novels. Cyborgs are no longer Earth-bound, nor do they necessarily retain humanoid forms. For "moldies"—"artificial life form[s] made of a soft plastic that was mottled and veined with gene-tweaked molds and algae" (1997, 1)—now work with and for humans and reproduce themselves. But "moldies" also risk being captured by Moon-based "loonie moldies" who need the influx and unity of their species in order to strengthen the Nest and thus to pursue their destiny (1997, 145–146).

In Shirley's trilogy, in contrast, the "becomings" proceed less along the "molecular" and more on the "molar" level of political consciousness-raising, with the most unlikely characters finding the means to oppose and expose the fascist SA. The most striking is undoubtedly the truly "anomalous" Rickenharp, the retro (i.e., 1960s–1970s), drugged-out rock star who inadvertently joins the New Resistance cause. Trapped and wounded during an SA dragnet in Paris, Rickenharp devises an ingenious, but suicidal means of diverting SA attention to allow his comrades to escape: he climbs to the top of the Arch of Triumph with monster amp, rhythm box, and guitar in hand to play his "last gig" to the attacking SA troops (1985, 304). Yet this ego/death-trip has a serious function, and gives the trilogy its name, for his "song called 'Youth'" is captured on video as the megadozers, the Jaegernauts, roll in to reduce the Arch to dust. The globally broadcast image of Rickenharp defies censorship, for the sounds of his song from atop the Arch spread across "the Grid" to inspire further resistance. The importance of this "cybernetwork" is further emphasized by the battle for control of FirStep, the space-based "web of information" that the New Resistance prevents the SA from converting into an impenetrable headquarters, and then use themselves to oversee the global resistance (Shirley 1988a).

However, the most threatening forms of becoming occur in *Eclipse Corona*, with the proliferation of drug-enhanced "wetware," experimental implants that stimulate an often uncontrollable war drive in NATO and fascist SA forces alike. In response to this "informatics of domination," a wetware counterresistance called "the Plateau" is developed:

> It was the Plateau, Jerome thought, that really scared the shit out of the feds. It had possibilities.... "They're holding the Plateau back," his brain-chip wholesaler had told him, "because they're afraid of what worldwide electronic telepathy might bring down on them. Like, everyone will collate information, use it to see through the bastards' game, throw the assbites out of office." (1990a, 27, 31)

The scene of the jailbreak, made by Jerome–Jessie–Eddie–Bones–Swish through the combined cyberlink of the "pack," is a veritable cybernetic deconstruction. Yet, as their "five chips become One" (1990a, 34), they teeter on the edge of "another realm through a break in the psychic clouds: the Plateau, the whispering plane of brain chips linked to forbidden frequencies, an electronic haven for doing deals unseen by cops, . . . a place roamed by the wolves of wetware" (1990a, 33; also 1988b). This link is the first of the successful efforts to tap into the Plateau's potential for communion, a breakthrough to cyberspace that works on the molecular level in tandem with the molar, political struggle. For not only do these links weaken and finally destroy the SA's grasp on the "informatics of domination," they also serve to thwart the genocidal plan of the New Resistance's own corporate benefactor, Witcher, to seize control of global informatics.

While this tempting, transcendent merging with the information matrix exists in tandem with other plot elements in both Shirley's and Rucker's narrative "clusters," the "becomings" in as well as of cyberspace form the fundamental link between the novels of Gibson's "Sprawl" trilogy. Deleuze and Guattari conceptualize this merging as a "becoming-imperceptible" occurring on "the plane of consistency," bringing "into coexistence any number of multiplicities, with any number of dimensions . . . the intersection of all concrete forms" (ATP, 251; MP, 307–308). The terror that Shirley's Jerome et al. feel in the face of the infinite expanse of the Plateau is the loss of the subject, or rather the intensity of participating in multiple subjectivities. Yet Deleuze and Guattari propose cartographic coordinates for such "composable individuations": "A degree, an intensity, is an individual, a *Haecceity* that enters into composition with other degrees, other intensities, to form another individual" (ATP, 253; MP, 310).[11] Plotting "distributions of intensity," of "affects" as "latitude" in relation to longitudinal "relations of movement and rest, speed and slowness" (ATP, 260; MP, 318), Deleuze and Guattari follow Spinoza's lead in proposing a

> mode of individuation very different from that of a person, subject, thing or substance. We reserve the name *haecceity* for it. A season, a winter, a summer, an hour, a date have a perfect individuality lacking nothing, even though this individuality is different from that of a thing or a subject. They are haecceities in the sense that they consist entirely of relations of movement and rest between molecules or particles, capacities to affect and be affected. (ATP, 261; MP, 318)

The "involution" of just such individuation lies at the narrative core of Gibson's "Sprawl" tales: in *Neuromancer,* the complicated plot into which the cybercowboy, Case, and his biotechnologically enhanced partner, Molly, are drawn is generated by an haecceity-type "becoming," that is, the distribution of intensity, of affect by Wintermute, an enormous complex of AI (artificial intelligence), in order to interface and merge with its counterpart, Neuromancer. To create this unprecedented and illegal mode of individuation, Wintermute must "distribute" human agents and cybernetic technology in ways that allow them to penetrate the restraining ICE surrounding the corporate databank of the Tessier–Ashpool family, and thus circumvent global regulations that police and attempt to prevent such dangerous cyberinfractions as this megamerger of AI. The "becoming-sentient" of the cybernetic matrix with which *Neuromancer* ends forms the backdrop of the transformed behavior of cyberspace in *Count Zero*—the infusion of "affect" with which certain characters come to terms by explaining these becomings as manifestations of gods of voodoo. In *Mona Lisa Overdrive*, the ultimate phase is reached as human subjectivities achieve a "haecceity": affect and interface within the cybernetic "becoming." In the final pages, the characters embark with the expanded AI on a new phase, toward merger with "another matrix, another sentience" that is signaling its presence from outer space. While Bruce Sterling has dismissed Gibson's narrative moves toward transcendence as "just a feature of the genre, like feedback in rock music" (1989b, 100), the very possibilities of diverse and merged subjectivities prevalent in the cyberpunk novels suggest affective relations quite difficult to enunciate, yet potentially quite real as a field of "becoming" in daily life.

CYBER/PLATEAUS

In the final sentences of Haraway's "Manifesto for Cyborgs," she establishes a bridge to another line of inquiry on "becomings" and the "informatics of domination" by insisting that the "dream" of cyborg imagery is

> not of a common language, but of a powerful infidel heteroglossia. It is an imagination of a feminist speaking in tongues to strike fear into the circuits of the super savers of the New Right. It means both building and destroying machines, identities, categories, relationships, spaces, stories. Although both are bound in the spiral dance, I would rather be a cyborg than a goddess. (1990; 1991b, 181)

I juxtapose this "dream" to three sets of images. This first is a suggestion from Gabriele Schwab that "we can observe a network of textual links . . . between cultural representations of the body and social practices involving the body (like medicine or education) or other forms of body politics" via the "phantasmatic intertextuality . . . filtered through or even controlled by the media or other cybernetic systems" (1989, 195). Schwab points to toys—such as "Masters of the Universe" action figures and computer software like "Kidwriter" (to which we might add hardware like the hand-held Nintendo "Gameboy" and its interchangeable software clips)— and concludes that this "imaginary and socially sanctioned cyborgization is, as far as childhood culture is concerned, a predominantly male enterprise in the most traditional sense" (1989, 197). The second image is from John Shirley's short story, "A Walk through Beirut," in which a blond, minimally clad woman asserts her presence on the street by means of a constant musical onslaught produced from a boom box with speakers mounted in her crotch (1996). The third image comes from Howard Rheingold's speculation on "teledildonics and beyond": "Thirty years from now, when portable telediddlers become ubiquitous, most people will use them to have sexual experiences with other people, at a distance, in combinations and configurations undreamed of by precybernetic voluptuaries. . . . Or so the scenario goes" (1991, 345).[12]

Such images might suggest a new twist on Luce Irigaray's celebrated essay (1977), to be retitled "When Our Woofers Speak Together." However, these juxtapositions raise certain questions left open in the preceding section, to wit: Do the representations of gender, both in cyberpunk novels and in the concept of "becomings," really speak in tongues that could strike the fear that Haraway evokes into conservative circuitry? And to what extent do these tales constitute constraining "myths" that reinforce the "informatics of domination" by reproducing stereotypes and leaving dualisms intact? At a conference on cyberpunk during which Shirley read "A Walk through Beirut," the novelist Elizabeth Hand leveled these same charges at the "SF Boys' Club" of cyberpunk, insisting that only a small group of SF writers such as Angela Carter, Ginette Winterson, Joanna Russ, and Alice Sheldon are currently engaging the possibilities of constituting an "infidel heteroglossia" (Hand 1991).[13] In remarks made at the same conference, Larry McCaffery insisted that, rather than to consider some "beyond" of cyberpunk, it would be more productive to consider the cybernetic conflicts and biotechnological incursions at the heart of these novels as an expression of a postmodern fiction exploring the very fabric of our daily life "as it already is" (1991a).[14]

It is into this *différend* that I introduce a particular aspect of "becomings" proposed by Deleuze and Guattari as "becomings-woman" (*les devenirs-femme*). Early in the development of their idea of "becomings" in Plateau 10 of *A Thousand Plateaus,* they insist that "exclusive importance should not be attached to becomings-animal" (*les devenirs-animal*) on which they seem to concentrate their analysis. Proposing "regions" that constitute "a kind of order or apparent progression for the segments of becoming in which we find ourselves" (ATP, 272; MP, 333), Deleuze and Guattari suggest that these becomings-animal "are segments occupying a median region. On the near side, we encounter becomings-woman, becomings-child. . . . On the far side, we find becomings-elementary, -cellular, -molecular, and even becomings-imperceptible" (ATP, 248; MP, 304). In a parenthetical remark, they add, "(becoming-woman, more than any other becoming, possesses a special introductory power; it is not so much that women are witches, but that sorcery proceeds by way of this becoming-woman)" (ATP, 248; MP, 304 my emphasis).

To address this topic, one that has given rise to much commentary and criticism, I must return to the importance that Deleuze and Guattari bestow on the "sorcerer" concept. They see the "sorcerer" as an agent of " 'anomic' phenomena pervading societies that are not degradations of the mythic order but irreducible dynamisms drawing lines of flight and implying other forms of expression than those of myth" (ATP, 237; MP, 290). Further on, Deleuze and Guattari suggest a general definition of "becoming":

> Starting from the forms one has, the subject one is, the organs one has, or the functions one fulfills, becoming is to extract particles between which one establishes the relations of movement and rest, speed and slowness that are *closest* to what one is becoming, and through which one becomes. This is the sense in which becoming is the process of desire. (ATP, 272; MP, 334)

In this way, "all becomings are molecular" through what they call the "extraction" and "emission of particles" that establish a "haecceity," that is, a "thisness," of speed and affect as "a molecular zone" of various relations (ATP, 275; MP, 337). So, passages into the "contagion of the pack" and into the "anomalous" and its "relation to a multiplicity" (ATP, 243–244; MP, 298), discussed heretofore in terms of "becomings-animal," may be prepared and rendered possible in the complex region or process called "becoming-woman."

As in all the plateaus they consider, Deleuze and Guattari distinguish two parallel, intersecting planes in order to develop an understanding of these diverse "becomings." On one plane, a molar entity is "the woman as defined by her form, endowed with organs and functions and assigned as a subject" (ATP, 275; MP, 337). As such, Deleuze and Guattari maintain that women must "conduct a molar politics, with a view to winning back their own organism, their own history, their own subjectivity" (ATP, 276; MP, 338). On another plane, the molecular plane, "becoming-woman" is a function of "emitting particles that enter the relation of movement and rest, or the zone of proximity, of a microfemininity, in other words, that produce in us a molecular woman, create the molecular woman" (ATP, 275; MP, 338). Since the manner in which these planes intersect is clearly of great importance, Deleuze and Guattari are quick to insist that "we do not mean to say that a creation of this kind is the prerogative of the man, but on the contrary that the woman as a molar entity *has to become-woman* in order that the man also becomes- or can become-woman" (ATP, 275–276; MP, 338).

These claims certainly demand further explanation. Let us recall, first, the manner in which the "myth system" would ground, according to Haraway, a new way of looking at science and technology, and thereby of challenging the "informatics of domination." This new way of looking would rely not on a drive "to produce total theory," Haraway argues, but rather on "an intimate experience of boundaries, their construction and deconstruction" (1990; 1991b, 181).[15] Similarly, "becomings" would rely on the "anomalous," that is, on the singular Anomal as complement to the becoming of an Animal within the "pack," the multiplicity, at "the cutting edge of deterritorialization" (ATP, 243–244; MP, 298). This Anomal is a necessary "phenomenon of bordering" through which a "multiplicity" is composed "by the lines and dimensions it encompasses in 'intension,' " as opposed to "extension" (ATP, 245; MP, 299). For this borderline of the multiplicity, say Deleuze and Guattari, "is in no way a center but rather the enveloping line or farthest dimension, as a function of which it is possible to count the others, all those lines or dimensions [that] constitute the pack at a given moment (beyond the borderline, the multiplicity changes nature)" (ATP, 245; MP, 299–300).

Moreover, since "sorcerers have always held the anomalous position, at the edge of the fields or woods," in positions of "affinity with alliance, with the pact" (ATP, 246; MP, 301), the "becomings-woman" would constitute a particular means of access to

> an entire politics of becomings-animal, as well as a politics of sorcery, which is elaborated in assemblages that are neither those of the family nor of religion nor of the State. Instead, these politics express minoritarian groups, or groups that are oppressed, prohibited, in revolt, or always on the fringe of recognized institutions, groups all the more secret for being extrinsic, in other words, anomic. (ATP, 247; MP, 302)

In other words, rather than comprehending "becoming-woman" as a starting point that would eventually be abandoned once "becomings" proceed on to some other more "advanced" phase, we can envisage "becoming-woman" as the very dynamic zone intermezzo. That is, it is this zone or process of "becomings" that all struggles of schizoanalysis and rhizomatics pass in order to gain their political and desiring force such that "becomings-woman" are never abandoned even as one traverses other zones or processes of "becomings." The "two-fold thought" engages "becoming-woman" as its very multiplanar dynamic, just as "becoming-woman" encompasses the "two-fold thought" as a way to help it envisage, indeed to make possible, further and simultaneous "becomings."[16]

As I suggested in Chapter 4, Deleuze and Guattari explore these concepts with illustrative examples drawn from Virginia Woolf and Proust, among other authors. I choose, rather, to reconstitute the locus and power of "becomings" introduced by "woman" through a consideration of several characters in cyberpunk tales. Gibson's favorite character is Molly Millions, to whom he refers, in an interview with Timothy Leary, as "a female lead who beats the shit out of everybody" (Gibson 1989, 61). Molly appears first in the short story "Johnny Mnemonic" (in Gibson 1986a, 1–22). There she is portrayed as a biotechnologically altered anomalous figure who saves the eponymous character, Johnny, by slaying a Japanese mob assassin in a duel, thereby sealing a partnership to deal in the data previously stored for rich clients in Johnny's biochip implants. Molly's subsequent activities in *Neuromancer,* however mercenary and financially motivated, enable her new partner, Case, to find a form of cybernetic redemption through repeated, near-fatal cerebral mergers with the "haecceities" of the Matrix. Here, Molly continues to exemplify the anomalous figure of alliance, even an ambiguous feminist exploitation of the cyborg image.[17] Cast as lethal enforcer, potential castrator (with surgically implanted razors under her burgundy-colored nails), and usurper of the male gaze (thanks to surgically inset mirrorshades), Molly returns the reflection of the "other" while skillfully transacting business, often with a mere flick of the hand or head in the street-code called "jive." Moreover, it is literally through her gaze that Case (and the reader) directly follow the action in the two crucial scenes of cyberscams thanks to a video-broadcast unit mounted behind the mirrorshades. With Case's assistance at the cyberconsole, Molly's penetration of the Tessier–Ashpool mansion, Straylight, permits the twin AI's, Wintermute and Neuromancer, to achieve their illegal merger and "becoming-sentient," thereby initiating unfathomable "becomings" of the cyberspace Matrix itself.

In *Count Zero,* Molly's only "appearance" is in a reference by the software dealer, Finn, to her Straylight run seven years earlier, that Finn links directly to the "becoming-sentient," to the "weird shit happening in the Matrix" (Gibson 1986b, 123–124). But *Count Zero* does present the "becomings" of another woman, Angela Mitchell, a teenager inhabited via biosoft implants by the "voices" of the Matrix. That she owes these to the surreptitious efforts of her scientist father—who, in turn, was manipulated in his own work on biochips by the sentient AI entities encountered in

Neuromancer (Gibson 1984)—suggests the rhizomatic links inherent to these processes. Angie's trajectory leads her briefly into the role of Virgin for a voodoo cult—her "voices" are those of their "gods"—and then into the public arena as a "simstim" (simulated stimuli) star, thereby creating new and broader collective assemblages of "becomings."

In *Mona Lisa Overdrive* (Gibson 1988), set seven years later, Molly returns as Sally Shears. Here, she successfully parries the blackmail threat posed by the avenging clone of the Tessier–Ashpool family, Lady 3Jane and, in the process, enables the completion of the merger of cyberspace AI "haecceities." However, despite this biotechnological and streetwise stance of power, Molly remains steadfastly locked into the molar plane, or what the cyberpunks refer to less technically as "meat." While along for the "ride" behind Molly's optical field in *Neuromancer,* Case finds the passive role "irritating," even threatening, as when Molly playfully causes him to gasp as she strolls down the street fingering her (and therefore his) nipple through their sensorial interface. Later, on the eve of their multiphased invasion of the Tessier–Ashpool estate, Molly reveals to Case that she financed the purchase of her biotech hardware on her earnings as a "meat puppet"—that is, as a prostitute whose software programming allowed her subjectivity to be bypassed during "working" hours.[18] However, the potential for depicting a woman's *jouissance,* and even a man's experience of it, is severely limited since Molly (and thus Case) endure intense pain throughout the novel following the leg injury sustained by Molly on the first cyberspace run. Case henceforth remains the "star attraction," as Fred Pfeil notes:

> Jacked in, he rides wildly up against and through the giant walls of corporate-conglomerate "ice" to the secret lairs, simultaneously located in cyberspace and the material world, where the darkest secrets and powers are hid. (1990, 89)

In contrast to Molly's (and eventually Case's) limitation to the molar plane, Angela Mitchell is the medium in *Count Zero* of the "funny stuff out there, out on the console cowboy circuit. . . . Ghosts, voices" (1986b, 124), of the "haecceities" of the voodoo "loa of communication," Legba. However, her role as cybersorceress merging with the "becoming-sentient" of the Matrix through direct cerebral link seems unwitting given her father's Faustian arrangement with the Matrix itself. In *Mona Lisa Overdrive,* Angela is reunited with her companion from the previous novel, Count Zero himself, the cybercowboy Bobby Newmark, who now is sustained permanently by mechanical life support, having been transformed into a vast database with only the flimsiest corporal link to the molar/meat. *Mona Lisa Overdrive* is truly the novel of "becomings," in which all the characters undergo various degrees of transformation brought about by the sentient "becoming-imperceptible" of AI, and Angela finally joins Bobby beyond "meat," in the virtual reality maintained by the megabase of the Matrix for "becomings-imperceptible" of humans. Yet, despite access to these troubling "haecceities," Angela is the exception confirming the rule of women like Mona, Molly, and Kumiko, who remain on the material, sensory plane.[19]

Another dualism arises in cyberpunk novels, however, that seems to contradict, or at least to stand in tension alongside, the meat/cybersentience dualism. While the most evident villain in the cyberpunk subgenre is usually the corporate "informatics of domination," the recurrent figure of potential domination in the "Sprawl" trilogy is a clone, like the vat-sustained Virek in *Count Zero* and the clones of the Tessier–Ashpool family in *Neuromancer,* of which Lady 3Jane returns with and for a vengeance in *Mona Lisa Overdrive.* Gabriele Schwab contends that the clone has "become a new mythological figure at the horizon of the postmodern imagination," a figure "invested with fantasies of immortality, doubling, endless mirroring, and phantasmatic redefinitions of death" (1989, 198). However, clones play a distinctly different role in these and other cyberpunk novels. There, clones and posthuman cyborgs, like Manchile the Meatbopper in Rucker's *Wetware* (1988), represent the evil and/or fatal horizon of technological progress feeding on humankind, with Manchile as the embodiment of "filiation" eschewing "alliance." However, once his own generative program aborts, Manchile acts not only to liberate Earth-bound cyborgs from their Asimov constraints, but also to permit further "becomings" of cellular automata, in between software and hardware in the first two novels, and then beyond wetware toward "the strange attractor of consciousness" (Rucker 1997, 180).[20] The evil/fatal status of the clone emerges not only in Gibson's novels, but in those of Shirley, Rucker, Sterling (*Schismatrix* [1985]), and Greg Bear (*Blood Music* [1985a], *Eon* [1985b], and even *Eternity* [1988], albeit somewhat more equivocally). These continuities suggest that "becomings" must be kept in check when the body (read: male body) is threatened, possibly leading us to conclude, with Alice Jardine, that "man is always the subject of any becoming, even if 'he' is a woman" (1985, 217).

From this perspective, the "informatics of domination" do indeed seem to provide grounds for concern for "their effects on the flesh" (Jardine 1987, 152). However, we can also consider the "becomings" in these novels from the perspective of the predominantly "negative valence" that biological and brain-function concepts have had in science fiction. In this light, the limits that I have attributed to these "becomings" may not stem solely from cyberpunk's filiation to the horror genre as it relates to the body's vulnerability (Csicsery-Ronay 1988, 272–273). As Joseph Miller

suggests, the negative valence is also a product "of the historical winnow-
ing of the centristic philosophy" (1989, 205). That is, like geocentrism and
anthropocentrism,

> "telecentrism" (to coin a term), the implicit faith in mind as inexplicable
> and irreducible center of the universe, last bastion of Cartesian duality, is
> now crumbling under the reductionistic onslaught of neuroscience in
> league with the aforementioned cognitive science. These sciences, along
> with the behavioristic approaches of the psychological and ethological
> disciplines, ultimately imply that there is nothing special about mind. . . .
> The very idea of artificial intelligence, as the final extension of neuronal
> reductionism, is an assault on the last bastion of human uniqueness,
> consciousness itself. (1989, 205)

So, these metaphysics—the unlimited metamorphosis in the quest for
that "cyberspace beyond . . . ," the "line of flight" through which an
emission of particles tends toward "becoming-imperceptible," the development of "cyborg identity" in response to "informatics of domination"—
all suggest the role of processes of destabilization at work in these
different texts, but processes that may be viewed differently depending
on the discursive angle one adopts. The pursuit of processes that encompass "becoming-imperceptible" may indeed by viewed as a nostalgic return
to the cybernetic "soul," or even to the "logos," the phallogocentric
folding into a center, of the outside within.[21] While Jardine's (1985)
critique of Deleuze and Guattari concerning woman's disappearance
seems to equate the molar, fixed plane with the molecular plane of
dispersion and destabilization of affects, molecular "becomings" are precisely what Deleuze and Guattari, cyberpunk authors (however inade-
quately), and Haraway attempt to negotiate. For all, the notion of
"becoming-imperceptible" is as applicable to men as to women, and for
Deleuze–Guattari and Haraway, at least, these "becomings" hardly correspond to a "teleological" perspective. Even though Haraway's "Manifesto"
might be said to embrace the "becoming-imperceptible" as a starting
point, whether or not "becomings-woman," both thematic and discursive,
allow women (characters and authors) to come along for the journey is
still a hotly contested topic not only in current science fiction debates,
but also in feminism.[22]
    It is no doubt significant that the writers chosen by Haraway as
exemplary storytellers "exploring what it means to be embodied in
high-tech worlds" are Joanna Russ, Samuel Delany, John Varley, James
Tiptree Jr. (aka Alice Sheldon), Octavia Butler, and Vonda McIntyre
(Haraway 1990; 1991b, 173).[23] While Shirley situates these writers within
what he calls the science fiction "over-ground" (1989a, 32), Haraway sees

them as "theorists for cyborgs" who reveal their strategic explorations of "bodily boundaries and social order." Haraway contends further that this molecular dispersion of "cyborg identity" extends beyond fictional "theorists," notably to works by an anthropologist (Mary Douglas), French feminists (Luce Irigaray, Monique Wittig), American feminists (Susan Griffin, Adrienne Rich), and women of color (Audre Lorde, Cherrie Moraga). Through this "cyborg identity," she maintains, "there are also great riches for feminists in explicitly embracing the possibilities inherent in the breakdown of clean distinctions between organism and machine and similar distinctions structuring the Western self" (1990; 1991b, 174). And "for all their differences," Haraway insists that these writers "know how to write the body; how to weave eroticism, cosmology, and politics from imagery of embodiment, and especially for Wittig, from imagery of fragmentation and reconstitution of bodies" (1990; 1991b, 174).[24]

"Cyborg identity" emphasizes the molecular fracture and dispersion toward "lines of flight." This implicit link between identity and its destabilization is derived not so much from common projects or even from common epistemological fields as from multiple sites of activity, of enunciation, of affect, in short, from the multiplicity of "plateaus." Moreover, if "cyborg writing" is indeed "about the power to survive not on the basis of original innocence, but on the basis of seizing the tools to mark the world that marked them as other" (Haraway 1990; 1991b, 217), we can understand the cyperpunks, if not as "theorists," then as "practitioners," and better still, as "pragmatists for cyborgs." Despite all their well-noted limitations and masculinist proclivities, they seized tools, notably the cybernetic, neuroscientific, and biotechnological technologies that mark us imperceptibly and daily as "other." A more critical view maintains that their message "didn't go far enough" and remained "too elitist to be truly revolutionary" (Shepherd 1989, 116). However, if we consider ongoing body/mind/technology advances in fields such as prosthetic devices, virtual reality, and cloning as of the late 1990s, the directions in which cyberpunk writers pushed their practice may only seem fantastic (although persistently elitist and privileged) for ever briefer periods of time. As Peter Fitting suggests, the concept of cyberspace (for Gibson and others) can be understood

> as an attempt to grasp the complexity of the whole world system through a concrete representation of its unseen networks and structures, of its invisible data transfers and capital flows . . . [and as] a way of making the abstract and unseen comprehensible, a visualization of the notion of cognitive mapping. (1991, 311)

Where does the proliferation of technology in everyday life leave the writer (and reader) of science fiction? As we have seen in the 1990s, the line between speculative fiction and daily life has become increasingly murky as the result of the proliferation of different technologies, applications, and practices, all the more complex given the sensationalistic media spins that surround these issues.[25] For science fiction, the innovation might have to come from outside science fiction, from those authors writing what Bruce Sterling calls "slipstream," "a kind of writing that simply makes you feel very strange; the way that living in the late twentieth century makes you feel, if you are a person of a certain sensibility" (1989a, 78).[26] For John Shirley, the science fiction underground, "pressing through the rift made by the thin edge of the cyberpunk wedge" and thriving in small SF underground journals, promises "an even more important influx of information and stylistic rebirth" (1989a, 32). Elizabeth Hand demonstrates, first in *Winterlong* (1990), next in *Aestival Tide* (1992), and then in *Icarus Descending* (1993), that writerly excesses and transgressions obliquely pose alternate modes of biology, morality, and sexuality as both thematic and discursive paths for "becomings." And Pat Cadigan's novels, particularly *Fools* (1992), provide nearly apocalyptic visions of cyborg "becomings" as the "I" of the subject tends toward increasing fragility through interface multiplications (through mindplay/affect in *Mindplayers* [1987], through viral cyberlinks in *Synners* [1991]) until the text itself, in *Fools,* translates the mutating subjectivities in transformation.[27]

Many other writers and practices come to mind, but these reflections and juxtapositions of theoretical and narrative plots suffice to suggest numerous openings, rather than closures. Whatever the limitations from a feminist perspective both of this fiction and of the possibilities for "becomings-woman," the cyberpunk writers as well as Deleuze and Guattari emphasize the stakes for envisaging "becomings" and "haecceities" in simultaneously abstract and concrete terms. Kenneth Surin points to our era's development of new forms of knowledges, logics, and topologies, and he refers to Deleuze's suggestion in *The Fold* that the "time of 'rhizomatic structure' may indeed be the time of an invention of a 'new' Baroque" (1997, 12). These new logics and topologies participate in "generating principles of integration that allow radically different mechanisms to function in concert" (12), and not surprisingly, Surin argues that the "cyberspaces" projected in cyberpunk fictions "represent in many ways a culmination, impressed more and more deeply into our cultures, of [principles of integration that allow radically different mechanisms to function in concert]" (13).[28] As Deleuze and Guattari express it so succinctly: "For you will yield nothing to haecceities unless you realize that

that is what you are, and that you are nothing but that. . . . Or at least you can have it, you can reach it" (ATP, 262; MP, 320). These statements, imagery, and topologies provide the theoretical bases not only to develop further narrative speculation, as we have seen, but also to help us envisage sites "of the potent fusion of the technical, textual, organic, mythic and political" (Haraway 1990; 1991b, 25), perhaps even to realize the potential of new "becomings" as a vital element of our actuality, present and future.

6 NOMAD LOVE AND THE WAR MACHINE

MICHEL TOURNIER'S *GILLES AND JEANNE*

> Any important literary work is like the Trojan Horse at the time it is produced. Any work with a new form operates as a war machine, because its design and goal is to pulverize the old forms and literary conventions. It is always produced in hostile territory. And the stranger it appears, nonconforming, unassimilable, the longer it will take for the Trojan Horse to be accepted.
>
> —*Monique Wittig, "The Trojan Horse"*
> (*in* The Straight Mind *1992)*

In this chapter, I develop a literary animation concerning Deleuze and Guattari's concept of the "war machine" through a reading of Michel Tournier's tale of material knowledge and mystical excess, *Gilles and Jeanne* (1983). In the section entitled "The Mythic Dimension" of his intellectual autobiography, *The Wind Spirit,* Tournier reminisces about his association with Gilles Deleuze at the Lycée Carnot in the early 1940s, and what he calls there the Deleuzian "fresh, undigested, bitter taste of newness" (1988, 128) also emerges in Tournier's own work. One notes in particular the tension between *écriture* (writing) and *sens* (meaning, sense), in what Colin Davis calls "his simultaneous identification with both nomad and sedentary, when the former values the journey and the latter only the destination" (1988, 205). It is the connection between "becoming," "nomadology," and the war machine in Tournier's remythologized *récit* (tale) *Gilles and Jeanne* that I propose to explore.

143

In Tournier's tale *Gilles and Jeanne,* Jeanne d'Arc's quest and martyrdom are depicted for the transmutation that they incite in the life and soul of a character based on a notorious figure from French history, her comrade-in-arms, the noble Gilles de Rais.[1] Through the brief but intense period of military campaigns that Jeanne and Gilles share, the chevalier is transformed from merely one "of those country squires from Brittany and the Vendée who had thrown in their lot with the Dauphin Charles" (GJ, 5; 9) into an isolated, tormented warlord waging his own private, roving battle with forces known only to him. While rewriting his previous novel about an "ogre," *Le roi des Aulnes* [*The Ogre*],[2] Tournier reinscribes the myth of Gilles de Rais in order to liken this transformation to an alchemical process of "becoming," ignited by Gilles's initial contact with Jeanne d'Arc and perpetuated through the subsequent phases that constitute his tale.

From the perspective of the concept of "becoming" and its relation to "nomadology," I will map out textual coordinates, plotted through the Deleuze–Guattarian connection, that will help us to understand the productive force of "becoming."[3] I wish to consider how Tournier deploys in his tale a textual "assemblage" that, "in its multiplicity, necessarily acts on semiotic flows, material flows, and social flows simultaneously" (MPEng, 22–23; MPFr, 33–34), and thereby creates a tale of rupture and displacement, even of exile within the grip of feudal society. The particular semiotic and social perspective that the Deleuze–Guattarian discourse provides allows me to illustrate the trajectory of Tournier's tale through the five phases of its textual and thematic progression. In this progression, Gilles is portrayed as a "war machine" under the dominion, and territoriality, of the State apparatus. He traverses various states of "becoming" via progressive nomadization and radical deterritorialization inscribed within the confines of his feudal domain. He reaches a limit, of course, precisely where the "war machine" exceeds the dictates of the State apparatus and must be sanctioned and reterritorialized—brought back fully under its control. By studying this representation of a cruel and ambiguous nomadism which has so shocked some readers,[4] I suggest that it is precisely through this ambiguity, this lack of closure and finality, both textual and moral, that Tournier problematizes cultural traditions and political structures. At the same time, my use of nomadological terminology animates a reading/writing practice in order to develop possibilities of fragmentation echoed thematically within the text.

THE WAR MACHINE

Let us consider, first, the concept of the "war machine" as it relates to nomadology and is thus developed in *A Thousand Plateaus.* Conceived as a means of developing a "thought" (*pensée*) that is not classical or arborescent—that is, a thought "whose relationship with the outside is [not] mediated by some form of interiority" such as the soul or consciousness (Patton 1984, 61)—nomadology expresses counterthoughts, "violent in their acts and discontinuous in their appearances," an "outside thought" that places "thought in an immediate relation . . . with the forces of the outside, in short to make thought a war machine" (MPEng, 376–377; MPFr, 467).[5] Against the universalizing aspirations of the classical image of thought and the striation of mental space that it effects, this nomadic thought allies itself not with "a universal thinking subject but, on the contrary, with a singular race"; it grounds itself not "in an all-encompassing totality but is, on the contrary, deployed in a horizonless milieu that is a smooth space, steppe, desert or sea" (MPEng, 379; MPFr, 469). It is from this perspective that war machines must be understood as distinct from the military institution. Deploying both a thought and a desire fundamentally at odds with the State apparatus, the war machine is an assemblage of creative force that "in no way has war as its object," but constitutes rather a transformational energy that Deleuze and Guattari call "the passage of mutant flows" (MPEng, 229–230; MPFr, 280).

The conflict of Gilles de Rais commences here, at the intersection of exteriority and interiority, at the boundary of the dominion of the State apparatus vis-à-vis the war machine, on the one hand, and of the impetus of his own "becomings" vis-à-vis the State/war machine complex, on the other. In the initial phase of the tale, Gilles has just thrown in his lot as a vassal to Charles VII, and is thereby appropriated by the military objectives of the feudal State apparatus. However, Gilles de Rais's submission to the influence of Jeanne d'Arc, prompted by the "purity that radiates from her face" (GJ, 10; 15), unleashes the simultaneously creative and conflictual assemblage of desire, the "mutant flows" of "nomad love," which propel him toward a "becoming" entirely outside the hierarchizing constraints of the State. At the same time, this "becoming" is directed toward an ultimate interiority and sedentary order that will cause his downfall even as it brings on his "glory."

The initial contrast of Jeanne d'Arc with those around her is presented starkly: "And, indeed, she did seem to glide along on invisible wings above the animal [*bête*] as it furiously pounded the earth with its four iron shoes" (GJ, 10; 16). This *bête* refers not only literally to Jeanne's new steed, but metaphorically to the war machine that envelops her, a machine that is appropriated by the violence of the State apparatus, whose order she and it will struggle to reestablish. But the particular war machine that Jeanne harnesses "bears witness to another kind of justice, one of incomprehensible cruelty at times, but at others of unequaled pity as well" (MPEng, 352; MPFr, 435). Moreover, this war machine bears witness "to other relations with women, with animals, . . . all things in relations of becoming. . . . In every respect, the war machine is of another species, another nature, another origin than the State apparatus" (MPEng, 352; MPFr, 435–436).

It is to this "other species" and to the possibilities it suggests that Gilles de Rais is attracted, and thereby lifted from the "fate of a country squire from a particularly backward province" (GJ, 11–12; 18) into a process of "becoming" that Tournier describes as "the intoxicating and dangerous fusion of sanctity and war" (GJ, 13; 19). Under her tutelage, Gilles "followed Jeanne as the body obeys the soul, as she herself obeyed her 'voices' " (GJ, 14; 21). For these "voices" function for Gilles and Jeanne alike as the guiding impulse of their particular war machine. During their fireside chats, through the example of her visions, her voices, and her quest, Jeanne is able to articulate for Gilles the confused mass of "obscure things" that, he exclaims, "I can't understand and that I am afraid I will understand one day" (GJ, 16; 23). "Jeanne," Gilles confesses, "I believe each of us has his voices. Good voices and bad voices. . . . The voices I heard in my childhood and youth were always those of evil and sin" (GJ, 20; 25–26). And he offers Jeanne his own interpretation of her quest, whose meaning is located at the junction of interiority and exteriority: "You have not come only to save the Dauphin Charles and his kingdom. You must also save the young lord Gilles de Rais! Make him hear your voice. Jeanne, I never want to leave your side. Jeanne, you are a saint, make a saint of me!" (GJ, 18; 26).

During the subsequent campaigns, Gilles is able to express his particular kind of love for Jeanne not merely through the perils that he shares with her in the field, but more importantly in the assemblage of movement, speed, and affect that constitutes a war machine, a "nomad love." He proclaims this to her as she lies wounded before the doors of Paris:

> "But I love you above all for the purity that is inside you and that nothing can tarnish."
> Looking down, he saw her [knee] wound.
> "Will you accept the only kiss that I ask of you?"
> He bent down and laid his lips for a long time on Jeanne's wound.
> He then stood up and licked his lips.
> "I have communicated with your blood. I am bound to you forever. Henceforth I shall follow you wherever you go. Whether to heaven or to hell!" (GJ, 23–24; 33)

This vow will determine the destiny of Gilles de Rais once Jeanne d'Arc is captured by the English, tried, found guilty of heresy and witchcraft, and burned at the stake despite the futile efforts of Gilles to liberate her. Even before her execution, his life had already taken on new dimensions: "Neither war nor politics held his interest [following Jeanne's capture] . . . all that mattered to him now was that personal, mystical adventure that had begun on the day that he had met Jeanne" (GJ, 27; 36). After Gilles witnesses her execution, hearing her cries, "Jésus! Jésus! Jésus!" inexorably ringing in his ears, "something had changed inside him: he had the face of a lying, pernicious, dissolute, blaspheming invoker of devils" (GJ, 35; 45). Thus begins the process of "becoming" a unique, maleficent, and perverse war machine, an expression of the transformative nomad love: "A beaten, broken man, he went on and buried himself in his fortresses in the Vendée. For three years, he became a caterpillar. When the malign metamorphosis was complete, he emerged, an infernal angel, unfurling his wings" (GJ, 35; 45).

BECOMINGS

This process of "becoming" had already commenced during Gilles's intense interaction with Jeanne. His inspiration derives from Jeanne's mode of "becoming-woman," the molecular politics that unfold for this particular girl-child. "The girl is certainly not defined by virginity," Deleuze and Guattari claim; "she is defined by a relation of movement and rest, speed and slowness, by a combination of atoms, an emission of particles: haecceity" (MPEng, 276; MPFr, 339).[6] These are the very attributes of the nomadic war machine pursuing its fluid path. Further, "it is also certain that girls and children draw their strength . . . from the becoming-molecular they cause to pass between sexes and ages, the becoming-child of the adult as well as of the child, the becoming-woman of the man as well as of the woman" (MPEng, 276–277; MPFr, 339–340). The "becoming-molecular" thus defines the "nomad love" between Gilles and Jeanne: an affective exchange—of "atoms, particles"—valuable not for terrestrial carnality, but for the transmutation of the chevalier into child, woman, mystic—in other words, "becomings" that propel the war machine further *dehors*, outside the striated borders of subjectivity so oppressively circumscribed by the State apparatus. So, in the tale's second segment, as Gilles comes into his "huge fortune" and gains "free rein" (GJ, 36; *le champ libre*, 46) with the death of his grandfather, he finds himself quite literally territorialized through possession of his newly inherited lands.[7] While the translation has Gilles admit that "these things mean nothing to me" (GJ, 37), the French version—"je n'ai pas le sens de ces choses" (GJ, 47)—suggests the ambiguous play of "sense" as no direction as well as no meaning, a missing "logic of sense" familiar to a Deleuzian perspective.[8] Gilles thus rejects the sedentary implications of this territorialization and affirms his purpose in the journey toward "the outside" inspired by his true master/mistress, the "Janus–Jeanne" (GJ, 38; *Jeanne bifrons*, 48):

> "Jeanne the holy, Jeanne the chaste, Jeanne the victorious under the standard of St. Michael! Jeanne the monster in woman's shape, condemned to the stake for sorcery, heresy, schismaticism, change of sex, blasphemy and apostasy," he recited. (GJ, 38; 48)

As his grandfather perceives on his deathbed, this metamorphosis into "excessive sanctity" is an ominous portend; the grandfather predicts, "My greed is going to place an immense fortune at the service of your fanaticism. I tremble to think what will come of it all!" (GJ, 38; 49).

We can see here an important facet of what Davis (1988) calls Tournier's "treatment of paradox" in *Gilles and Jeanne* (GJ, 129). Despite the explicit territorialization within the feudal matrix, or perhaps because of it, this war machine is henceforth increasingly divorced from the State apparatus and is defined in terms of its own nomadic exteriority and speed, though it does draw strength and authority from the sedentary feudal State structure. As Deleuze and Guattari remark, not only is "the war machine's form of exteriority ... such that it exists only in its own metamorphoses," it is "in terms ... of coexistence and competition *in a perpetual field of interaction*, that we must conceive of exteriority and interiority, war machines of metamorphosis and State apparatuses of identity, bands and kingdoms, megamachines and empires" (MPEng, 360–361; MPFr, 446). Thus, now in possession of an immense fortune, Gilles can turn apparent "good works" toward his own ends. By founding a community (*collégiale*) dedicated to the Holy Innocents, Gilles can devote his energies to preying sexually on boys by "recruiting and examining the young singers of his foundation from the point of view of their voices—and the rest. Indeed it was not enough that they should have a divine voice, since, being divine, they should also look divine in face and body" (GJ, 39–40; 51).

This activity participates in a new form of "becoming," one of musical expression that "is inseparable from a becoming-woman, a becoming-child, a becoming-animal that constitute its content" (MPEng, 299; MPFr, 367). Conceived as "the adventure of the refrain," this music, especially as practiced in Gilles's *collégiale*, "is a deterritorialization of the voice, which becomes less and less tied to language" (MPEng, 302; MPFr, 271). Through this machinic force, "the musical voice itself becomes-child at the same time as the child becomes-sonorous, purely sonorous" (MPEng, 304; MPFr, 373). With the confused support of his confessor, the Reverend Eustache Blanchet, "God's medium before the penitent" (GJ, 43; 55), Gilles can thus strive toward becoming "something other than a child, a child belonging to a different, strangely sensual and celestial, world" (MPEng, 304; MPFr, 373). He indulges his taste for nomadic recruitment for the *collégiale*, and thereby attains new thresholds of deterritorialization, "no longer that of a properly vocal becoming-woman or becoming-child, but that of a becoming-molecular in which the voice itself is instrumentalized" (MPEng, 308; MPFr, 378).

This instrumental "becoming-molecular" can be seen in terms of another project, or assemblage, that Gilles undertakes. He commissions a fresco depicting the Massacre of the Holy Innocents for his chapel's walls. The artist "had costumed the figures like the men, soldiers, women, and children of his own period, and placed them in a village that was supposed to be Bethlehem, but in which everybody could recognize the houses of Machecoul," with "their lord Rais behind the features of the cruel King of the Jews" (GJ, 40–41; 51–52). Gilles thus creates a dual, aural/visual assemblage of deterritorialization and molecular dispersion of sanctity and suffering: "The anguished chants of the angel-faced choirboys moved Gilles all the more intensely when he saw those children against the background of such horror and slaughter. Overcome with emotion, he would stand there leaning against a pillar, murmuring between sobs, 'Pity, pity, pity!' " (GJ, 41; 152). But this particular kind of pity, one of "immense pleasure" at the "beautiful sight" of the suffering of the children's "tender, panting," "bloodstained" bodies (GJ, 42; 53–54), recalls the ambiguous ecstasy of Gilles's "nomad love" for Jeanne, the purity and corporality of holiness and blood.

Recruitment for the *collégiale* is but a prelude to the new pleasures of hunting "that other game, which was so special and so delicious" (GJ, 44; 56). In this nomadic recruitment across Gilles's vast territory, the figure of the "horseman galloping through plains and forests" (44; 57) fuels the "dark, cruel scenes" with their traits of speed and affect in the nomadic pursuit:

> A woman rushes out after a young boy, seizes him and takes him into her house. The horseman is swathed in a large cloak, which floats around the horse. With loud beating of hooves he crosses the castle drawbridge. He is now standing, motionless, legs apart, at the entrance of the armoury.
> The lord's voice is heard.
> "Well?"
> The horseman opens his cloak. A young boy is clinging to him. He falls down, then tries to rise clumsily.
> "Well done!" says the voice. (GJ, 45; 57)

This nomadic pursuit is the very stuff of legend, of myth, of fairy tales: of the witch called La Meffraye (she who arouses fear); of the woodcutter's son Poucet (Tom Thumb) who "saves" his brothers from the woods by leading them to the château of Tiffauges . . . never to emerge again (GJ, 46–48; 58–61).[9] And the "torrent of black smoke, gushing out of the castle's biggest chimney" ("torrent de fumée noire, vomi par la plus grosse chéminée du château"), this "stink of burning flesh" (GJ, 49; "puanteur de charogne calcinée" 62), disturb even the Reverend Blanchet. He agrees to undertake a mission on behalf of the exalted and obsessed *seigneur*, "after a particularly delirious night." Having learned that in "a place far away to the south, in Tuscany . . . scientists, artists and philosophers, it seemed, had combined their forces and intelligence to create a new golden age that would soon spread to the whole of mankind," Blanchet sets out to "investigate these novelties on the spot. Perhaps he would bring back to the Vendée some teaching, some object, even perhaps some man capable of tearing the *seigneur* de Rais from his dark chimeras" (GJ, 50; 63). Thus, the priest is propelled into the coordinates of new "spaces" and of mutant, "ambulant science."

SPACES

Before discussing the "spaces" and "science" that Blanchet encounters on his arrival in Florence, let us consider more fully how Tournier has situated Gilles in a "mixed state," the particularly ambiguous "space" constituted and inhabited in the early phases of the tale.[10] As a vassal to Charles VII and thus a participant in his cause, Gilles pursues the goals of the sedentary State apparatus alongside his comrade-in-arms, Jeanne. Deleuze and Guattari describe these goals as being *"to parcel out a closed space to people,* assigning each person a share and regulating the communication between shares" (MPEng, 380; MPFr, 472). One of the fundamental tasks of the State, say Deleuze and Guattari, is "to striate the space over which it reigns, or to utilize smooth spaces as a means of communication in the service of striated space." For this Gilles and Jeanne fought, to assure the control of the State apparatus over nomadism and migrations, "to establish a zone of rights over an entire 'exterior,' over all the flows traversing the ecumenon" (MPEng, 385; MPFr, 479). Whereas Jeanne took up arms in support of the State apparatus through a quite literal divine "calling," Gilles participates due to his rank in the hierarchy, at first, and then through a holy devotion to Jeanne.

Subsequently, however, it is this "capture of flows" that Tournier's Gilles implicitly opposes in his multiple "becomings." That is, despite (or because of) his own inscription in the striated space of the feudal hierarchy, Gilles's activities of "assemblage" run counter to the State's "need for fixed paths in well-defined directions, which restrict speed, regulate circulation, relativize movement, and measure in detail the relative movements of subjects and objects" (MPEng, 386; MPFr, 479). Notably, his "recruitment" activities, both for the *collégiale* and for his own ends, culminate in the ambiguous "savour of heresy or odor of sanctity" emanating from the château's chimney (GJ, 50; 63), and correspond to the war machine's constitution of a "smooth space" that the "nomad" occupies and holds. However, he does so not according to movement, but according to the nomadic traits of "immobility and speed, catatonia and rush, a 'stationary process' " (MPEng, 380–381; MPFr, 471–473).[11]

The smoke and odor that terrify Blanchet are but the exterior traces of this war machine's "becoming"—"spiritual voyages effected without relative movement, but in intensity, in one place" (MPEng, 381; MPFr, 473). From this open, smooth space of speed and distribution, of multiple sensorial assemblages (aural, visual, olfactory), Blanchet travels to the opposite pole, to the striated space par excellence of the *polis,* the city, in which "one closes off a surface and 'allocates' it according to determined intervals, assigned breaks" (MPEng, 481; MPFr, 600–601).

During his stay in Florence and his cultural initiation by the defrocked cleric, Francesco Prelati, Blanchet is dazed by the contrast between the poverty of his master's domain in the Vendée and the marvelous Florentine city space, striking for its own ascending, vertical "becoming," "that city, which at the time was a vast building site for palaces and churches with architects, painters and sculptors rushing hither and thither" (GJ, 54; 68). Furthermore, the splendor of the striated space encompasses another milieu of interiority, the spectacle of death "behind each tree, each street corner" (GJ, 58; 73), and this frightening, yet fascinating assemblage of graveyards, charnel houses, and gibbets inspires Prelati's mesmerizing exposition of his unorthodox religious and scientific views. For Prelati is inspired by the very abundance of riches and luxury around him to pursue "science, which opens all doors, all coffers, all safes" (GJ, 56; 70), in search of the "remedy for that purulent canker [of war, famine and epidemics]: gold." "Against mankind's moral wounds, the panacea is wealth," he tells Blanchet (GJ, 57; 72). And to Blanchet's horror, Prelati proclaims his faith in a new, quasi-mystical science: "If the good angel appeared on earth to cure all the wounds of body and soul, do you know what he would do? He would be an alchemical angel and manufacture gold!" (GJ, 57; 72). Referring to Florence's charnel houses and torture chambers, Prelati proclaims, "We must plunge, Father Blanchet, we must have the courage to plunge into the darkness in order to bring back light," and further claims that even the Devil "might have a purpose" (GJ, 59–60; 75). Moreover, Prelati's views on modern art resonate ominously with the "becomings" of Gilles de Rais, for Prelati extols the preeminence of anatomy, of the Tuscans' love of the skeleton, "and not only the skeleton, but also the muscles, the viscera, the entrails, the glands . . . and the blood, my dear father, the blood!" (GJ, 61–62; 78).[12]

Given his predilections, this curious prelate is uniquely prepared to receive the tale that Blanchet recounts of the particular "becoming" of his master: "He surrounds himself with extravagant luxury. He eats like a wolf. He drinks like a donkey . . . he dirties himself like a pig" (GJ, 63–64; 79–82). Prelati thus learns that Gilles's transformation following Jeanne's death was toward a "becoming-animal." Upon his return from Jeanne's execution in Rouen, Gilles's face was "bestial": "There was something wild about his features, almost the face of a werewolf" (GJ, 64; 81). Moreover, Prelati learns that Gilles's despair is not marked by weeping, that instead "he laughs, he roars like a wild beast. He rushes forward, driven by his passions, like a furious bull" (GJ, 65; 82). And Blanchet pleads, "Some use must be found for his strength, it must be given some direction, raised upward! Could you do that, François Prélat?" (GJ, 64–65; 82). But it is when Prelati learns all about Gilles's futile attempts "to force Jeanne's wandering soul" to return—first, embodied by a youthful actor in the Mystery of the Siege of Orleans commissioned by Gilles, then through his belief in the false Jeanne who subsequently appeared—that Prelati can admit, "I think I have understood the heart and soul of the Sire of Rais" (GJ, 68–69; 87). Blanchet concludes, "I am looking . . . I am looking for someone who can give him back a sense of direction. . . . How can I put it? Give him back the vertical, transcendent dimension that he lost when he lost Jeanne," a speech to which Prelati "listened with passionate attention, realizing the role that he might play in that man's destiny" (GJ, 64; 80).

Culled from, yet transformed by, the splendor and carnage of the Florentine striated space—"so filled with marvels, yet so repulsive by disease," says Blanchet (GJ, 71; 88)—Prelati's "science" is based on the ambiguity so fundamental to Tournier's nomadism that "the transcendent dimension is never presented as a realm of harmony and absolute justice in which earthly conflicts are resolved" (Davis 1988, 134). For Prelati maintains that "the light of heaven and the flames of hell are closer than is often thought," and that "man, steeped in mire, yet animated by the breath of God, needs an intercessor between God and himself . . . one who is his accomplice in all his evil thoughts and deeds, but one who also has entry to heaven" (GJ, 72; 89–90). Thus Prelati justifies his hermeneutic role by evoking man's need "to consult witches, to appeal to magi, to call up Beelzebub in magic circles," in order not only "to discover a truth," but also "to master that truth" (GJ, 73; 89–90). Despite Blanchet's protests against Prelati's modern science "nourished on blood and filth," the priest sadly admits that Prelati's description, "hands too strong, a head too weak," portrays exactly the childlike quality of Gilles begging forgiveness for his crimes (GJ, 73; 91). Prelati thus exults: "If there are crimes, we shall treat them with light! We shall see well enough what becomes of those swarming Gothic serpents when heated by the sunlight of Florence" (GJ, 74; 92). In other words, as a professional alchemist, he would offer to Gilles a horizontal science affirming "a 'more' or an excess, and lodg[ing] itself in that excess, that deviation" (MPEng, 370; MPFr, 459), a scientific field of smooth space whose heterogeneity and multiplicity relate directly to Prelati's insistence on the benefits of his practice: "Have gold, more gold, and yet more gold and all the rest will be given unto you, genius and talent, beauty and nobility, glory and pleasure, and even, by some incredible paradox, disinterest, generosity and charity!" (GJ, 56; 70).

NOMADIC SCIENCE

The tale's fourth segment thus commences with the return of Blanchet and Prelati to the smooth, horizontal space constituted by Gilles's war machine in the Vendée countryside, a space now set for the development of a horizontal, "nomad science" opposed to the royal science's practice of "reproduction, iteration and reiteration" (MPEng, 372; MPFr, 460). The alternate model, as Deleuze and Guattari describe it, "consists in being distributed by turbulence across a smooth space, in producing a movement that holds space and simultaneously affects all of its points, instead of being held by space in a local movement from one specified point to another" (MPEng, 363; MPFr, 449–450). This model suggests an alternate "scientific procedure," an "itineration" based not on reproducing, but on "following":

> One is obliged to follow when one is in search of the "singularities" of a matter, or rather of a material, and not out to discover a form; when one escapes the force of gravity to enter a field of celerity; when one ceases to contemplate the course of a laminar flow in a determinate direction, to be carried away by a vortical flow; when one engages in a continuous variation of variables, instead of extracting constants from them, etc. (MPEng, 372; MPFr, 461)[13]

All of these traits—the quest for "singularities" of matter, the field of celerity, the vortical flow, and the continuous variation of variables—characterize the alchemical "ambulant or itinerant science" that Prelati exercises outside the purview of "the reproductive royal sciences"; he will function as "a type of ambulant scientist whom State scientists are forever fighting or integrating or allying with" (MPEng, 373; MPFr 462). Deleuze and Guattari describe this "'savant' of nomad science" as "caught between a rock and a hard place, between the war machine that nourishes and inspires them"—that is, Prelati's and Gilles de Rais's nomadic pursuit of his particular mode of "becoming"—"and the State that imposes upon them an order of reasons" (MPEng, 362; MPFr, 448)—an apparatus dominated by feudal and religious absolutism.

At the château of Tiffauges, Prelati assures Gilles that the cost of revealing the "truths that were once unspoken" will be "whatever price they are worth. . . . An infinite price!" (GJ, 77; 96). But first the cleric must understand more fully the space into which he has ventured, the men who "were little more human than the forest that hemmed them in on every side" (GJ, 76; 94). Thus, as Prelati encounters the male court with which Gilles surrounds himself, he is dazzled at the spectacle of this "animal brutality and innocence," and wonders, "How can I convert all that brute force to my subtle ends?" (GJ, 79–80; 99–100), that is, how can he transform the raw material of this war machine according to the variable precepts of a nomadic science. Prelati accompanies Gilles and his henchmen on their nomadic hunting trips in order to discover "the key to that desolate land that he had been seeking since his arrival" (GJ, 82; 102–103). Prelati is astonished by the striated confines of the "huge Gaulish forests," and especially by "that huge ballroom chimney in which whole tree trunks burnt" (GJ, 82; 103). However, standing on the dunes overlooking the smooth space of the storm-swept sea, from which Gilles seems to derive particular strength and inspiration, Prelati realizes that "the ocean represented the tool, the weapon that he now had in his hands. . . . He now knew the direction of his mission: to touch with an ardent hand the purulent wound of that country and force it to rise, to stand up" (GJ, 82–83; 103).

Here the narrator plays on multiple perspectives to point out the manner in which Prelati would henceforth lead Gilles into new "becomings": first, the narrator suggests that "Blanchet was not entirely wrong in thinking that Prelati would influence his master in the direction of the sacred. That was certainly how the Tuscan adventurer conceived his role at the court of the Seigneur de Rais" (GJ, 83; 103). Then, the narrator renders his own judgment of the ambiguous "becoming" that will unfold:

> But Prelati was quite incapable of imagining the terrible course that this salvation would take. Gilles, stunned by Jeanne's execution, dragged himself along the ground like an animal. Prelati would raise him up, but only to encourage him in the diabolical vocation to which Gilles believed himself to have been called ever since Jeanne had been found guilty of the sixteen charges. (GJ, 83; 104)[14]

To succeed in his task, "the Florentine used everything he could lay his hands on," particularly his understanding of Gilles's taste for young boys, "to convince his master that only a curtain of flames separated him from heaven and that the alchemical science alone could enable him to cross it" (GJ, 86; 107). In the heights of the alchemical laboratory in the attic of the château, Prelati and Gilles explore what Deleuze and Guattari call the "ambulant science," "the connection between content and expression in themselves, each of these two terms encompassing form and matter," a matter "essentially laden with singularities (which constitute a form of content)," and an expression "inseparable from pertinent traits (which constitute a matter of expression)" (MPEng, 369; MPFr, 457). Tournier writes that for "the pilgrim of the sky—as the searching alchemist is called" (GJ, 87; 108), the scientific experiments with "the fundamental ambiguity of fire, which is both life and death, purity and passion, sanctity and damnation" (GJ, 87; 108), are "an art as much as a technique" (MPEng, 369; MPFr, 457), resulting in "the phenomenon of inversion, as an excess of cold causes a burning, or as the paroxysm of love merges with hate," an inversion either benign or malign (GJ, 87; 108). Such a process, declares Prelati, explains Jeanne's destiny, her agony at the stake having been "the zero level at which a benign transmutation was to begin," preceding her eventual rehabilitation, beatification, and canonization; "but the trial by fire was the ineluctable pivot of this change of direction" (GJ, 88; 109). It is thus to the hunger of Barron, one of Satan's lieutenants, that Gilles must henceforth sacrifice the children so that their flesh might "open up . . . the incandescent gates of hell" (GJ, 88; 110). Says Prelati, "Instead of degrading yourself with them, you will save yourself and them with you. You will descend, like Jeanne, to the bottom of the burning pit, and you will rise again, like her, in a radiant light!" (GJ, 90; 111–112).

THE "APPARATUS OF CAPTURE"

These "sublime labours of transmutation" (GJ, 90; 112) are short-lived, however. One cause of this brevity is the fundamental ambiguity of Prelati's "art," the uncontrollable nature of the malign inversion "because of the interdependence of malign and benign . . . that already coincide in the same state and the same actions" (Davis 1988, 133–134). Moreover, this "accursed game" also causes a ripple effect as "sinister rumors traveled across the country" (GJ, 90; 112), and eventually the weight of the feudal and religious State apparatus crashes down on the experiments of Gilles and Prelati. Initially threatened by a surprise visit to Tiffauges by the calculating Dauphin Louis and his court, Gilles finds his transgressions brought to the attention of his peers by an infraction against the feudal code, his commission of public sacrilege in the church of Saint-Etienne-de-Mermorte. Then, besieged in his castle of Machecoul, abandoned by all his henchmen, Gilles surrenders to the troops representing both arms of the State structure, those of Jean V, duke of Brittany, and those of Jean de Malestroit, bishop of Nantes. Thus the "apparatus of capture" comes to bear on Gilles not only because of the public rumors regarding murder, sodomy, and devil worship, but because of "what was really at stake—that immense fortune, those fortresses, those lands, all that countless loot! It was high-flying banditry, with a regal quarry on which all the great wild beasts of the region were converging!" (GJ, 99–100; 122–123). In response to the forty-nine articles of indictment, Gilles attacks the judges in a similar vein: "All of you here present care not a fig for crimes and heresies. . . . What is at stake is the immense loot that your quivering nostrils can scent" (GJ, 103; 127). That is, the "outside thought" and "becomings" of Gilles's nomadic pursuit provide the pretext for a quite literal reterritorialization of the feudal domain from which Gilles drew his strength, but in support of which he was impelled toward the "ambulant," alchemical quest for gold.

Thus, the final segment, nearly one-third of the tale, presents a complex and ambiguous dénouement to this destiny. On one level, excerpts from the trial and testimony of witnesses, henchmen, the savant Prelati, and finally the master Gilles de Rais, provide gruesome details of the latter's crimes, while revealing both the limits that the State apparatus must impose on such an excentric war machine and the means of this appropriation or "capture" by the State. On another level, the accomplishment of the State's royal "unity of composition," of "interior essence" (MPEng, 427; MPFr, 532), is effected thanks to Gilles's willingness now to pursue his nomadic quest of "inversion" via the paths of interiority. For, as Deleuze and Guattari insist, "the State cannot effect a capture unless what is captured . . . escapes under new forms, as towns or war machines" (MPEng, 435; MPFr, 542). On the one hand, the extensive representation of detailed testimony in these four short, but intense chapters provides an example of the open and explicit ceremony through which the secular and clerical will was exercised, a ceremony that preceded the veiling of confessional questions after the Middle Ages.[15] On the other hand, through this same confessional process, Gilles undergoes a penultimate sequence of "becomings": first, he is the "great lord, haughty, violent and relaxed" (GJ, 101; 125)—the mask of his earliest incarnation before encountering Jeanne d'Arc. Then, when confronted with the threat of excommunication (GJ, 105–106; 129–131), he appears as "a desperate wretch, both bestial and puerile, clinging to all those whom he believed could bring him help and safety" (GJ, 101; 125)—the mask of himself after

Jeanne's execution. Finally, having confessed to his crimes and submitted to his accusers, Gilles "stood, stiff and motionless as a statue, through the endless procession of witnesses" (GJ, 108; 134), but also definitively "inhabited by the memory of Jeanne" thanks to which he "went to the stake as a Christian, radiantly at peace with himself and his God" (GJ, 101; 125).

Thus, to evince the "power of metamorphosis" of war machines, which "allows them to be captured by States, but also to resist that capture and rise up again in other forms, with other 'objects' besides war" (MPEng, 437; MPFr, 545), Gilles must avoid excommunication so that his quest for ascension through conflagration can attain its ultimate goal. Confronted by this threat, Gilles reverts to an apparently childlike innocence, exclaiming, "'You have no right! The Church is my mother! I appeal to my mother! . . . I have no wish to be left out in the cold far from my mother's bosom. Help! Help!' And he dashed over towards his judges and threw himself, weeping, into Malestroit's arms" (GJ, 105–106; 131). So, his subsequent submission consists of an apparently sincere, but nonetheless strategic, confession of his crimes so that the decree of excommunication might be lifted:

> "For my part I recognize the absolute truth of the appalling evidence brought against me. . . . I beseech you to impose without weakness or delay the heaviest possible penalty, convinced as I am that it will still be too light for my infamy. But, at the same time, I beg you to pray ardently for me and, if your charity is capable of it, to love me as a mother loves the most wretched of her children." (GJ, 107; 132–133)

As Prelati explains the principles of nomadic "science" before the tribunal, his apparently blasphemous interpretations of Scriptures, and of Gilles's destiny, still command attention, for "these theologians, great lovers of subtle disputes, could not but cock their ears." To submit Gilles to a "benign inversion, like the one that transmutes ignoble lead into gold," says Prelati, would result in his "becoming a saint of light." For the "malign inversion," that is, Gilles's "crimes under the invocation of the devil," would lead directly to the "right path" of the benign (GJ, 119–120; 147–148):

> "Who knows whether, one day, the witch of Rouen will not be rehabilitated, washed of all accusation, honored and celebrated? Who can say whether, one day, she will not be canonized at the court of Rome, the little shepherdess of Domrémy? St. Jeanne! What light will then not fall upon Gilles de Rais, who always followed her like a shadow? And who can say whether, in this same movement, we shall not also venerate her faithful companion: St. Gilles de Rais?" (GJ, 121; 149)

This faith in the ultimate "becoming" of his "nomad love" is carried serenely by Gilles to the pyre, as he exhorts his henchmen, "I shall precede you, therefore, to the gate of heaven. Follow me in my salvation, as you have followed me in my crimes" (GJ, 123; 152), and finally evokes his guiding light, amid the flames, "a celestial cry that echoed like a distant bell: 'Jeanne! Jeanne! Jeanne!' " (GJ, 124; 152).

Thus, that "the crimes of Gilles de Rais are neither explained nor justified by Prelati's most bold hypotheses concerning the convertibility of Evil into Good" hardly qualifies *Gilles and Jeanne* as a failure (Davis 1988, 134). For the ambiguity, paradox, indeed the undecidability for which Davis criticizes this text are, in fact, a significant mark of the tale's powerful complexity. What Davis calls the "core of *Gilles and Jeanne*," "the unsolved but urgent enigma of ethical limits and the limits of ethics" (Davis 1988, 134), is the perpetually recurring dilemma of our own century as well, one that has spawned more than its share of bloodthirsty "ogres." But the ethical ambiguity in Tournier's tale extends beyond malevolent individual *illuminés* to apply as well to the State apparatus, to its justice *in extremis*. Indeed, Gilles's condemnation of his judges—"You have negotiated the buying of this or that parcel of my goods on fabulously profitable terms. No, you are not judges: you are debtors. I am not a defendant: I am a creditor" (GJ, 103; 127)—recalls the (post)modern conundrum of the demand for individual "ethical limits" within institutional apparatuses that reveal themselves so frequently to be indifferent, at best, to observing any such limits. As Rosello concludes quite succinctly, "Tournier's *récit* thus causes to appear (and perhaps to denounce) all forms of violence and to show that sometimes, Christian justice and the judiciary system, as they are used in a period of 'delirium,' are basically not different from the most brutal primitive sacrifice" (1989, 94; my translation). Whether the result of individual violence or State-sanctioned operations of "capture," the ethical uncertainty that Tournier maintains, and the limits of such ethics that he questions in *Gilles and Jeanne*, are part of our own limits and uncertainties, both scriptural and existential.

Throughout this analysis, I have tried to indicate the focal elements for a reading along nomadological lines. I have emphasized the key oscillations between the sovereign/State apparatus—its military and religious appropriation of the war machine by "royal science" and "law"—and the excentric forces of metamorphoses, of "becomings" of the war machine and its traits of speed, "smooth space," and "ambulant science" inspired by the initial "nomad love." Such an appropriation becomes necessary whenever the war machine is developed not through a "line of destruction" (with war as its object), but rather through "the drawing of a creative line of flight, the composition of a smooth space and of the movement of people in that space" (MPEng, 422; MPFr 526). While Gilles de Rais's quest required inhuman cruelty and destructive brutality, this desire, say Deleuze and Guattari, "has nothing to do with a natural or spontaneous determination; there is no desire but assembling, assembled, desire" (MPEng, 399; MPFr, 497). Gilles's goals as well as Prelati's were always "beyond" the appropriation or "capture" characteristic of the State apparatus and its science. However abominable the effects of their practice, they functioned in a regime of strategic affects, "the active discharge of emotion, the counterattack, . . . projectiles just like weapons" (MPEng, 400; MPFr 498).

For this "beyond"—in Gilles's case, toward ascension and *dépassement* into sanctity via the necessarily limited, barbaric tools at his disposal—is extolled by the same State apparatus that arrests (and yet, ironically, helps realize) his path toward "becoming." As Deleuze and Guattari argue, "There is a relation between the affect and the weapon, as witnessed not only in mythology, but also in the *chanson de geste,* and the chivalric novel or novel of courtly love" (MPEng, 400; MPFr, 498), even of the nomadic kind. This "becoming" is a movement toward the smooth space of a nomad horizon of "flight" (in sainthood or in damnation), and this spiritual and existential decoding is inevitably overcoded and captured by and within the boundaries of the State hierarchies. As I hope I have made clear, then, the remythologizing that Tournier effectuates on the story of Gilles and Jeanne lends itself, in turn, to textual "animation" that reveals itself as much a rereading as a rewriting. That is, like Tournier's own work, an "animation" is necessarily compelled by desire, "assembling" nomadological connections between points, always intermezzo, seeking the metamorphoses of the Deleuzian "bitter novelty."

7
OF *HECCÉITÉS* AND *RITOURNELLES*
"SPACES OF AFFECT" AND THE CAJUN DANCE ARENA

PROLOGUE: MEMOIRS OF A DANCER

> That night I dreamed of South Louisiana, of
> blue herons standing among flooded cypress
> trees, fields of sugarcane beaten with purple
> and gold light in the fall, the smell of
> smoldering hickory and pork dripping into the
> ash in our smokehouse, the way billows of fog
> rolled out the swamp in the morning, so thick
> and white that sound—a bass flopping, a
> bullfrog falling off a log into the water—came
> to you inside a wet bubble. . . .
>
> *–James Lee Burke,* Black Cherry Blues *(1989)*

In this chapter, I turn to Deleuze and Guattari's concepts of
the "minor" and "deterritorialization," proposed initially in
their "literary" analysis of Kafka's works, in order to situate
these and other concepts in relation to sociocultural intersections. To do so, I develop an animation of concepts derived
from *A Thousand Plateaus, heccéités* and *ritournelles,* within the
context of Cajun dance and music spaces. I first consider
popular representations of Cajun music and dance spaces;
then, the traditional thematics of the Cajun music repertoire
in relation to more recent compositions; and, finally, the

reconstitution of "spaces of affect" within Cajun dance arenas. In this way, I reflect on the ways in which lines between "minor" and "major" cultures shift and even disappear through complex processes of cultural "de-" and "reterritorializations."

In the months before I first set foot on a Cajun dance floor, the names "Beausoleil" and "Maple Leaf" appeared in the events listing of the weekly *Lagniappe* (the New Orleans activities supplement to the *Times-Picayune* newspaper) like something at once joyous and forbidding. What would the Maple Leaf bar, situated in an obscure neighborhood in uptown New Orleans, be like? Who would be there? What kind of crowd would the Cajun band Beausoleil attract? What kind of music would be played? And how would I, could I, respond? During the years that followed, I would learn the answers to these and many other questions, not only with Beausoleil, but especially with Filé, at the Maple Leaf bar every Thursday night, and for a while, Wayne Toups and ZydeCajun across the river in Algiers. But it was Beausoleil that kept drawing me, and so many others, back to that narrow, crowded dance floor.

The last time I spent with Beausoleil before I moved north, I mostly stood on the benches along the walls, at once gazing and listening while surrounded by the melodious sounds and intense movement of dancing bodies below. Leaning against the wall behind the sound board, gripping a Dixie beer, I enjoyed watching the band rip out one tune after another to the quivering, stationary mass of standees jostling up front for position and perhaps for an occasional glimpse of the band, while the dancers maneuvered alongside one another at their own peril much further back. And yet, I saw all this less than I felt it, the space and its/my shifting feelings engulfing me as much as any well-executed dance turn or accordion solo.

When the band reached the final number before the break, I descended with my partner into this near frenzied tumult, to become immersed in the sweat and heat, to feel the menacingly slick floor beneath us, to discover yet again, despite or maybe through, the forced proximity of the crowd, a wonderful synchrony of movement, sound, and story sung in the plaintive tones of the Cajun French idiom.

*   *   *

It is another night at the Maple Leaf, this time on a balmy New Year's Eve with Dewey Balfa and his band performing. Given the holiday eve, the crowd contained many regular dancers seeking celebration in a familiar milieu, as well as assorted merrymakers who were unfamiliar with the site, but open to all possibilities. Doing a great job filling the "Guy Lombardo" role, Dewey Balfa was, as ever, an ambassador of Cajun music providing a gentle narration that wove one song to the next and welcomed all the dancers and spectators in to the dance/music dialogue. As the evening unfolded toward the new year, we spontaneously became a community of dancers in growing harmony with the movement from waltz to two-step and with the messages that Balfa and his musicians joyfully and plaintively expressed in each song.

*   *   *

On a hot weekend in early June, the morning humidity in Mamou promises a familiar Louisiana late spring day. Like every year at this time, the weather is bright, with only the occasional cloud. The villagers of Mamou have been preparing their annual Cajun music festival for months. We arrive Friday night for the community ceremony and evening dance. The festival queen, who must be sixty-five or older, is crowned after demonstrating the requisite skills: dancing a waltz and a two-step, and reciting a recipe and telling a joke in Cajun French. We dance throughout the evening under the stars to the sounds of Marc and Ann Savoy, their smiling, celebratory renditions becoming more and more excited as the hours (and the years) flow by.

It is Saturday's day-long event, though, that the celebrants await most eagerly. Many people, especially the seniors, arrive early to stake out their sites near the dance floor by means of strategic placement of lawn chairs. As the sun and heat rise in tandem, the dancers waltz, two-step, and jitterbug around the wooden platform that passes for a dance floor. Styles (of dance, of clothes) clash and collide between locals and visitors from near and far, but also eventually manage to merge on the dance floor. The music remains steadfastly "traditional" since the sounds of the blues, rock, and country are banned by the festival organizers. Meanwhile, on the fringe of the crowd, competitive events take place—sack races and the egg toss for children; arm wrestling, *boudin* eating, and beer drinking for adults—while the pungent odors of the locally prepared foods waft in all directions.

*   *   *

It is a frigid late December night in the western Chicago suburbs. We had spent several hours during the afternoon applying a hair dryer to the door locks on our car so that we could drive to Fitzgerald's in Berwyn where Beausoleil will play two sets to what we hoped would be a sparse crowd that might allow plenty of room for dancing. Instead, we find a packed house, with the vast majority of patrons attending as observers, onlookers, in no way interested in making room for dancing.

As strangers to the suburb and to the Cajun music-as-concert scene, we feel distanced from the surroundings, apprehensive about what might follow. Indeed, during the first set—an amazingly short sixty minutes of well-performed, but fairly uninspired music—we and the few scattered couples on the floor have to struggle to make a space to dance, at times hurling our bodies against static onlookers. But during the break, as the crowd thins out somewhat, we converse with our fellow dancers, exchange stories, and discover that there is even a "Chicago Cajun Connection" newsletter and a home-grown Chicago Cajun band that holds regular *fais dodos* (Cajun music and dance parties).

Then, during the second set, we are able to coalesce with each other's movements and with the music, exchanging partners and even inviting new partners from the crowd. Gradually, we gain ground both spatially and affectively, so that nearly everyone in the audience is either dancing or at least moving to the beat. Beausoleil's second set lasts well over an hour, and when they return to the closing ovation, they provide an exuberant forty-five-minute encore. When we depart late that night to our home five hours away, we do so with a handful of names and addresses, and invitations to return to Chicago with a place to stay for the next Cajun music/dance event.

SPACES OF AFFECT

> Since Orpheus, we know we must never turn back to look at what we love, or risk destroying it.
>
> *–Roland Barthes,* Critical Essays *(1964)*

Forms and Feeling

During the mid- to late 1980s, an exotic, yet confused mix of things Cajun and Creole became "hot," in the senses both of spicy and popular, most notably in cuisine and music. Blending conjoined, though distinct traditions—the fast-paced zydeco music of Afro-Caribbean origins with the more rustic Cajun musical sounds—various corporations vied during the decade's final years to employ rhythms and images ostensibly inspired by these traditions to advertise products as diverse as motor vehicles, fast food, laundry detergent, and potato chips. While this trend still lingers in the 1990s (e.g., in the form of ads for Maalox, apparently set in an appropriately spicy Louisiana locale), that it had run its course became fairly evident in the mercifully short-lived TV series "Broken Badges" (Fall 1990) in which a New Orleans–Cajun detective named Beau Jean (played by Miguel Ferrer) was displaced to southern California to add linguistic exoticism and leadership of sorts to an undercover team of occupationally handicapped police officers. Despite such dilution and distortion of ethnic identities in the mass media, a concurrent movement of affirmation, begun in the 1960s, developed quietly, yet forcefully in southern Louisiana through the efforts of creative and innovative indigenous Louisiana artists in diverse forms of musical and dance expression.

The focus of this chapter is the manner in which Cajun identities in their multiplicity emerge in the dynamic and creative exchange between Cajun musicians and their fans. The preceding "memoirs" offer some reflections on my participation in dance arenas animated by different Cajun bands. I understand these vignettes as serving, first, to present some of the experiences of one observer-participant and unabashed fan who remains enthralled by the dynamic music/dance interchange constitutive of what I call "spaces of affect." With this term, I wish to express and explore the transformation of Cajun dance arenas by the fleeting, yet intense circulation of "feeling" evoked through the evolving music and dance forms that participants perform therein.[1] Second, these "memoirs" introduce the intersection of dancers' and spectators' practices that contribute to producing such feelings, and indicate the extent to which spectators are as much involved in the "affective security" of the dancer–musician interchange as these performers themselves (Hanna 1979, 27).[2] Third, these vignettes begin to suggest the fluid "borders" that constitute such sites and experiences. The most obvious "border" involves the spectators' relation to the dancers, on the edge of the floor, yet engulfed and united by the all-encompassing music/dance expression. Other "borders" include the different geographical locales in which these music/dance events occur, and the cultural "landscapes," that is, the "spaces of affect," that are created wherever Cajun music and dance are performed: rural bars in Acadiana (the Cajun region stretching across southern Louisiana from the Texas border to just west of New Orleans); dance-music restaurants in Acadiana and in "the City" (New Orleans) itself; and local events, such as concerts and festivals, large and small, held throughout southern Louisiana and across the United States and beyond, devoted to the different expressions of Cajun music.

These affective profiles thus serve to frame a brief explanation of the theoretical model at the base of this study. I employ the formulation "spaces of affect" as a means to conceptualize both the "forms" characterizing diverse modes of collective assemblage, and the "feelings" evoked through these various "forms." Just as dancers perform waltzes and two-steps as couples in variable response to the anticipated musical performance, the musicians prepare in each venue to provide a musical support in expectation of the physical, that is, performative dance demands that audiences produce. I am interested in considering several intersections of Cajun music/dance forms: how particular music/dance arenas invite and, in some ways, construct gatherings of particular assemblages of musicians and dancers/spectators; how the artistic expression enhances these forms within different venues; how these forms place participants, musicians, and dancers/fans alike into active, performative dialogue; and how these forms and expressions thereby create a unique "structure of feeling,"[3] a "space of affect" that may vary as event from one venue to another, but is no less important, even vital, for the appreciation by all participants.

These same experiences contribute, moreover, to producing the often contradictory and conflicting preferences among musicians and fans toward actual musical and dance practices. I understand these artistic expressions and responses to them as implicated in the ever-present "instability of the frontiers" determined by complex conditions of the surrounding sociopolitical (hegemonic) formation (Laclau and Mouffe 1985, 136). This instability produces, in turn, shifting modes of both the self-representation and the specificity of Cajun identities. Notably, with the integrity of an inherited tradition of music and dance perceived as "threatened" by the influences of innovative, contemporary music and dance forms, some fans tend to resist such "innovation" by seeking to "preserve" what they understand as originary and authentic forms. At the same time, however, many entrepreneurs and cultural revivalists have successfully exploited the increasing demand inside as well as "outside" Louisiana for cultural forms that showcase "Cajun identity" (Ancelet 1992). Recalling Lipsitz's reminder about popular culture, that "hegemony is not just imposed on society from the top; it is struggled for from below" (1990, 15), we can understand why the very efforts to accommodate such demands participate in the shifting construction of such "identity" by themselves extending and influencing the processes of cultural representation.

Following an initial section in which I provide a brief narrative of the origins of the French Cajuns of southern Louisiana, I proceed to an examination of movement and affect in the Cajun dance arena. I suggest that we try to understand this process in both dialogical and dialectical terms based on the "objective social locations" of these cultural identities, an approach that might enable us "to see experience as a source of both real knowledge and social mystification" (Mohanty 1993, 54). To consider how the modes of representation previously examined are manifested in the realm of Cajun dance, I study the dance/music relationship as an "affective economy" (Grossberg 1988, 285) by drawing upon and extending the conception of the "thisness" of events that Gilles Deleuze and Félix Guattari call "haecceities" (ATP, 260–262; MP, 318–320). I also describe the constitution of "thisness" in the (music/dance) event in terms of the *ritournelle* (recurring) aspect of the Cajun dance/music interchange, drawing examples from selected recordings and from videotapes now available commercially or from folklore researchers (see Severn 1991). My purpose is to study the means by which the repetition of themes, images, and cadences creates a "rhythm" that underlies the specific "event" of the Cajun "dance arena," and in doing so, to establish a bridge between the music repertoire understood as oral text communicated musically and the lively dialogue engaged through the dance response to this music.[4]

Global and Local Relations

I believe that establishing the contrast of different and repeatedly created "spaces of affect" helps us to situate both the diverse responses from fans, dancers, and musicians to (Cajun) musical innovation and the conflicts to which innovations and resultant responses give rise. These "spaces" also provide a broad framework for understanding the apparent contradiction of musicians' search for renewal beyond the local, often quite strict, demands of respect for a particular heritage. For such tensions regarding self-representation and creative innovation are, in fact, those that arise for any ethnic minority that perceives its cultural identity as beset, distorted, and diminished in relation to more dominant cultural forces.[5] Moreover, this chapter draws connections between Deleuze–Guattarian concepts and recent work in critical theory, notably the area of scholarly inquiry known broadly as "cultural studies."[6] Consulting *Cultural Studies* (Grossberg, Nelson, and Treichler 1992), the collection of essays that, in many ways, "defines" this field, albeit quite broadly, one can glean some understanding of the concepts that structure this volume, and especially the focal importance of the intersection between the "global" and the "local." I understand this distinction as operating in the *Cultural Studies* volume in terms of particular "practices": on the one hand, the focus on "global" (national or multinational) hegemonic "practices" and structures that overshadow and even threaten regional and specific activities and expressions; on the other hand, the focus on the "local" as possible modes of resistance to such "global" practices, that is, local expressions that by their very existence and continuing transmission can offer living contradictions to the often homogenizing effect of "global" assimilation.

Taken conceptually, however, we can also envisage the "global"/"local" dyad in a concomitant fashion: while the former term may point to broadly applicable theoretical tools that can engage critically the diverse facets of specific, everyday practices within "local" sites, the latter, pointing to "local exigencies and political demands," may tend to underestimate "the values of the lines linking the various sites of cultural studies" (Grossberg 1993, 3). In regards to the *Cultural Studies* volume, one could argue that whatever the methodological, disciplinary, and even political differences between the volume's various contributors, there exists a consistent, if usually implicit, negotiation of the "global"/"local" dyad in both senses that I have suggested. Such a negotiation helps us to clarify the sources of tensions inherent to the otherwise elusively defined field of "cultural studies," the "global" taken as both totalizing danger and critical potential that intersects with "local" practices and circumspection in possibly enlivening and possibly threatening ways.[7] Indeed, as Grossberg argues, "If the relation between the global and [the] local is itself an articulated one, with each existing in and constituting the other, cultural studies needs to map the lines connecting them" (1993, 3). Reflecting on this same conjuncture, Michael Bérubé concludes that in engaging in "cultural studies," "one has to negotiate a busy, Bakhtinian intersection of competing sociolects—where the lived subjectivities of ordinary people stand, ideally, in a mutually transformative relation to theories about the lived subjectivities of ordinary people" (1994, 166).

As a scholar of French culture attempting to understand "cultural studies" within the context of poststructuralist theories and their relation to Francophone studies, I read the *Cultural Studies* volume and related discussions with special interest. For, upon consulting the volume's essays and especially its index in some detail, I confirmed a long-held suspicion regarding an apparently "global" assumption for undertaking the examination of "local" practices. With the exception of the essays written by Meaghan Morris (1992) and Elspeth Probyn (1992), this large volume totally ignores the corpus of works by Gilles Deleuze and Félix Guattari. This refusal to heed the Deleuze–Guattarian view implicitly points to the practical limitations imposed on certain voices of poststructuralist theory for critically approaching the "local." Such a limitation might well lead one to conclude, for example, that the Deleuze–Guattari critical corpus is of no utility whatsoever in "cultural studies" research. Without denying the possible "danger," notably the risk of totalizing effects on particular "local" practices, posed by the complex conceptual terminology developed throughout the Deleuze–Guattari corpus, I wish to challenge both the general limitation and this particular conclusion in terms of the "global"/"local" dyad. By employing two complementary "global" concepts proposed in *A Thousand Plateaus* as theoretical tools for examining specific "local" practices, I will first argue that these tools provide purchase for defining and understanding a specific set of folkloric interests and pursuits. I will then propose these terms and analyses as a way of beginning to redress what Jody Berland has identified as a limitation of discussion of cultural technologies, music "rarely conceived spatially . . . in relation to the changing production of spaces for listeners" (in Grossberg, Nelson, and Treichler 1992, 39). These analyses will enable me, I hope, to envisage "cultural studies" as a means of straddling a zone "in-between" the "local" and the "global" by functioning as a "territorial-izing machine" that "attempts to map the sorts of places people can occupy and how they can occupy them" (Grossberg 1993, 15), in terms of their possibilities for investment, empowerment, and even resistance.

Cultural Origins

As background for this analysis, I wish to present a brief account of the process of globalization and reterritorialization within the cultural forms that I will subsequently discuss. To consider issues of the French and Acadian origins within southern Louisiana, one must distinguish the original European explorers and founders of the Louisiana Territory from the subsequent waves of settlers who had previously emigrated to *Acadie* (Nova Scotia) in Canada during the seventeenth century, and who were subsequently forced to resettle elsewhere a century later. French explorers founded Louisiana in 1682. The contested term *Creole* refers to the native-born descendants of these first French settlers (as distinct from French immigrants), as well as to the descendants of slaves of Afro-Caribbean origin born in Louisiana.[8] By the middle of the eight-eenth century, New Orleans had developed into an important urban center "with a population of political and military officials who, along with the more successful merchants and merchant/planters from the Mississippi River settlements above and below the city, constituted the upper echelons of an increasingly stratified social order" (Dormon 1983, 19). The outlands of the colony, its woods, swamps, bayous, and prairies, however, were sparsely populated, and thus this French Catholic colony with land available for expansion had much to offer Francophone migrants.

In fact, unbeknownst to them, the Acadian ancestors of the popula-tion later known as "Cajuns" would soon need just such a site. For after the English colonization of French Canada in the early eighteenth century, the descendants of the settlers in *Acadie* refused to forswear their Catholic faith and pledge allegiance to the British king. So, following decades of tension between Protestant British military authorities and the French-speaking Catholic population, the Nova Scotian governor Charles Lawrence took steps in 1754 and 1755 to isolate and then expel the *Acadiens* from the Bay of Fundy region. Lawrence ordered a mass deportation that has come to be known as "Le Grand Dérangement" (the Great Upheaval). After several decades of wandering along various circui-tous routes, most of the expelled *Acadiens* and resettled in southern Louisiana between 1765 and 1785.[9] Meanwhile, a change of administra-tion had taken place in the Louisiana colony: in 1763 the Treaty of Paris brought an end to the French and Indian War and shifted Louisiana to

Spanish control. Spain would govern the area until 1803, when it returned briefly to French control before it was sold to the United States.

The *Acadien* refugees were welcomed by the Spanish, however, for the products of their farming and cattle-raising would eventually provide the New Orleans area with sustenance and economic development that were sorely needed. But, in return for Spanish land grants upon arrival, the refugees had to accept assignment to specific regions, specifically to the southwestern prairies of the Opelousas and Attakapas areas west of the Atchafalaya River, and to the forests and bayous of the Mississippi River of the Cabannocé area to the west and southwest of New Orleans. As Brasseaux explains, despite the geographical differences of the sites, the original settlers experienced similar problems "often linked to a rapidly expanding population—epidemic disease and the growing scarcity of arable land—as well as the inevitable clashes between the exiles and neighboring sociocultural groups, particularly the long-established and aristocratic Creoles" (1987, 114). Thus, the groups of settlers remained aloof from the French Creoles, yet through trade and other encounters, they often intermarried with their rural neighbors, including Creoles of Afro-Caribbean descent. The mostly rural *Acadiens*, whose name evolved by deformation to *Cajuns*, adapted well and quickly in their new environment. Some prospered to the point that by the end of the eighteenth century slaveholding became an accepted practice for those realizing "that development of a habitation from commercial agriculture required amounts of labor far beyond the capacity of the family labor pool" (Brasseaux 1987, 193). This prosperity continued unabated throughout the nineteenth century, but because of the Civil War, most of their socioeconomic structures collapsed and were not rebuilt until well into the next century. The Cajuns' subsequent assimilation to American culture occurred quite slowly until after World War II, then accelerated with exposure to cultural and technological influences from outside the region.[10]

The development of Cajun music is directly related to the spaces in which social gatherings took place in the rural communities, especially the *bals de maison* (house dances) held regularly in the homes of individuals. Although the Acadian refugees arrived without instruments and their musicians had to mime fiddle sounds, "by the late 1770s most of the fiddlers had achieved a comfortable existence and enjoyed the leisure time to make, or the financial resources to purchase, new instruments" (Brasseaux 1987, 147). A tradition developed following the dictum "After a week of hard work follows a night of hard play," with local musicians providing the rhythms in the limited dance space, and a common meal and refreshments were shared by all participants. In these *bals de maison* (also known as the *fais dodo* in reference to the children encouraged by parents to sleep ["fais dodo"] in the "cry room" near the dance floor), Cajun families socialized, young men and women courted, and the musicians and dancers honed their skills. Eventually this tradition extended beyond the private homes to dances held in public halls. Cajun music is a complex blend of German, Spanish, Scottish, Irish, Anglo-American, Afro-Caribbean, and Native American influences with a base of French and French Acadian folk traditions; indeed, it is what Louisianans would call "un vrai gumbo."[11]

In the late 1920s, recording began to extend the music of southern Louisiana, especially through radio shows. The first recording, "Allons à Lafayette," was made in 1928 by Joseph and Cleoma Falcon. Over the next thirty years, the fortunes of Cajun music were linked to successive waves of musical influences that usually overwhelmed the rural form, for example, Nashville and Texas country swing and big band influences in the 1930s. Indeed, Cajun music was relegated to a distinctly secondary position as rural clubs provided the styles drawn from other regions (Texas) and national trends (swing bands) that would attract more customers. This diminishment of the region's forms was buttressed by state legislation forbidding Cajuns from speaking French in schools (see Daigle 1972/1987, 65–67). Despite the generally dismissive attitude toward the traditional music (evident in its derogatory appellation, "chank-a-chank"), with the return of GIs to Louisiana following World War II came a slow but growing interest in this music, thanks especially to compositions for and revival of the accordion by musicians such as Iry Lejeune and Nathan Abshire, and to efforts by Floyd Soileau to provide Cajun music recordings on the Swallow record label (Broven 1987, 234–245).

Despite renewed interest during the 1950s, traditional Cajun music lost considerable ground with the rise of rock 'n' roll (and its Louisiana version, "swamp pop") in the late 1950s (see Broven 1987, 179–233), and especially in the 1960s with the "British musical invasion." At the same time, however, the various national folk festivals nurtured a growing interest in ethnic musical expression. The revival of Cajun music is generally dated from the appearance at the 1964 Newport Folk Festival of Gladius Thibodeaux, Louis "Vinesse" Lejeune, and Dewey Balfa, who together received a standing ovation. Balfa returned to Louisiana as a veritable ambassador of Louisiana Cajun music who worked to bring Cajun music into greater view and to encourage younger musicians to adopt and adapt French Cajun musical forms.[12] He fulfilled that role admirably to the end of his life. The Cajun cultural "renaissance" has since proceeded on a number of fronts.[13] These areas include the linguistic, pedagogical, and culinary domains, of course,[14] but also the diffusion of the diverse musical trends through the proliferation of "folkways initiatives" (such as the different locales of Jean Laffitte National Park), as well as radio and television shows devoted to Cajun music (Daigle 1987, 12–13; Ancelet 1992, 262–264). Moreover, the growing interest in Cajun musical and dance expression has provided the greatest impetus toward access to the specific cultural heritage.[15] However, as I will describe in the final section below, this access does not exist without tensions that relate to global/local issues, particularly between fans of more "progressive" (e.g., zydeco/rhythm-and-blues oriented bands, such as Zachary Richard, Wayne Toups and ZydeCajun, Filé, Bruce Daigrepont, and Beausoleil) musicians who record and perform nationally and internationally, and fans of more "traditional," local musicians (e.g., Savoy-Doucet Band, Balfa Toujours, among many other) who tend to limit the range of their performances and recording activities.[16]

Constructing Minor(ity) Identity

Having briefly traced the origins of the French Cajuns of southern Louisiana, particularly in terms of folk practices that relate to the development of dance and music forms, I now wish to suggest how sociocultural representations reveal the important relationship between memory and history, a link that provides the bridge to consideration of constructing "minor(ity) identity." Besides constituting a question of theoretical interest, the matter of "minor(ity) identity" is at the crux of much debate on taste and styles in music and dance in southern Louisiana. In fact, identity in this region is precisely constructed on the basis of many complex attributes, some of which, like the Cajun dialect, are quite distinct, although beleaguered, while others are highly problematic (most notably, racial origin). Indeed, many such attributes contribute to defining "tradition" (in Cajun dance, music, festivities, and rituals), and even of maintaining what some would call the "purity," others the "authenticity," of "traditions" in the face of perceived threats from "outside" influences. We may thus understand the relationship of the horizontal (of "inside"/"outside") to the vertical (of "above"/"below") through the distinction of national/global versus regional/local oppositions.

In this light, I place the suffix "-ity" in parentheses within my section heading with two goals in mind: first, since the attribution of "minority" status to this particular social group of predominantly European origins may appear incongruous, the parentheses placed in the term "minor(ity)" is a way to emphasize both the marginal status of this ethnic group of French and French-Canadian heritage within American national culture and the fact of their predominantly willing integration into this very culture. However, the first use of the parenthetical markers connects to a second, to the specific valence that the term "minor" acquires in Deleuze and Guattari's writing, first in *Kafka: Toward a Minor Literature,* then in *A Thousand Plateaus.* Among many theorists who have employed the Deleuze–Guattarian "minor" for their work, Fredric Jameson cogently suggests that this concept "has the advantage of cutting across some of our stereotypes or doxa about the political as the subversive, the critical, the negative, by restaging an affiliated conception of art in the new forcefield of what can be called the ideology of marginality and difference" (1992, 173). He succinctly defines this codification of the "minor" as that which "works within the dominant ... [to] undermin[e] it by adapting it," such that "selective modes of speaking are 'intensified' in a very special way, transformed into a private language" (1992, 173). Jameson goes on to suggest two specific traits of this use of language (or representation): on the one hand, the limits "designated by the excess of intensity" articulated through pitch and intonation; on the other hand, the disappearance of the individual subject "behind the beleaguered collective which thus speaks all the more resonantly through it" (1992, 173). Since "this is a very different conception of aesthetic subversion from that of the breaking of forms," Jameson concludes that such " 'minor' aesthetics" or "symbolic 'restricted codes' ... forfeit any grand progress on towards the status of a new hegemonic discourse; unlike Hollywood style, they can never, by definition, become the dominant of a radically new situation or a radically new cultural sphere" (1992, 173–174).

I use "minor(ity)," then, to emphasize at once the linguistic, discursive, and sociopolitical facets that constitute the "minor" status of Cajun culture and identity, constructed at the nexus of tension and conflict between vertical (above/below) and horizontal (outside/inside) sociocultural relations. Jameson's reference to the hegemonic dominance of "Hollywood style" as distinct from, but connected to, a " 'minor' aesthetics," provides an approach for reflecting on specific elements of conflict inherent to the concept of "minor(ity) identity." If one studies, for example, the central *bal de maison* sequence in the commercially successful film *The Big Easy* (1987), one can understand how the segment constitutes the film's moral and narrative turning point.[17] Following this scene representing Cajun dancing and revelry at a *fais do-do* (house dance) with "real" Cajun musicians (Dewey Balfa and friends), the protagonist distances himself from the corrupt police activity in which he is implicated and reorients an open murder investigation in a direction that will quickly lead to legal, moral, and even familial resolution. The stereotypical representation of Cajun "identity" evident in such mass-media constructions obscures all nuances and complexities of the cultural practices depicted. Moreover, the exploitation of actual agents of these practices, particularly the musicians, for both narrative and discursive ends also suggests the power that "the dominant" wields in adapting "minor(ity)" cultures, rather than the reverse as Jameson would have it.[18] This process often occurs through the willingness of these very cultural agents to be included in such exploitation, wittingly or not, and often with quite disturbing results. In *The Big Easy*, even the limited use of Cajun dialect (sung and spoken) and the performance of dance effectively allow the filmmakers to employ the most poignant site of cultural expression and of potential family and community harmony both to express the simplistic moral message and to bring "law" and "civilization" finally to the "lawless" and the "uncivilized." This particular construction of " 'minor(ity)' identity" through the Cajun music and dance arena reveals not simply the obvious strategic use of specific cultural practices, but also the filmmakers' awareness of the potential for cinematic representation contained in the skilled deployment of these very practices.

Understanding such strategies of construction allows me now to consider further these music and dance practices, notably the effective, if not necessarily subversive, development of the music repertoire and dance sites for the expression and definition of a multiplicity of "minor(ity)" identities. For through the music and dance practices and sites of this cultural expression, we can understand the conflict of "global" and "local" forces, between willing assimilation to the national American paradigm (e.g., education, capitalism, cultural expression) and the fierce, even desperate struggle to maintain the practices that define the "traditions" and rituals of local culture. Of particular import is the debate among and between Cajun dancers/fans and musicians concerning trends toward modernizing traditional and new songs alike through heterogeneous modes of instrumentation, rhythms, and themes. Without attempting to adjudicate a seemingly irreconcilable cultural and aesthetic dispute regarding "dilution" versus innovation, I wish to consider how the different music/dance responses illustrate the extent to which the reconstitution of "spaces of affect" is determined by the allegiance of dancers/spectators to one sensibility or the other. For this allegiance serves as a specific means for Cajuns and Cajun music and dance fans of representing (or affirming) specific cultural identities in relation to the dominant cultural formation through articulation of " 'minor' aesthetics," and thereby of participating actively in "adapting" the local, seemingly dominated, cultural forms and practices, to the exigencies of the global and the dominant.

OF *HECCÉITÉS* AND *RITOURNELLES*

> Every lament is always a lament for language,
> just as all praise is principally praise of the
> name. These are the extremes that define the
> domain and the scope of human language, its
> way of referring to things. Lament arises when
> nature feels betrayed by meaning; when the
> name perfectly says the thing, language
> culminates in the song of praise, in the
> sanctification of the name.
>
> –*Giorgio Agamben,* The Coming Community *(1993)*

Spaces and *Heccéités*

In order to situate Cajun music/dance forms at the intersection of the
global and local "spatial practices," I posit a process of reconstitution of
feeling that I call "spaces of affect," through which Cajun musicians and
fans (dancers and spectators alike) together engage in continuous dialogical exchange as responses to their reciprocal (musical and dance) performances.[19] The formulation "spaces of affect" precisely constitutes a
"global"/"local" intersection as a way of envisaging (global) modes of
reciprocal dynamics and collective assemblages occurring in the (local)
Cajun dance arena in terms of *heccéités* (i.e., the "thisness" of events).[20]
The components of *heccéités,* the affect and speed that constitute an
"event," provide a precise means to understand the reconfigurations in
Cajun dance arenas of "spatial practices" through dialogic interaction
between musicians and dancers/ spectators. These are "affective investments" through which "the body [understood as more than simply a
semantic space and less than a unity defining our identity] is placed into
an apparently immediate relation to the world" (Grossberg 1986b, 185;
see also Grossberg 1988; 1992). Specifically, just as dancers form couples
to waltz, two-step, and jitterbug in variable responses to the anticipated
musical performance, the musicians prepare in each dance site to provide
the musical style(s) that anticipate the physical, that is, performative,
dance demands of the particular audience. These assemblages are based
therefore on traits of *heccéités,* the mutual "relations of movement and
rest" and the capacities of participants on both sides of the stage front
"to affect and be affected" in interactive exchange (ATP, 261; MP, 318).
As Henri Lefebvre notes, music and dance rhythms "embrace both [the]
cyclical and [the] linear," and it is "through the mediation of rhythms (in
all three senses of 'mediation': means, medium, intermediary) [that] an

animated space comes into being which is an extension of the space of bodies" ([1974] 1991, 206–207).

Furthermore, the concept of *ritournelles* serves to describe more precisely the "event" under scrutiny—not only the music (lyrics and rhythms) that drives the dance performance, but also the physical repetition of steps and movements through which the dancers' propulsion enables them to engage in dialogue with each other as well as with the musicians. I maintain that these variable experiences of speed and affect circulating intensely between musicians and dancers/spectators contribute both to the incessant reconstitution of "spaces of affect" within specific performance arenas and to the often contradictory and usually conflicting preferences of musicians and fans alike regarding concomitant musical and dance practices, a conflict to which I will return in this chapter's final section.[21]

Admittedly, any written discussion is inherently hampered by the inability to offer readers the experiences of live music and dance performances and necessarily distanced from the actual physical structures within which such experiences habitually occur.[22] I hope nonetheless to communicate some effects of *heccéités* and *ritournelles,* first, by asking the reader to cast her/his memories back in time and space to those peak "events" when feelings and movement coalesced into indescribably, ineffably privileged experiences, the kind that occur all too infrequently as we get older. It might have been on a playground on a warm spring night with a few friends gathered around, or in a summer camp activity with hundreds of children, or alone on a rooftop or in a field gazing at the stars. It might have been on a sailboat, or surfing, or on dangerous white water, or on a lonely trail. It might have been with a lover, a child, in a foreign country, in the street, or in the backyard over the grill. It might even have been in front of the classroom, or around a seminar table with students and colleagues, or alone with pencil in hand or before the computer monitor, in those fleeting moments of creation and understanding. Giorgio Agamben speaks of the "halo" as "this supplement added to perfection—something like the vibration of that which is perfect, the glow at its edges . . . the individuation of a beatitude, the becoming singular of that which is perfect" (1993, 55). Although one may rarely think of attaining "perfection," the "becoming singular" is quite evident through the joy derived from what it is "we do" without apologies.

If the lyrical "excess" that I have just produced seems more appropriate for an article on Lamartine than on either "local" Cajun dance spaces or on "global" theoretical discourse, this affective evocation remains entirely within the problematics of *heccéités,* that is, the "in-between" zone in which "local" investments and resistance engage broader issues of enunciation, articulation, and power, the very "becoming of place and space" (Grossberg, 1996, 177). Deleuze and Guattari ask, "What is the individuality of a day, a season, an event?" They respond that "a degree, an intensity, is an individual, a *Haecceity* that enters into composition with other degrees, other intensities, to form another individual." And just as "these degrees of participation . . . imply a flutter, a vibration in the form itself that is not reducible to the properties of a subject . . . that prevent[s] the heat of the whole from increasing," this is all the more reason "to effect distributions of intensity, to establish latitudes that are 'deformedly deformed,' speeds, slownesses, and degrees of all kinds corresponding to a body or set of bodies taken as longitude: a cartography" (ATP, 253; MP, 310). They muse on the variety of modes of individuations, of *heccéités*, that "consist entirely of relations of movement and rest between molecules and particles, capacities to affect and be affected" (ATP, 261; MP, 318): demonology, *contes,* haiku; wind in Charlotte Brontë, "five in the evening" in Lorca, meteorology in Tournier, a walk through the crowd in Virginia Woolf, agroup of girls in Proust (ATP, 261–263, 271; MP, 318–321, 332–333). And were one tempted to accept "an oversimplified conciliation, as though there were on the one hand formed subjects, of the thing or person type, and on the other hand spatio-temporal coordinates of the haecceity type," Deleuze and Guattari insist:

> You will yield nothing to haecceities unless you realize that that is what your are, and that you are nothing but that. . . . You are longitude and latitude, a set of speeds and slownesses between formed particles, a set of nonsubjectified affects. You have the individuality of a day, a season, a year, a *life* (regardless of its duration)—a climate, a wind, a fog, a swarm, a pack (regardless of its regularity). Or at least you can have it, you can reach it. (ATP, 262; MP, 320)

But where are the Cajuns? the reader may well ask at this point. Where do "local" practices (Cajun dance and music) intersect all this talk of molecules and particles, this swarm of "global" concepts? The analysis that I propose is precisely an attempt to understand the "event," specifically in the Cajun music/dance arena, from an "in-between" perspective by proposing the concept of *heccéités* as consisting not "simply of a decor or backdrop that situates subjects, or of appendages that hold things and people to the ground" (ATP, 262; MP, 320–321). Rather, I wish to understand *heccéités* in the music/dance arena as "the entire assemblage in its *individuated aggregate,* . . . defined by a longitude and a latitude, by speeds and affects, independently of forms and subjects, which belong to another plane" (ATP, 262, my emphasis; MP, 321). This facet of my project, to situate the "global"/"local" through a perhaps ineffable "in-between" of *heccéités* conceived in it-/themselves, leads to a quandary that Guattari recognized: "As soon as one decides to quantify an affect, one loses its qualitative dimensions and its power of singularization, of heterogenesis, in other words, its eventful compositions, the 'haecceities' that it promulgates" (Guattari 1990, 67).[23] Yet, if *heccéités* are elusive when "quantified," it is through the concept of *ritournelles* that I hope to extend my consideration of the "individuated aggregate" within the Cajun music/dance arena.

Ritournelles and Affective Territories

I have selected a waltz performed by the group Beausoleil on their album *Bayou Boogie* for two purposes: the song serves both as an exemplar for discussing the multiple connotations of the concept of *ritournelle,* and as a starting point to illustrate, however approximately, the possibilities of rhythm, movement, speed, and affect that contribute to forming *heccéités* within the focal "events." By providing both stanzas and the refrain, I wish to emphasize the recurrence of similar locutions that correspond to the regular, 3/4 waltz meter:

La Valse du Malchanceux	The Unlucky [Man's] Waltz
C'est ça la valse après jouer	That's the waltz that was playing
Quand moi, j'ai fait mon idée	When I made up my mind
C'est ça la valse après jouer	That's the waltz that was playing
Chez ma belle j'ai parti	When I set out for her house
C'est ça la valse après jouer	That's the waltz that was playing
Quand à ma belle j'ai demandé	When I asked for my sweetheart's hand
C'est ça la valse après jouer	That's the waltz that was playing
Quand ses parents m'ont refusé.	When her parents refused me.
[Refrain]	[Refrain]
C'est ça la valse veux tu me joues sur le lit de ma mort	That's the waltz I want you to play for me on my deathbed
C'est ça la valse veux tu me joues le jour que je va mourir	That's the waltz I want you to play for me on the day that I die
C'est ça la valse veux tu me joues jusqu'à la porte du cimetière	That's the waltz I want you to play for me up to the gates of the cemetery
C'est ça la valse que moi j'appelle la valse du malchanceux.	That's the waltz that I call the unlucky man's waltz.
[2]	[2]
C'est ça la valse après siffler mais dans le temps que je courtisais	That's the waltz that I was whistling at the time I was courting her
C'est ça la valse après jouer quand je l'ai volée	That's the waltz I was playing when I stole her away
C'est ça la valse après jouer quand ils m'ont fait la marier	That's the waltz I was playing when they made me marry her
C'est ça la valse après jouer quand on s'est séparé.	That's the waltz that was playing when we separated.[24]

Whereas the term translates as "refrain,"[25] I am interested in the way in which the lyrics of this waltz "return," properly speaking, in the stanzas as well. For the repeated lyrics, "C'est ça la valse après jouer . . . ," forms an incantation that combines the two forms of temporality of *heccéités,* *Aeon,* "the indefinite time of the event, the floating line that knows only speeds and continually divides that which transpires into an already-there that is at the same time not-yet-here," and *Chronos,* "the time of measure that situates things and persons, develops a form, and determines a subject" (ATP, 262; MP, 320). The verb "jouer" in each line, except at the start of Stanza 2, suggests this oscillation between temporalities since its use creates a "becoming-music" that permeates all thought and activity, linking the present "C'est ça la valse" to the indistinct past established in the Cajun locution "après" preceding an infinitive. Then, in the refrain itself, this "return" is modified in an explicitly dialogic manner, no longer the "après jouer" of an indefinite past, but the plaintive "veux tu me joues" of an indistinct and yet inevitable future. The final verse of the refrain offers a closure of sorts through the self-referential manner of announcing the title, yet it also provides the lyrical bridge that leads the song into its instrumental phases and thus to the very moments in which the response to the dialogic plea, "veux tu me joues," is actualized.[26]

Thus, "music exists," say Deleuze and Guattari, "because the refrain exists also, because music takes up the refrain, lays hold of it as a content in a form of expression, because it forms a block with it in order to take it somewhere else" (ATP, 300; MP, 368). This movement "somewhere else" occurs, they argue, through music's submitting the refrain to the "very special treatment of the diagonal or transversal," a treatment that consists in "uproot[ing] the refrain from its territoriality" through music's "creative, active operation . . . [of] deterritorializing the refrain" (ATP, 300; MP, 368–369). In the next section I will address ways in which such "deterritorializing" occurs in geopolitical terms, but for the moment, I wish to remain on the dance floor, as it were. There the dancers respond directly to the implicit dialogic "plea" of the Cajun song not so much in response to the actual lyrics as through the "creative operation," for example, of the 3/4 meter that defines the waltz.

These observations allow us to consider a second facet of the "individuated aggregate" within *heccéités.* A distinct trait or code of the actual waltz performance in the Cajun dance arena is the smooth walking step that assures the constant counterclockwise pattern of flows.[27] Yet Deleuze and Guattari insist that "rhythm is not meter or cadence; . . . Meter is dogmatic, but rhythm is critical; it ties together critical moments" (ATP, 313; MP, 385). The walking step of the Cajun waltz is linear while also determining spatial *ritournelles* that are at once territorializing, that is, in the "becoming expressive of rhythm or melody" (ATP, 316; MP,

388), and yet in constant movement toward deterritorialization, what Deleuze and Guattari call "territorial motifs" that form "rhythmic faces or characters" in relationship to "territorial counterpoints" that form "melodic landscapes" (ATP, 317–318; MP, 389–391).

Such a constant interplay of "expressive qualities" forms appropriative "signatures that are the constituting mark of a domain, an abode" (ATP, 316; MP, 389). This interplay is evident, I believe, from particular dance responses that the waltz generates in the dance arena, with several circular patterns usually contained within each other, all propelled by the rhythmic support from and dialogue with the musicians' expression. In the Cajun dance arena, each couple forms a unit with its own territorial individuation, and the very convention of the "lead" (male) and "following" (female) assures the smooth integration of this individuation into the assemblage.[28] The individuated aggregate thus responds to a rhythm "caught up in a becoming," say Deleuze and Guattari, "that sweeps up the distances between characters, making them rhythmic characters that are themselves more or less distant, more or less combinable (intervals)" (ATP, 320; MP, 393). One only needs to experience dancing with a novice partner, male or female, or even more pointedly, alongside couples unable or unwilling to follow the coded "flow," to understand Deleuze and Guattari's formula: "It is a question of keeping at a distance the forces of chaos knocking at the door" (ATP, 320; MP, 393). For such chaos, and even physical damage, can result on the dance floor through ineffective communication from the "lead" through hands, arms, and often cheek-to-cheek contact, or, as is more often the case, between couples ineffectively maintaining the territorial "critical distance." In their machinic discourse that preceded *A Thousand Plateaus,* Deleuze and Guattari provide a telling description of the relations between machines and desire that seems appropriate here: "The dancer combines with the floor to compose a machine under the perilous conditions of love and death" (Guattari 1995, 121; AOFr, 464).

Thus, to this fluid individuation of "becoming-expressive of rhythms," of the "signature" marking the domain or abode on the dance arena, corresponds a certain "decoding" or deterritorializing within the dance arena as the couples continue moving around the floor. Whatever the flourishes introduced by the "lead" that the partner "follows"—for example, turnout combinations and even back-and-forth shuffles (the *varsovienne*) in uncrowded dance arenas; the simple conversational step (rocking back and forth in place) in crowded spaces (Plater, Speyrer, and Speyrer 1993, 53–56, 106)—their movements shift the partners into different patterns within the counterclockwise flow, allowing such "expressive qualities" at once to mark a familiar abode (e.g., the shared "style" of the coded waltz repertoire) and yet to maintain the territorial "critical distance" of distinct spatial differentiation. This combination of affect and speeds/slownesses thus contributes to maintaining a tension between deterritorializing, apparently "decoding" forces of movement and the simultaneously territorializing function in the dance arena.

Then at each song's end another facet of the *ritournelle* becomes evident as the couples clear the dance floor and situate themselves as spectators on the sides until the first strains of the next song call them back to the floor, or leave them to participate as observers. In discussing the "event" in *Pourparlers* as well as in *The Fold* (76–82; *Le Pli* 103–112), Deleuze insists that "the event is inseparable from *temps morts* . . . [that are] in the event itself, it gives to the event its thickness [*épaisseur*]" (P, 218; N, 160; my translation). That is, the moments of alternation between songs are as constitutive of the *heccéité*, understood as "event," as are the activities in the music/dance *ritournelle*. Thus, the *temps mort* (literally, the "dead time," or suspended moment) is the complementary face of the flow continuing from one song to the next since it is in this "moment" that socializing occurs, that dancers can trade instructions on steps or simply rest and recoup their energy. Moreover, the "signature" of this domain or abode manifests itself further at the juncture of the *temps mort,* for it is in this "pause" that the musicians prepare and the dancers anticipate the regular alternation between waltz (3/4) and two-step (4/4) meters. Indeed, any deviation from the equal alternation between these two forms, waltz to two-step/jitterbug and back to waltz, serves to "sign" or characterize the particular dance arena as more "traditional," that is, with a dominance of waltzes, or more "progressive," that is, with a dominance of two-step/jitterbug numbers.

Similarly, the kinds of dance steps chosen by dancers in response to songs of the faster 4/4 beat mark the particular dance arena and its possibilities for reconstitution of "spaces of affect." In certain dance halls, especially in rural Louisiana, that attract an audience of older dancers, the two-step is *de rigueur* as the dance response "appropriate" to songs of the 4/4 beat, and performers of the Cajun jitterbug are sometimes actively discouraged from practicing this step. To understand why, the participant in the Cajun dance arena immediately notes the flow and transformation of patterns therein, not only in comparison to the usually regular counterclockwise flow of the waltz space, but especially in terms of the possible lateral shifts occurring during a two-step number. That is, the two-step dance arena appears as a faster, fluid version of the waltz floor since both are walking steps, with the two-step requiring a regular rhythmic shift of the feet through eight beats.[29] The two-step also generates the complex deterritorializing effect that occurs with the waltz pattern, that is, of a quite literal, counterclockwise *ritournelle* around the dance floor, with variable configurations of flows and speeds held in check by the size of both the dance assemblage and the space.

This effect is altered dramatically, however, when even one couple shifts from the two-step to the jitterbug. In the typical dance arena, for example, at Randol's Restaurant in Lafayette, Louisiana, a few couples on the periphery of the dance floor may be able to maintain the fluid counterclockwise, two-step movement throughout the song, but they can do so only by carefully negotiating their dance pattern around and between the couples performing the more static jitterbug moves. Of course, each couple performing the latter remains constantly in motion. However, they simultaneously and necessarily stake out a specific "territory" on the dance floor by engaging in the regular push–pull, rotating parallelogram of the basic move combined with the intricate upper-body arm movements that can make the well-performed jitterbug so dazzling. Despite the dynamic impression that a jitterbug performance creates, one implicit statement that dancers make in shifting from the two-step to the jitterbug concerns their regard for the fragility of the territorial boundaries established in the fluid, counterclockwise movements of the two-step. Indeed, those dancers who maintain a steadfast allegiance to one step or the other may find their efforts thwarted, for example, by the aggregate of jitterbug couples who effectively block the possibility for counterclockwise flow or, conversely, by the two-steppers who tend to move forward against and even through the jitterbug pairs.[30]

Here we encounter the fundamental question of "distinction," the "judgment of taste" to which Pierre Bourdieu has devoted an exhaustive examination. As he points out, "Explicit aesthetic choices are in fact often constituted in opposition to the choices of the groups closest in social space, with whom the competition is most direct and most immediate" (1984, 60). Deleuze and Guattari speak of this as "the disjunction noticeable between the code and the territory," the latter "aris[ing] in a free margin of the code" and formed "at the level of a certain decoding" (ATP, 322; MP, 396). The implicit message communicated by the choice of steps in the dance performance, for example, may correspond for some dancers to their affirmation of cultural identity, that is, to a certain means of determining margins and differentiating their own "becoming-expressive" in relation to such margins. Grossberg is thus correct in arguing that shared taste for some texts (and practices, I would maintain) "does not in fact guarantee that [the] common taste describes a common relationship. Taste merely describes people's different abilities to find pleasure in a particular body of texts [and practices] rather than another" (1992, 42). Still, as Bourdieu argues, "the most intolerable thing for those who regard themselves as the possessors of legitimate culture is the sacrilegious reuniting of tastes which taste dictates shall be separated" (1984, 56–57). The assertion of "taste" clearly manifests itself toward the conventions admissible in certain dance arenas, notably the predilection for less "embellished" waltz moves or for the two-step over the jitterbug. The specific territorial differences are thus marked through the code (i.e., conventions) evidently shared by some dancers, and despite its complexity and fluidity, this message comes across clearly to the musicians. For they are likely to respond directly to the performers' and spectators' particular modes of "becoming-expressive" through their own variable musical modes of "becoming-dance," yet attentive to the fluctuations of "taste" manifested in particular dance arenas.

Text/Pretext and Dialogue

The links between music and dance performances lead us to note several other facets of *ritournelles* that occur within the Cajun music/dance arena. First, however the limited, but vital repertoire of Cajun songs may be interpreted by musicians observing both differing elements of cultural tradition and manifestations of fans' tastes, it is clear that the repertoire's dissemination through recordings certainly constitutes important linguistic and cultural statements about musical self-representation and affirmation of Cajun identity. Yet the reconstitution of "spaces of affect" relies not on these recordings, but on the live performance of the songs, usually the same songs within the Cajun repertoire. Moreover, since most dancers/spectators are now unlikely to understand these lyrics, the frequent experience of these songs is in the form of a pretext for dancing and socializing in bars, restaurants, and (now less frequently) *bals de maison*. This alternate and, I would argue, principal status of the songs does not necessarily preclude a linguistic communication. However, certain examples—notably, the Bruce Daigrepont Band's usual venue (Sunday evenings at the New Orleans club, Tipitina's) or, until a few years ago, Thursday night sets of the group Filé at the Maple Leaf in New Orleans—are quite revealing. The vast majority of spectators and dancers at these events do not understand French, much less Cajun French; they do not even hear clearly, much less attend to the "message" contained in these lyrics.[31] Yet the dancers and musicians have no difficulty whatsoever in reconstituting the exhilarating "spaces of affect" through their mutual "becoming-music"/"becoming-dance."

Thus, the corresponding active appreciation of Cajun music by musicians and dancers/spectators alike is a sociocultural phenomenon that creates different "spaces of affect" in given Cajun dance arenas, where "music is a deterritorialization of the voice, which becomes less and less tied to language" (ATP, 302; MP, 371). This observation leads me to another component of this "affective economy" (Grossberg 1988, 285): the overall lack of uniformity in the dancers'/fans' response. This component allows us to illustrate one final facet of *ritournelles* and also to address the aforementioned "geopolitical" aspect of deterritorialization by comparing urban Cajun music/dance sites to rural settings. As I have previously noted, the reconstitution of "spaces of affect" is determined by the allegiance of dancers/spectators to particular musical sensibilities toward Cajun music, and this allegiance goes to the heart of the complex tensions existing in southern Louisiana regarding Cajun self-representation in relation to the dominant cultural formation. This is at once a question of the "frames" into which musicians and dancers/spectators may be situated vis-à-vis the cultural "event" and one of the dialogical relationship that develops among and between musicians and dancers/spectators.[32]

On the one hand, considerations of "distinction" place couples in constant communication regarding the steps that territorialize the dance arena to greater or lesser degrees. Thus, borrowing from Lewis (1992, 195), "inner games" may unfold on the dance floor and thus constitute "nested" subterritories therein in relation (and even resistance) to the more general flow of dance movement. However, whatever the differences and difficulties of articulations of "taste" toward the dance steps (and musical interpretations), the *heccéités*, with their variables of rest and speed and their concomitant expression and investment of affect, extend across and around the dance floor, encompassing even those not participating in the active dance movement per se. Indeed, by my use of the terms "dancers/spectators" throughout this chapter, I have meant to suggest this all-encompassing articulation that is constitutive of "spaces of affect," an expression enveloping spectators and musicians as well as dancers in the "dance flow."

On the other hand, without precluding the model of "nested frames," I prefer to envisage this dance space by drawing from M. M. Bakhtin to argue that *ritournelles* in all their forms develop in a "dialogical" relationship between musicians and dancers/spectators (see Bakhtin 1981, 270–275). In many rural dance halls and at certain festivals held in southern Louisiana, centrifugal relations prevail between musicians and dancers. That is, these relations are oriented outward, away from the musicians, with an emphasis on the performance of the dancers, in synch with the musicians' expression, but beyond them. In these centrifugal contexts, not only do the musical groups most locally popular respect the fans' desire for familiar and relatively simplified musical forms, some local populations themselves (usually older fans) frown on, if not actively discourage, the responsive dance innovations, notably the Cajun jitterbug, that frequently accompany the more "progressive" musical cadences. Elsewhere, such as in many urban dance arenas, and especially in concert and festival settings outside Louisiana, the centripetal or musician-oriented relation occurs. Such circumstances (to entertain usually passive audiences and free-form, rock-nourished dancers) create demands on musicians for the "fusion" and experimental sounds that bands like Beausoleil, Filé, and Wayne Toups and ZydeCajun bring to their music.[33]

This negotiation of "centripetal"/"centrifugal" relations between dancers/spectators and musicians allows us to address how the "global" and the "local" intersect within the elements of *heccéités* and *ritournelles*. The contrasting dance sites and modes of exchange therein certainly determine different possibilities for reconstitution of "spaces of affect," possibilities that concern the "global" appropriation of Cajun cultural forms by apparently external, American mass culture. It is clear that the creation of renewed "spaces of affect" through the dynamic interaction between musicians and dancers/spectators allows Cajuns (and even so-called Cajuns-by-choice) to participate literally and figuratively in the "two-step" of self-representation. However, this process is complicated, I maintain, by the shifting articulations of Cajun identity in relation to the ever-present "instability of frontiers" imposed from conditions of the surrounding hegemonic formation (Laclau and Mouffe 1985, 136). That is, the joyful, affirmative strength that emerges in musical lyrics and forms (including dance steps) may strike back and at times assert its own counterinvasive mode of territoriality in the face of various forms of appropriation. Indeed, just as many lyrics in Cajun music emphasize precisely this individual integrity in the face of adversity, the attitudes of fans and musicians alike clearly support Bourdieu's contention about marking "distinction," that "the song [and, I would argue in this context, the dance], as a cultural property which (like photography) is almost universally accessible and genuinely common . . . calls for particular vigilance from those who intend to mark their difference" (1984, 60). Thus, whereas certain groups (notably, some chapters of the Cajun French Music Association) explicitly "prohibit" members from dancing the jitterbug (aka "the jig") at Association-sponsored events, other fans (particularly among the fluid uptown New Orleans dance crowd) appear to insist on more free-form interpretations of the dance steps, waltz and jitterbug alike.

Yet, in the very negotiation between seemingly conflicting articulatory practices, particularly between apparently "outside" and even "global" forces in relation to a locally perceived "inside" of the cultural frame, musicians often express, and their fans often exhibit, a deterritorializing ambivalence toward the musical and cultural identity and heritage being reinforced. For, in seeking to reach ever wider audiences and thereby attain greater popularity and economic rewards, musicians necessarily contribute to the inherently equivocal articulations and thus to an active reterritorialization by the dominant cultural formation. That is, in seeking an audience beyond what is frequently viewed as the confines, or limited "market," of Cajun society in southern Louisiana, musicians and their fans often willingly participate in the appropriation of the culture's forms of expression by these same "invasive" forces. To the literal commodification of Cajun music and zydeco (e.g., in Frito-Lay and Burger King commercials), one can also add examples of such commercialized cultural re-presentations as the film *The Big Easy* (and its television adaptation for cable) and the 1990 Dolly Parton/Louisiana ABC television special.[34]

A final example will illustrate how facets of *ritournelles* in the dynamic dancer–musician dialogue can help clarify the apparent sociocultural ambivalence through strategies that arise from "global"/"local" negotiations. For one dance/music segment in particular, available commercially, suggests the active and prevalent possibilities of communication between dancers and Cajun musicians, precisely through the fusion of rock, zydeco, and Cajun sounds responding to the pressures of "global" forces of the American music industry. The final scene from the Les Blank et al. documentary, *J'Ai Été au Bal: The Cajun and Zydeco Music of Louisiana,* emphasizes both the centripetal, musician-oriented dialogic pole and the centrifugal, "becoming-dance" of this music, performances-in-dialogue that take place by featuring dancers responding to the music of Wayne Toups and his band ZydeCajun. This name alone defines a deliberate musical fusion, as Toups says, "a new wave Cajun; it's Cajun music of the future" (1990, 162).[35]

Toups's poignant introductory statement reveals his awareness of the precarious equilibrium between innovation and tradition.[36] The filmmakers then introduce the final number that stands in sharp contrast to the film's previous Cajun performances in terms of its setting, instrumentation, and especially Toups's distinctive musical and fashion statements. Besides the location on the porch of a race-track shelter (a modern version of the traditional site for the *bal de maison*) and the predominantly young crowd of dancers, the instrumental break presents not the traditional fiddle, but instead electric piano and guitar, followed then by Toups's own impassioned performance on electrified accordion. The instrumental finale is Toups's showcase, with the accordionist—clad in muscle shirt, headband, and garish jams—emphasizing the transformative power of the traditional lyrics of the song "Allons à Lafayette," from music to dance and back again, with electrified instrumentation and the mixture of Cajun, zydeco, and rock cadences. As for the dancers, because of the accelerated 4/4 beat, the two-step simply becomes too difficult, especially on a dance floor through which the smooth negotiating necessary for this step would be impossible. Thus, the jitterbug is an entirely appropriate response to the pace set not only by the energetic beat, but also by the territorializing elements in this particular "becoming-expressive of rhythm or melody" (ATP, 316; MP, 388).

This film segment brings into sharp relief the strategies deliberately pursued by bands like Toups's ZydeCajun and Michael Doucet's Beausoleil in order to negotiate implicitly the "global"/"local" pressures. While surviving commercially with recording contracts and attracting listeners and dancers, new and old alike, with their "fusion" sound, these bands also seek to integrate and thereby to develop and extend their cultural heritage with and through this very sound. Live performances of these and other groups show the extent to which they remain concerned (though certainly not in the terms that I adopt) with maintaining the waltz/two-step *ritournelle*, with enhancing the *heccéités*, that is, the combined elements of speed and affect, and thus and especially with maximizing the performance dialogue between musicians and dancers/spectators in venues outside as well as within Louisiana.[37] Thus, in contrast to critics (notably Ancelet 1990, 1992; Marc Savoy 1988) who have addressed the "global"/"local" conflict in the apocalyptic or oppositional terms of dilution of Cajun heritage, I understand this dialectic as variations on *l'invention du quotidien* (the invention of daily life), that is, the negotiated and shifting construction of diverse "spatial practices."

It is precisely the continuing capacity to define diverse "spaces of affect" through the constitutive facets of *ritournelles* in Cajun music and dance that assures future possibilities of innovation and renewed self-definition within the Cajun heritage. The Deleuze–Guattari methodological perspectives that I continue to explore are productive, I believe, for understanding the expressive potentials and thresholds inherent to the "local" intersections of dance and musical performances. For while "global" concepts, such as *heccéités* and *ritournelles*, allow us to examine the varied forms of the dance/music dialogue in which dancers/spectators and musicians engage at each dance/music site, these concepts also help establish connections toward the ongoing sociocultural dialectic engaged in the same sites, in the dance arenas upon which the "local" and the "global" intersect and often collide. These geopolitical negotiations of "forms and feelings" are precisely the proper focus of a "cultural studies" understood not in a limited, "territorialized" sense of dueling disciplines, but rather as "(de)territorializing" openings toward and negotiations between adjoining theoretical and conceptual articulations and strategies.

* * *

That night I dreamed of South Louisiana, of . . . pelicans sailing out of the sun over the breakers out on the Gulf, the palm trees ragged and green and clacking in the salt breeze, and the crab and crawfish boils and fish fries that went on year-round, as though there were no end to a season and death had no sway in our lives, and finally the song that always broke my heart, "La Jolie Blonde," which in a moment made the year 1945. Our yard was abloom with hibiscus and blue and pink hydrangeas and the neighbors come on horseback to the fais-dodo under our oaks.

–*James Lee Burke,* Black Cherry Blues *(1989)*

SECTION

III POST-TEXTS

8 PRAGMATIC/ MACHINIC

DISCUSSION WITH FÉLIX GUATTARI (19 MARCH 1985)

For Michael Current

The following discussion with Félix Guattari took place in his apartment in Paris. With the help of a number of friends, I had prepared a set of questions, and had contacted him to see if he might be available to answer them. He responded immediately, indicating his willingness to meet with me. Prior to the trip, I had also contacted Gilles Deleuze to arrange an extended interview. Although his schedule and health prevented him from seeing me for a long session, I did visit him at his apartment the night before the session with Guattari.

I met Guattari in his sixth *arrondissement* apartment, near the Odéon, and we spent about three hours talking, took a break to do errands in the neighborhood, and have lunch, and then continued talking for a few more hours. He was extremely generous with his time, more than willing to consider anything I threw his way, and—as the reader will note—extremely patient with me. Shortly after the interview, I realized that I had overdone the barrage of prepared questions and topics to be treated and should have limited the subjects to a few key questions that we could have considered in greater detail. Also, while preparing this exchange for distribution and publication, I have winced more than once upon rereading some of my remarks. Yet, despite the demands I made upon his good nature and patience, Guattari spoke entirely without reserve and even outlined quite extensively some of the elements of his ongoing work.

Although I tried to interest several journals in this interview in the following years, its length as well as a low regard for Guattari in the North

American critical community, combined to make its publication impossible. Only through Internet contacts on the Deleuze–Guattari List have I seen the demand for a more thorough and equitable account of Guattari's contributions to his collaboration with Deleuze and of his own highly speculative work. Now, a decade after the interview, some of the topics that we discussed seem dated, but I have retained most of these in the text because they do shed light on Guattari's thinking, particularly on politics and culture. While I have also reviewed my translation, I have refrained from "regularizing" it too completely in order to leave intact as much of the spontaneity of Guattari's verbal pyrotechnics as possible.

Toward the end of our talk, the doorbell rang, and while Guattari answered it, I excused myself for a few minutes. When I returned, he introduced me to a lean, greying man, Toni Negri, whose mail Guattari was receiving and who had an appointment with Guattari. I took my leave, and saw Guattari only once more, in 1990, in Baton Rouge at Louisiana State University, where he presented an edited version of his *Les trois écologies* (*The Three Ecologies*; 1989b, 1989c).

I. Pragmatic
1. "Deleuze-Thought"
2. Molecular Revolutions in Europe
3. French Politics under Mitterand
4. Deleuze and Guattari and Psychoanalysis
5. The Americanization of Europe
6. Left and Right Readings of Deleuze–Guattari

I.   PRAGMATIC

1.   "Deleuze-Thought"

CS: Referring to the front cover of *SubStance* 44–45 (Stivale 1984a), once again the name "Gilles Deleuze" blocks out the name of Félix Guattari. This blockage, that quite often occurs when someone refers to the schizoanalytic project, seems to correspond to the effect you emphasized in "Machine and Structure" (PT, 240–248; MR, 111–119),[1] the effect of transforming a proper name into a common noun, that is, erasing the individual. How do you react to these two effects, the blockage of your name and the "figuration" of Gilles Deleuze's name?

FG: I can't give you a simple answer because I think that behind this little phenomenon there are some contradictory elements. There is a rather negative aspect, which is that some people have considered

Deleuze's collaboration with me as deforming his philosophical thought and leading him into analytical and political tracks where he somehow went astray. So, some people have tried to present this collaboration, often in some unpleasant ways, as an unfortunate episode in Gilles Deleuze's life, and have therefore displayed toward me the infantile attitude of quite simply denying my existence. Sometimes, one even sees references to *L'Anti-Oedipe* or *Mille pla-teaux* in which my name is quite simply omitted, in which I no longer exist at all. So, let's just say that this is one dimension of malice of a political nature.

One could also look at this dimension from another perspective: one could say, OK, in the long run, "Deleuze" has become a common noun, or in any case a common noun not only for him and me, but for a certain number of people who participate in "Deleuze-thought" [*la pensée deleuze*], as we would have said years ago "Mao-thought." "Deleuze-thought" does exist; Michel Foucault insisted on that to some extent, in a rather humorous way, saying that this century would be Deleuzian, and I hope so (Foucault 1994, 2:76; 1977, 165). That doesn't mean that the century will be connected to the thought of Gilles Deleuze, but will comprise a certain reassemblage of theoretical activity vis-à-vis university institutions and power institutions of all kinds.

CS: What are your current projects, and don't you have a book which will appear soon on your clinical work?

FG: I have two books which are going to appear, a book with Toni Negri, *Les nouveaux espaces de liberté* (Guattari and Negri 1985)[2]; then, a collection of articles dating from the last three or four years. I thought of calling it *Les années d'hiver* (Guattari 1986a), but I don't know. Then there is a third collection which will be texts on schizoanalysis.[3]

2. Molecular Revolutions in Europe

CS: You spoke to me earlier about the Collège International de Philoso-phie.[4] So what are your goals in this activity and your hopes for this institution, and in terms of the schizoanalytic enterprise, how do you understand your participation there?

FG: I warned you ahead of time: I don't understand it at all now! (*Laughter*)

CS: Right, you just mentioned that you no longer are involved there, that you no longer belong to the Collège?

FG: No. The people, not the founders, who have taken control of this institution, sometimes by means that recall more the life within small political groups than a self-respecting, purely scientific activity, the people who thus brought off this operation are not devoid of qualities quite generally, but they have a conception of philosophy that, in my opinion, is traditional in its exercise and that therefore does not allow the construction of a new institution since, after all, the way they want to develop philosophical studies could be done entirely in the framework of existing university institutions.

CS: How do they understand philosophy?

FG: Well, you understand, this Collège de Philosophie, we had the idea, with a certain number of friends, Jean-Pierre Faye in particular, immediately after the arrival of the Socialists in France in 1981. The idea was to develop completely new forms of collective reflection, particularly in the field of relationships between science and philosophy, art and philosophy, and for my part, in the domains of reflection about urbanism, education, health, and psychiatric questions. It was therefore a conception, let's say, much closer to that of the Encyclopedists of the eighteenth century than to university philosophy as it has developed, and in my opinion, as it has dried up philosophy. So, instead of accepting the idea of a multipolarity entirely necessary for the project as I just defined it, the present team, which took control of the Collège de Philosophie, created a sole central body that distributes transitory seminars, without much continuity, uniquely directed in the end toward subjects that recall an education in the history of philosophy, obviously with some interesting innovations, of course, but subjects that finally don't allow one to do anything more than present a complementary teaching. These subjects don't allow us to undertake or to establish research or "think" teams with people who are not in the university field of philosophy, therefore to develop a mediating or interfacing perspective in completely new ways.

So, Jean-Pierre Faye and I were entirely prepared to collaborate with these people devoted to this way of thinking, but provided that they had their precisely delimited territory and didn't attempt to invade and direct the Collège de Philosophie like a political bureau with a central committee whose general secretary would direct the so-called philosophical organizations. We have therefore decided to constitute something else, another European college of philosophy, hoping to have the means to realize its development.

CS: Given that you're considering a European college, what is happening in Europe as far as "molecular revolutions" are concerned? Are there any "molecular revolutions" taking place in Europe or in France?

FG: That's an interesting and embarrassing question at the same time because one might think—a lot of people think—that this whole dimension I called "molecular"—this dimension of interrogation of the relationship between subjectivity and all kinds of things, the body, time, work, problems of daily life, all the becomings of subjectivity addressed by these molecular revolutions—one might think that it was a passing phenomenon, connected to the events of the 1960s, to the new culture of the 1960s, a flash in the pan, perhaps a dream, a fantasy, with no tomorrow. Today [1985], everything seems to have returned to order, and it's now the era of the "New Conservatism," something that you know quite well in the United States.

But, people like me who continue to think that, on the contrary, this movement continues, whatever the difficulties and uncertainties might be, we are taken either for visionaries or completely "retro" and unhinged. Well, I willingly accept this outlook, much more willingly than many other things, because basically . . . I think that, in 1968, not much happened. It was a great awakening, a huge thunderclap, but not much happened. What has been important is what occurred afterward, and what hasn't ceased occurring ever since. Thus, the molecular revolutions on the order of the liberation of women have been very important in their scope and results, and they are continuing across the entire planet. I am thinking to some extent of what I encountered in Brazil, of the immense struggles of liberation of women that must be undertaken in the Third World.

There is at present a very profound upheaval of subjectivity in France developing around the questions of immigrants and of the emergence of new cultures, of migrant cultures connected to the second generation of immigrants. This is something that is manifested in paradoxical ways, such as the most reactionary racism we see developing in France around the movement of Jean-Marie Le Pen,[5] but also, quite the contrary, manifested through styles, through young people opening up to another sensitivity, another relationship with the body, particularly in dance and music. These also belong to molecular revolutions. There is also a considerable development, which, in my opinion, has an important future, around the Green, alternative, ecological, pacifist movements. This is very evident in Germany, but these movements are developing now in France, Belgium, Spain, and so on.

So, you'll say to me: But really, what is this catch-all, this huge washtub in which you are putting these very different and often violent movements, for example the movements of nationalistic struggles (the Basques, the Irish, the Corsicans), and then women's, pacifist movements, nonviolent movements? Isn't all that a bit incoherent? Well, I don't think so because, once again, the molecular revolution is not something that will constitute a program. It's something that develops precisely in the direction of diversity, of a multiplicity of perspectives, of creating the conditions for the maximum impetus of processes of singularization. It's not a question of creating agreement; on the contrary, the less we agree, the more we create an area, a field of vitality in different branches of this phylum of molecular revolution, and the more we reinforce this area. It's a completely different logic from the organizational, arborescent logic that we know in political or union movements.

OK, I persist in thinking that there is indeed a development in the molecular revolution. But then if we don't want to turn it into a vague global label, there are several questions that arise; there are two, I'm not going to develop them, I'll simply point them out. There is a theoretical question and a practical question:

1. The theoretical question is that, in order to account for these correspondences, the "elective affinities" (to use a title from Goethe) between diverse, sometimes contradictory, even antagonistic movements, we must forge new analytical instruments, new concepts, because it's not the shared trait that counts there, but rather the transversality, the crossing of abstract machines that constitute a subjectivity and that are incarnated, that live in very different regions and domains and, I repeat, that can be contradictory and antagonistic. That is therefore an entire problematic, an entire analytic, of subjectivity which must be developed in order to understand, to account for, to plot the map of [*cartographier*] what these molecular revolutions are.

2. That brings us to the second aspect, which is that we cannot be content with these analogies and affinities; we must also try to construct a social practice, to construct new modes of intervention, this time no longer in molecular, but molar relationships, in political and social power relations, in order to avoid watching the systematic, recurring defeat that we knew during the 1970s, particularly in Italy with the enormous rise of repression linked to an event, in itself repressive, which was the rise of terrorism. Through its methods, its violence, and its dogmatism, terrorism gives aid to the State repression which it is fighting. There is a sort of complicity, there again transversal. So, in this case, we are no longer only on the theoretical plane, but on the plane of experimentation, of new forms of interactions, of movement construction that respects the diversity, the sensitivities, the particularities of interventions, and that is nonetheless capable of constituting antagonistic machines of struggle to intervene in power relations.

I really can't develop much for you on that; this is simply to tell you that there is at least a beginning of such an experimentation showing that this is not entirely a dream, not only mere formulae like I tossed them out ten, fifteen years ago; and this movement, I believe that it's the German Greens who are giving us not its model, but its direction, since the German model is of course not transposable. But it's true that the German Greens not only are people whose activity is quite in touch with daily life, who are concerned with problems relating to children, education, psychiatry, and so on, who are concerned with the environment and with struggles for peace. They are also people who are now capable of establishing very important power relations at the heart of German politics, and who intervene on the Third World front, for example, having intervened in solidarity with the French *Canaques*,[6] or who intervene in Europe to develop similar movements. That interests me greatly, the multifunctionality of this movement, this departure from something that is a central apparatus with its program, its political bureau, with its secretariat. You see, I've returned again to the same terms I used when we were talking about the Collège de Philosophie.

CS: That is, the Greens seem to work on all strata, on both molar and molecular strata, of the Third World . . .

FG: Right, and on artistic strata and philosophical strata.

3.   French Politics under Mitterand

CS: I'd like to continue the discussion in this political direction. You wrote an article last year entitled "The Left as Processual Passion" (in Guattari 1986a, 51–54; Genosko 1996, 259–261), and you spoke about several aspects of the current political scene. I'd like to know how you see this scene, not only from a political perspective, but from an intellectual one as well. For example, in this article, you spoke of Mitterand's government, and you said, "The Socialist politicos settled into the sites of power without any reexamination of the existing institutions"; that Mitterand, "at first, let the different dogmatic tendencies in his government pull in opposing directions, then resigned himself to installing a tumultuous management team whose terminological differences from Reagan's 'Chicago Boys' must not mask the fact that this team is leading us toward the same kinds of aberrations."[7] Could you develop these comments by explaining the resemblance that you see between Mitterand's and Reagan's politics?

FG: It is not exactly a resemblance. There is, let's say, a methodological resemblance which is that these are people, whatever their origins, their education, who have come to think that there was only one possible political and economic approach, which they deduced from economic indices, and the like, the idea that they could govern on the basis of the existing and functioning economic axiomatic.

But, very schematically, here is how I see things: current world capitalism has taken control of the entirety of productive activities and activities of social life on the whole planet by succeeding in a double operation, an operation permeating worldwide [*de mondialisation*] that consisted in rendering homogeneous the Eastern State capitalistic countries and then a totally peripheral Third World capitalism in an identical system of economic markets, thus of economic semiotizations. This operation has completely reduced the possibilities; that is, at the limit, we no longer have the dual relationship between imperialistic countries and colonized countries. All are at once colonized and imperialistic in a multicentering of imperialism. This is quite an operation, that is, it's a new alliance between the deep-rooted capitalism of Western countries and the new capitalisms constituted by the "nomenclatura" of the Eastern countries and the kinds of aristocracies in Third World countries. One incident that I'll point out to you, which in fact would be entirely superficial, in my opinion, is lumping together Japanese capitalism with American and European capitalisms. For I have the impression that we have yet to understand that it's a completely different capitalism from the others, that Japanese capitalism does not function at all on the same bases. I don't want to develop this point, but it would be quite interesting to do so.

The other operation of this capitalism is an operation of integration, that is, its objective is not an immediate profit, a direct power, but rather to capture subjectivities from within, if I can use this term.[8] And to do so, what better technique is there to capture subjectivities than to produce them oneself? It's like those old science fiction films with invader themes, the body snatchers; integrated world capitalism takes the place of the subjectivity, it doesn't have to mess around with class struggles, with conflicts: it expropriates the subjectivity directly because it produces subjectivity itself. It's quite relaxed about it; let's say that this is an ideal which this capitalism partially attains. How does it do it? By producing subjectivity, that is, it produces quite precisely the semiotic chains, the ways of representing the world to oneself, the forms of sensitivity, the forms of curriculum, of education, of evolution; it furnishes different age groups, different categories of the population, with a mode of functioning in the same way that it would put computer chips in cars, to guarantee their semiotic functioning.

Yet, with this in mind, this subjectivity is not necessarily uniform, but rather very differentiated. It is differentiated as a function of the requirements of production, as a function of racial segregations, as a function of sexual segregations, as a function of x differences, because the objective is not to create a universal subjectivity, but to continue to reproduce something that guarantees power with a certain number of capitalistic elites that are totally traditional, as we can witness quite well with Thatcherism and Reaganism. They aren't in the process of creating a renewed and universal humanity, not at all; they want to continue the traditions of American, Japanese, Russian, and so on, aristocracies.

Thus, there is a double movement, of deterritorialization of subjectivities in an informational and cybernetic direction of adjacencies of subjectivity in matters of production, but a movement of reterritorialization of subjectivities in order to assign them to a place, and especially to keep them in this place and to control them well, to place them under house arrest, to block their circulation, their flows. This is the meaning of all the measures leading to unemployment, to the segregation of entire economic spaces, to racism, and the like: to keep the population in place. One of the best ways of keeping them in place would have been to develop politics of guilt such as those in the great universalist religious communities. But that didn't work too well, these politics of interiorization and guilt, which explains the collapse of theories like psychoanalysis. Now it's much more a systemic thought that asserts itself: it's a matter of creating systemic poles that guarantee that the functions of desire, functions of rupture of balance will manifest themselves the least possible. What is the best procedure? Much better than guilt is systematic endangering: you're sitting in a place, you might have a tiny functionary's job, you might be a top-level manager; that's not important. It's absolutely necessary that you are convinced that, at any moment, you could be thrown out of this job. That concerns the nonguarantees of welfare as well as the superguarantees of the salaried professions, with their contracts, perquisites, dachas, and so on. From this point of view, it's the same in Russia as in the United States. You are not guaranteed; you are not guaranteed by a connection, by a territory, by a profession, by a corporation; you are essentially endangered because you depend on this system which, from one day to the next, as a function of some requirement of production or simply some requirement of power or social control, might say to you: now, it's over. You might have been the biggest TV star with tens of millions of fans crazy about you, but in the next instant, all that could end immediately if there were any dissension that suddenly resulted in your no longer functioning in the register of functions we agree to promote for the production of subjectivity. So it's that kind of instrument, I believe, that gives this power to integrated world capitalism.

And so, in that case, what does a Socialist government do when it comes to power in France? At the beginning, it thinks that it will be able to change all of that, it thinks that it will be able to change television, hierarchical relationships, relationships with immigrants, and so on. And there is astonishment for six months during the grace period. And then, since it has no antagonistic instrument, no different social practice, no specific production of subjectivity, since the government is itself molded by bureaucratization, by hierarchical spirit, by the segregation formed by the integrated model of capitalism, necessarily it discovers with astonishment that it can do nothing, that it is completely the prisoner of inflation, of mechanisms that render impossible the development of a production and a social life in such a country subjugated by the overall machinery of world capitalism. A guy I know well, sort of a friend, Jack Lang [the minister of culture], discovered this immediately: he made a few harmless statements, that might have passed totally without notice, at the UNESCO convention that I attended. Then he found that he had set off an explosion because he had dared to touch a tiny wire, a tiny wheel of this mechanism of subjectivation. He dared to say: after all, this American cinema is something that has taken much too great an importance vis-à-vis the potential Third World productions. There was a frightening scandal! He had to beat a retreat because he questioned—like during the Inquisition—he questioned fundamental dogma relating to this production of subjectivity.

CS: You have said about the Socialist government that by committing itself to "an absurd one-upsmanship with the Right in the area of security, of austerity, and of conservatism," the Left has not contributed "to the assemblage of new collective modes of enunciation." What collective modes of enunciation did you foresee?

FG: Listen, from 1977 to 1981, a group of friends and I organized a movement, that wasn't very powerful, but wasn't entirely negligible either, whose images I have here [FG indicates the different posters on his living room walls], that was called the Free Radio Movement. We developed about a hundred free radio stations, an experimentation, a new mode of expression somewhat similar to what happened in

Italy. Before 1981, the Socialists supported us; François Mitterand even came to some of our stations, and there was a lawsuit (I lost it, by the way, I lost quite a few). When they came to power, they created a committee on free radios; they undertook the most incredible machinations with their Socialist militants, people who aren't directly venal in terms of money, but who are part of the venality of power, an administrative venality. To speak bluntly, they appointed their buddies, people who knew absolutely nothing about free radios. The result: at the end of two years, all the stations were dead, and all had been invaded, just like the invaders we were talking about, by municipal interests, by private capitalists, by the large newspapers who already had all the power, by other stations, that resulted in their quite simply killing the Free Radio Movement. I think that if a rightist government had remained in place, we would have continued to struggle and to achieve things. It sufficed that the Socialists came to power in order to liquidate all that.

I've given you the example of free radios, but I can give you the example of attempts at pedagogical and educational renovations. They liquidated it all; no, not everything, since there are nonetheless some experimental high schools like Gabriel Cohn-Bendit's, one of my friends.[9] But, after all, one sees clearly today, and I said this directly to Laurent Fabius [then Mitterand's prime minister], that [Jean-Pierre] Chevènement is the most conservative minister of national education that we have seen during the Fifth Republic. I could go on and on: in the domain of alternatives to psychiatry, there was an incredible offensive of calumny, of destruction of the alternative network through the lawsuit undertaken against Claude Sigala, claiming that he had raped little boys, I don't know what else.

I could make a complete enumeration for all the potentialities; they weren't enormous, it wasn't May 1968, but some beginnings, some new kinds of practices, compositions of new attitudes, of new assemblages, of all that have been systematically crushed. Not that the Socialists did this voluntarily; they didn't realize what they were doing, that's the worst part! They didn't realize what they were doing!

CS: So, this failure of the Left from a political perspective could be extended undoubtedly to the intellectual domain.

FG: Well, there, the failure has been total.

CS: You also said in this article, "A whole soup of supposed 'new philosophy,' of 'postmodernism,' of 'social implosion,' and I could go on, finally ended up by poisoning the atmosphere and by contributing to the discouragement of attempts at political commitment at the heart of the intellectual milieu."

FG: Well, the Socialists weren't responsible for that; it had begun well before. But it's true that despite the sometimes considerable efforts by the Ministry of Culture, the result is quite nil in all domains. For example, in the domain of cinema, French cinema is alive from an economic point of view, but it doesn't at all have the richness of German cinema or other kinds because in this domain as well, the assemblages of enunciations remained entirely traditional, in the publishing houses, in the classical systems of production, and so on.

CS: And your work in *change International?*[10]

FG: They helped us a bit, at the beginning, and then they dropped us. This was, in my opinion, a very interesting and very promising undertaking, but we didn't have the resources, and as you know, for a journal with that kind of ambition, one has to have resources.

CS: So it no longer exists?

FG: No. Well, there is an issue coming out, we're still going to put out one or two issues, but what we wanted to create was a powerful monthly, international journal. Instead, the Socialists spent billions to support stupidities like the *Nouvelles littéraires* journal. And I mean billions! It's shameful.

4.   Deleuze and Guattari and Psychoanalysis

CS: Regarding the current intellectual scene, in a recent issue of *Magazine littéraire*, D. A. Grisoni claimed that *Mille plateaux* proves that "the desiring vein" has disappeared . . .

FG: Yeh, I saw that! (*Laughter*)

CS: . . . and he called Deleuze "dried up" (Grisoni 1983, 78). What do you think of this? What is your conception of the schizoanalytic enterprise right now, and what aspects of the two volumes of *Capitalism and Schizophrenia* appear to you as the most valid?

FG: They're not valid at all! Me, I don't know, I don't care! It's not my problem! It's however you want it, whatever use you want to make of it. Right now, I'm working, Deleuze is working a lot. I'm working with a group of friends on the possible directions of schizoanalysis; yes, I'm theorizing in my own way. If people don't care about it, that's their business; but I don't care either, so that works out well.

CS: That's precisely what Deleuze said yesterday evening: I understand quite well that people don't care about my work because I don't care about theirs either.

FG: Right, so there's no problem. You see, we didn't even discuss it, but we had the same answer! (*Laughter*)

CS: Deleuze and I spoke briefly about the book by Jean-Paul Aron, *Les modernes* (1984).[11] What astounded me was that despite his way of presenting things, he really liked *Anti-Oedipus*. What particularly struck me in his statement about *Anti-Oedipus* was that "despite a few bites, the doctor [Lacan] is the sacred precursor of schizoanalysis and of the hyper-sophisticated industry of desiring machines" (Aron 1984, 285). A question that one asks in reading *Anti-Oedipus* is what is the place of Lacanian psychoanalysis in the schizoanalytic project? One gets the impression that you distance yourselves from most of the thinkers presented, but that Lacan has a rather privileged place to the extent that there is no rupture.

FG: In my opinion, what you are saying is not completely accurate because it's true in the beginning of *Anti-Oedipus,* and then if you look, en route, it's less and less true because, obviously, we didn't write at the end the same way as we did in the beginning, and then it's not true at all throughout *A Thousand Plateaus*—there, it's all over. This means the following: Deleuze never took Lacan seriously at all, but for me, that was very important. It's true that I've gone through a whole process of clarification, which didn't occur quickly, and I haven't finally measured, dare I say it, the superficial character of Lacan. That will seem funny, but in the end, I think that's how Deleuze and Foucault . . . I remember certain conversations of that period, and I realize that they considered all that as rather simplistic, superficial. That seems funny because it's such a sophisticated, complicated language.

So, I'm nearly forced to make personal confidences about this because, if I don't, this won't be clear. What was important for me with Lacan is that it was an event in my life, an event to meet this totally bizarre, extraordinary guy with extraordinary, crazy even, acting talent, with an astounding cultural background. I was a student at the Sorbonne, I was bored shitless in courses with Lagache, Zazzo, I don't remember who, and then I went to Lacan's seminar. I have to say that it represented an entirely unforeseen richness and inventiveness in the university. That's what Lacan was; he was above all a guy with guts; you can say all you want about Lacan, but you can't say the contrary, he had no lack of guts. He possessed a depth of freedom that he inherited from a rather blessed period, I have to say, the period before the war, the period of surrealism, a period with a kind of gratuitous violence. One thinks of Gide's Lafcadio.

He had a dadaist humor, a violence at the same time, a cruelty; he was a very cruel guy, Lacan, very harsh.

As for Deleuze, it wasn't the same because he acquired this freedom vis-à-vis concepts, this kind of sovereign distance in his work. Deleuze was never a follower of anyone, it seems to me, or of nearly anyone. I wasn't in the same kind of work, and it was important for me to have a model of rupture, if I can call it that, all the more so since I was involved in extreme leftist organizations, but still traditionalist from many perspectives. There was all the weight of Sartre's thought, of Marxist thought, creating a whole environment that it wasn't easy to eliminate. So, I think that's what Lacan was. Moreover, it's certain that his reading of Freud opened possibilities for me to cross through and into different ways of thinking. It's only recently that I have discovered to what extent he read Freud entirely in bad faith. In other words, he really just made anything he wanted out of Freud because, if one really reads Freud, one realizes that it has very little to do with Lacanism. (*Laughter*)

CS: Could you specify in which writings or essays Lacan seems to read this way?

FG: The whole Lacanian extrapolation about the signifier, in my opinion, is absolutely un-Freudian, because Freud's way of constructing categories relating to the primary processes was also a way of making their cartography that, in my opinion, was much closer to schizoanalysis, that is, much closer to a sometimes nearly delirious development—why not?—in order to account for how the dream and how phobia function, and so on. There is a Freudian creativity that is much closer to theater, to myth, to the dream, and which has little to do with this structuralist, systemic, mathematizing, I don't know how to say it, this mathemic thought of Lacan. First of all, the greatest difference, there as well, is at the level of the enunciation considered in its globality. Freud and his Freudian contemporaries wrote something, wrote monographs. Then, in the history of psychoanalysis, and notably in this kind of structuralist vacillation, there are no monographs. It's a meta-meta-meta-theorization; they speak about textual exegesis in the nth degree, and one always returns to the original monograph, little Hans, Schreber, the Wolf Man, the Rat Man (see AO, Chap. 2; ATP, Chap. 2). So all that is ridiculous. It's as if we had the Bible, the Bible according to Schreber, the Bible according to Dora. This is interesting, this comparison could be pushed quite far. I think that there is the invention of the modelization of subjectivity, an order of this invention of subjectivity that was that of the [Freudian] apostles: it comes, it goes, but I mean that it's moving much more quickly now than at that time, that is, we won't have to wait two thousand years to put that religion in question, it seems to me.

CS: It also seems to me that there are many more apostles who have betrayed their master than apostles who betrayed Jesus.

FG: I was thinking more of the apostles, I see them more as Freud's first psychoanalyses; then, it's the Church Fathers who are the traitors. Understand, with the apostles, there is something magnificent in Freud, he's like a guy who has fallen hopelessly in love with his patients, without realizing it, more or less; a guy who introduced some very heterodoxical practices, nearly incestuous when you think of what was the spirit of medicine at that period. So, he had an emotion, there was a Freudian event of creation, an entirely original Freudian scene, and all that has been completely buried by exegesis, by the Freudian religions.

CS: A few minutes ago, you mentioned Foucault. I asked Deleuze this question about Foucault yesterday evening: what are your thoughts on Foucault nearly a year after his death? How do you react to this absence, and can we yet judge the importance of Foucault's work?

FG: It's difficult for me to respond because, quite the contrary to Deleuze, I was never influenced by Foucault's work. It interested me, of course, but it was never of great importance. I can't judge it. Quite possibly, it will have a great impact in different fields.[12]

CS: Deleuze told me something very interesting: he said that Foucault's presence kept imbeciles from speaking too loudly, and that if Foucault didn't exactly block all aberrations, he nonetheless blocked imbeciles, and now the imbeciles will be unleashed. And, in terms of Aron's book, *Les modernes,* he said that this book wouldn't have been possible while Foucault was alive, that no one would have dared publish it.

FG: Oh, you think so?

CS: I really don't know, but in any case, when it's a matter of machinations on the right . . .

FG: It's certain that Foucault had a very important authority and impact.

5.   The Americanization of Europe

CS: There's another question I want to return to. In terms of capitalism in the world, I'd like to consider the question of the Americanization that penetrates everywhere, for example, the *Dallas* effect. There is even a French *Dallas, Châteauvallon* . . .

FG: It's not bad either. It's better than *Dallas,* I find.

CS: Of course, for the French. But when you like J. R. . . .

FG: That's true. J. R. is a great character, quite formidable.

CS: But what strikes me in your writing, especially in *Rhizome,* is the impression of a kind of romanticism about America, references to the American nomadism, the country of continuous displacement, deterritorialization . . .

FG: Burroughs, Ginsberg . . .

CS: Right, and one gets the impression of a special America, and we Americans who read your texts, we know our America, and here in France, as a tourist this time, I see the changes, the penetration of our culture that has occurred over the last few years, the plastification, the fast food restaurants everywhere . . .

FG: Ah, it's incredible. And in the popular social strata, among the youth, they babble this kind of slang, they've completely identified with it, it's incredible. It's all over Europe, everywhere, the linguistic phenomenon of the incorporation of American rock. It's really surprising.

CS: So there are two conceptions of America: this nomadic conception which you present in your works, but that is finally a romantic conception in light of the practice of Americanization, the penetration of America and, of course, of capitalism. It seems that one does not go with the other, so how do you explain this difference? It's not really a contradiction, but simply a distance between two conceptions of America.

FG: Well, that's complicated. I'm not very clear about that because . . . I went to America occasionally, especially during the 1970s and then afterward, during the 1980s, I've gone to Japan, to Brazil, and to Mexico a lot, and I've no longer wanted to go to the United States. I haven't considered it well, I haven't understood why.

You know, it's not certain that this is a romantic vision. Americans are often jerks; they have a pragmatic relationship with things; they are dumb, and sometimes this is great because they don't have any background as compared to Europeans, Italians, but there is an American functionalism that makes us pass into this a-signifying register, that transports a fabulous creationism, fabulous anyhow in the technical–scientific domain, because they are really a scientific people; they don't look for complications, it works or it doesn't, they move on to something else.

I met an American last summer, I was in California, at Stanford, I don't know where. I was on a tour to study the problems of mental health, a mission for the Ministry of Exterior Affairs. Americans are people who receive you very well, who take time to talk, which isn't the case here, not the same kind of welcome. So, each person that I met gave me an hour for discussion, and there, this young psychiatrist explained what had happened after the Kennedy Act, the liquidation of the big psychiatric hospitals and the establishment in his sector of halfway houses, a kind of day hospital to replace the big hospitals. He made a diagram chart, I remember, there was a graph with double entries, there were all the dimensions of these establishments, a remarkable organization of what had been developed. So, he finished presenting all that to me, and then the conversation finally ended, but there still remained ten minutes because we had an hour for our discussion, so there was no reason to leave. And I asked him a final question: "And so, how did all that work? What was the result?" He broke out laughing: "Nil. Zero. It didn't work at all!" I said: "Oh, really?" He said: "Yes, it's just a program we made, but it didn't work at all!" That was like a thunderbolt for me that this guy had made this entire development, and then it didn't work, so let's do something else. We see this well in [Gregory] Bateson's work: he makes a program on something, it works, but that doesn't matter, they move on to something else because they were on contract.[13] That's what I find to be the marvelous a-signifying freedom, going on to something else, going on to something else. They massacre Vietnamese for years, then afterward, oh, well, no, that was stupid, let's go on to something else.

So I wonder if that isn't the rather invading, Yankee side of Americans that makes us ask what they're up to, what they're looking for. But one shouldn't try too hard to discover what they're looking for or what they're up to. It's the same for the Japanese, but with an entire background of mysticism, of religiosity, that also exists in the United States, but without being structured the same way.

CS: But where could we insert this question of nomadism? We have this "go on to something else" nomadism, so perhaps that's it, Kerouac, going on to something else . . .

FG: And next, and next, and next, constantly, constantly, and now, and now.

CS: . . . but his kind of incessant deterritorialization only exists in extreme cases, so to speak.

FG: But, no, that's not true. Jean-Paul Sartre, when he made his trip to America—that must have been in 1947 or thereabouts—wrote a magnificent article about American cities. He explained that American cities aren't cities in the European sense, that is, they have no contours. They are crisscrossed by avenues, they have no limit. In my terminology, this means that these are deterritorialized cities. America is entirely deterritorialized. "Deterritorialized" means that instead of having obstacles or having land, things, curves, there are lines, trains, planes, everything crossing, everything sliding, demographic flows sliding everywhere, and on top of that, there are extraordinary reterritorializations. Henry Miller in Brooklyn, Faulkner in a certain sense, because for Faulkner, to what extent isn't it a misreading to situate him as an archaic writer of American life? Isn't he rather a mythical reterritorialization about deterritorialized America? We'd need to debate that; I'm not able to undertake it about Faulkner. Anyway, how does one make oneself a "body without organs," how does one make oneself a little territory, a life, a warmth, a childhood, in this American mess, in this whole mishmash spread out all over? Look at the extraordinary poetry of shop windows in New York! You know the shop windows in France or in Italy. But there, in New York, most of the windows speak, even on the main streets where you have side by side expensive windows and then places where you find piles of any old thing; one finds there a kind of accumulation of vistas like that, where there are marvelously beautiful things from an architectural perspective, and then there is a dump, a maximum, and then a mess.

CS: I do understand the difference between cities, the constant sliding across territorialities between city and suburb. But quite simply, this invasion, the body snatchers, America as body snatcher, the grip of capitalism in other countries, for me . . . well, perhaps that all belongs to the same process of deterritorialization: there is no territory, either in individual existence or in capitalistic flows: they invade everything, everywhere, everybody, everywhere in the world, without limits, without borders, crossing and invading France.

FG: But don't you think that this deterritorialization, catastrophic from many perspectives, is precisely the occasion for extraordinary reterritorializations? That is, it's difficult to make oneself a territory on the Moon, really; it's more complicated than going out to the French countryside. America is a bit like the Moon, it's very complicated, and precisely these traits create a difference from the Japanese as well because the Japanese have means of reterritorialization, a very ancient civilization, they have insignia, emblems of this reterritorialization, corporal techniques, and the like. Whereas there, in America, they are forced to reinvent everything, these kinds of continental Galeries Lafayette [Paris department store], anything. So that becomes a formidable exercise: to create music with a tradition of religious music is difficult, but creating music with just anything, like that, with these piles of metal, it's something else altogether. And when they succeed, it's fantastic.

But look: take the American mystery novel whose basic material is all this deterritorializing trivia, and look at what warmth of intimacy, of suspense, of subjectivity that you grab to stay warm, to sleep, to feel good, to feel sheltered; it's really something. With what do they create that? What are they talking about? These aren't tales of chivalry. American cinema as well has a lot of that: look at the power of American culture to produce a more than tolerable and comfortable subjectivity, warm, passionate, exciting, in this pile of metal, this heap of shit, this load of stupidities, as I said earlier. Isn't that really quite a feat? It's nonetheless a civilization that has created some extraordinary forms of subjectivation. Jazz . . . do you realize? Jazz has a great impact on the level of world culture. Line up cinema, jazz, the mystery novel. I'll leave painting aside because I find that, in the long run, it's not a very noticeable success because it really belongs to capitalistic deterritorialization, seriously, with some exceptions, but for me, it's really a lot less convincing.

CS: I think that the problem for me is that I'm too close to daily life in the States, and I see so much stupidity in all these areas. In cinema, one constantly sees exploitation of the body, of the individual. In music, there is so much shit . . .

FG: That's true; when one hears the classical music that people listen to in the United States, it's overwhelming. Won't you ever get fed up with Rachmaninoff, Tchaikovsky, and all that . . . ?

CS: I was really thinking about popular music, where all that might happen, where changes did occur during the 1970s. But what always strikes me is that the music comes from England to invade America, and then America reterritorializes what the English do, and they lose everything. That began with the colonies and continues today. But, perhaps its my own problem, being too close to this daily life, and not being able to see this abstract machine which you are outlining. But, on the other hand, the reproach made by friends who read *A Thousand Plateaus* and other works is really that in regards to American nomadism, this deterritorialization, they'd like to believe in it, but isn't the general schizoanalytic enterprise in the long run a utopic dream without any future?

FG: I'm sorry to interrupt you, but in any case, the idea of a utopic dream just doesn't hold water. A dream is necessarily utopic, in any case. We participated a little in that America, that kind of New West. It was our dream, our very own America. You are telling me that it's not yours! I find that fascinating, but you aren't going to reproach me for having dreamt my dream! You have a whole generation of American writers who created a dream about Europe, about Greece, who landed here like these were colonies, but I'm not going to reproach them for having perceived in their own way, "What is this Europe you saw here?," that's just not possible! What one has to know is: Has it been useful for you that we had that dream? Has it been useful for us that you had that dream, that some American writers had a particular dream about Europe before the war? For me, yes, that certainly was useful. I haven't looked at Europe in the same way because there is this deterritorialized vision by relay from American writers. Miller's vision of Paris, for me, is enormous, is fundamental! I'm sorry that Deleuze and Guattari's vision of the United States hasn't been at all useful for you, but we can't all have the same talent as Miller! (*Laughter*)

6.   Left and Right Readings of Deleuze and Guattari

CS: That's not at all what I said, but it's a question that comes from a friend who is working on *Anti-Oedipus* and is waiting for the translation of *Mille plateaux*. He is trying to use the developments of schizoanalysis in his work on the philosophy of communication, how effects of communication are produced on sociological as well as philosophical levels. So, he is attempting to present this thought, and his students, from another generation of thinkers, reveal a certain cynicism that dominates all Western societies, not only in the United States, but a cynicism that sees Marxism, or any thought attempting to outline a theory and a practice, merely as being a utopic dream finally leading nowhere.

FG: But that all belongs to the same reactionary stupidity, it's the Restoration, the great Restoration. That's not really important because other generations will soon discover, will soon say, "Oh, that's right . . . " That's the dregs of history, it's valueless. But that still doesn't prove that there isn't a potential America, an America of nomadism. Some people still exist . . . I was thinking of Julian Beck, of Judith Molina, the former members of the Living Theater. Just because they've been completely marginalized is no reason to ignore their existence. They still exist nonetheless.

CS: There's another reproach made about *Anti-Oedipus,* and you might lump it together with the previous objection, regarding a kind of recuperation of schizoanalytic thought by the right. There was recently an article in *Le nouvel observateur* (Anquetil 1984), an article about a book by Michel Noir, *1988: Le grand rendez-vous* (Noir 1984), where he uses *Mille plateaux* and a book by Prigogine as the organizing model for a new rightist thought.

FG: Oh, really? I didn't know about it. Do you have it there?

CS: Yes. [*FG peruses the article*] So here are two kinds of reproach: in the States, some people think that here is a thought that merely boils down to a utopic dream, and others say, right, but this schizoanalysis is a thought without any ideological specificity, if you will; that is, either the Left or the Right can make use of it. It's this question of the toolbox: a little earlier, when I questioned you about the use of schizoanalysis, you said, Yes, in the end, I continue to work, and what people do with schizoanalysis doesn't interest me, they can take it or leave it, but I'm busy with our work. That's all well and good, but here is French neoliberalism, a rightist intellectual using it. Still again, that may not matter at all to you . . .

FG: Oh, not at all because what does it mean to attach a name like that, to hook our names onto it as a reference? Is it true, does it correspond to anything? It's quite simply a paradox. And then there is another aspect of this thing: this Left–Right split is absolutely evident in social struggles, in power relations, as shown in the current reactionary upheaval, the rise of racism. But on the level of thought, it's not at all clear. Let's take a very simple example, the example of schools: I'm for free schools,[14] not free schools run by priests, but I'm for the liberation of schools, I'm in favor of dismantling national education, and so on. So, is this a theme of the Right or the Left? A while ago, Gérard Soulier, a law professor who organized a prisoners' review on culture in prisons, did a study on drugs, and he quoted me as explaining that I was for the elimination of all repression of the spread of drugs since that was the best way to avoid an escalation of dealers, of criminality, and the like, and right beside this, he placed an identical statement word for word from Milton Friedman! Understand?

II. Machinic
1. "Minor literature"
2. *A Thousand Plateaus*: A "Speculative Cartography"
3. *A Thousand Plateaus*: "Becoming-Woman"
4. *A Thousand Plateaus*: The "Body without Organs"

   5. *A Thousand Plateaus*: Modes of Encoding and A-signifying
      Semiotics
   6. *A Thousand Plateaus*: The "War Machine" and "Striated"
      versus "Smooth" Space

II.   MACHINIC

1.   "Minor Literature"

CS: You have often referred to works by particular American authors as
forms of deterritorialization, and I'd like to situate these reflections in
relation to what you've said about "minor literature" [*littérature mineure*]. Specifically, when you speak of one or several "minor literature(s),"
are these necessarily forms of deterritorialization, and if so, how?

FG: In Kafka's writing, this kind of deterritorialization of language is
obvious. That is, his work is located on an edge, a border, at the limit
of a huge aggregate in order to deterritorialize, a way of fighting a kind
of "en-sobering," of making sober, an active return to sobriety of
language.[15] One finds this process of deterritorialization, for example,
in Samuel Beckett's works, an impoverishment that at the same time
is a placing into intensity, an intensification of expression. So, I hadn't
thought about it, but, in fact, one could make an equation by saying
that whenever a marginality, a minority, becomes active, takes the word
power [*puissance de verbe*], transforms itself into becoming, and not
merely submitting to it, identical with its condition, but in active,
processual becoming, it engenders a singular trajectory that is necessarily deterritorializing because, precisely, it's a minority that begins
to subvert a majority, a consensus, a great aggregate. As long as a
minority, a cloud, is on a border, a limit, an exteriority of a great whole,
it's something that is rejected, something that is, by definition, marginalized. But here, this point, this object, begins to proliferate, to use
categories suggested by Prigogine and Stengers (1979), begins to
amplify, to recompose something that is no longer a totality, but that
makes a former totality shift, detotalizes, deterritorializes an entity.

   For example, to return to what we were saying earlier about the
German Greens, one could say that this is more or less what seems
to be produced: a few marginals, whom everybody made fun of,
created an upheaval in Parliament, and became representatives. They
behave totally differently, for example, they have a rotation system,
they change every two years, which makes quite a mess in the
German or European Parliaments. And one realizes that the issues
they are developing, that were marginal issues, are becoming not
major issues, but issues that upset the whole society, not only their
ecological theme because, in fact, people realize that the German

forests are devastated, and that the Greens have been announcing it for twenty years; but also because these are attitudes that question the regular hierarchy, the orders of value, and so on, and this is what I call the process of singularization: what was ranked as being ordered, coordinated, referenced, now one no longer knows: What is the face? What are they doing? What is the reference? The system of values is inverted.

I lived that myself during May 1968. I had the impression sometimes of walking on the ceiling, of not knowing any more what was going on, when I found myself in the occupied areas of the Sorbonne where I had been a student, where I had been completely bored, the Amphitheater Richelieu invaded by students writing graffiti everywhere. What was the order of the referenced, of the organized, of the coordinated is located in the order of process because, suddenly, there are singular elements that quit their enclosure, their singularity, their isolation, and begin to be a kind of exploratory probe, a producing probe, precisely engendering systems of autoreference. Instead of being referenced, they are producers of new types of reference, they are themselves their own referential until the moment when they are rearticulated, recoordinated.

CS: So, this idea of "minor literature" is an autoproduction, the production of new territories. And the question one asks is why you limit your examples, you and Deleuze, to reference points in the twentieth century? Aren't there writers in previous centuries who can also reveal these kinds of deterritorialization?

FG: Yes, certainly. It's a problem of familiarity. It's a little difficult because . . . I may be saying something stupid, but it seems to me that the examples of eruption of "becoming-minor" either have been completely buried, or have taken on considerable importance. For example, Jean-Jacques Rousseau could have been a minor writer, but on the contrary, he has a fantastic importance as perhaps Artaud will have tomorrow, being classified as a principal writer of the twentieth century. I even think this is presently taking place.

So, I don't know. One really has to see the "minor" a bit in its nascent state, one has to see it a bit closer to oneself because the historically distant "minor" has perhaps a different impact. I don't know, I haven't thought about this question.

2. *A Thousand Plateaus*: A "Speculative Cartography"

[FG's answers to the following sets of questions correspond to the various schema that he was preparing in the mid- to late 1980s for his seminars and, eventually, for publication in *Cartographies schizoanalytiques,* neither of which I had access to at the time. In revising the text below, I attempted to clarify the dense conceptual terrain, to the extent possible, with reference to CS.][16]

CS: I'd like to ask several questions going into some detail about *A Thousand Plateaus.* Referring to two terms, "faciality" [the subject of Plateau 7, "Year Zero–Faciality"], and another term, "heccéité" [introduced in Plateau 10, "1730–Becoming-Intense, Becoming-Animal, Becoming-Imperceptible . . . "], could you explain what place these concepts hold in rhizoanalysis and to what regimes of signs they correspond? For example, what is the relationship of "faciality" with "black holes," and what is the function of "haecceity" in the cartographic process?

FG: Oh, là là. That's enormous. I'd really have to develop a very complex overview. We need to consider a separate speculative cartography, divided between two logics: a cardologic, that is, the logic of discursive aggregates, and an ordologic, the logic of bodies without organs.[17]

Under the first logic, there are discursive systems, there is always an aggregate to connect to another aggregate, it engenders a meaning effect, that can refer you to another meaning effect, creating a double articulation. There is the arbitrary nature of the relationship: for example, one might be a phonological chain and the other the semantic content, but the double articulation can be triple because there is no primacy of the double articulation. But each time that there are these deep structures of meaning, there are also what I call "primary modules of enunciation" that then correspond to an ordological aggregate, that is, they aren't discursive. With this in mind, they nonetheless compose subjective agglomerations as well, agglomerates, constellations, but that do not accede to expression in the direction of discursive differentiation, but that emerge in a phenomenon of countermeaning, which at one moment is a statement [*énoncé*], for example, the dream—by the way, I'm going to do an analysis of the dream from this perspective[18]—which is caught in paradigmatic coordinates, in energetic coordinates; it [the statement] also serves in the other direction as enunciator [*énonciateur*].

So let's say that there is triple division [*tripartition*] of the referential or autoreferential activity of enunciation that goes in the direction of the discursivity-logic (the cardologic) such that one can bracket, completely set aside, the problematic of enunciation. But where the problematic reappears is when a statement functions as organizer of the enunciation; in that case, it's according to completely different logical norms because the statement functions to agglomerate, to juxtapose, primary enunciators (under the ordologic). It's in this way that we see the double impact of a statement that can work, function, both in the direction of discursive aggregates and in the direction of what I call "synapses."

So, we can divide a graph into four categories: the categories of "material and indicative Fluxes" and of "machinic Phylums" [under the cardologic], and the categories of "existential Territories" and of "incorporeal Universes" [under the ordologic].[19] The incorporeal Universes would be precisely everything that becomes detached from this primary enunciation, all the pseudo-deep structures of enunciation because here (under the ordologic) everything is flat, whereas (under the cardologic) there are effectively deep structures with all kinds of paradigms that intersect.[20] So, when all the coordinates are unified, these are capitalistic coordinates; if not unified, these are what one can call regional or local coordinates.[21]

All this is to tell you that with "faciality," you have a face there (under the machinic Phylum, in the synapses), a face that can be situated in different coordinates, it's big, it's small, it's white, it's like this or that; one can put it in all the paradigmatic coordinates. One can make a content analysis: what is that face? But certain traits of this face can be detached from this cardology and function in the ordological logic, and then it's the father's superego-ish mustache, the grimace, or the gaze of Christ looking at you, and that then is a discursive chain, but that doesn't function in those cardological coordinates, but functions to put on a mask, to coagulate, to constellate, some subjective enunciators. It's a bit in the general lineage of the Lacanian object small-a, it's a generalized function of the object small-c or transitional object.[22] It's this kind of object that one finds in dreams, in phantasms, in delirium, or in religion. It's an object that functions on two registers: in one register, let's say, of an aesthetic unconscious because we can say that it has an aesthetic unconscious, and in a machinic unconscious. So, the haecceity is the fact that it occurs as an event, but when it emerges, it has always-already been there, it is always everywhere. It's like the smile of the Cheshire cat in Lewis Carroll's *Alice,* it's everywhere, in the entire universe.

So there remains a paradox to consider, this logic of the event that is dated, situated, articulated by a particular use, a sign-function. But the sign has this double import, that's why a few years ago—this is another theme—I preferred to talk about a "point-sign" entity, because it's a sign insofar as being a surplus-value of meaning that emerges from this relationship of repetition. But it begins to function as a point of materialization of enunciation at the same time as it is this element that is going to catalyze an existential constellation. It's something that isn't at all extraordinary in the long run since, if you think about it, in the entire cybernetic economy, there is the "formalism" function of significations that are articulated in many signs, but there is also the material function of the sign that functions like a signal, like a release mechanism [*déclencheur*], a material release mechanism with its own energy, with its own consistency, with threshold phenomena. So I think that it's entirely essential to forge a "point-sign" category in which semiotics has an impact in release effects [*effets de déclenchement*]. There is a particular moment when a sign passes into act, but its way of passing into act is something inscribed in machines, in recordings, in releases, in release mechanisms; I'm working on this subject in an article for one of Prigogine's colloquia where I'll speak, an article on semiotic energetics. There is a semiotic energetics as well.[23]

CS: How could one translate this schema into political terms?

FG: In political terms, one asks: What are the statements, what are the representations of images, of echoes, of faces that, at a certain moment, result in this: instead of hearing/understanding [*entendre*] a discourse, a statement is existentializing, and an effect of subjectivity is crystallized, an effect not only crystallized on the mode of representation, but on the mode of enacting [*mise en acte*]? All at once, that [effect] begins to exist. That's when saying is existing; it's no longer when saying is doing or when saying is making-exist. From this results the fact that there's a particular usage of language since a mode of politics can be completely aberrant from the point of view of meaning, like a ritual usage or religious activity. The whole question is knowing if this usage can be compatible with a perspective of desire, with an aesthetic perspective, or another operation, or if it's a way to construct an a-subjective subjectivity.

3. *A Thousand Plateaus:* "Becoming-Woman"

CS: I'd like to return to one of the areas you touched on earlier, that is, feminism, in order to consider the term "becoming-woman," whether this conception still functions, if it was a conception that had a historical specificity at a given moment or if it's still valid today. It's a term to which certain feminists react in a very negative way.

FG: In the United States? Because that's not everywhere, there are some feminists who react to it quite well.

CS: In the United States and in France.

FG: About the "becoming-woman" question? I didn't know.

CS: Oh yes. One objection is that one finds "becoming-woman," especially in *A Thousand Plateaus,* in a kind of progression—becoming-woman, becoming-animal, becoming-child, then becoming-molecular, and finally becoming-imperceptible—and so the question: Why "woman" at the beginning of this progression? Why is there this sort of questioning of femininity? Where is the woman, where is the woman's body in all that?[24]

FG: There is no rigorous dialectic, there is no series of connections like *The Phenomenology of Mind.* But simply, the departure from binary power relations, from phallic relations, is on the side of the "woman" alternative; the promotion of a new kind of gentleness, a new kind of domestic relationship; the departure from this, one might say, elementary dimension of power that the conjugal unit represents, it's on the side of woman and on the side of the child such that, in some ways, the promotion of values, of a new semiotics of the body and sexuality, passes necessarily through the woman, through "becoming-woman." And this "becoming-woman" isn't reserved to women, this could be a "becoming-homosexual." ... To present this simply, brutally: if you want to be a writer, if you want to have a "becoming-letters," you are necessarily caught in a "becoming-woman." That might be manifested to a great extent through homosexuality, admitted or not, but this is a departure from a "grasping," power's will to circumscribe that exists in the world of masculine power values. Let's say that this is the first sphere of explosion of phallic power, therefore of binary power, of the surface–depth power [*pouvoir figure-fond*] of affirmation. Obviously, it doesn't end there, for this "becoming-woman" is nonetheless to a great extent in a relationship, even indirect, of dependence vis-à-vis masculine power so that it might rapidly be reconverted into the form of masculinized power.

There are other becomings that are much more multivocal, that are much more liberated from this bi-univocity, from these binary relations of woman–man, yin–yang, and so on. So these are the other "becomings" that you've enumerated that ... well, it's obvious that animal-becomings, for example in Kafka, offer an exploratory spectrum of intensities, of sensitivities, that is much larger than a simple binary alternative, that also exists in Kafka, but there are binary machinic alternatives in his work: think of his magnificent short story, "Blumfeld," where you have a little pingpong ball bouncing like that. So, the "becoming-woman" has no priority, it's no more of a matrix than a "becoming-plant," than a "becoming-animal," than a "becoming-abstract," than a "becoming-molecular"; it's a direction. Toward what? Quite simply, toward another logic, or rather a logic I've called "machinic," an existential machinic, that is, no longer a reading of a pure representation, but a composition of the world, the production of a body without organs in the sense that the organs there are no longer in a relationship of surface–depth positionality, do not postulate a totality itself referenced on other totalities, on other systems of signification that are, in the end, forms of power. Rather, these are forms of intensity, forms of existence-position that construct time as they represent it, exactly like in art, forms that construct coordinates of existence at the same time as they live them.

4.   *A Thousand Plateaus*: The "Body without Organs"

CS: You've suggested this term "body without organs" that continues to cause problems for your readers, and I'd like to pursue this idea: in Plateau 6 of *A Thousand Plateaus,* the chapter "How Do You Make Yourself Make a Body without Organs?," you compare the relationship between the organism and the body without organs to the relationship between two key terms suggested to Carlos Castaneda by don Juan in *Tales of Power,* the "Tonal" [the organism, significance, the subject, all that is organized and organizing in/for these elements], and the "Nagual" [the whole of the Tonal in conditions of experimentation, of flow, of becomings, but without destruction of the Tonal] (Castaneda 1974; ATP, 161–162; MP, 199–200). This correspondence between your terms and the Tonal/Nagual couple created some problems for me to the extent that the Nagual seems to correspond to the general "plane of consistency," to the bodies without organs which you pluralize in this plateau. Could you explain the difference between the various forms of bodies without organs— for example, you designate a particular body without organs for junkies and some other very specific forms of bodies without organs— and the more general Body without Organs?

FG: Listen. In this, I think we'd get quickly locked into a misunderstanding if I passed the time making a zoological description of bodies without organs, a taxonomy of bodies without organs since, as I just told you, to make oneself a body without organs, starting with drugs, with a love experience, with poetry, with any creation, is essentially to produce a cartography, that has this particular characteristic: that one cannot distinguish it [the cartography] from the existential territory which [the cartography] represents. There is no difference between the map and the territory. That means that there is no transposition, that there is no translatability, and therefore no possible taxonomy. The modelization here is a producer of existence.

So you'll say: in that case, why use general terms like "body without organs," and the like (and God knows that with Deleuze, we've had no trouble creating them)? Yes, but then one must distinguish between what I call a "speculative cartography," concepts of transmodelization, and then the instruments of direct modelization, that is, a concrete cartography. To push the paradox to its limit, I'd say that the interest of a speculative cartography is that it be as far away as possible, that it have no pretension of accounting for concrete cartographies. This is its difference from a scientific activity. Science is conceived to propose the semiotization which accounts for practical experience. For us, it's just the opposite! The less we'll account for things, the farther we'll be from these concrete cartographies, those of Castaneda or psychotics (which are more or less the same in this case), and the more we can hope to profit from this activity of speculative cartography.

That appears absurd, but think about aesthetics: aesthetics isn't something that gives you recipes to make a work of art. And in some ways, for it to make an impact, it must be totally disconnected, unaligned vis-à-vis this perspective of accounting for a pragmatic or artistic activity. The speculative cartography, just like any theology or philosophy, isn't there to provide an inventory of these different modes of invention of existence, of sensitivity, of productions of new types of intensity.

5.   *A Thousand Plateaus*: Modes of Encoding and A-signifying Semiotics

CS: What you just said reminds me of something in *La révolution moléculaire*, where you distinguish different modes of encoding. The third order of these modes of encoding is the mode of a-signifying semiotics, that is, signs functioning and producing in the Real, on the very level of the Real. As an example, you suggested physics; does this connect with what you just said about science, that is, science as a means of directly recognizing processes in the Real or an a-signifying semiotics, opposed to other forms of semiotics?

FG: Let's understand each other. The same semiotic material can be functioning in different registers. A material can both be caught in paradigmatic chains of production, chains of signification [under the cardologic], but at the same time can function in an a-signifying register [the ordologic]. So what determines the difference? In one case, a signifier functions in what one might call a logic of discursive aggregates, that is, a logic of representation. In the other case, it functions in something that isn't entirely a logic, what I've called an existential machinic, a logic of bodies without organs, a machinic of bodies without organs. In that case, what are we talking about? We're no longer talking about representing, but of enunciating, of creating what one might call an existential statement [*énonciation existentielle*], a production of subjectivity, a production of new coordinates, an autocoordination, an autoreferentiation. In the domain of the logic of discursive aggregates (the cardologic), there's an exo-referentiation; there's a referent, like in Peircian semiotics, where there is always a third term, a ternary nature which refers at one remove to the semiotic reference, whereas there (under the ordologic), it's the same mechanism, inside this ternary nature, it's the autopositionality of subjectivity that asserts itself there, that asserts itself on all sorts of levels, on a modular level or on an incomplete level. It's a very complex level of collective assemblage.

So, just like this example of the domain that has "speech acts" at the level of enunciation, that has an engendering pragmatic of subjectivity through speech acts (to use [John] Searle's [1969] categories, and so on), there are also "science acts" or "art acts" that produce an enunciation and not a subjectivity. A scientific enunciation that produces quarks or a reading of the "Big Bang" of the universe, what occurs there? It produces semiotic entities that allow us to think about and connect completely disparate events. But we can't say that these semiotic events are in a relationship of correspondence with a being who might be caught in a relationship of denotation. These entities obviously produce a vision of the world, they produce a world, they produce universes of reference that have their own logic in the same way that a musician like Debussy, at one point, invented a new type of relationship of musical writing, a new type of scale, a new type of melodic and harmonic line, and suddenly produced new universes and fertilized an entire series of machinic phyla for the future of music. It's a universe production, an enunciation production. In one sense, it's true that at this vital level of the semiotic production of enunciation, I think that one can liken scientific activity to artistic activity, not to devalue it, but on the contrary, to reevaluate it. I think that in this case, considering the work of people like [Thomas] Kuhn (1970) and a certain number of epistemologists, one might give greater value to the character of creativity and collective creation brought forth by traditionally opposed fields like science, social activity, art, and the like (*Pause*).[25]

You don't look very satisfied.

CS: I'm still trying to situate the idea of an a-signifying semiotic.

FG: OK, here it is. What is important in this a-signifying character, in this a-signifying vacillation of chains that elsewhere could be meaningful? It's the following: first, a spectrum of a-signifying, discreet signs in limited number gives a power of representation, that is, on a spectrum that I master, that I articulate, I can pretend to take account of a signified description [*tableau signifié*], on an initial level. But obviously, this doesn't stop here. This subjectivation that I lose starting from this a-signifying spectrum, gives me an extraordinary surplus-value of power; that is, it opens fields of the possible that aren't at all in a bi-univocal relationship with the description presented. When Debussy invented a pentatonic scale, he wrote his own music; perhaps he felt it at a level we might call "his inspiration," but he engendered abstract machinic relationships, a new musical logic that has implications, that represents trees of implication or, we really must say, rhizomes of implication, completely unforeseen in all sorts of other levels, including levels that aren't, strictly speaking, musical. It is precisely on the condition that this constitution, that this semiotic arbitrarization occurs, to generalize Saussure's notion of "arbitrary" in regard to signifier and signified, that there also will be the creation of these coefficients of the possible. If the representation of coding codes too much on the signified description, the signifier is like a cybernetic "feedback" and, in the long run, does not carry an important coefficient of creativity, of transversality. On the other hand, as soon as there is this arbitrarization and this creation of a spectrum that plays on its own register as an abstract machine, then there are possibilities of unheard-of connections, there is a possible crossover from one order to another, and then, moreover, there is a considerable multiplication of what I call these spectrums of the possible.

CS: I'd like to connect this idea to popular, modern music: do you think that there are groups or singers who are going in this direction?

FG: I'll take the example of a musician who isn't at all a popular musician, who's really difficult to categorize, Aperghis, who creates gestual music and theater and who composes his music simultaneously with his gestures. One can really see that he creates a gestual spectrum, a spectrum of expression, a possibility of nearly baroque composition, in the sense of baroque music by Bach or Handel, from the simple fact that he creates this detachment of a gesture out of gesticulation itself, a detachment of faciality out of faces, and the like. There is an entire scenic writing, an entire deterritorialization of scenes onto an aggregate that brings this along.

So, some examples: I don't see why you want me to give

examples of popular music which are generally reterritorializations. However, there is one that immediately occurs to me, it's break dancing and music, all these dances which are both hyperterritorialized and hypercorporeal, but that, at the same time, make us discover spectrums of possible utilization, completely unforeseen traits of corporality, and that invent a new grace of entirely unheard-of possibilities of corporality. I've also been fascinated—but this isn't popular music either—by Chicago blues, the Chicago school, because these monstrous, elephantine instruments like the bass, they begin to fly with unheard-of lightness and richness. . . .

Here's another amazing work of composition, a record by Bonzo Goes to Washington entitled "Five Minutes," a CCC Club Mix.

CS: Oh, right, it's developed from Reagan's statement on the radio announcing that he was ready to drop the bomb on the Russians in five minutes.

FG: That's it. Let's listen to this:

[*Song: In a slowed-down recording, Ronald Reagan says in a bass voice: "My fellow Americans, I'm pleased to tell you today that I've signed legislation that would outlaw Russia forever. We begin bombing in five minutes." There follows a very rhythmic music dominated by drumbeat and bass guitar, on top of which the lyrics consist of the recurrence of various syllables of Reagan's statement, repeated in such a way as to create a "song." For example:*

"Bombing in five minutes, bombing in five minutes, I'm pleased to tell you today that, I'm pleased to tell you today that, to tell you today, to tell you today, to tell you today, to tell you today, Bombing in five minutes, five minutes . . . "

This continues for about five minutes with different variations between rhythms and Reagan's words, sometimes accelerated, sometimes slowed down, but always distorted.]

CS: One of the "composers" of this "mix," Jerry Harrison, is one of the four members of Talking Heads, and Bootsy Collins is the leader of a group called The Rubber Band, a group of black singers who are, in some ways, precursors of break music.

6.   *A Thousand Plateaus:* The "War Machine" and "Striated" versus "Smooth" Space

CS: I have a final question about a term which you suggest in *A Thousand Plateaus* in Plateau 12, the concept of "war machine." This concept is paradoxical to the extent that it does not have "war" as its object, and that this term is currently used in the militaristic milieu to designate the military apparatus of the superpowers. But the "war machine," if I understand it correctly, is a machine against this militarism. So, there's a dual problem: first, how does one resolve this paradox, but also, for the translators of your works, especially of *A Thousand Plateaus,* doesn't this term "war machine" run the risk of stifling acceptance of these concepts?

FG: It's not a matter of a power formation, but of machinic, deterritorialized elements, that are placed into operation in a social situation, of which military incarnation does not acknowledge the character that, when it's a war machine, it can be a scientific war machine, an aesthetic war machine, a loving war machine. Courtly love is a kind of war machine of "becomings-woman," the transformation of relationships with women. And that refers back to machinic phyla, and the war machine is its abstract, mutational name.

Why do we call it "war machine"? Because, after all, it is the coveted object of State power that constitutes an army seeking to take hold of this war machine, just as capitalism wants to capture all the technical–scientific machines and all the elements of deterritorialization to incorporate it into its segmentarity. [see ATP, Chap. 13] So, to some extent, we accept the ambiguity since the problem remains complete; there isn't a good war machine and a bad, a good science and a bad. There is this fact that the most deterritorialized elements and, let's say, the most potentially creative are precisely at the heart of armies, of State machines, of oppressive powers, just as fascism is really an example as equally at the heart of desire.

CS: In the schema you just developed [of the "speculative cartography"], where do you situate the concepts of "striated" and "smooth" space?

FG: "Striated" space is all that comes under the energetic-spatio-temporal coordinates [i.e., the material and indicative Fluxes; see Guattari 1992, 88; 1995, 60]; it's numbered space (under the cardologic), whereas there (under the ordologic), it's the numbering domain. So, one can't call it a space, that's saying too much, it's just "smoothness," both in a content and in an absolute ethericity (*ethergété*). For example, subjectivity is presented like a continuum: in subjectivity, there is your subjectivity, there's the whole world, there's no possibility of numbering subjectivity; and yet, it is singular, it maintains differential relations of intensity.

So, "striated" space is the energetic-spatio-temporal; I'd like to make a logical category out of energy. Under the category of material and indicative Fluxes, the modules are primary modules of actuation, and on these modules of actuation are developed the deep and pseudo–deep structures. The symmetrical difference is that there (under the machinic Phylums), there are surplus-values that give a space of coordinates of differentiation, but there (under the ordologic), there is a total phenomenological flattening, that is, it relates to analyses by [John] Searle (1969, 1983) and other phenomenologists, that, after all, an existence's relation of intelligibility passes through a sort of total solipsism of existential relationships. One only has knowledge of an existence insofar as one is oneself in the field of existential, and even imperialistic, relationships.

I've presented my whole seminar for three years on this; I've received a stack of reports up to here by psychoanalysts.

Under the machinic Phylums are situated the synapses, that is, the points of reversal in which the module, instead of going in the direction of differentiation, goes from a differentiated point toward points which are nondifferentiatable, there and there [under the ordologic]; there are no deep structures at that level, all the parenthesism is called forth. Let's say that there [under the existential territory], it's visual perception, the sex, so that it's all the same to have an existential access to visual perception or to sex or to a collective enunciation; there is no means to pry it loose [décoller]. Sartre described it, I had a sexual appreciation of the charismatic leader, I exist it/him [je l'existe], I can't put him in the same coordinates, it's the same object that hands him over to me, this idea of existential "grasping."

CS: Are "synapses" faciality as well?

FG: Well, no, that was only one example; they could be anything, they could be a partial object, a haecceity, a refrain [ritournelle], anything. That was a way of providing an example.

CS: And you said, about the synapses, that they also relate to the object small-a?

FG: For me, yes, it's a generalization. Just as my notion of "machine" was a generalization of Lacan's "small-a" notion, the notion of "machinic Phylums" is the double play of the machine that is both in the order of mechanical coordinates, let's say, and at the same time, is life itself, both the most mechanical and the most living. Because it's from there that the fields of the possible are created as well as the existential agglomeration.

But then, if we start off in that direction, toward this kind of analysis, we'll never get out of it.

9 COMMENTS ON A MEETING WITH GILLES DELEUZE (18 MARCH 1985)

POSTINGS

Date: Sun, 05 Nov 95 22:30:37 +0100 [16:30 EST]
From: Melissa McMahon
To: deleuze-guattari@jefferson.village.virginia.edu
Subject: Deleuze is dead . . .

*****

Date: Sun, 05 Nov 95 18:25:57 EST
From: Charles J. Stivale
Subject: Re: Deleuze is dead
To: deleuze-guattari@jefferson.village.virginia.edu
In-Reply-To: Message of Sun, 5 Nov 1995 22:30:37 +0100

When I heard of Michael Current's death several years ago [Current was the original moderator of the Deleuze–Guattari List], I had a very similar, overpowering feeling of loss, although I'd never "met" Michael face to face, rather the intensity of his words. Reading Melissa's message, I found myself . . . laughing . . . this is the way he wanted to go. A short while later, I found the words, in *Pourparlers* [*Negotiations*] that began reverberating when I read Melissa's post:

"That's what subjectification is about: bringing a curve into the line, making it curve back on itself, and making force impinge on itself. So we get ways of living with what would otherwise be unendurable. What Foucault says is that we can only avoid death and madness if we make existing into a 'way,' an 'art.' It's idiotic to say Foucault discovers or reintroduces a hidden subject after having rejected it. There's no subject, but a production of subjectivity: subjectivity has to be produced, when its time arrives, precisely because there is no subject. The time

comes once we've worked through knowledge and power; it's that work that forces us to frame the new question, it couldn't have been framed before. Subjectivity is in no sense a knowledge formation or power function that Foucault hadn't previously recognized; subjectification is an artistic activity distinct from, and lying outside, knowledge and power. In this respect Foucault's a Nietzschean, discovering an artistic will out on the final line. Subjectification, that's to say the process of folding the line outside, mustn't be seen as just a way of protecting oneself, taking shelter. It's rather the only way of confronting the line, riding it: you may be heading for death, suicide, but as Foucault says in a strange conversation with Schroeter, suicide then becomes an art it takes a lifetime to learn" (P, 154; N, 113–114).
CJ Stivale

*****

Date: Mon, 6 Nov 1995 18:16:32 +0000 (GMT)
From: "F.S.T."
To: deleuze-guattari@jefferson.village.virginia.edu
Subject: Re: Deleuze is dead

Well, I do agree with your "practice" of practicing and by practicing constructing subjectivity. That's all about D&G and their machinic analysis. However, I have to mention the risk we are crossing when it comes to research, for instance, or to the practice of dealing with human beings. How [does] this practice of constructing practice [constitute] practice-ide? Does it make sense? I mean, when you mentioned about suicide, it came to me: [what is it like] when we are in a psychoanalytic practice? Your teenager, your daughter, for instance, [might] come and say that s/he will commit suicide! Well, how [does] this practice [have] to be interpreted without becom[ing] a moral practice? How to be ethical in this sense? I am posing this question for us to think [about] because when I (we) come to practice this practice of thinking in my (our?) practice of being psychoanalysts, for instance, I (we) are constantly in need of analyzing these practices and our practice of analyzing these practices. That's the moment, these are the questions that people are imposing to me to be answered, right now, in my practice as a psychoanalyst researcher. Who would like to discuss it with me?
F.S.T.

*****

Date: Wed, 08 Nov 95 06:49:58 EST
From: CSTIVAL@cms.cc.wayne.edu
Subject: Re: Deleuze is dead
To: deleuze-guattari@jefferson.village.virginia.edu
To: F.S.T

I do not at all feel capable of responding in any adequate manner to the perplexing and complex questions you raise about practice of practice and of constructing subjectivity, especially not from a clinical/practicing psychoanalytical perspective. The reason I respond at all is that (a) in quoting my initial post to the list following the announcement of Deleuze's suicide, I feel directly drawn in to your questions, and (b) your questions are important, so I would hate to see them ignored, even if my response is unsatisfactory.

Unfortunately, my difficulty is hampered by the enunciation of your questions: you refer to a risk we run in discussing suicide as if it were just another practice of constructing subjectivity, asking if this might not be "practicezide," i.e., the death of the constructing practice itself? What moral and/or ethical stance would one take necessarily in counseling a teenager, one's daughter for instance, who announces she's contemplating suicide? You conclude that we need to take care both to analyze the practices we study and to analyze that very analysis of these constructing practices.

All that I can say is that the citation I provided from Deleuze in *Pourparlers* (text taken from Martin Joughin's translation in *Negotiations*) in which he refers to Foucault and to suicide, was meant not to provide a justification, nor a game-plan, as it were, for a recourse to an extreme constructing practice, but just as a way for me (and for others who might find it useful) to begin to get a hold on an act that initially seemed so inconceivable. I do not consider Deleuze's statement a template for action. Counseling a teenager or child or spouse or friend in such dire circumstances is a delicate process, and frankly has little if anything to do with Deleuze's decision and act. For whatever reasons, he took it upon himself to go out by the means that were at his disposal. Whether one leaves it at that, or then tries also to theorize the event ("line of flight," "tool box," "BwO" . . .), I guess that's up to each of us to work through in our own way. . . .

I'm hoping to share with this list soon some comments I wrote in 1985 following my meeting with Deleuze in Paris. One thing he said then was "What counts is one's work." Finding those notes and my brief correspondence with him, rediscovering his wit, generosity, and kindness in my files, has been a real joy.
CJ Stivale

End of File

BACKGROUND

The preceding sequence of posts following Deleuze's death triggered my recollection of meeting him in 1985, and also of having jotted down notes on that meeting immediately thereafter. Some introductory remarks are in order to explain how my meeting with Gilles Deleuze came about.

For several years prior to a trip I made to France in March 1985, I had maintained a sporadic correspondence with Deleuze. This began when I tried to contact him in May–June 1983 during a trip to Paris, without success. As I had the temerity to attach to the note a copy of my *SubStance* article on *Anti-Oedipus* (1981), he kindly responded with a short note of his own, dated 8 June 83, indicating that for health reasons, he was currently away from Paris, but hoped to be in better shape during my next "passage."

I responded with a rather lengthy letter, outlining my work, and including an essay that I had written for publication on a trilogy of novels by the nineteenth-century French novelist Jules Vallès. I particularly raised the prospect of a special issue of *SubStance* that I was then attempting to organize on his work, and for which I would gladly include something from him, possibly on the topic of where he might locate the schizo-/rhizoanalytic project in the middle of the 1980s. His response (22 August 1983), again extremely generous, gave me some very important suggestions about my study of Vallès's trilogy, but he confessed that "I am late all the time, and that's why, if you succeed in organizing the special issue that you mentioned, I'm afraid I cannot prepare a special text for it. But I could send you some excerpts from what I'm currently doing, on cinema, that will appear in France."

During the fall and winter of 1983–1984, I prepared the *SubStance* issue that appeared as volume 44–45 (1984), and sent several letters to Deleuze asking if he was still interested in contributing. He responded (15 February 1984) to say that he was sorry but he would be unable to contribute to it, "not having anything currently that can be published separately." However, he indicated his willingness to allow me to translate a short excerpt from his cinema book, which I eventually did include in the issue.

Later in the year (November), I wrote to Deleuze to send him the final table of contents of the issue, and also to ask him if he would agree to an interview about his own writings and those with Guattari. His response (5 December 1984) indicated that he would be glad to meet me the following March during my trip to Paris, but rather than take part in an oral interview, he would prefer to prepare one based on written questions consulted ahead of time, to which he would answer in written form. As I had heard from Guattari agreeing to meet with me as well, but for an oral interview, I began preparing an enormous list of questions for each writer. In the case of Guattari, the resultant interview, in the preceding chapter, is a slightly modified version of the text published in *PRE/TEXT* (Stivale 1993). As for Deleuze, I was able to visit him for a drink in his apartment in the seventeenth *arrondissement*, rue de Bizerte, the evening before the interview with Guattari.

In retrospect, I realize now the extent to which I misunderstood completely Deleuze's interest in my activities. Having viewed his interview with Claire Parnet in the *Abécédaire*, I now better comprehend how importunate my communications were, especially in light of statements he makes about his ill health and *vieillesse* (old age). Stating how much he enjoys having been "let go" (*lâché*) and being no longer burdened by society in his retirement, Deleuze admits that what is really bothersome is when something catches hold of him again, for example, when someone who thinks Deleuze still belongs to society asks him for an interview. When that happens, Deleuze says he feels like asking if the person is feeling OK ("*ça va pas, la tête?*"), and hasn't anyone told the person that Deleuze is old and society has let go of him? (ABC 1996, "M comme Maladie" [I as in Illness]).

What follows is an account of my discussion with Deleuze that I drafted immediately afterward, in French, in order to share it with friends and colleagues in France that I would meet there. I've revised it only slightly, but include parenthetically the text of certain of the prepared questions to which he graciously responded while I was there. I have one reservation about this account: because Deleuze was expressly reluctant to engage in an oral interview, I have been likewise reluctant to disseminate it widely. However, I think some of his thoughts, rendered frankly and spontaneously, need to be aired, so I take upon myself the responsibility (or blame) for sharing them now. In fact, many of his comments to me have now become public knowledge through the broadcast and commercial sale of Deleuze's *Abécédaire*.

COMMENTS ON A MEETING

After I explained to Deleuze where I came from and the origins of the *SubStance* issue entitled "Gilles Deleuze," we began talking about the American philosophical tradition and American thought, and we discussed the distinction between analytic philosophers in America and so-called continental philosophers. I explained to him that the "*continentaux*" were beginning to makes some inroads in the United States, and he stated that the analytical philosophers were responsible for killing off what he considered to be "la pensée américaine valable" (valid American thought), for example, by writers like Kerouac, e. e. cummings, Henry James, and even philosophers like Whitehead and others. He was surprised by my impression that, in the United States, scientific questions and research were dominant in relation to the humanities, by my remark that while philosophy was a discipline within the humanities, analytic philosophers were able to align themselves with scientists to the extent that both groups reached their "incontestable conclusions" through proof and reasoning. I described some U.S. discussion groups in which no one ever said anything that called into question the bases of the scientific method, instead practicing a hermetic approach to consider scientific questions. Deleuze did not understand how things could work that way, but he had encountered similar tendencies in some scientific writing in France. But I answered that in both scientific and literary writing in France, there was a great difference from the United States, since in France they knew how to write and to express themselves well. He agreed that one could not separate ideas from style, that if ideas were present, there would also be style.

In any event, we spoke considerably about the American situation, and Deleuze spoke about it, telling me that we are in a difficult period, that there are good and bad periods: for example, at the time of the French liberation in 1944, or in 1968, there were things happening (*des choses qui bougeaient*), and also things that were being invented, during which people discovered new and interesting things. But now, it was hollow, both in America and in France. I answered that the establishment of the International College of Philosophy, by the Socialist government, seemed positive, and he said, Yes, it's a government initiative, but that the government was not able to change tendencies that deeply propel societies. So, indeed, the College of Philosophy was interesting, he said, but constituted very little in relation to what was really occurring in France. I tried to press the question regarding the College, and he said that Félix would certainly have something to say about it. He said that Félix was one of the men he loved the most in the world, that he was enormously talkative, with opinions on everything, and that was completely opposite to Deleuze.

We touched on another topic, the material question of his analysis in *L'image-movement* (1983; *Cinema 1: The Movement-Image*), in which there are a considerable number of references to a wide array of films. So I wanted to know what sort of material support he had, how he worked, with a VCR or a movieola? In response, he laughed aloud, saying, "Not at all." I said, "So it came from the *fonds deleuze* [the Deleuze archives]," what he had in his head? He said Yes, from all that he could recall. But he continued, saying that one did not need to see the films again if one possessed an idea. That is what's essential: with a small idea that one could communicate, no material support was needed; one simply needs to reflect, to present the small idea, thus to show how films, for example, are linked to this small idea. He said that, in the final analysis, he wasn't interested in the cinema; the only thing that interested him was philosophy, and he only delivered his ideas to cinema in the light of philosophy. I said, "So why write two volumes on cinema?" He answered that he didn't know why, that there was an idea that he had to communicate, but that there was very little depth in the first volume. The second volume, *L'image-temps* (1985; *Cinema 2: The Time-Image*), presented him with many more problems, requiring much more work. He really seemed to say that this work was not very important, that there was much more to be done, for example, philosophy. And work, that he conceptualized in an interesting way: when I told him I wanted to get my book on Vallès published, he said, Yes, that's essential, to work; one shouldn't have to be bothered with publication; that gets done all by itself, but it's the work that counts! I was tempted, but did not say, that this view is easily expressed by him, a famous writer, but for those struggling to get published, it's a little bit more difficult since one has to deal with both simultaneously.

There was another moment, toward the end of our discussion, which was gauged by the level of whiskey in my glass. When I'd swallowed the last drop, it was clear to me that he felt that the discussion was ending. So I said that I had written to him about the written questions that I was supposed to prepare, and asked if he was still willing to answer them. He then explained how much he held interviews in complete horror, and the only reason he had said yes to the written questions was in order not to have to say yes to the oral ones! Then, he said that if I really felt strongly about him answering these questions, he would do so, but could not promise me when. When he told me that I could send him the questions, I responded that I had them with me, so he said, "So show them, show them." I said, "Wait; after what you've just said, I want us to agree to the following procedure before you look at them: if there is something in these questions that interests you, go ahead and answer it. After what you've just said, though, since questions are a priori uninteresting for you, there won't be anything to answer! I hope, though, that there might be something interesting in them, but if something in them bothers you, just drop them." He then began looking through them and said finally, "But these questions are serious."

He then began to react to certain ones; for example, "In *Le nouvel observateur*, they have published that you intend to undertake an essay entitled 'What Is Philosophy?'" He asked, They've published that in *Le nouvel observateur*? He said he didn't know how they could have learned that since he'd only mentioned it to a few close friends. I said, Yes, and that's what got printed, and he agreed, Yes, that's what got printed, but indicated that he didn't understand at all how. But later, he returned to this idea of what is philosophy: he spoke of a painting by Francis Bacon that he had in his apartment, and of the importance of true creation, of people who can express their ideas (people who have no ideas, he told me directly, you can read Vallès for twenty years, and if you don't have your little idea, it's a waste of time; but if you have your little idea, then you have to read Vallès completely, fully [*à fond*] and communicate this little idea); speaking of Bacon, he said that Bacon succeeds in creating this painting, but never manages to paint a little wave: Bacon creates a water spout, but not a little wave. And he, Deleuze, would like to succeed in creating a little wave (*une petite vague*), that is, an essay called "What Is Philosophy?"

Then, regarding a question about "postmodernism" ("What is the relationship between your theoretical projects and practices and those of other so-called post-modern [or even poststructuralist] works, for example, by Baudrillard, Lyotard, or Serres? Does the term 'postmodern' have a meaning, and if so what? If not, how might he conceive of the contemporary intellectual conjuncture?"), he laughed at the idea of "postmodernism": he referred (somewhat inexplicably) to philosophers of the Chicago School, that this was just a way for them to amuse themselves by creating a "postmodernism," nothing of real interest. Regarding the question on Baudrillard and another on Jean-Paul Aron, both of whom I cited ("How do you respond to Aron's statement, in *Les modernes,* that thanks to Deleuze's contribution, *Anti-Oedipus* does not cut it bridges with 'legal culture,' maintaining 'literary civility, clannish complicity, fraternal smiles at Lyotard, Serres, Clavel, kindly gestures to Sartre, insistent homage to Marx, and especially writing a hymn to Lacan?'"), he said that he noticed I was quoting cretins, real imbeciles, this Baudrillard, this Aron. About Baudrillard, Deleuze admitted that he himself had so much difficulty expressing *one* idea in a book, even one that was long, and that the work of formulating clearly one small idea was very hard for him. So to see these people creating books in a quarter hour, without much thought, really irritated him, he found it absurd (*aberrant*), not at all serious, the kind of thing that really drove him to despair. As for Aron, about whom and whose book, *Les modernes,* he spoke at length, he said it wasn't a nasty book, but was vulgar, not even a book, something poorly written and of little import.

As he leafed through the questions, he came back to Aron because of a question about Foucault ("Foucault is dead. What reflections does this disappearance evoke for you?"). He said that Foucault's death was something terrible, not only because Foucault died, but because France lost a very important presence who caused imbeciles to hesitate to speak out, knowing that Foucault was there to respond. For example, Aron would never have written his book were Foucault still alive. Not that Foucault would have read it, not at all, but simply Aron would not have dared to write it. Deleuze maintained that Foucault did not function as "safeguard" (*garde-fou*), but rather as an "imbecile-guard" (*garde-imbécile*), and with the passing of Foucault, the imbeciles would be unleashed. He ended by saying that there really was no one now to replace Foucault, that there was a vacuum. And he himself, he said, was unable to do it.

He did not say much at all about *Anti-Oedipus.* I spoke to him briefly about our experience reading it together at the University of Illinois, about the trouble that some philosophers had with it. I mentioned how one Sartrean philosopher could well accept to read Lacan, but that from the first paragraph of *Anti-Oedipus,* he felt himself under attack, could not understand at all what was happening, and wanted to undermine our own activity, to makes us drop *Anti-Oedipus* for something else. He finally left the group after three meetings. Deleuze nodded that he understood completely; for him what they write is absolutely worthless, so he understood how what he wrote would be worthless for them as well, and that he expected nothing any different.

When I told Deleuze that I was working through *A Thousand Plateaus* and this work was what interested us the most, he laughed as if this were the funniest thing he had ever heard, that someone would continue delving into *A Thousand Plateaus.* In any case, he looked at these questions and told me that he would answer them during the summer vacation, and he added that, if he said yes, it was a sworn promise. I was very happy finally because he looked through these questions as if he really found them of interest. Surely he was being extremely polite, but he had no need to make such a formal commitment as he did. So we'll see what happens next.

FINAL COMMENT

Again, in retrospect a number of his comments became much clearer in light of his interviews with Parnet in *L'Abécédaire.* For example, his initial comments on critical currents in philosophy and the proper task of doing philosophy correspond to numerous points in *L'Abécédaire,* particularly in "H as History of Philosophy" and "U comme Un" (O as in One). The question of the importance of style arises in "L as in Literature" and "R as in Resistance." Deleuze discusses at considerable length in "C as in Culture" the topic of cultural high and low points. And the crucial importance of the "idea" for any form of creativity arises in "I as in Idea" and "Q as in Question." Two other comments in *L'Abécédaire* gave me particular pause for reflection in light of meeting him in the apartment where the lengthy interviews were filmed. At one point, to Deleuze's comments about discussing Primo Lévi's writings (on the Nazi death camps) as a form of resistance and also how the work of artists resists by unleashing "forces of life," Parnet objects that art does not suffice, that Primo Lévi ended his life with suicide long afterward. To this Deleuze responds, "He committed suicide personally, he couldn't hold on any longer, so he committed suicide to his personal life. But there are four pages or twelve pages or a hundred pages by Primo Lévi that will remain to constitute an eternal resistance" (R as in Resistance). Later, while refuting the received notion that philosophy and science would deal with universals, Deleuze takes as an example the formula "All bodies fall," and insists: "What is important is not that all bodies fall. What is important is the fall and the singularities of the fall" ("U comme Un" [O as in One]).

In any event, I did not consider the promise Deleuze made to answer my questions to be binding since he had provided more than his share of answers during our meeting. That same year, he published the second volume on cinema, *L'image-temps*; in 1986, he published *Foucault*. As ever, he had his own "petite idée" to pursue . . .

10 COMMENT PEUT-ON "ÊTRE DELEUZIEN"?
THE GIFT OF PEDAGOGY

> Let us speak about friends then, but I will not
> speak to you of friends as such. I belong
> perhaps to a rather old-fashioned generation
> for whom friendship is something at once
> capital and superstitious.... Friendship for
> me is a kind of secret Freemasonry, but one
> also making certain points visible.
>
> –*Michel Foucault, "La scène de la philosophie"*
> *(22 April 1978) [1994, 3:588–589]*

This chapter takes its departure point from a title or, more accurately, from an expression. No sooner had I proposed this title to Lawrence Kritzman (for one of the Twentieth-Century French Studies Division panels of the 1996 MLA convention) than I recognized the dilemma, or at least the conundrum, in the question. "Comment peut-on être deleuzien?" (How can one be Deleuzian?) is an obvious allusion to Montesquieu's well-known, ironic formulation in the *Lettres persanes* (*Persian Letters*), "Comment peut-on être Persan?" (How can one be Persian?), which evokes at once the haughty elitism of eighteenth-century Parisians gazing at the oriental "other" and Montesquieu's self-deprecating humor in placing this question addressed to the *Persian* in the mouth of a Parisian.

Besides occasionally feeling like this "other" in the poststructuralist critical domain of the past two decades, many commentators on Deleuze's works, written by him alone or in partnership with Félix Guattari, have found themselves confronted with the reference in my titular question, the "être deleuzien" enunciated by Michel Foucault in his now overexploi-

235

ted declaration that "un jour ce siècle sera peut-être deleuzien" (1994, 2:76). In confronting this "epochality" of Deleuzean thought, Kenneth Surin argues that, to give any substance to Foucault's claim, "the thought that is 'deleuzean' has to be read in terms of the episteme, but, equally, the episteme has to be approached in terms of the thought" (Surin 1997, 11). As rendered in an English translation—"Perhaps one day this century will be known as Deleuzian"—Foucault's statement is complicated by its transposition into the passive voice. For the century to "be known as Deleuzian" suggests that an assemblage of privileged knowers will somehow come to recognize the "être deleuzien" of this century and even of or among themselves. Or as Keith Ansell-Pearson puts it succinctly, "It is to be hoped that this century will not, as predicted, come to be known as 'Deleuzian,' in which his thought would acquire the status of a singular event. For at such a point, Deleuze would become well and truly dead" (1997a, 13).

Foucault's own explanation, now buried in a four-volume collection of interviews and occasional pieces, *Dits et écrits,* was originally given during a 1978 interview published in the Japanese journal *Sekai* (1994, 3:571–595). Opening "Theatrum philosophicum" with a wink aimed at the few Deleuzian initiates in 1970 who would read this review-essay in *Critique* on Deleuze's *Différence et répétition* and *Logique du sens* (1994, 2:75–99), Foucault had implied that one day, perhaps inevitably, "le siècle" or "l'opinion commune" (common opinion) would come to recognize itself as "deleuzien"; eight years later, he added, "Et je dirais que ca n'empêchera pas que Deleuze est un philosophe important" ("And I would say that this takes nothing away from Deleuze being an important philosopher") (1994, 3:589). As for Deleuze, he understood Foucault's formulation as a manifestation of his "diabolical sense of humor," but also as a way of expressing "that I was the most naïve among the philosophers of our generation":

> Among us, themes like multiplicity, difference, repetition were common, but I proposed concepts in nearly raw form [*presque bruts*], whereas others worked via greater modes of mediation. I was never affected by the overcoming of metaphysics or the death of philosophy, and the renunciation of the Whole, the One, the subject, all this was no tragedy for me. I never broke off from a kind of empiricism that proceeds by a direct exposition of concepts. I never went through structure, nor through linguistics or psychoanalysis, or through science, or even through history, because I believe that philosophy has its own raw material which allows it to enter into external relations, all the more necessary, with these disciplines. Perhaps that is what Foucault meant: I was not the best, but the most naïve, a kind of raw piece of art, if one can say that; not the most profound, but the most innocent [the most unencumbered by a guilt of

"doing philosophy"]. (Maggiori 1995, 9; translation by Chauderlot and Stivale)

If the recent number of published translations is any indicator, Deleuze's works (and those of Deleuze and Guattari) have entered into a distinct process of machinic assemblages and metamodelization, to put the situation in Deleuze–Guattarian terms. That is, despite or perhaps because of the work at once serious and snickering that we undertake in studying Deleuze and Guattari, their writings now function as cogs in the machinery of sociocultural and material interrelations and representations extending into many domains: pedagogy, university institutionalization and professionalization, and competition between academic and commercial presses—to name but a few. In short, their works are now in circulation as part of what has come to be called "cultural capital," in an oddly schizo sort of way that Deleuze and Guattari might have appreciated, or might not have. Of course, preparing a text such as this—this book, with its new chapters, sections previously presented or published and now revised, references, and list of works cited—is to participate quite obviously in those very machinic assemblages. My hope here, in "closing," is to reflect briefly on certain paths that might allow me if not to leave this "siècle deleuzien" behind, then perhaps to scramble its tracks a bit—or at least to explore my own practices and modes of apprenticeship, along with those of Deleuze and Guattari in their final collaboration, *What Is Philosophy?*

ÊTRE ANTI-OEDIPE/BEING ANTI-OEDIPAL

In thinking of ways to answer the somewhat facetious question in the chapter title, the most obvious one comes from Guattari himself. When I asked him in 1985 what aspects of *Capitalism and Schizophrenia* he thought remained the most valid, he replied, "Ils ne sont valables en rien! Moi, je ne sais pas! Je m'en fous! Ce n'est pas mon problème! C'est comme on veut, on fait l'usage qu'on veut" [They're not valid at all! Me, I don't know, I don't care! It's not my problem! It's however you want it, whatever use you want to make of it]. As tempting as it might be to accept this apparently outright rejection of the operative query, such a gesture would be tantamount to falling into what Foucault, in his English Preface to *Anti-Oedipus,* calls one of the main "traps" (*pièges*) of the Deleuze–Guattarian enterprise, its humor: "so many invitations to let oneself be put out, to take one's leave of the text and slam the door shut" (AO, xiv; Foucault 1994, 3:136). Yet, as Foucault maintains here, it is precisely through this use of humor and play that something essential and highly serious takes place: "the tracking down of all varieties of fascism, from the enormous ones that surround and crush us to the petty ones that constitute the tyrannical bitterness of our everyday lives" (AO, xiv; Foucault 1994, 3:136).

Referring to *Anti-Oedipus* (and asking Deleuze and Guattari's forgiveness for doing so) as "the first book of ethics to be written in France in quite a long time," Foucault then suggests one reason for the book's broad appeal beyond a specialist readership: "Being anti-oedipal has become a life style, a way of thinking and living" (AO, xiii; Foucault 1994, 3:134–145: "être anti-OEdipe est devenu un style de vie, un mode de pensée et de vie"). He goes on to specify a set of goals and principles that accords with this antifascist "art of living" as a "guide to everyday life": "Free political action from all unitary and totalizing paranoia"; "develop action, thought, and desires by proliferation, ... not by subdivision"; "prefer what is positive and multiple ... over uniformity, ... unities ... systems, [over what is] sedentary"; avoid sadness in political militancy; "use political practice as an intensifier of thought"; " 'de-individualize' by means of multiplication and displacement"; and "do not become enamored of power" (AO, xiv; Foucault 1994, 3:135). One understands why Foucault asked Deleuze and Guattari's forgiveness in advance: their sense of humor and their rejection of ceremony would seem to run counter to such an exercise of "metamodelization," however well meant. Nevertheless, I want to elaborate Foucault's "way of thinking and living" (even at the risk of pursuing what Deleuze and Guattari would no doubt reject), namely, as a "two-fold thought" that brings into play a number of principles geared not to an "être" (being), but to a "devenir" (becoming) or, if you will, a "devenir deleuze–guattarien":

- a principle of becoming in and through constant mutation, displayed and enfolded in the profusion of multiplicities developed, for example, in Plateau 10 of *A Thousand Plateaus*;
- a principle of becoming *à cheval*, a *chevauchement*, astride the Anglophone–Francophone divide, by means of mutations of linguistic cross-fertilizations and monstrous realizations;
- a principle of *intermezzo, dans le milieu*, in the middle, intersections at once of microrelations to ongoing processes of smooth becomings in diverse projects, however disparate, and of macrorelations, debates in a "milieu" or a "profession," in well-configured and striated domains that are nonetheless fertile possibilities for the production of becomings, circumstances permitting;
- a principle of transversality, of reciprocities, of contaminations, and lines of flight out on some edge, but also of *fuites*, leakages,

as in the unsuspected transpositions of creativity and apparent madness so well understood by Guattari in his clinical work and political practice;

- the principle of linkages, of connectivity, the culmination of all the preceding principles, as exemplified by the cyberspatial overlaps and engagements that give rise there not merely to production and creativity, but to the repressions, aggressions, and abuses symptomatic of what Deleuze and Guattari call "cancerous Bodies without Organs."

All of these principles underlie modes of becoming and therefore inform modes of practice. Fundamental to practice (and to my notion of the "two-fold thought") is a complex principle simply designated as "apprenticeship," a term employed by Michael Hardt in his book on Deleuze's early writings (1993) and that Deleuze uses himself to describe his work on the history of philosophy as a long apprenticeship (ABC, "H as in History of Philosophy"). Yet I think "apprenticeship" needs to be envisaged from those perspectives that Deleuze and Guattari developed throughout their collaboration together and with others, namely, the perspectives of "friendship," or *intermezzo* (working with or between each other), and a relationship with "the outside" based on "intercessors." Apprenticeship, friendship, and intercessors are concepts developed in Deleuze and Guattari's final collaborative effort, *What Is Philosophy?* Through the intersection of these concepts, the authors address philosophy as an "image of thought" and thereby envelop it frankly and explicitly within the schizo-/rhizoanalytic project.

IMAGE(S) OF A "TWO-FOLD THOUGHT"

In the manner of Deleuze and Guattari's earlier works, *What Is Philosophy?* is a collaborative work of "speculative fiction" that emphasizes, in a deliberately and generously pedagogical way, the process of constructing ideas, systems, and arguments so that these might inhabit a universe parallel to our own while seeking ultimately to displace it. By extending their previous development of multiplicity, becomings, and the image of thought, this collaboration constitutes a concerted instruction in the fundamental elements of the work the authors have undertaken, alone and together, for forty years. After having "done philosophy" for so long and with a fervor that precluded asking such questions, Deleuze and Guattari recognize that they have reached "that point of nonstyle where one can finally say, 'What is it I have been doing all my life?'" (WIP, 1; Q, 7). This interrogation takes on a sense of urgency with their insistence that, of the "three ages of the concept" (encyclopedia, pedagogy, commercial professional formation), "only the second can safeguard us from falling from the heights of the first into the disaster of the third—an absolute disaster for thought whatever its benefits might be, of course, from the viewpoint of universal capitalism" (WIP, 12; Q, 17). Even if their answers have appeared in various forms throughout all their previous works, *What Is Philosophy?* is the occasion for clarifying these thoughts once and for all, *between* friends and, one senses, *for* their friends and students.

The book divides neatly into two parts of three chapters divided by the central Chapter 4, devoted to "Geophilosophy," that completes Part I. The authors carefully situate their introductory remarks on friendship as an initial example of how the kernel of philosophical activity, the "concept," develops "conceptual personae" as the necessary "condition for the exercise of thought" (WIP, 3-4; Q, 8-9). They insist further that "concepts" must be constructed "in an intuition specific to them: a field, a plane, and a ground that must not be confused with them but that shelters their seeds and the personae who cultivate them" (WIP, 7; Q, 12). Here we see the focal nexus for the book's first three chapters, for Deleuze and Guattari lay out the elements of the new "image of thought," what philosophy "is" in terms of its creative processes and three instances: the concept, the plane of immanence, and conceptual personae. The authors implicitly link the concept's pedagogy and ontology to Deleuze's earliest development of the "image of thought" through the formula "The concept is real without being actual, ideal without being abstract" (see Appendix, p. 254). Hence the concept's self-referentiality, "its endoconsistency and its exoconsistency," constitute the bases for Deleuze and Guattari's "constructivism [that] unites the relative and the absolute" (WIP, 22; Q, 27). And truly, the activity of creating philosophical concepts cannot be taken for granted since philosophy—like a painter's taste for colors—requires a "taste for concepts": "[A philosopher] can determine a concept only through a measureless creation whose only rule is a plane of immanence he lays out and whose only compass are the strange personae to which it gives life" (WIP, 78; Q, 75–76).

In the final paragraphs of Chapter 3, Deleuze and Guattari distinguish their dynamic and creative conception of philosophy from two sets of rival perspectives: on the one hand, from "problems concerning the extensional conditions of propositions assimilable to those of science" (WIP, 79; Q, 76), and on the other hand, from the domains of criticism and history that "brandish ready-made old concepts like skeletons intended to intimidate any creation" (WIP, 83; Q, 80–81). To the former distinction, they respond in Part II's three chapters with a detailed consideration of "Philosophy, Science, Logic, and Art," while the latter distinction, on the history of philosophy, receives crucial and intensive attention in the chapter on "Geophilosophy." In some ways, the book's second part is the obverse of the first: once the conditions and instances of philosophy have been carefully developed in the initial chapters, Deleuze and Guattari are free to respond to its conceptual rivals by scrutinizing the object of each domain. They define science's object as "functions that are presented as propositions in discursive systems" (WIP, 117; Q, 111), then contrast the philosophical concept with the elements of scientific functions, functives. Similarly, they distinguish concepts from the elements of logical propositions, prospects, and then juxtapose concepts to the artistic "bloc of sensations, that is to say, a compound of percepts and of affects" (WIP, 164; Q, 154).

These separate and successive discussions provide the basis for considering them together in the conclusion, entitled provocatively "From Chaos to the Brain." Suggesting that "we require just a little order to protect us from chaos" in the whirlwind of ideas, they argue that "art, science, and philosophy require more: they cast planes over the chaos" (WIP, 201-202; Q, 189-190). As if returning "from the land of the dead," the philosopher, the scientist, and the artist each bring back different "invocations" or "epiphanies" that Deleuze and Guattari trace through the successive struggles against chaos in philosophy, science, and art (WIP, 203–208; Q, 190–196). Concluding that "the brain is the junction—not the unity—of the three planes" (WIP, 208; Q, 196), the authors express their abiding interest in "the problems of interference between the planes that join up in the brain" (WIP, 216; Q, 203). In the final lines of the book, Deleuze and Guattari emphasize the importance of philosophy's maintaining openings, not closure, through development of "a nonphilosophical comprehension just as art needs nonart and science needs nonscience," three Nos that are needed "at every moment of their becoming or their development." And through this mode of becoming "is extracted from chaos the shadow of the 'people to come' in the form that art, but also philosophy and science, summon forth: mass-people, world-people, brain-people, chaos-people—nonthinking thought that lodges in the three" (WIP, 218; Q, 205–206).

Although this is the "final word" of *What Is Philosophy?*, the evocation of a new "people to come" harkens back to the central Chapter 4, on "Geophilosophy." As Jean-Jacques Lecercle has noted, this is the book's fulcrum, lying outside any systematic schema, in which "the other of the concept makes its appearance," that is, "the Figure" (1996, 46). But this "other" emerges only through an image of thought "tak[ing] place in the relationship of territory to the earth." Each of these is comprehended as two components of "two zones of indiscernibility"—"deterritorialization (from territory to the earth) and reterritorialization (from earth to territory)"—that Deleuze and Guattari carefully consider in terms of the Greek model of philosophy in the West (WIP, 85–86; Q, 81–82). This chapter can be read as both the philosophical analog of Chapter 3 of *Anti-Oedipus* and as a philosophical complement to the plateaus on "becomings," "the war machine," and "the apparatus of capture" (10, 12, and 13, respectively) in *A Thousand Plateaus.*

In confronting the concept as territory, Deleuze and Guattari consider its "past form, present form and, perhaps, a form to come" (WIP, 100; Q, 97). Whereas Greece did not yet possess concepts but did possess the plane of immanence that we no longer possess, philosophy's present reterritorialization is "on the modern democratic State and human rights," or would be if a "universal" of either truly existed (WIP, 102; Q, 98). As for the future form, Deleuze and Guattari present something of a fervent manifesto that rejects any "philosophy of communication that claims to restore the society of friends, or even of wise men, by forming a universal opinion as 'consensus' able to moralize nations, States, and the market" (WIP, 107; Q, 103). They turn rather to a "double becoming that constitutes the people to come and the new earth. The philosopher must become nonphilosopher so that nonphilosophy becomes the earth and people of philosophy" (WIP, 109; Q, 105). This "becoming-people" shares with creations of philosophy and of art "unimaginable sufferings that forewarn of the advent of a people. They have resistance in common— their resistance to death, to servitude, to the intolerable, to shame, and to the present." It is here that deterritorialization and reterritorialization meet, in this "double becoming," in the "becoming stranger to oneself, to one's language and nation"—in short, "the peculiarity of the philosopher and philosophy, their 'style'" (WIP, 110; Q, 105–106). The image of thought is thus conceived as experimentation that "is always something in the process of creating itself [*ce qui est en train de se faire*]—the new, remarkable, and interesting that replace the appearance of truth and are more demanding than it is" (WIP, 111; Q, 106, translation modified). This "becoming-other" corresponds to Foucault's sense of "the actual": "not what we are but, rather, what we become, what we are in the process of becoming" (WIP, 112; Q, 107; see Foucault 1972).

This gloss of *What Is Philosophy?* is no doubt an all-too-brief treatment of a crucial philosophical and creative reflection. Yet it may help the reader understand the overarching concerns of Deleuze and Guattari in extending this pedagogy of the concept explicitly into philosophy, the domain they have, of course, never ceased examining in their own special manner throughout their careers. I wish to consider apprenticeship and friendship further by approaching questions posed to me online by a cyberfriend and colleague, Greg Seigworth, who asked: "What do Deleuze and Guattari have to say to the contemporary moment? How do we take them up, put their work and perspectives into practice?" These questions arrived from Greg as email in mid-August 1996, nearly a year after we had first "encountered" each other's thoughts and words online through exchange on the Deleuze–Guattari List discussion. Our particular topic then, pursued intermittently off and on ever since, relates to cultural studies, how global and theoretical concepts proposed by Deleuze and Guattari might be translated or animated within diverse practices of cultural studies. The preceding Chapters 3, 5, and 7 are my most direct responses to these queries, and I return here to the online, Internet processes in order to address apprenticeship and friendship in terms of *intercesseurs* (intercessors or mediators).

Besides showing well-deserved and growing respect, my use of a colleague's and online interlocutor's proper name serves to introduce Deleuze and Guattari's argument that "for concepts, proper names are intrinsic *conceptual personae* who haunt a particular plane of consistency" (WIP, 24; Q, 29). If we take "cultural studies" to designate such a plane, then the conceptual personae that haunt and populate diverse discussion lists provide active animation of this plane in a Deleuze–Guattarian practice of philosophy. Now, Deleuze and Guattari declare flatly that "philosophers have very little time for discussion . . . since the participants never talk about the same thing," a view easily confirmed by anyone who has read or engaged in online discussion. Moreover, since what counts for Deleuze and Guattari is "creating concepts for the undiscussible problem posed," they conclude that "conversation is always superfluous" and that "those who criticize without creating . . . are the plague of philosophy" (WIP, 28; Q, 32–33). However, their exemplar of such a perpetrator, someone who rendered impossible free discussion among friends, is Socrates: "He turned the friend into the friend of the single concept, and the concept into the pitiless monologue that eliminates rivals one by one" (WIP, 29; Q, 33). Deleuze and Guattari value a different mode of exchange, one that values the concept not "by reference to what it prevents," but rather "for its incomparable position and its own creation" (WIP, 31; Q, 34).

Borrowing a well-used metaphor from Mallarmé (see Appendix, note 13), Deleuze and Guattari also maintain that philosophy "throws its numbered dice" (WIP, 28; Q, 32), and that its concepts are, in fact, "the outcome of throws of the dice" (WIP, 35; Q, 38). This gaming "table," this "plateau," this "slice"—this net—is the plane of immanence that "has no other regions than the tribes populating and moving about on it" (WIP, 35–37; Q, 38–39). While "it is the plane that secures conceptual linkages with ever-increasing connections," concepts themselves "secure the populating of the plane on an always renewed and valuable curve" (WIP, 37; Q, 39). And maintaining that this plane is "the image thought gives itself of what it means to think, to make use of thought, to find one's bearings in thought," Deleuze and Guattari insist that this "image" retains "only what thought claims by right," its constitution by "infinite movement or the movement of the infinite" (WIP, 37; Q, 39–40).

Despite obvious risks in extending these reflections into a particular domain such as cyberspace or cultural studies, and despite many suggestions to the contrary, online discussion has the potential to displace the confining, territorializing "pitiless monologue" that Deleuze and Guattari distinguish from the opening toward the creation of concepts. Here one might well select from among the growing string of caveats about the manifold shortcomings of Internet access and exchange. I argue, rather, that the plane of immanence, defined by Deleuze and Guattari as philosophy's "earth or deterritorialization, the foundation on which it creates concepts" (WIP, 41; Q, 44), does encompass prephilosophical domains as seemingly heterogeneous as cyberspace and cultural studies. No doubt, indifference and the dangers of experimentation that thinking can entail are not foreign to online exchange, and formal limitations also exist as seemingly inherent to the medium, such as spamming, flaming, lurking, and lagging, to name but a few (see Chapter 3). Deleuze and Guattari pursue their reflection in terms that surely resonate with online engagement:

> Precisely because the plane of immanence is prephilosophical and does not immediately take effect with concepts, it implies a sort of groping experimentation and its layout resorts to measures that are not very respectable, rational, or reasonable. These measures belong to the order of dreams, of pathological processes, esoteric experiences, drunkenness, and excess. We head for the horizon, on the plane of immanence, and we return with bloodshot eyes, yet they are the eyes of the mind. Even Descartes had his dream. To think is always to follow the witch's flight. (WIP, 41; Q, 44)

Perhaps because they question in various ways respectability, rationality, and whatever one considers as reasonable, these measures succeed in provoking "the disapproval of public opinions," from all quarters of the sociopolitical spectrum. Deleuze and Guattari maintain that such measures point to important consequences and processes, that "one does not think without becoming something else, something that does not think—an animal, a molecule, a particle—and that comes back to thought and revives it" (WIP, 42, Q, 44). There is nothing elegant in this process of thought, "which involves much suffering without glory," for "if thought searches, it is less in the manner of someone who possesses a method than that of a dog that seems to be making uncoordinated leaps" (WIP, 55; Q, 55).

At this juncture, I wish to reintroduce, with Deleuze and Guattari, the term "intercessor" because, in their view, it is the reader who must reconstitute conceptual personae, "carry[ing] out the movements that describe the author's plane of immanence and . . . play[ing] a part in the very creation of the author's concepts" (WIP, 63; Q, 62). Whether these conceptual personae are named or nameless, sympathetic or antipathetic, "the philosopher is only the envelope of his principal conceptual personae and of all the other personae who are the intercessors, the real subjects of his/her philosophy." And Deleuze and Guattari insist in this respect that: "I am no longer myself but thought's aptitude for finding itself and spreading across a plane that passes through me at several places" (WIP, 64; Q, 62).

"I am no longer myself . . . ," "Je est un autre . . . ": To the dice roll of philosophy, we need to add the crucial connection between Deleuze and Guattari and Arthur Rimbaud. In "becoming something else," I am/become "thought's aptitude for finding itself," like some inexorable homing device, by "spreading across a plane" into which I am inserted, onto which I am inscribed, yet passing "through me at several places." Returning to the intersecting planes of online exchange and cultural studies, I again evoke the "philosopher's 'heteronyms' " called Greg, or Gil, or Larry, or Karen, not as embodied professors-scholars-writers, but as the intercessors of concepts, as conceptual personae, agents for "thought's aptitude for finding itself." That is, these intercessors play the invaluable role defined by Deleuze and Guattari of "show[ing] thought's territories, its absolute deterritorializations and reterritorializations." Through online exchange as well as in the varying intersections and analyses that constitute cultural studies, the "personalized features [of these intercessors of thought's aptitude] are closely linked to the diagrammatic features of thought and the intensive features of concepts." Whether or not these conceptual personae stammer, break off, lurk, or fall silent is of little import. For "stammerer, friend, or judge do not lose their concrete existence," Deleuze and Guattari argue, "but, on the contrary, take on a new one as thought's internal conditions for its real exercise with this or that conceptual persona." And the imbricated role of apprenticeship and pedagogy through the "image of thought" becomes altogether evident in this light:

> This is not two friends who engage in thought; rather, it is thought itself that requires the thinker to be a friend so that thought is divided up within itself and can be exercised. It is thought itself which requires this division of thought between friends. These are no longer empirical, psychological, and social determinations, still less abstractions, but intercessors, crystals, or seeds of thought. (WIP, 69; Q, 67–68)

In short, the dynamic features described by Deleuze and Guattari create "a thought that 'slides' with new substances of being, with wave or snow, and turn the thinker into a sort of surfer as conceptual persona" (WIP, 71; Q, 70).

These remarks should not be construed as sublimely romanticizing the potential for online interaction, since here and in Chapter 3 I have been at pains to qualify the limits of such exchange. Nor is this consideration of Deleuze–Guattarian philosophy an attempt to devalue "real life," face-to-face dialogue, although such "real life" exchange should not be unduly idealized either. However, one can argue without too much risk that were it not for the cyberspatial net, many extremely productive intersections of ideas and potential creations of concepts would have been impossible face to face, between interlocutors who live and work hundreds and even thousands of miles apart. In the best of circumstances (a phrase I cannot overemphasize), such exchange of the conceptual personae as intercessors "establishes a correspondence between each throw of the [chance-chaos] dice and the intensive features of a concept that will occupy this or that region of the table" (WIP, 75; Q, 73). This correspondence entails risks and danger, wherever and however they take place, and circumstances are not often, or usually, optimal or "best." This activity, like most that result in lasting creation, requires patience, tenacity, and hard work. Yet, even in such conditions, exciting possibilities exist to which online engagement of conceptual personae can give rise and cultural studies themselves can contribute while also deriving considerable benefit.

DEVENIRS DELEUZIENS/DELEUZIAN-BECOMINGS

As Deleuze states in *Pourparlers*, "[Mediators] can be people—for a philosopher, artists or scientists; for a scientist, philosophers or artists—but things too, even plants or animals, as in Castaneda. Whether they're real or imaginary, animate or inanimate, you have to form your mediators" (N, 125; P, 171). Calling this a relation in "a series," he adds, "If you're not in some series, even a completely imaginary one, you're lost," and although he concludes here by saying, "Félix Guattari and I are one another's mediators" (N, 125; P, 171), it is his reference to Carlos Castaneda that seizes my attention. For this reference may lead toward an answer to the question in my title, while also elaborating more fully the "two-fold thought."

Deleuze and Guattari's collaborative work is punctuated by crucial references to the early volumes of Carlos Castaneda's "conversations" with don Juan Matus, especially *Tales of Power* (1974). Castaneda's particular form of apprenticeship to don Juan appears to be a reconceptualized student–teacher relationship. As we know quite well, this relationship can entail a considerable sacrifice of time and energy, and much patience, on the part of the teacher in hopes of inducing some sort of insight that may be resisted or accepted, readily or grudgingly, by the student. Moreover, it is only as the student extends his or her horizons of understanding, or better still, recognizes new possibilities for deterritorialization (however relative and fleeting), that he or she comes to apprehend more fully the import of the gift of knowledge, and the concomitant sacrifice that was proffered through the intensive pedagogical exchange. The teachings of don Juan Matus, as recorded and later revisited in Castaneda's narrative, provide at least three perspectives on their joint trajectory toward knowledge and power that relate to the Deleuze–Guattarian project:

First, the evolving phases and circumstances of Castaneda's apprenticeship described in his first four volumes bring into stark relief the inherent resistance to possible deterritorialization that complicates the sacrifices made and the gifts proffered in the master–apprentice or teacher–student relationship (Castaneda 1968, 1971, 1972, 1974). At several key moments, Castaneda feels obliged to break off his apprenticeship completely, for reasons explicitly related to perceived threats to his "objectivity" and ability to maintain his preestablished, rational belief system. Each time this happens it is only after several years of reflection that he can resume his apprenticeship and reveal new details about the circumstances that he had originally related. He thereby reconceptualizes what has gone before in order better to pursue his search further, into new territories. These break-flows suggest the extent to which various processes of production and antiproduction and their diverse becomings can operate within a particular mode of apprenticeship, indeed as the very dynamic of the pedagogical exchange.

Second, the Castaneda–don Juan exchange might also allow us to consider apprenticeship in terms of a "space of affect," that is, the "thisness" of events that Deleuze and Guattari call "haecceity." The haecceity's combination of relative "speed" and "feeling" corresponds here to a precipitation of the gift of knowledge as a result of both sacrifices made and concomitant resistance maintained—yet another set of break-flows that also establish an affective rhythm within the teaching/learning process. This precipitation becomes evident in the second through fourth volumes as Castaneda, having somehow resolved his fear upon reviewing his earlier experiences, hurries to resituate successively each series of field notes, and recognizes the previously unappreciated (and predictably misunderstood) depth of the teachings made available to him by the sorcerer (*brujo*) don Juan.

Third, that the *brujo* conceives of his teaching and Castaneda's apprenticeship as coterminous with the latter's acquisition of "power" (as defined by don Juan) is quite relevant for understanding the potential of the gift of knowledge to carry the student toward a point "beyond," or better perhaps, "outside," the gift. The exchange between teacher and student is one in which the latter's understanding and applications of the gift can transform the former's sacrifice in unexpected ways, leading the student not simply to "power" (at once threatening and beneficent), but also to insight about the use of this "power" and knowledge, that is, to wisdom. This concept of "power" would seem to be at odds with one of the principles elaborated by Foucault from his reading of *Anti-Oedipus*—"do not become enamored of power"—but in fact the relation to "power" in don Juan's teachings is anything but a love affair. Rather, it constitutes a practical means by which to approach one's existence—relationships and circumstances—at once cautiously and efficiently, that is, out on an edge productive of the dismantlings of hierarchies, yet with a foothold maintained in a plane of consistency. In Plateau 6 of *A Thousand Plateaus*, Deleuze and Guattari ask,

> What does it mean to disarticulate, to cease to be an organism? How can we convey how easy it is, and the extent to which we do it every day? And how necessary caution is, the art of dosages, since overdose is a danger. You don't do it with a sledgehammer, you use a very fine file. (MPEng, 160; MPFr, 198)

They then refer specifically to don Juan's pedagogy, describing how Castaneda is compelled

> first to find a "place," . . . then to find "allies," and then gradually to give up interpretation, to construct flow by flow and segment by segment lines of experimentation, becoming-animal, becoming-molecular, etc. For the BwO is all of that: necessarily a Place, necessarily a Plane, necessarily a Collectivity (assembling elements, things, plants, animals, tools, people, powers, and fragments of all of these . . .). (MPEng, 161; MPFr, 199–200; see Castaneda 1974, 102–209)

For some readers, this brief excursus into apprenticeship, teaching, and learning as an exchange between Castaneda and don Juan may beg the many "unresolved" questions around the veracity and authenticity (or lack thereof) in Castaneda's research (see Fikes 1993; Murray 1981; Noel 1976). However, this exchange has given me some reference points, oriented me between the static, striated confines of an "être deleuzien" and a dynamic "devenir/devenir deleuze–guattarien"—becoming as a process of teaching and learning, hardly undertaken and never finished, but always to be recommenced. Diverse "devenirs deleuziens" participate, or at least have the potential to do so, in the dimensions and sociocultural strata opened up through various activities that we might designate as "rhizomatic" and to which Brian Massumi has recently addressed himself in an essay conveniently entitled "Becoming-Deleuzian" (1996). Among a number of provocative insights, Massumi argues that the Deleuze text "challenges the reader to do something with it," and that through this pragmatic, rather than dogmatic, insistence, "Readers are invited to fuse with the work in order to carry one or several concepts across their zone of indiscernibility with it, into new and discernibly different circumstances" (1996, 401).

While the reference points I have sought here would seem to contradict the concept of continual "becomings," I can formulate some questions about possible "rhizomatic activities" between "intercessors" in an array of media and circumstances: what concrete, actual, even pertinent examples of fusion and new modes of discernibility can clarify these "devenirs deleuziens" as an intersection of strata and everyday life? What forms of teaching and learning, of apprenticeship in its many senses, are available to extend these "becomings"? In what ways could one articulate how "one," as an individual, might construct such forms of apprenticeship such that they would not appear merely banal, anecdotal, inapplicable, even inhospitable to interlocutors? In considering the "image of thought" on Internet lists in this chapter's previous section, I might have included more examples of the online engagement of "intercessors," as I did at the end of Chapter 3. Yet moving into the specific has the possible disadvantage of missing the processual aspect, the "becomings" between "intercessors," by reducing them to mere anecdote.

However, by providing above Greg Seigworth's questions sent to me via email, I do offer a very brief fragment of such an exchange between "intercessors." When I received the questions in August 1996, I printed out the message and filed it as something to which I would return in its proper moment. As is often the case with such interventions, the questions chose their own times to assert themselves, to remain with me throughout the fall and winter. These questions obliquely impelled certain aspects of the paper entitled "Comment peut-on 'être deleuzien'?" that I gave in December 1996, and revise here. These questions also began to enfold themselves within the pages of this book that I composed and revised throughout 1997. Yet another "intercessor" of long standing, Larry Grossberg, further impelled these questions into my work by inviting me to speak to his cultural studies group at the University of North Carolina in March 1997. While there, my continuing engagement with *What Is Philosophy?* conjoined with Greg's questions to impel me further to compose a version of the pages with which I close this book. Direct discussions between "intercessors"—Grossberg, Seigworth, Karen

Ocana, and many others—that occurred at the International Communication Association convention in Montreal helped these questions—and these pages—to undergo new mutations and revisions, inducing further becomings. "I am no longer myself," say Deleuze and Guattari, "but thought's aptitude for finding itself and spreading across a place that passes through me at several places" (WIP, 63–64; Q, 62).

What I find fundamental to these processes, whatever the media, is the learning–teaching exchange that Deleuze and Guattari address in nearly every recorded conversation, and especially in the filmed *Abécédaire* that one can view as an extended, far-ranging lesson over eight hours. I refer specifically to the authors' concern for the work of *intercesseurs* as a means to further their (and our) work, to extend concepts and to find new ones. These are not limits to which we remain necessarily bound, but to paraphrase Manuel De Landa, they constitute that little plot of land to which we can return after a hard day of deterritorializing (see Davis 1992, 48). And yet the process of exchange in apprenticeship can lead back to that edge of the world with which Castaneda was confronted again and again, that helped him experiment and "to see," that is, to become a "seer" in the sense that both Rimbaud and don Juan understood it. The "becomings" that I evoke must occur through reconnections, experimentations, and transmissions (pedagogical, cyberspatial, and affective, as you prefer). In *What Is Philosophy?*, the "becomings" that Deleuze and Guattari develop in their final collaboration suggest the complex ways in which the "two-fold thought" proceeds through its own steps, toward a pedagogy of the concept that is at the same time an experimentation and an opening toward further creations. It is through such becomings and experimentations that thought might somehow punctuate striated frameworks, even minimally, and thereby produce zones of mutual apprenticeship, friendship, and, with a little luck or work, "devenirs monstrueux," "becoming(s)-monstrous."

APPENDIX

GILLES DELEUZE, "HOW DO WE RECOGNIZE STRUCTURALISM?"

The text under consideration here, "A quoi reconnaît-on le structuralisme?" (How Do We Recognize Structuralism?), was written in 1967, shortly before the start of Deleuze and Guattari's collaboration.[1] Bearing many marks of Deleuze's ongoing reflections that would result in the publication of *Différence et répétition* (1968b) and *Logique du sens* (1969), this essay might seem to be what one online interlocutor has called a "throwback" text that raises puzzling questions particularly in the context of our post-poststructuralist, cultural studies-nourished critical awareness in the 1990s. Yet, having considered above Deleuze's own conception of his early reading and writing, I wish to offer some commentary that relates this essay (Deleuze 1973b; hereafter cited in the following translation and abbreviated as HDW ["How Do We . . . "] with page references to the current volume) both to Deleuze's writings and to his eventual collaboration with Guattari. The reader is, of course, free to bypass this introduction in order to consult the essay directly.

STRUCTURALISM(S): AGGRESSIVE, INTERPRETATIVE

Following his books on Nietzsche (1962, 1965) and an initial version of his study on Proust (1964a),[2] Deleuze undertakes a reflection on the pair "difference"/"repetition," and their links to the concepts of expression and subjectivity (1968b) and of sense, identity, art and desire (extended in *Logique du sens*). In the structuralism essay, he explores the relation of these concepts to (then) contemporary critical perspectives and thereby elucidates an idiosyncratic conceptualization of "structuralism." By developing seven (or eight) criteria for "recognizing structuralism" as well as its diverse practices, Deleuze offers a superb example of his "loving," yet "monstrous" re-view of different works by the main "structuralist" proponents, already implicated in what would become known in North America as "poststructuralism": Lévi-Strauss, Althusser, Lacan, and Foucault.[3]

Under the guise of respecting customary practices of providing "samples" like so many bits of fabric or wares, Deleuze "names names" transversally by linking individual writers qua structuralists through the means by which they "recognize structuralism," particularly how they discern "the language proper to a domain" (HDW, pp. 258–259). If we recall Foucault's above-cited statement (Chapter 1, p. 5), made three years before *Logique du sens*, that Lévi-Strauss and Lacan indicated to contemporaries the "surface effect" of meaning and how "system" "sustains us in time and space," we can best orient the procedure that Deleuze follows and the links that he makes in this essay. To discover traits for recognizing the "system," or what he calls "series," Deleuze discerns criteria by which he can carefully disengage and "assemble" the particular practices of key writers. He thus pursues his practice of *enculage*, of "taking an author from behind," but equally making the author "actually say all I had him saying," through a particular mode of "depersonalization through love" (N, 6–7; P, 15–16). Thus, despite or because of the diversity of the projects pursued by the different authors cited, Deleuze both extends and adapts what he proposes as the following distinct criteria: (1) the symbolic, (2) the local or positional, (3) the differential and the singular, (4) the *differenciator* and *differenciation*, (5) the serial, (6) the empty square, and finally (7) and (8) "from the subject to practice."

The opening section is indicative of his "assemblage" process. Deleuze first makes what for us is now a familiar distinction between the "real," the "imaginary," and the "symbolic" (i.e., the three orders identified by Jacques Lacan). He then insists that this "symbolic" does not derive merely from forms, figures, or essences, but that it is fundamentally "the production of the original and specific theoretical object" (HDW, p. 261). Let us note the dynamic aspect, the production of this "object," which will contribute to the development of the "two-fold thought" in important ways. Deleuze defines structuralism's productive enterprise as both "aggressive"—in denouncing "the general misunderstanding" about the "symbolic" category—and "interpretative"—in employing this category to renew interpretations of works and their links to language, ideas, and action (HDW, p. 261). For readers of the collaborative works by Deleuze and Guattari, particularly *Anti-Oedipus*, the following statement indicates the fruitful line of inquiry and critique they later pursue: "Romanticism and symbolism, but also Freudianism and Marxism, thus become the object of profound reinterpretations. . . . But this reinterpretation only has value to the extent that it animates new works that are those of today, as if the symbolic were the source, inseparably, of living interpretation and creation" (HDW, p. 262).[4]

Having emphasized the "symbolic" in Section 1, and thereby seeming to foreground the importance of the Lacanian perspective, Deleuze proceeds in the subsequent sections to nuance his understanding not only of this crucial term, but also of the very concept of "structure." The second criterion, the local or positional, helps Deleuze explain what the symbolic is not; specifically, it is not real or imaginary. Rather, it is relational, having a sense as both meaning and direction within "a topological space . . . pure *spatium* constituted bit by bit as an order of proximity" (HDW, p. 262). Here Deleuze can address the question of subjectivity with reference to particular proponents of "structuralism": the constitution of subjectivity through distributions in relation to production (Althusser), determinations (Foucault), and signifying displacement (Lacan). The results of this relationship for structuralism are, first, that it regards sense (especially an overproduction of sense) as a "positional effect" (HDW, p. 263), that is, dependent on relational assemblages within particular domains for the (over)production of sense. Second, structuralism tends to emphasize combinatory and positional play and theater. Third, Deleuze asserts that structuralism is "inseparable from a new materialism, a new atheism, a new antihumanism" (HDW, pp. 263–264).

To situate this perspective in terms of a structuralist proponent mentioned, but unexamined in Deleuze's essay, Roland Barthes, I read Deleuze's perspective certainly as having little similarity to the "heroic structuralism," for example, of Barthes's "Introduction à l'analyse structurale des récits" (1966). However, the relational elements that Barthes develops in two different texts before and after this "Introduction" are worth considering in this context. In "L'activité structuraliste" (from 1963, in Barthes 1964 [1972]), Barthes stakes out the positional relations between analysis (dissection) and creation (assemblage), a multidisciplinary practice that participates in what Deleuze calls "reinterpretation . . . that animates new works which are those of today" (HDW, p. 262). Seven years later in S/Z (1970 [1974]), Barthes returns forcefully to the positional relations, but then in order to prepare the terrain for a concerted destabilization of signification. The movement of structuralism into the "heroic" confidence in defining relational significations typified the increasing formalism of the mid-1960s that many structuralist acolytes extolled, Barthes included. It is to his credit, then, that Barthes pushed his reflection toward a thorough interrogation of the stability of the author, the subject, and the possibilities of formal multiplicity, a stance that only became more pronounced and complex in his writings of the 1970s.[5]

Deleuze's development of the third and fourth criteria suggests, however, that any such comparisons for "recognizing structuralism" are risky and approximate, at best. Regarding the third criterion, of the differential and the singular, Deleuze affirms the consistency of a "positional symbolic" along two axes: on the one hand, an axis of reciprocal determination of symbolic elements kept in differential relationship among themselves; on the other hand, an axis of singularities, that is, of symbolic elements distributed as *singular* points that thereby determine a corresponding space of the structure. According to these two axes, Deleuze defines structure as based on multiple relationships, elements and points that one must seek in different domains: for example, kinship systems (Lévi-Strauss), "libidinal movements" of the body (Serge Leclaire), and modes of production (Althusser) (HDW, pp. 265–267).[6]

Then, in the essay's fourth section, Deleuze considers where and how such multiplicity of structures emerges in their diverse elements, points, and relationships. He begins by exploring the distinction between the actual and the virtual and draws from Proust (and behind him, from Bergson) to define the virtual as "real without being actual, ideal without being abstract" (HDW, p. 267).[7] Structuralism would play a crucial role in understanding how the virtual and the actual communicate since, as Deleuze argues, "to discern the structure of a domain is to determine an entire virtuality of coexistence that preexists the beings, objects, and works of this domain" (HDW, p. 268). Yet he also emphasizes the necessity for distinguishing "the total structure of a domain as an ensemble of virtual coexistence" from "substructures that correspond to diverse actualizations in the domain" (HDW, p. 268). He thereby posits a double process: on the one hand, there is a structure's "undifferenciation" as virtuality while being "totally and completely differentiated"; on the other hand, there is a structure's "differenciation" through the virtual's actualization, that is, through the structure's embodiment in particular forms. Insisting on this "complex" of different/ciation of "structure," Deleuze describes structuralism's ability at once to constitute "in itself a system of elements and of differential relations," and to actualize the virtual by "differenciating" species and parts (HDW, p. 269).[8] Structure functions, then, to enable the actualization of the virtual that "presents a dynamic multiplicity in which the process of differentiation creates the original arrangement or coherence of actual being: This is the multiplicity of organization" (Hardt 1993, 41).

Deleuze provides several examples: first, he points to Georges Dumézil's work on comparative religions as showing how species and parts are differenciated by the structure that, itself, achieves actualization through them. Referring to the way that "gods of religion" are realized at once within differential relations and as functions in proximity to singularities, Deleuze says, "It is precisely here that the border passes between the imaginary and the symbolic: the imaginary tends to reflect and to resituate around each term the total effect of a wholistic mechanism, whereas the symbolic structure assures the differentiation of terms and the differenciation of effects" (HDW, p. 269). That is, while the terms may be associated with distinct species of differential relations, the effects assure the actualization of the structure through singularities. Developing a second example, Deleuze considers the extent to which "structures are unconscious, necessarily overlaid with their products and effects," with links at once to the psychoanalytic and the economic domains. Forming problems and questions "resolved only to the extent that the corresponding structure is instantiated and according to the way it is instantiated," this differential or structural unconscious is no simple operation, but rather is problematizing, questioning, and serial (HDW, pp. 270-271).

The interplay between differential relations and singularities would seem quite adequate to recast structuralism from a renewed perspective. Deleuze proceeds further, however, in the fifth and sixth sections, by providing what we might consider to be signature concepts that link "structure" at once to production of sense and to production of desire (still conceptualized within the Lacanian framework). For all that precedes, claims Deleuze, cannot function without restoring structure's "other half," and so one must consider structure's inherently "serial" organization. Citing specific examples—Lévi-Strauss on totemism, Lacan's interpretations of Poe's "The Purloined Letter" and Freud's "Rat Man" (HDW, pp. 271-273)—Deleuze maintains that the structure's two constitutive series do not merely reflect each other. Rather, these series constantly undergo slippage, relative displacements, thanks to the differential relations into which the terms of each series enter. And Deleuze insists that we understand this displacement as fundamental, belonging "essentially to the places in the space of the structure." Hence the importance of metaphor and metonymy for structuralism: not at all figures of the imagination, these are structural factors, "even *the* two structural factors, in the sense that they express the two degrees of freedom of displacement, from one series to another and within the same series," thus preventing "the series that they animate from confusing or duplicating their terms in imaginary fashion" (HDW, p. 273).

In the sixth section, then, Deleuze explores this "properly structural or symbolic" displacement occurring as a result of "a wholly paradoxical object or element" that a structure envelops. Whereas the series "are constituted by symbolic terms and differential relations," this object is " 'eminently' symbolic . . . because it belongs to no series in particular." Rather, it functions as "the convergence point of the divergent series as such," immanent to both series simultaneously (HDW, pp. 273-274).[9] In each of the examples that Deleuze provides, this so-called object = x, belonging to no series in particular, traverses them and causes them to circulate while constantly displacing itself—the letter in Poe's tale, debt in "The Rat Man," the handkerchief in *Othello,* the crown in *Henry IV,* the "place of the king" in Foucault's opening description of Velasquez's painting in *The Order of Things* (1966a), "mana" as "floating signifier" for Lévi-Strauss, the "zero phoneme" for Jakobson, the portmanteau word for Lewis Carroll, a "letter which is Cosmos" in *Finnegan's Wake* (HDW, pp. 274–276). Besides the evident imbrication of this concept with its development in *Difference and Repetition* and *Logic of Sense*, the emergence of the "two-fold thought" is particularly striking in diverse passages on works by Joyce, Proust, Roussel, and Gombrowicz. Deleuze there situates the movement of heterogeneous series through this disparate, displacing "object," suggesting most notably that in songs, "the refrain encompasses an object = x, while the verses form the divergent series through which this object circulates" (HDW, p. 274; see also DREng, 123; DRFR, 160–161).[10]

Deleuze draws an explicit Lacanian connection to the "object = x," developed in *Difference and Repetition* and *Logic of Sense* as well: "Debt, letter, handkerchief, or crown, the nature of this object is specified by Lacan: it is always displaced in relation to itself. Its peculiar property is not to be where one looks for it, and conversely, also to be found where it is not. One would say that it 'is missing from its place' [*il manque à sa place*]" (HDW, p. 275).[11] Deleuze's reliance on the Lacanian constructs becomes apparent as we see the extent to which the very consistency of the "object = x," and that of structuralism as well, is neither "recognizable [n]or identifiable," but is related by Deleuze directly to the Lacanian "phallus." This functions, says Deleuze, "as the symbolic organ that founds sexuality *in its entirety* as system or structure," and "that does not coincide with its identity, always found there where it is not since it is not there where one looks for it, always displaced in relation to itself, *from the side of the mother*" (HDW, p. 277).[12] Deleuze is quick, though, to insist that "the phallus is not a final word," that in another order, of economics, for example, the empty square is determined differently. Just as carefully, Deleuze seeks to deflect an impression of positing a complete relativism, insisting that "in each structural order, certainly, the object = x is not at all something unknowable, something purely undetermined." Yet, although "perfectly determinable . . . , it is simply not assignable," and so, "for each order of structure [linguistic, familial, economic, sexual, etc.], the object = x is the empty or perforated site that permits this order to be articulated with the others, in a space that entails as many directions as orders" (HDW, pp. 277–278).

Concluding the essay's lengthy sixth part with four requirements for the empty square's important function in any structure (HDW, p. 279), Deleuze then completes this analysis by linking "subject" to "practice," addressing the question of actualization of structure through which places are filled and occupied by "real beings" (HDW, p. 279). On one hand, Deleuze sees this subject as "less a subject than subjected [*assujetti*]," and far from suppressing the subject, structuralism seeks to break it up, distribute it, shift it, dissipate it as "an always nomad subject" (HDW, p. 280). On the other hand, two structural "accidents" can occur, either to separate the empty square from this nomad subject, whereby "its emptiness becomes a veritable lack, a lacuna"; or to conjoin the square with this accompanying subject to such an extent that "its mobility is lost in the effect of a sedentary or fixed plenitude," for example, "the two pathological aspects of psychosis" (HDW, p. 280). Changing from one order to another (e.g., economic, psychic, or linguistic), these accidents are immanent to the event, interior to the structure, and not of contingent or exterior character.

In order that "the empty place . . . be given over to the subject that must accompany it on new paths, without occupying or deserting it," there is what Deleuze calls a "structuralist *hero*" that is "neither God nor man, neither personal nor universal." Rather, this "hero" is defined by its "resistant and creative force," by its "agility in following and safeguarding the displacements," and by its "power to cause relations to vary and to redistribute singularities" (HDW, p. 281). This "hero" or "mutation point" defines a praxis, "or rather the very site where praxis must take hold," and, according to Deleuze, structuralism "is not only inseparable from the works that it creates, but also from a practice in relation to the products that it interprets." Anticipating the intersection of psychic and social orders that will dominate *Anti-Oedipus*, Deleuze maintains, "whether this practice is therapeutic or political, it designates a point of permanent revolution, or of permanent transfer" (HDW, p. 281). However, such a movement "from subject to practice" has yet to be realized, Deleuze warns, for these last two criteria are "the criteria of the future," whereas the six criteria previously developed already function at the different structural levels as a means for conceptualizing the " 'effects' . . . at the conclusion of a 'process,' of a properly structural, differenciated production" (HDW, pp. 281–282).

In completing this examination of Deleuze's essay, I must point out that Deleuze would subsequently express severe misgivings about structuralism in different texts. In *Dialogues*, he criticizes the French for being "too human, too historical, too concerned with the future and the pasts," for spending "their time in in-depth analysis," for not knowing "how to become . . . how to trace lines, to follow a channel." Then, as an example, he refers to structuralism:

> It is a system of points and positions, which operates by cuts which are supposedly significant instead of proceeding by thrusts and cracking. It warps the lines of flight instead of following them and tracing them and extending them in a social field. (DEng, 37; DFr, 48)

Moreover, as Melissa McMahon pointed out to me (in private correspondence), Deleuze possessed a love for the power of the false, employing in his work a seemingly irreconcilable device of betraying while remaining faithful, of appropriating his subject to his own concerns while freeing it up simultaneously. Thus, what he says to Michel Cressole about his work on historical figures of philosophy would be no less appropriate for understanding the essay on structuralism: "I saw myself as taking an author from behind and giving him a child that would be his own offspring, yet monstrous . . . because it resulted from all sorts of shifting, slipping, dislocations, and hidden emissions that I really enjoyed" (N, 6; P, 15). As McMahon concludes, perhaps Deleuze's reluctance to reprint this essay during his life or to see it appear in translation arose from a sense that the irony and monstrosity that he enjoyed producing were not sufficiently emphatic or evident in this reinterpretation of structuralism.

GILLES DELEUZE, "HOW DO WE RECOGNIZE STRUCTURALISM?"

Translated by Melissa McMahon and Charles J. Stivale

We used to ask not long ago, "What is existentialism?"; now we ask "What is structuralism?" These questions are of keen interest, but only on the condition of being currently pertinent, of bearing on works actually in progress. *We are in 1967.* Thus we cannot invoke the unfinished character of these works in order to avoid replying, for it is this character alone that endows the question with a sense. The question "What is structuralism?" is required henceforth to undergo certain transformations. In the first place, *who* is structuralist? In the current moment, certain customs prevail; rightly or wrongly, it is customary to name names [*désigner*], to provide "samples" [*échantillonner*]: a linguist like Roman Jakobson; a sociologist like Claude Lévi-Strauss; a psychoanalyst like Jacques Lacan; a philosopher renewing epistemology, like Michel Foucault; a Marxist philosopher again taking up the problem of the interpretation of Marxism, like Louis Althusser; a literary critic like Roland Barthes; writers like those of the *Tel Quel* group. . . . Of these, some do not reject the word "structuralism," and use "structure," "structural." Others prefer the Saussurean term "system." These are very different kinds of thinkers, and from different generations, and some have exercised a real influence on others. But of greatest import is the extreme diversity of the domains that they explore. Each of them discovers problems, methods, solutions that are analogically related, as if sharing in a free atmosphere or spirit of the time, but one that distributes itself into singular creations and discoveries in each of these domains. -Ism words, in this sense, are perfectly justified.

There is good reason to ascribe the origin of structuralism to linguistics: not only Saussure, but the Moscow and Prague schools. And if structuralism then extends into other domains, this occurs henceforth without it being a question of analogy, nor merely in order to establish methods "equivalent" to those that first succeeded for the analysis of language. In truth, language is the only thing that can properly be said to have structure, be it an esoteric or even a nonverbal language. There is a structure of the unconscious only to the extent that the unconscious speaks and is language. There is a structure of bodies only to the extent that bodies are supposed to speak with a language that is one of symptoms. Even things possess a structure only insofar as they maintain a silent discourse, which is the language of signs. So the question "What is structuralism?" is further transformed—It is better to ask, What do we recognize in those that we call structuralists? And what do they themselves recognize?—since one does not recognize people, in a visible manner, except by the invisible and imperceptible things that they recognize in their own fashion. How do the structuralists go about recognizing a language in something, the language proper to a domain? What do they discover in this domain? We thus propose only to discern certain *formal* criteria of recognition, the simplest ones, by invoking in each case the example of cited authors, whatever the diversity of their works and projects.

I. First Criterion: The Symbolic

We are used to, almost conditioned to, a certain distinction or correlation between the real and the imaginary. All of our thought maintains a dialectical play between these two notions. Even when classical philosophy speaks of pure intelligence or understanding, it is still a matter of a faculty defined by its aptitude to grasp the heart of the real [*le réel en son fond*], the real "in truth," the real such as it is, in opposition to, but also in relation to, the forces [*puissances*] of imagination. Let us cite some creative movements that are quite different: Romanticism, Symbolism, Surrealism. . . . In so doing, we invoke at once the transcendent point where the real and the imaginary interpenetrate and unite, and their sharp border, like the cutting edge of their difference. In any case, we go no further than the opposition and complementarity of the imaginary and the real—at least in the traditional interpretation of Romanticism, Symbolism, etc. Even

Freudianism is interpreted from the perspective of two principles: the reality principle with its power to disappoint, the pleasure principle with its hallucinatory power of satisfaction. With all the more reason methods like those of Jung and Bachelard are wholly inscribed within the real and the imaginary, within the frame of their complex relations, transcendent unity and liminary tension, fusion and cutting edge.

The first criterion of structuralism, however, is the discovery and recognition of a third order, a third reign: that of the symbolic. The refusal to confuse the symbolic with the imaginary, as much as with the real, constitutes the first dimension of structuralism. There again, everything began with linguistics: beyond the word in its reality and its resonant parts [*parties sonores*], beyond images and concepts associated with words, the structuralist linguist discovers an element of quite another nature, a structural object. And perhaps it is in this symbolic element that the novelists of the *Tel Quel* group wish to locate themselves, as much to renew the resonant realities [*réalités sonores*] as the associated narratives. Beyond the history of men, and the history of ideas, Michel Foucault discovers a deeper, subterranean ground that forms the object of what he calls "the archaeology of thought." Behind real men and their real relations, behind ideologies and their imaginary relations, Louis Althusser discovers a deeper domain as object of science and of philosophy.

We already had many fathers, in psychoanalysis: first of all, a real father, but also father-images. And all our dramas occurred in the strained relations of the real and the imaginary. Jacques Lacan discovers a third, more fundamental father, a symbolic father or Name-of-the-father. Not just the real and the imaginary, but their relations, and the disturbances of these relations, must be thought of as the limit of a process in which they constitute themselves in relation to the symbolic. In Lacan's work, in the work of other structuralists as well, the symbolic as element of the structure constitutes the principle of a genesis: structure is incarnated in realities and images according to determinable series. Moreover, the structure constitutes series in incarnating itself, but is not derived from them since it is deeper than them, being the substratum for all the strata of the real as for all the heights [*ciels*] of imagination. Inversely, catastrophes that are proper to the symbolic structural order take into account the apparent disturbances of the real and the imaginary: thus, in the case of "The Wolf Man" as Lacan interprets it, the theme of castration reappears in the real since it remains nonsymbolized ("foreclosure"), in the hallucinatory form of the cut finger.[13]

We can enumerate the real, the imaginary, and the symbolic: 1, 2, 3. But perhaps these numerals have as much an ordinal as a cardinal value. For the real in itself is not separable from a certain ideal of unification or of totalization: the real tends toward one, it is one in its "truth." As soon as we see two in "one," as soon as we start to duplicate [*dédoublons*], the imaginary appears in person, even if it is in the real that its action is carried out. For example, the real father is one, or wants to be according to his law; but the image of the father is always double in itself, cleaved according to a law of the dual [*une loi de duel*]. It is projected onto two persons at least, one assuming the role of the play-father, the father-buffoon, and the other, the role of the working and ideal father: like the Prince of Wales [Prince Hal] in Shakespeare, who passes from one father image to the other, from Falstaff to the Crown. The imaginary is defined by games of mirroring, of duplication, of reversed identification and projection, always in the mode of the double.[14] But perhaps, in turn, the symbolic is three, and not merely the third beyond the real and the imaginary. There is always a third to be sought in the symbolic itself; structure is at least triadic, without which it would not "circulate"—a third at once unreal, and yet not imaginable.

We will see why later; but already the first criterion consists of this: the positing of a symbolic order, irreducible to the orders of the real and the imaginary, and deeper than them. We do not know at all yet what this symbolic element consists of. We can say at least that the corresponding structure has no relationship with a sensible form, nor with a figure of the imagination, nor with an intelligible essence. It has nothing to do with a *form*: for structure is not at all defined by an autonomy of the whole, by a preeminence [*pregnance*] of the whole over its parts, by a Gestalt that would operate in the real and in perception. Structure is defined, on the contrary, by the nature of certain atomic elements that claim to account both for the formation of wholes and for the variation of their parts. It has nothing to do either with *figures* of the imagination, although structuralism is riddled with reflections on rhetoric, metaphor, and metonymy, for these figures themselves imply structural displacements that must account for both the literal and the figurative. It has nothing to do finally with an *essence,* for it is a matter of a combinatory formula [*une combinatoire*] supporting formal elements that by themselves have neither form, nor signification, nor representation, nor content, nor given empirical reality, nor hypothetical functional model, nor intelligibility behind appearances. No one has better determined the status of the structure as identical to the "Theory" itself than Louis Althusser—and the symbolic must be understood as the production of the original and specific theoretical object.

Sometimes structuralism is aggressive, as when it denounces the general misunderstanding of this ultimate symbolic category, beyond the imaginary and the real. Sometimes it is interpretative, as when it renews our interpretation of works in relation to this category, and claims to discover an original point at which language is constituted, in which works elaborate themselves, and where ideas and actions are bound together. Romanticism and Symbolism, but also Freudianism and Marxism, thus become the object of profound reinterpretations. Further still, it is the mythical, poetic, philosophical, or practical works themselves that are subject to structural interpretation. But this reinterpretation only has value to the extent that it animates new works that are those of today, as if the symbolic were the source, inseparably, of living interpretation and creation.

II. Second Criterion: Local or Positional

What does the symbolic element of the structure consist of? We sense the need to go slowly, to state repeatedly, first of all, what it is not. Distinct from the real and the imaginary, it cannot be defined either by preexisting realities to which it would refer and that it would designate, nor by the imaginary or conceptual contents that it would implicate, and which would give to it a signification. The elements of a structure have neither extrinsic designation nor intrinsic signification. Then what is left? As Lévi-Strauss recalls rigorously, they have nothing other than a *sense* [*un sens* = meaning and direction]: a sense that is necessarily and uniquely "positional" (Lévi-Strauss 1963, 636–637). It is not a matter of a location [*place*] in a real spatial expanse, nor of sites [*lieux*] in imaginary extensions, but rather of places and sites in a properly structural space, that is, a topological space. Space is what is structural, but an unextended, preextensive space, pure *spatium* constituted bit by bit as an order of proximity, in which the notion of proximity [*voisinage*] first of all has precisely an ordinal sense and not a signification in extension.[15] Or in genetic biology: the genes are part of a structure to the extent that they are inseparable from "loci," sites capable of changing their relation within the chromosome. In short, places in a purely structural space are primary in relation to the things and real beings that come to occupy them, primary also in relation to the always somewhat imaginary roles and events that necessarily appear when they are occupied.

The scientific ambition of structuralism is not quantitative, but topological and relational, a principal that Lévi-Strauss constantly maintains. And when Althusser speaks of economic structure, he specifies that the true "subjects" there are not those who come to occupy the places, that is, concrete individuals or real men, no more than the true objects there are the roles that they fulfill and the events that are produced. Rather, these "subjects" are above all the places in a topological and structural space defined by relations of production (Althusser 1965b, 2:157 [1979, 180]). When Foucault defines determinations such as death, desire, work, or play, he does not consider them as dimensions of empirical human existence, but above all as the qualifications of places and positions that will render mortal and dying, or desiring, or workman-like, or playful, those who come to occupy them, but who only come to occupy them secondarily, fulfilling their roles according to an order of proximity that is an order of the structure itself. That is why Foucault can propose a new distribution of the empirical and the transcendental, the latter finding itself defined by an order of places independently of those who occupy them empirically (Foucault 1966a, 329–333 [1970, 318–322]). Structuralism cannot be separated from a new transcendental philosophy, in which the sites prevail over whatever fills them. Father, mother, etc., are first of all sites in a structure; and if we are mortal, it is by moving into the line, by coming to a particular site, marked in the structure following this topological order of proximities (even when we do so ahead of our turn).

"It is not only the subject," says Lacan, "but subjects grasped in their intersubjectivity, who line up . . . and who model their very being on the moment of the signifying chain which traverses them . . . The displace-ment of the signifier determines subjects in their acts, in their destiny, in their refusals, in their blindnesses, in their conquests and in their fate, their innate gifts and social acquisition notwithstanding, without regard for character or sex" (Lacan 1966, 30; 1972, 60).

One could not say more clearly that empirical psychology is not only founded on, but determined by, a transcendental topology.

Several consequences follow from this local or positional criterion. First of all, if the symbolic elements have no extrinsic designation nor intrinsic signification, but only a positional sense, it follows necessarily and by right that *sense always results from the combination of elements that are not themselves signifying* (Lévi-Strauss 1963, 637). As Lévi-Strauss says in his discussion with Paul Ricoeur, sense is always a result, an effect: not merely an effect like a product, but an optical effect, a language effect, a positional effect. There is, profoundly, a non-sense of sense, from which sense itself results. Not that we return in this way to what was once called a philosophy of the absurd since, for it, sense itself is lacking, essentially. For structuralism, on the contrary, there is always too much sense, an overproduction, an overdetermination of sense, always produced in excess by the combination of places in the structure. (Hence the importance, in Althusser's work, for example, of the concept of *overdetermination*.)[16] Non-sense is not at all the absurd or the opposite of sense, but rather that which gives value to sense and produces it by circulating in the structure. Structuralism owes nothing to Albert Camus, but much to Lewis Carroll.[17]

The second consequence is structuralism's inclination for certain games and a certain kind of theater, for certain play and theatrical spaces. It is no accident that Lévi-Strauss often refers to the theory of games, and accords such importance to playing cards. As does Lacan to his game metaphors that are more than metaphors: not only the moving object [*le furet*, literally, "the ferret"; or, the moving token in *jeu de furet*, the game of hunt-the-slipper] that darts around the structure, but also the dummy hand [*la place du mort*] that circulates in bridge. The noblest games, such as chess, are those that organize a combinatory system of places in a pure *spatium* infinitely deeper than the real extension of the chessboard and the imaginary extension of each piece. Or when Althusser interrupts his commentary on Marx to talk about theater, but a theater that is neither of reality nor of ideas, a pure theater of places and positions, the principle of which he sees in Brecht,[18] and that would today perhaps find its most extreme expression in Armand Gatti's work. In short, the very manifesto of structuralism must be sought in the famous formula, eminently poetic and theatrical: To think is to cast a throw of the dice [*Penser, c'est émettre un coup de dés*].[19]

The third consequence is that structuralism is inseparable from a new materialism, a new atheism, a new antihumanism. For if the place is primary in relation to whatever occupies it, it certainly will not suffice to replace God with man in order to change the structure. And if this place is the dummy hand [*la place du mort*, i.e., the dead man's place], the death of God surely means the death of man as well, in favor, we hope, of something yet to come, but which could only come within the structure and through its mutation. This is how we understand the imaginary character of man for Foucault or the ideological character of humanism for Althusser.

III. Third Criterion: The Differential and the Singular

What, then, do these symbolic elements or units of position finally consist of? Let us return to the linguistic model. What is distinct both from the voiced elements, and the associated concepts and images, is called a phoneme, the smallest linguistic unit capable of differentiating two words of diverse meanings: for example, *b*illard [billiard] and *p*illard [pillager]. It is clear that the phoneme is embodied in letters, syllables, and sounds, but that it is not reducible to them. Moreover, letters, syllables, and sounds give it an independence, whereas in itself the phoneme is inseparable from the phonemic relation that unites it to other phonemes: b/p. Phonemes do not exist independently of the relations into which they enter and through which they reciprocally determine each other.[20]

We can distinguish three types of relation. A first type is established between elements that enjoy independence or autonomy: for example, $3 + 2$, or even $2/3$. The elements are real, and these relations must themselves be said to be real. A second type of relationship, for example,

$x^2 + y^2 - R^2 = 0$, is established between terms for which the value is not specified, but that, *in each case,* must however have a determined value. Such relations can be called imaginary. But the third type is established between elements that have no determined value themselves, and that nevertheless determine each other reciprocally in the relation: thus $ydy + xdx = 0$, or $dy/dx = -x/y$. Such relationships are symbolic, and the corresponding elements are held in a differential relationship. Dy is totally undetermined in relation to y, dx is totally undetermined in relation to x: each one has neither existence, nor value, nor signification. And yet the relation dy/dx is totally determined, the two elements determining each other reciprocally in the relation.[21] This process of a reciprocal determination is at the heart of a relationship that allows one to define the symbolic nature. Sometimes the origins of structuralism are sought in the area of axiomatics, and it is true that Bourbaki, for example, uses the word "structure." But this use, it seems to us, is in a very different sense, that of relations between nonspecified elements, not even qualitatively specified, whereas in structuralism elements specify each other reciprocally in relations. In this sense, axiomatics would still be imaginary, not symbolic, properly speaking. The mathematical origin of structuralism must be sought rather in the domain of differential calculus, specifically in the interpretation that Weierstrass and Russell gave to it, a *static and ordinal* interpretation, which definitively liberates calculus from all reference to the infinitely small, and integrates it into a pure logic of relations.

Corresponding to the determination of differential relations are singularities, distributions of singular points that characterize curves or figures (a triangle, for example, has three singular points). In this way, the determination of phonemic relations proper to a given language ascribes singularities in proximity to which the vocalizations and significations of the language are constituted. *The reciprocal determination* of symbolic elements continues henceforth into *the complete determination* of singular points that constitute a space corresponding to these elements. The crucial notion of singularity, taken literally, seems to belong to all the domains in which there is structure. The general formula, "To think is to cast a throw of the dice," itself refers to the singularities represented by the sharply outlined points on the dice. Every structure presents the following two aspects: a system of differential relations according to which the symbolic elements determine themselves reciprocally, and a system of singularities corresponding to these relations and tracing the space of the structure. Every structure is a multiplicity. The question "Is there structure in any domain whatsoever?" must be specified in the following way: in a given domain, can one uncover symbolic elements, differential relations, and singular points that are proper to it? Symbolic elements are incarnated in the real beings and objects of the domain considered; the differential relations are actualized in real relations between these beings; the singularities are so many places in the structure, which distributes the imaginary attitudes or roles of the beings or objects that come to occupy them.[22]

It is not a matter of mathematical metaphors. In each domain, one must find elements, relationships, and points. When Lévi-Strauss undertakes the study of elementary kinship structures, he not only considers the real fathers in a society, nor only the father-images that run through the myths of that society. He claims to discover real kinship phonemes, that is, *kinemes* [*parentèmes*], positional units that do not exist independently of the differential relations into which they enter and that determine each other reciprocally. It is in this way that the four relations— brother/sister, husband/wife, father/son, maternal uncle/sister's son— form the simplest structure. And to this combinatory system of "kinship names" correspond in a complex way, but without resembling them, the "kinship attitudes" that complete [*effectuer*] the singularities determined in the system. One could just as well proceed in the opposite manner: start from singularities in order to determine the differential relations between ultimate symbolic elements. Thus, taking the example of the Oedipus myth, Lévi-Strauss starts from the singularities of the story (Oedipus marries his mother, kills his father, immolates the Sphinx, is named "Clubfoot," etc.) in order to infer from them the differential relations between "mythemes" that are determined reciprocally (overestimation of kinship relations, underestimation of kinship relations, negation of aboriginality, persistence of aboriginality) (Lévi-Strauss 1958, 1:235–242 [1963, 1:213–218]). In any case, the symbolic elements and their relations always determine the nature of the beings and objects that come to complete them, while the singularities form an order of positions that simultaneously determines the roles and the attitudes of these beings insofar as they occupy them. The determination of the structure is therefore completed in a theory of attitudes that explain its functioning.

Singularities correspond with the symbolic elements and their relations, but do not resemble them. One could say, rather, that singularities "symbolize" with them, derive from them, since every determination of differential relations entails a distribution of singular points. Yet, for example: the values of differential relations are incarnated in species, whereas singularities are incarnated in the organic parts corresponding to each species. The former constitute variables, the latter constitute functions. The former constitute within a structure the domain of *appellations,* the latter the domain of *attitudes.*[23] Lévi-Strauss insisted on this double aspect—derived, yet irreducible—of attitudes in relation to appellations (Lévi-Strauss 1958, 1:343–344 [1963, 1:310–312]). A disciple of Lacan, Serge Leclaire, shows in another field how the symbolic elements of the unconscious necessarily refer to "libidinal movements" of the body, incarnating the singularities of the structure in such and such a place (Leclaire 1967, 97–105). In this sense, every structure is psychosomatic, or rather represents a category-attitude complex.

Let us consider the interpretation of Marxism by Althusser and his collaborators: above all, the relations of production are determined there as differential relations that are established not between real men or concrete individuals, but between objects and agents which, first of all, have a symbolic value (object of production, instrument of production, labor force, immediate workers, immediate nonworkers, such as they are held in relations of property and appropriation).[24] Each mode of production is thus characterized by singularities corresponding to the values of the relations. And if it is obvious that concrete men come to occupy the places and carry forth the elements of the structure, this happens by fulfilling the role that the structural place assigns to them (e.g., the "capitalist"), and by serving as supports for the structural relations. This occurs to such an extent that "the true subjects are not these occupants and functionaries . . . but the definition and distribution of these places and these functions." The true subject is the structure itself: the differential and the singular, the differential relations and the singular points, the reciprocal determination and the complete determination.

IV. Fourth Criterion: The Differenciator, Differenciation

Structures are necessarily unconscious, by virtue of the elements, relations and points that compose them. Every structure is an infrastructure, a microstructure. In a certain way, they are not actual. What is actual is that in which the structure is incarnated or rather as what the structure constitutes in its incarnation. But in itself, it is neither actual nor fictional, neither real nor possible. Jakobson poses the problem of the status of the phoneme, which is not to be confused with any actual letter, syllable, or sound, no more than it is a fiction, or an associated image (Jakobson and Halle 1963 [1956]). Perhaps the word "virtuality" would precisely designate the mode of the structure or the object of theory, on the condition that we eliminate any vagueness about the word. For the virtual has a reality that is proper to it, but that does not merge with any actual reality, any present or past actuality. The virtual has an ideality that is proper to it, but that does not merge with any possible image, any abstract idea. We will say of structure: *real without being actual, ideal without being abstract.*[25] This is why Lévi-Strauss often presents the structure as a sort of ideal reservoir or repertoire, in which everything coexists virtually, but where the actualization is necessarily carried out according to exclusive rules, always implicating partial combinations and unconscious choices. To discern the structure of a domain is to determine an entire virtuality of coexistence that preexists the beings, objects, and works of this domain. Every structure is a multiplicity of virtual coexistence. Louis Althusser, for example, shows in this sense that the originality of Marx (his anti-Hegelianism) resides in the manner in which the social system is defined by a coexistence of elements and economic relations, without one being able to engender them successively according to the illusion of a false dialectic.[26]

What is it that coexists in the structure? All the elements, the relations, and relational values, all the singularities proper to the domain considered. Such a coexistence does not imply any confusion, nor any indetermination, for the relationships and differential elements coexist in a completely and perfectly determined whole. Except that this whole is not actualized as such. What is actualized, here and now, are particular relations, relational values, and distributions of singularities; others are actualized elsewhere or at other times. There is no total language [*langue*] embodying all the possible phonemes and phonemic relations. But the virtual totality of the language system [*langage*] is actualized following exclusive rules in diverse, specific languages, of which each embodies certain relationships, relational values, and singularities. There is no total society, but each social form embodies certain elements, relationships, and production values (e.g., "capitalism"). We must therefore distinguish between the total structure of a domain as an ensemble of virtual coexistence, and the substructures that correspond to diverse actualizations in the domain. Of the structure as virtuality, we must say that it is still undifferenciated, even though it is totally and completely differentiated. Of structures that are embodied in a particular actual form (present or past), we must say that they are differenciated, and that for them to be actualized is precisely to be differenciated. The structure is inseparable from this double aspect, or from this complex that one can designate under the name of different/ciation, where t/c constitutes the universally determined phonemic relationship.[27]

All differenciation, all actualization is carried out along two paths: species and parts. The differential relations are incarnated in qualitatively distinct species, while the corresponding singularities are incarnated in the parts and extended figures that characterize each species: hence, the language species, and the parts of each one in the vicinity of the singularities of the linguistic structure; the specifically defined social modes of production and the organized parts corresponding to each one of these modes, etc. One will notice that the process of actualization always implies an internal temporality, variable according to what is actualized. Not only does each type of social production have a global internal temporality, but its organized parts have particular rhythms. As regards time, the position of structuralism is thus quite clear: time is always a time of actualization, according to which the elements of virtual coexistence are carried out at diverse rhythms. Time goes from the virtual to the actual, that is, from structure to its actualizations, and not from one actual form to another. Or at least time conceived as a relation of succession of two actual forms makes do with expressing abstractly the internal times of the structure or structures that are effectuated in depth in these two forms, and the differential relations between these times. And precisely because the structure is not actualized without being differenciated in space and time, hence without differenciating the species and the parts that carry it out, we must say in this sense that structure *produces* these species and these parts themselves. It produces them as differenciated species and parts, such that one can no more oppose the genetic to the structural than time to structure. Genesis, like time, goes from the virtual to the actual, from the structure to its actualization; the two notions of multiple internal time and static ordinal genesis are in this sense inseparable from the play of structures.[28]

We must insist on this differenciating role. Structure is in itself a system of elements and of differential relations, but it also differenciates the species and parts, the beings and functions in which the structure is actualized. It is differential in itself, and differenciating in its effect. Commenting on Lévi-Strauss's work, Jean Pouillon defined the problem of structuralism: "[Can one elaborate] a system of differences that leads neither to their simple juxtaposition, nor to their artificial erasure?" (Pouillon 1956, 155). In this regard, the work of Georges Dumézil is exemplary, even from the point of view of structuralism: no one has better analyzed the generic and specific differences between religions, and also the differences in parts and functions between the gods of a particular, single religion. For the gods of a religion, for example, Jupiter, Mars, and Quirinus, incarnate elements and differential relations, at the same time as they find their attitudes and functions in proximity to the singularities of the system or "parts of the society" considered. They are thus essentially differenciated by the structure that is actualized or carried out in them, and that produces them by being actualized. It is true that each of them, considered solely in its actuality, attracts and reflects the function of the others, such that one risks no longer discovering anything of this originary differenciation that produces them from the virtual to the actual. But it is precisely here that the border passes between the imaginary and the symbolic: the imaginary tends to reflect and to resituate around each term the total effect of a wholistic mechanism, whereas the symbolic structure assures the differentiation of terms and the differenciation of effects. Hence the hostility of structuralism toward the methods of the imaginary: Lacan's critique of Jung, and the critique of Bachelard by proponents of

"New Criticism." The imagination duplicates and reflects, it projects and identifies, it loses itself in a play of mirrors, but the distinctions that it makes, like the assimilations that it carries out, are surface effects that hide the otherwise subtle differential mechanisms of symbolic thought. Commenting on Dumézil, Edmond Ortigues does well to say: "When one approaches the material imagination, the differential function diminishes, one tends toward equivalences; when one approaches the formative elements of society, the differential function increases, one tends toward distinctive values [*valences*]" (Ortigues 1962, 197).[29]

Structures are unconscious, necessarily overlaid by their products or effects. An economic structure never exists in a pure form, but is covered over by the juridical, political, and ideological relations in which it is incarnated. One can only *read*, find, retrieve the structures through these effects. The terms and relations that actualize them, the species and parts that effectuate them, are as much forms of interference [*brouillage*] as forms of expression. This is why one of Lacan's disciples, J.-A. Miller, develops the concept of a "metonymic causality,"[30] or Althusser, the concept of a properly structural causality, in order to account for the very particular presence of a structure in its effects, and for the way in which it differenciates these effects, at the same time as these latter assimilate and integrate it (Althusser 1965b, 2:169–177 [1979, 187–193]). The unconscious of the structure is a differential unconscious. One might believe, then, that structuralism goes back to a pre-Freudian conception: doesn't Freud understand the unconscious as a mode of the conflict of forces or of the opposition of desires, whereas Leibnizian metaphysics already proposed the idea of a differential unconscious of minute perceptions? But even in Freud's writing, there is the whole problem of the origin of the unconscious, of its constitution as "language," which goes beyond the level of desire, of associated images and relations of opposition. Inversely, the differential unconscious is not constituted by minute perceptions of the real and by passages to the limit, but rather by variations of differential relations in a symbolic system as functions of distributions of singularities. Lévi-Strauss is right to say that the unconscious is made neither of desires nor of representations, that it is "always empty," consisting solely in the structural laws that it imposes on representations and on desires (Lévi-Strauss 1958, 224 [1963, 203]).

For the unconscious is always a problem, though not in the sense that would call its existence into question. Rather, the unconscious by itself forms the problems and questions that are resolved only to the extent that the corresponding structure is instantiated [*s'effectue*] and always according to the way that it is instantiated. For a problem always gains the solution that it deserves based on the manner in which it is posed, and on the symbolic field used to pose it. Althusser can present the economic structure of a society as the field of problems that the society poses for itself, that it is determined to pose for itself, and that it resolves according to its own means, that is, according to the lines of differenciation along which the structure is actualized (taking into account the absurdities, ignominies, and cruelties that these "solutions" involve by reason of the structure). Likewise, Serge Leclaire, following Lacan, can distinguish psychoses and neuroses, and different kinds of neuroses, less by types of conflict than by modes of questions that always find the answer that they deserve as a function of the symbolic field in which they are posed: thus the hysterical question is not that of the obsessive (Leclaire 1956).[31] In all of this, problems and questions do not designate a provisional and subjective moment in the elaboration of our knowledge, but on the contrary, designate a perfectly objective category, full and complete "objectalities" [*objectités*] that are the structure's own. The structural unconscious is at once differential, problematizing, and questioning. And, as we shall see, it is finally serial.[32]

V. Fifth Criterion: Serial

All of the preceding, however, still seems incapable of functioning, for we have only been able to define half of the structure. A structure only starts to move, and become animated, if we restore its other half. Indeed, the symbolic elements that we have previously defined, taken in their differential relations, are organized necessarily in series. But so organized, they relate to another series, constituted by other symbolic elements and by other relations: this reference to a second series is easily explained by recalling that singularities derive from the terms and relations of the first, but are not limited simply to reproducing or reflecting them. They thus organize themselves in another series capable of an autonomous development, or at least they necessarily relate the first to this other series. So it is for phonemes and morphemes; or for the economic, and other social series; or for Foucault's triple series, linguistic, economic and biological, etc. The question of knowing if the first series forms a basis and in which sense, if it is signifying, the others only being signified, is a complex question the nature of which we cannot yet assess. One must state simply that every structure is serial, multiserial, and would not function without this condition.

When Lévi-Strauss again takes up the study of totemism, he shows the extent to which the phenomenon is poorly understood as long as it is interpreted in terms of imagination. For according to its law, the *imagination* necessarily conceives totemism as the operation by which a man or a group are identified with an animal. But *symbolically*, it is quite a different matter, not the imaginary identification of one term with another, but the structural homology of two series of terms: on the one hand, a series of animal species taken as elements of differential relations, on the other hand, a series of social positions themselves caught symbolically in their own relations. This confrontation occurs "between these two systems of differences," these two series of elements and relations (Lévi-Strauss 1962, 112 [1963, 77–78]).[33]

The unconscious, according to Lacan, is neither individual nor collective, but intersubjective, which is to say that it implies a development in terms of series: not only the signifier and the signified, but the two series at a minimum organize themselves in quite a variable manner according to the domain under consideration.[34] In one of Lacan's most famous texts, he comments on "The Purloined Letter" by Edgar Allan Poe, showing how the "structure" puts into play two series, the places of which are occupied by variable subjects. First series: the king who does not see the letter, the queen who is thrilled at having so cleverly hidden it by leaving it out in the open, the minister who sees everything and takes possession of the letter. Second series: the police who find nothing at the minister's hotel; the minister who is thrilled at having so cleverly hidden the letter by leaving it out in the open; Dupin who sees everything and takes back possession of the letter (Lacan 1966, 15; 1972, 44). Already in a previous text, Lacan examined the case of "The Rat Man" on the basis of a double series, paternal and filial, in which each put into play four relational terms according to an order of places: debt–friend, rich woman–poor woman (Lacan 1953 [Evans 1979]).

It goes without saying that the organization of the constitutive series of a structure supposes a veritable *mise en scène* and, in each case, requires precise evaluations and interpretations. There is no general rule at all; we touch here on the point at which structuralism implies, from one perspective, a true creation, and from another, an initiative and a discovery that is not without its risks. The determination of a structure occurs not only through a choice of basic symbolic elements and the differential relations into which they enter, nor merely through a distribution of the singular points that correspond to them. The determination also occurs through the constitution of a second series, at least, that maintains complex relations with the first. And if the structure defines a problematic field, a field of problems, it is in the sense that the nature of the problem reveals its proper objectivity in this serial constitution, which sometimes makes structuralism seem close to music. Phillipe Sollers writes a novel, *Drame*, punctuated [*rhythmé*] by the expressions "Problem" and "Missing" [*"Manqué"*], in the course of which tentative series are elaborated ("a chain of maritime memories passes through his right arm . . . the left leg, on the other hand, seemed to be riddled with mineral groupings").[35] Or consider Jean-Pierre Faye's attempt in *Analogues,* concerning a serial coexistence of narrative modes.

But what keeps the two series from simply reflecting one another, and henceforth identifying each of their terms one to one? The whole of the structure would then fall back into the state of a figure of imagination. The factor that allays such a threat is seemingly quite strange. Indeed, the terms of each series are in themselves inseparable from the slippages [*décalages*] or displacements that they undergo in relation to the terms of the other. They are thus inseparable from the variation of differential relations. In the case of the purloined letter, the minister in the second series comes to the place that the queen had occupied in the first one. In the filial series of "The Rat Man," the poor woman comes to occupy the friend's place in relation to the debt. Or again, in the double series of birds and twins cited by Lévi-Strauss, the twins are the "people from on high" in relation to the people from below, necessarily coming to occupy the place of the "birds from below," not of the birds from on high (Lévi-Strauss 1962, 115 [1963, 79–81]). This relative displacement of the two series is not at all secondary; it does not come to affect a term from the outside and secondarily, as if giving it an imaginary disguise. On the contrary, the displacement is properly structural or symbolic: it belongs essentially to the places in the space of the structure, and thus regulates all the imaginary disguises of beings and objects that come secondarily to occupy these places. This is why structuralism brings so much attention to bear on metaphor and metonymy. These are not in any way figures of the imagination, but are, above all, structural factors. They are even *the* two structural factors, in the sense that they express the two degrees of freedom of displacement, from one series to another and within the same series. Far from being imaginary, they prevent the series that they animate from confusing or duplicating their terms in imaginary fashion. But what are these relative displacements, then, if they belong absolutely to the places in the structure?

VI. Sixth Criterion: The Empty Square (*La case vide*)

It appears that the structure envelops a wholly paradoxical object or element. Let us consider the case of the letter, in Edgar Allan Poe's story, as examined by Lacan; or the case of the debt, in "The Rat Man." It is obvious that this object is eminently symbolic, but we say "eminently" because it belongs to no series in particular: the letter is nevertheless present in both of Poe's series; the debt is present in both of the "Rat Man" series. Such an object is always present in the corresponding series, it traverses them and moves with them, it never ceases to circulate in them, and from one to the other, with an extraordinary agility. One might say that it is *its own* metaphor, and *its own* metonymy. The series in each case are constituted by symbolic terms and differential relations, but this object seems to be of another nature. In fact, it is in relation to the object that the variety of terms and the variation of differential relations are determined in each case. The two series of a structure are always divergent (by virtue of the laws of differenciation), but this singular object is the convergence point of the divergent series as such. It is "eminently" symbolic, but precisely because it is immanent to the two series at once. What else would we call it, if not Object = x, the riddle Object or the great Mobile element? We can nevertheless remain a bit doubtful: what Jacques Lacan invites us to discover in two cases, the particular role played by a letter or a debt—is it an artifice, strictly applicable to these cases, or rather is it a truly general method, valid for all the structurable domains, a criterion for every structure, as if a structure were not defined without assigning an object = x that ceaselessly traverses the series? As if the literary work, for example, or the work of art, but other *oeuvres* as well, those of society, those of illness, those of life in general, enveloped this very special object that assumes control over their structure. And as if it were always a matter of finding who is H,[36] or of discovering an x shrouded within the work. Such is the case with songs: the refrain encompasses an object = x, while the verses form the divergent series through which this object circulates. It is for this reason that songs truly present an elementary structure.[37]

A disciple of Lacan, André Green, signals the existence of the handkerchief that circulates in *Othello*, traversing all the series of the play (Green 1966, 32). We also spoke of the two series of the Prince of Wales, Falstaff or the father-buffoon, Henry IV or the royal father, the two images of the father. The crown is the object = x that traverses the two series, with different terms and under different relations. The moment when the prince tries on the crown, his father not yet dead, marks the passage from one series to the other, the change in symbolic terms and the variation of differential relations. The old dying king is angered, and believes that his son wants to identify with him prematurely. Yet responding quite capably in a splendid speech, the prince shows that the crown is not the object of an imaginary identification, but, on the contrary, is the eminently symbolic term that traverses all the series, the infamous series of Falstaff and the great royal series, and that permits the passage from one to the other at the heart of the same structure. As we saw, there was a first difference between the imaginary and the symbolic; the differenciating role of the symbolic, in opposition to the assimilating and reflecting role, doubling and duplicating, of the imaginary. But the second dividing line appears more clearly here: against the dual character of the imagination, the Third which essentially intervenes in the symbolic system, which distributes series, displaces them relatively, makes them communicate with each other, all the while preventing the one from imaginarily falling back on the other.

Debt, the letter, the handkerchief, or the crown—the nature of this object is specified by Lacan: it is always displaced in relation to itself. Its peculiar property is not to be where one looks for it, and conversely, also to be found where it is not. One would say that it "is missing from its place" [*il manque à sa place*] (and, in this, is not something real); further-more, that it does not coincide with its own resemblance (and, in this, is not an image); and that it does not coincide with its own identity (and, in this, is not a concept). "What is hidden is never what is *missing from its place*, as the call slip puts it when speaking of a volume lost in the library. And even if the book be on an adjacent shelf or in the next slot, it would be hidden there, however visibly that it may appear. For only something that can change its place can *literally* be said to be missing from it: that is, the symbolic. For the real, whatever upheaval we subject it to, is always in its place; it carries it glued to its heel, ignorant of what might exile it from it" (Lacan 1966, 25; 1972, 55; translation modified).[38] If the series that the object = *x* traverses necessarily present relative displacements in relation to each other, this is so because the *relative* places of their terms in the structure depend first on the *absolute* place of each, at each moment, in relation to the object = *x* that is always circulating, always displaced in relation to itself.[39] It is in this sense that the displacement, and more generally all the forms of exchange, does not constitute a characteristic added from the outside, but the fundamental property that allows the structure to be defined as an order of places subject to the variation of relations. The whole structure is driven by this originary Third, but that also fails to coincide with its own origin. Distributing the differences through the entire structure, making the differential relations vary with its displacements, the object = *x* constitutes the differenciating element of difference itself.

Games require the empty square, without which nothing would move forward or function. The object = *x* is not distinguishable from its place, but it is characteristic of this place that it constantly displaces itself, just as it is characteristic of the empty square to jump ceaselessly.[40] Lacan invokes the *dummy hand* in bridge, and in the admirable opening pages of *The Order of Things*, where he describes a painting by Velasquez, Foucault invokes the place of the king, in relation to which everything is displaced and slides, God, then man, without ever filling it (Foucault 1966a, 19–31 [1970, 3–16]). No structuralism is possible without this degree zero. Phillipe Sollers and Jean-Pierre Faye like to invoke the *blind spot* [*tache aveugle*], so designating this always mobile point that entails a certain blindness, but in relation to which writing becomes possible, because series organize themselves therein as veritable "liter-emes" [*lit-térèmes*].[41] In his effort to elaborate a concept of structural or metonymic causality, J.-A. Miller borrows from Frege the position of a *zero*, defined as lacking its own identity, and which conditions the serial constitution of numbers (Miller 1966, 44–49 [1977–1978, 26–32]). And even Lévi-Strauss, who in certain respects is the most positivist among the structuralists, the least romantic, the least inclined to welcome an elusive element, recognized in the "mana" or its equivalents the existence of a "floating signifier," with a symbolic zero value circulating in the structure (Lévi-Strauss 1950, 49–59).[42] In so doing, he connects with Jakobson's zero phoneme that does not by itself entail any differential character or phonetic value, but in relation to which all the phonemes are situated in their own differential relations.

If it is true that structural criticism has as its object the determination of "virtualities" in language that preexist the work, the work is itself structural when it sets out to express its own virtualities. Lewis Carroll, Joyce, invented "portmanteau" words, or more generally, esoteric words, to ensure the coincidence of verbal sound series and the simultaneity of associated story series.[43] In *Finnegan's Wake*, it is again a *letter* that is Cosmos, and that reunites all the series of the world. In Lewis Carroll's works, the portmanteau word connotes at least two basic series (speaking and eating, verbal series and alimentary series) that can themselves be subdivided, such as the Snark. It is incorrect to say that such a word has two meanings; in fact, it is of another order than words possessing a sense. It is the non-sense that animates at least the two series, but which provides them with sense by circulating through them. It is this non-sense, in its ubiquity, in its perpetual displacement, that produces sense in each series, and from one series to another, and that ceaselessly dislocates [*décaler*] the series in relation to each other. This word is the word = x insofar as it designates the object = x, the *problematic* object. As word = x, it traverses a series determined as that of the signifier; but at the same time, as object = x, it traverses the other series determined as that of the signified.[44] It never ceases at once to hollow out and to fill in the gap between the two series. Lévi-Strauss shows this in relation to the "mana" that he assimilates to the words "thingumajig" [*truc*] or "thingie" [*machin*]. As we have seen, this is how non-sense is not the absence of signification but, on the contrary, the excess of sense, or that which provides the signifier and signified with sense. Sense here emerges as the effect of the structure's functioning, in the animation of its component series. And, no doubt, portmanteau words are only one device among others to ensure this circulation. The techniques of Raymond Roussel, as Foucault has analyzed them, are of another nature, founded on differential phonemic relations, or on even more complex relations (see Foucault 1963 [1986]). In Mallarmé's works, we find systems of relations between series, and the moving parts that animate them, of yet another type. Our purpose is not to analyze the whole set of devices that have constituted and are still constituting modern literature, making use of an entire topography, an entire typography of the "book yet to come" [*livre à venir*]; our goal is only to indicate in all cases the efficacy of this two-sided empty square, at once word and object.

What does it consist of, this object $= x$? Is it and must it remain the perpetual object of a riddle, the *perpetuum mobile*? This would be a way of recalling the objective consistency that the category of the problematic takes on at the heart of structures. And in the long run, it is good that the question "How do we recognize structuralism?" leads to positing something that is not recognizable or identifiable. Let us consider Lacan's psychoanalytic response[45]: the object $= x$ is determined as phallus. But this phallus is neither the real organ, nor the series of associable or associated images: it is the symbolic phallus. However, it is indeed sexuality that is in question, a question of nothing else here, contrary to the pious and ever-renewed attempts in psychoanalysis to renounce or minimize sexual references. But the phallus appears not as a sexual given or as the empirical determination of one of the sexes. It appears rather as the symbolic organ that founds sexuality *in its entirety* as system or structure, and in relation to which the places occupied variously by men and women are distributed, as also the series of images and realities. In designating the object $= x$ as phallus, it is thus not a question of identifying this object, of conferring on it an identity, which is repellant to its nature. Quite the contrary, for the symbolic phallus is precisely that which does not coincide with its own identity, always found there where it is not since it is not there where one looks for it, always displaced in relation to itself, *from the side of the mother*. In this sense, it is certainly the letter and the debt, the handkerchief or the crown, the Snark and the "mana." Father, mother, etc., are symbolic elements held in differential relations. But the phallus is quite another thing, the object $= x$ that determines the relative place of the elements and the variable value of relations, making a structure of the entirety of sexuality. The relations vary as a function of the displacements of the object $= x$, as relations between "partial drives" constitutive of sexuality.[46]

Obviously the phallus is not a final word, and is even somewhat the locus of a question, of a "demand," that characterizes the empty square of the sexual structure. Questions, like answers, vary according to the structure under consideration, but never do they depend on our preferences, or on an order of abstract causality. It is obvious that the empty square of an economic structure, such as commodity exchange, must be determined in quite another way. It consists of "something" that is reducible neither to the terms of the exchange, nor to the exchange relation itself, but that forms an eminently symbolic third term in perpetual displacement, and as a function of which the relational variations will be defined. Such is *value* as expression of a "*generalized* labor," beyond any empirically observable quality, a locus of the question that runs through or traverses the economy as structure.[47]

A more general consequence follows from this, concerning the different "orders." From a structuralist perspective, it is no doubt unsatisfactory to resurrect the problem of whether there is a structure that determines all the others in the final instance. For example, which is first, value or the phallus, the economic fetish or the sexual fetish? For several reasons, these questions are meaningless. All structures are infrastructures. The structural orders—linguistic, familial, economic, sexual, etc.—are characterized by the form of their symbolic elements, the variety of their differential relations, the species of their singularities, finally and, above all, by the nature of the object = x that presides over their functioning. However, we could only establish an order of linear causality from one structure to another by conferring on the object = x in each case the type of identity that it essentially repudiates. Between structures, causality can only be a type of structural causality. In each structural order, certainly, the object = x is not at all something unknowable, something purely undetermined; it is perfectly determinable, including within its displacements and by the mode of displacement that characterizes it. It is simply not assignable: that is, it cannot be fixed to one place, nor identified with a genre or a species. Rather, it constitutes itself the ultimate genre of the structure or its total place: it thus has no identity except in order to lack this identity, and has no place except in order to be displaced in relation to all places. As a result, for each order of structure the object = x is the empty or perforated site that permits this order to be articulated with the others, in a space that entails as many directions as orders. The orders of the structure do not communicate in a common site, but they all communicate through their empty place or respective object = x. This is why, despite several of Lévi-Strauss's hasty pages, no privilege can be claimed for ethnographic social structures, by referring the psychoanalytic sexual structures to the empirical determination of a more or less desocialized individual. Even linguistic structures cannot pass as symbolic elements or as ultimate signifiers. Precisely to the extent that the other structures are not limited simply to applying by analogy methods borrowed from linguistics, but discover on their own account veritable languages, be they nonverbal, always entailing their signifiers, their symbolic elements, and their differential relations. Posing, for example, the problem of the relations between ethnography and psychoanalysis, Foucault is right to say: "They intersect at right angles; for the signifying chain by which the unique experience of the individual is constituted is perpendicular to the formal system on the basis of which the significations of a culture are constituted: at any given instant, the structure proper to individual experience finds a certain number of possible choices (and of excluded possibilities) in the systems of the society; inversely, at each of their points of choice the social structures encounter a certain number of possible individuals (and others who are not)" (Foucault 1966a, 392 [1970, 380]).[48]

And in each structure, the object = x must be disposed to give an account (1) of the way in which it subordinates within its order the other orders of structure, that then only intervene as dimensions of actualization; (2) of the way in which it is itself subordinated to the other orders in their own order (and no longer intervenes except in their own actualization); (3) of the way in which all the objects = x and all the orders of structure communicate with one another, each order defining a dimension of the space in which it is absolutely primary; and (4) of the conditions in which, at a given moment in history or in a given case, a particular dimension corresponding to a particular order of the structure is not deployed for itself and remains subordinated to the actualization of another order (the Lacanian concept of "foreclosure" would again be of decisive importance here).

VII. Final Criteria: From the Subject to Practice

In one sense, places are only filled or occupied by real beings to the extent that the structure is "actualized." But in another sense, we can say that places are already filled or occupied by symbolic elements, at the level of the structure itself. And the differential relations of these elements are the ones that determine the order of places in general. Thus there is a primary symbolic filling-in [*remplissement*] before any filling-in or occupation by real beings. Except that we again find the paradox of the empty square. For this is the only place that cannot and must not be filled, were it even by a symbolic element. It must retain the perfection of its emptiness in order to be displaced in relation to itself, and in order to circulate throughout the elements and the variety of relations. As symbolic, it must be for itself its own symbol, and eternally lack its other half that would be likely to come and occupy it. (This void is, however, not a nonbeing; or at least this nonbeing is not the being of the negative, but rather the positive being of the "problematic," the objective being of a problem and of a question.)[49] This is why Foucault can say: "It is no longer possible to think in our day other than in the void left by man's disappearance. For *this void does not create a deficiency; it does not constitute a lacuna that must be filled in.* It is nothing more and nothing less than the unfolding of a space in which it is once more possible to think" (Foucault 1966a, 353 [1970, 342]).

Nevertheless, if the empty square is not filled by a term, it is still accompanied by an eminently symbolic instance that follows all of its displacements, accompanied without being occupied or filled. And the two, the instance and the place, do not cease to lack each other, and to accompany each other in this manner. The *subject* is precisely the agency [*instance*] that follows the empty place: as Lacan says, it is less subject than subjected [*assujetti*]—subjected to the empty square, subjected to the phallus and to its displacements. Its agility is peerless, or should be. Thus, the subject is essentially intersubjective. To announce the death of God, or even the death of man, is nothing. What counts is *how*. Nietzsche showed already that God dies in several ways; and that the gods die, but from laughter, upon hearing one god say that he is the Only One. Structuralism is not at all a form of thought that suppresses the subject, but one that breaks it up and distributes it systematically, that contests the identity of the subject, that dissipates it and makes it shift from place to place, an always nomad subject, made of individuations, but impersonal ones, or of singularities, but preindividual ones.[50] This is the sense in which Foucault speaks of "dispersion"; and Lévi-Strauss can only define a subjective agency as depending on the Object conditions under which the systems of truth become convertible and, thus, "simultaneously receivable to several different subjects" (Lévi-Strauss 1964–1972, 1:19 [1964, 11]).

Henceforth, two great accidents of the structure may be defined. Either the empty and mobile square is no longer accompanied by a nomad subject that accentuates its trajectory, and its emptiness becomes a veritable lack, a lacuna. Or just the opposite, it is filled, occupied by what accompanies it, and its mobility is lost in the effect of a sedentary or fixed plenitude. One could just as well say, in linguistic terms, either that the "signifier" has disappeared, that the stream [*flot*] of the signified no longer finds any signifying element that marks it, or that the "signified" has faded away, that the chain of the signifier no longer finds any signified that traverses it: the two pathological aspects of psychosis.[51] One could say further, in theoanthropological terms, that either God makes the desert grow and hollows out a lacuna in the earth, or that man fills it, occupies the place, and in this vain permutation makes us pass from one accident to the other: this being the reason why man and God are the two sicknesses of the earth, that is to say, of the structure.

What is important is knowing according to what factors and at what moments these accidents are determined in structures of one order or another. Let us again consider the analyses of Althusser and his collaborators: on the one hand, they show in the economic order how the adventures of the empty square (Value as object = x) are marked by the goods, money, the fetish, capital, etc., that characterize the capitalist structure. On the other hand, they show how contradictions are thus born in the structure. Finally, they show how the real and the imaginary—that is, the real beings who come to occupy places and the ideologies that express the image that they make of it—are narrowly determined by the play of these structural adventures and the contradictions resulting from it. Not that the contradictions are at all imaginary: they are properly structural, and qualify the effects of the structure in the internal time that is proper to it. Thus it cannot be said that the contradiction is apparent, but rather that it is derived: it derives from the empty place and from its becoming in the structure. *As a general rule, the real, the imaginary, and their relations are always engendered secondarily by the functioning of the structure, which starts with having its primary effects in itself.* This is why what we were earlier calling accidents does not at all happen to the structure from the outside. On the contrary, it is a matter of an "immanent" tendency,[52] of ideal events that are part of the structure itself, and that symbolically affect its empty square or subject. We call them "accidents" in order better to emphasize not a contingent or exterior character, but this very special characteristic of the event, interior to the structure insofar as the structure can never be reduced to a simple essence.

Henceforth, a set of complex problems are posed for structuralism, concerning structural "mutations" (Foucault) or "forms of transition" from one structure to another (Althusser). It is always as a function of the empty square that the differential relations are open to new values or variations, and the singularities capable of new distributions, constitutive of another structure. The contradictions must yet be "resolved," that is, the empty place must be rid of the symbolic events that eclipse it or fill it, and be given over to the subject that must accompany it on new paths, without occupying or deserting it. Thus, there is a structuralist *hero*: neither God nor man, neither personal nor universal, it is without an identity, made of nonpersonal individuations and preindividual singularities. It assures the breakup [*l'éclatement*] of a structure affected by excess or deficiency; it opposes *its own* ideal event to the ideal events that we have just described.[53] For a new structure not to pursue adventures that again are analogous to those of the old structure, not to cause fatal contradictions to be reborn, depends on the resistant and creative force of this hero, on its agility in following and safeguarding the displacements, on its power to cause relations to vary and to redistribute singularities, always casting another throw of the dice. This mutation point precisely defines a praxis, or rather the very site where praxis must take hold. For structuralism is not only inseparable from the works that it creates, but also from a practice in relation to the products that it interprets. Whether this practice is therapeutic or political, it designates a point of permanent revolution, or of permanent transfer.

These last criteria, from the subject to practice, are the most obscure— the criteria of the future. Across the six preceding characteristics, we have sought only to juxtapose a system of echoes between authors who are very independent from each other, exploring very diverse domains, and as diverse as the theory that they themselves propose regarding these echoes. At the different levels of the structure, the real and the imaginary, real beings and ideologies, sense and contradiction, are "effects" that must be understood at the conclusion of a "process," of a properly structural, differenciated production: strange static genesis for physical (optical, sound, etc.) "effects." Books against structuralism (or those against the "New Novel") are strictly without importance; they cannot prevent structuralism from exerting a productivity that is that of our era. No book *against* anything ever has any importance; all that counts are books *for* something, and that know how to produce it.[54]

NOTES

Chapter 1

1. On the concept of weariness, see Deleuze's "L'épuisé" (The Exhausted) (1992). In *ABC 1996* ("F comme Fidélité" [L as in Loyalty]), Deleuze relates his conception of friendship directly to the Greek philosophical tradition and to Blanchot's thought. A summary in English of the sections of this eight-hour interview with Claire Parnet can be found online at http://www.langlab .wayne.edu/romance/FreDeleuze.html.

2. See Joughin (1990) for comments on "the fold" in Deleuze's work.

3. For a dense, yet remarkable "introduction" to the "in-between" of Deleuze–Guattarian thought, see Doel (1996).

4. The social and political framework of the 1960s is also of great import for understanding Deleuze's and Guattari's (particularly the latter's) writings, but is a project that exceeds the scope of this study. For alternative introductions to Deleuze and Guattari, see Bogue (1989, 1–11), Goodchild (1996b, 1–6); and Massumi (1992, 1–9). For readings that pursue a sequential approach to Deleuze's early works, see Cressole (1973) and Boundas (1993a). Bogue (1989, Chap. 1, "Deleuze's Nietzsche") also provides a precise situation of the major developments in Deleuze's reading strategies at this period. Hardt (1993) focuses on the early work of Deleuze, particularly on Bergson, Nietzsche, and Spinoza, as a means of fully appreciating his subsequent writings.

5. For a collection of abstracts on recent work devoted to Deleuze, see the online site for "Deleuze: A Symposium" (1996). In the Appendix, I provide the heretofore untranslated (into English) essay by Deleuze—completed with Melissa McMahon—dating from 1967, "A quoi reconnaît-on le structuralisme?" (1973b; "How Do We Recognize Structuralism?"). Preceding this translation, I provide a brief overview of key points of this essay.

6. Deleuze's *Abécédaire* is available commercially as a video from France, although still only in the SECAM (European) format, at least at this date (1998).

7. Some biographical details on Deleuze: Born in Paris in 1925, he completed secondary education at the Lycée Carnot, entered the Sorbonne, and

studied under professors Ferdinand Aliquié, Maurice de Gandillac, Jean Hyppolite, and Georges Canguilhem, and with fellow students and friends François Châtelet, Michel Butor, and Michel Tournier. After receiving his *agrégation* in 1948, he taught successively in Amiens and Orleans, before returning to Paris at the Lycée Louis-le-Grand. During this period (the 1950s), he frequented social and intellectual milieus in which he met Jacques Lacan, Jean Paulhan, and Pierre Klossowski. He taught the history of philosophy at the Sorbonne (1957–1960), worked as a research attaché at the CNRS (1960–1964), and then taught at the university in Lyon (1964–1969). He submitted the two theses, on Spinoza (1968a) and on "difference and repetition" (1968b), required for the award of a professorial chair in 1968. He met Foucault in Clermont-Ferrand in 1962, Guattari in Paris in 1968. From 1969 onward he was a professor at Paris–VIII Vincennes until his retirement in 1987.

For further details, see Lefort (1995), Maggiori (1995), and the personal tributes to Deleuze by Alain Badiou, Jean-Luc Nancy, Giorgio Agamben, Jean-François Lyotard, Jacques Derrida, and Jean-Pierre Faye in *Libération* (7 November 1995). In *ABC 1996* ("E comme Enfance" [C as in Childhood]), Deleuze offers disparate recollections of his childhood, including one about the *lycée* teacher, Pierre Halwachs, under whose tutelage Deleuze "[a] cessé d'être idiot" (stopped being an idiot) in his studies (see Stivale 1997c). In "P comme Professeur" (P as in Professor), Deleuze discusses the phases of his teaching career, and in "M comme Maladie" (M as in Malady), how his ill health functioned in his philosophical work. See also Jouary (1995) for a succinct overview (in French) of Deleuze's career, and Colombat (1996) for an overview of "Deleuze's death as an event." Burchell (1984) presents a succinct "Introduction to Deleuze" as the Preface to his translation of of Deleuze's essay on Michel Tournier (Deleuze 1984) that appears as one of five appendices to *Logic of Sense* (1969). See also essays included in the *Magazine littéraire* "Dossier" on Deleuze, introduced by Bellour (1988).

8. See the early article by Deleuze on Sartre, entitled quite frankly, "Il a été mon maître" [He has been my master] (1964b). Deleuze corroborates Tournier's depiction of their response to Sartre in an interview with Didier Eribon published the week following Deleuze's death (Deleuze 1995). Deleuze had previously described Sartre's influence to Claire Parnet as constituting

> our Outside, he was really the breath of fresh air from the backyard. . . . Among all the Sorbonne's probabilities, it was his unique combination which gave us the strength to tolerate the new restoration of order. And Sartre has never stopped being that, not a model, a method or an example, but a little fresh air—a gust of air even when he had just been to the Café Flore—an intellectual who singularly changed the situation of the intellectual. It is idiotic to wonder whether Sartre was the beginning or the end of something. Like all creative things and people, he is in the middle, he grows from the middle. (DEng, 12; DFr, 18–19)

On Sartre's role in restoring "the rights of immanence," see Q, 49; WIP, 47–48.

9. During an interview they gave together in July 1966, in which Deleuze and Foucault described their project to reedit Nietzsche's complete works, they

contrasted the impact of Nietzsche on contemporary Western thought to the
Sartrean legacy (the interview's format obscures which interlocutor is speaking):
"Nietzsche opened a wound in philosophical language. Despite efforts by special-
ists, the wound has never been healed. Look at Heidegger, increasingly obsessed
by Nietzsche throughout his long meditation; Jaspers as well. If Sartre is an
exception to the rule, this is perhaps because he ceased philosophizing a long time
ago" (Foucault 1994, 1:551). That is, as Foucault indicated in an interview also
printed in *La Quinzaine littéraire* two years later (March 1968), "It was around
1950-1955 [that] Sartre himself renounced, I believe, what one might call philosophical speculation properly defined, when he invested his philosophical activity
within a political pursuit" (1994, 1:663).

   10. Deleuze here enumerates some of these ways:

> By concentrating, in the first place, on authors who challenged the rationalist
> tradition in this history (I see a secret link between Lucretius, Hume, Spinoza, and
> Nietzsche, constituted by their critique of negativity, their cultivation of joy, the
> hate of interiority, the externality of forces and relations, the denunciation of
> power . . . and so on). What I most detested was Hegelianism and dialectics. My
> book on Kant [is] different; I like it, I did it as a book about an enemy that tries
> to show how his system works, its various cogs—the tribunal of Reason, the
> legitimate exercise of the faculties, our subjection to these made all the more
> hypocritical by our being characterized as legislators. (N, 5-6; P, 14-15)

See also *Dialogues* for Deleuze's reflections on this background (DEng, 12-19;
DFr, 18-26).

   11. Deleuze's 1965 book entitled *Nietzsche* (and several subsequent reeditions,
untranslated) consists of the following chapters: "La vie" (His life), "La philosophie" (His philosophy), "Dictionnaire des principaux personnages de Nietzsche"
(Dictionary of Nietzsche's principal characters), "L'oeuvre" (His works), and
"Extraits" (thirty-four excerpts, organized under six thematic subheadings), plus a
limited bibliography.

   12. I should clarify that Deleuze was also developing a third project at this
time, a book on Spinoza (1968a) that served as his "minor" thesis for the
professorial chair. In the translation's Preface, Deleuze describes the place of the
Spinoza book to Martin Joughin:

> What interested me most in Spinoza wasn't his Substance, but the composition of
> finite modes. . . . One finds [an immanence of being] only in him. This is why I
> consider myself a Spinozist. . . . In the book I'm writing at the moment, *What Is
> Philosophy?*, I try to return to this problem of absolute immanence, and to say why
> Spinoza is for me the "prince" of philosophers. (1968a [1990], 11)

In that book, Deleuze asks, "Will we ever be mature enough for a Spinozist
inspiration?" (WIP, 48; Q, 50).

   13. Cressole describes his reading as follows:

> I always used [*Anti-Oedipus*] as a fantastic toy, a book and laughter, hot nights of
> Marrakesch, a tube of lipstick, sparkling backfire from motorcycles, the expression
> "imperious violets," a frighteningly beautiful transvestite, science fiction with the
> mad savants Deleuze-Guattari. With this book, always having the same relation as

with the film (not always the same, it was called "The Faceless Man" then) that was showing at the cinema, right next to your place, where I had a stroke of good luck right after visiting you. From the upper balcony slightly askew in relation to the main floor, the film could only be watched there at an angle and, perhaps due to this angle, the viewers are the actors of an immense sucking and engorging [*emmanchement*], bits of film caught between trembling legs, little pieces of lovers' dialogue mixed with gasps of pleasure, characters in "The Faceless Man," torn from their pitiful Made-in-Hollywood adventure that everyone lost track of, are caressed with the faceless neighbor's thigh, the screen from in front or behind, as all are in front or behind us, nothing and no one in its place. When this is all over, like with *Anti-Oedipus,* no one will be able to recount the story, but everyone will say it was really great. (1973, 104)

On Cressole and Deleuze, see Millett (1997).

14. See Bennett (1977), Spivak (1976), and Ungar (1983) for illuminating discussions of the bases of structuralism and of the "heroic" years. See the two-volume work by Dosse (1991–1992) for a definitive history of structuralism.

15. Referring to this very essay, Toni Negri defines Deleuze's project following its composition in 1967:

Within an already defined field of immanence, how is one to regain a force, an ontological element, that might allow a dual escape, from the structuralist episte-mological horizon and from dialectics, while still maintaining a completely positive link [*relation*] to the real? *Difference and Repetition* and *Logic of Sense,* two great books on the history of postwar French philosophy, display the extreme refinement and the exhaustion of two lines that it was possible to follow within structuralism, on the one hand, a transcendental philosophy, and on the other, the empiricist logic on which Deleuze worked starting with Hume and that led him to consider perception as the exclusive means of knowing [*mode de connaissance*] and the "common name/noun" as the only definition of the concept. To this, one must add the relations Deleuze maintained with the Freudian tradition, more accurately the Lacanian tradition, that he observed a bit like a critical spectator, while trying to discover therein a creative and intersubjective symbolic element, beyond the real and the imaginary. Where is the "structuralist hero"? Where is the one, enclosed in the symbolic, who reactivates spatial topologies and makes them virtual? That is the question posed by Deleuze. (1996, 36–37).

I should emphasize that it is rather difficult to make structuralist–poststructu-ralist delimitations for Deleuze and Guattari: in Guattari's case (as I indicate here in Chapter 1), he gradually developed a critique of Lacanian psychoanalysis well before the publication of *Écrits* (1966), based on his own clinical practice and on debates generated from Lacan's lectures that he attended from the 1950s onward. For Deleuze, careful study of his works of the 1960s—on Nietzsche, on Proust, on Spinoza—indicates the extent to which his thought cannot be contained in neat "pre-" or "post-" rubrics (see Hardt 1993). For a contrary view that reduces Deleuze's *Proust et les signes* to the perspective of "structural poetics," see Thomas (1992).

16. Besides Grossberg and myself, the original working group consisted of Martin Allor, Charles Laufersweiler, S. P. Mohanty, and Phillip Sellars.

17. For a thorough analysis of this period, particularly as it relates to French psychoanalytic politics, see Turkle (1978; 1992).

18. In arriving at an initial understanding of this concept in 1979–1980, I tried to develop an overly simplified illustration of the "vital machinic progression" deployed in *Anti-Oedipus* (in a table appended to Stivale 1981, 57). Let us recall that beyond the situated function of their first collaborative work as a post-1968 manifesto, Deleuze and Guattari created new nuances of the key concept "body without organs," in relation to many others that they introduced subsequently, particularly in *A Thousand Plateaus*. Indeed, from the later perspective of intersecting "plateaus," Deleuze and Guattari seem to have deployed the "body without organs" as a strategic element for launching the first "plateaus" on psychoanalysis and Marxism, respectively, in Chapters 2 and 3 of *Anti-Oedipus*. For an altogether original reflection on "machinic thinking" in both Deleuze and Deleuze and Guattari, see Welchman (1997).

19. Deleuze's interest in Proust began well before *Anti-Oedipus,* with *Proust et les signes* (1964a). The first version, *Marcel Proust et les signes,* appeared in 1964, was subsequently retitled *Proust et les signes,* and was republished three times in augmented editions (1970, 1971, 1976). The most recent one consists of two sections: Part 1 is the 1964 edition's original seven chapters and conclusion; Part 2, entitled "La machine littéraire" (The literary machine) has five chapters: "Antilogos," "Les boîtes et les vases" (Boxes and vases), "Niveaux de la recherche" (Levels of [re]search), "Les trois machines" (Three machines), "Le style" (Style), and a conclusion, "Présence et fonction de la folie, l'Araignée" (Presence and function of madness, the Spider). The English translation, by Richard Howard, is of the third (1971) edition, already augmented with a new chapter, "Antilogos, or the Literary Machine," and conclusion, "The Image of Thought," clearly a result of Deleuze's developing *pensée à deux* with Guattari.

20. My own participation in these associations, frankly, has not been as conflicted as this passage may suggest. I have served and still do serve (in 1998) as a member of the MLA Delegate Assembly and have been active in the Midwest MLA as well. The organization and administration of these associations, nonetheless, are (and have been) quite evidently open to critique from positions all along the political spectrum (see Nelson [1997] for a somewhat hyperbolic, yet pertinent, leftist critique of the MLA).

21. Cohen (1993) draws upon Deleuze and Guattari (as well as Lyotard and Baudrillard) to develop a critique of academic institutions.

22. On "the minor," see essays collected in JanMohamed and Lloyd (1990) and Bhabha (1997).

23. Some biographical details on Guattari: Born in the Paris suburb of Colombes in 1930, Pierre Félix Guattari received an erratic education, having studied pharmacy, then philosophy, but earning no official degrees. An activist from his early years (particularly in the youth hostel movement through which he met Franz Fanon and Jean Oury), Guattari was influenced, with Oury, by François Tosquelles's ideas about similarities between imprisonment and psychiatric asylum internment. After Oury purchased the La Borde château (near Blois) in the early 1950s and founded the now famous clinic, Guattari worked as a therapist there from its beginning. He pursued practical research into antipsychiatric approaches to therapy and, while attending Lacan's lectures, underwent a seven-year analysis with Lacan in the 1960s. He became a psychoanalyst of Lacan's *Ecole freudienne* in 1969.

After a brief stint in Communist youth groups and then the French Communist Party, Guattari was expelled in 1956. He supported the Jeanson network in support of the Algerian *Front de libération nationale* (FLN) and continued political activism into the 1960s through the heterogeneous *Voix communiste* initiative. Concurrent to his vigorous political organizing (see below, Note 26), Guattari founded the journal *Recherches* in the 1960s, an issue of which (entitled "3 Billion Perverts" and touted as an "encyclopedia of homosexualities") resulted in its confiscation by the Pompidou government and Guattari's condemnation for "moral turpitude" (he received amnesty under Giscard d'Estaing). Guattari's initiatives in the late 1970s and 1980s included support for the Italian "Autonomy" movement, for the Free Radio movement, and in defense of Italian political prisoners, among whom was Toni Negri. Besides lecturing abroad extensively during the 1980s, Guattari cofounded the International College of Philosophy, another journal, *Chimères,* and became closely allied to the Green movements (one of his final books is *Les trois écologies* [1989b; *The Three Ecologies*]). Guattari died in 1992 at La Borde (see Maggiori 1992; Marongiu, Ragon, Perrignon, and Hennion 1992; Roudinesco 1992).

24. As Elisabeth Roudinesco notes, in January 1980, following the dissolution of Lacan's *Ecole freudienne,* Jacques-Alain Miller expressed his dismay at the "foutoir" (mess) that reigned in the *Ecole* due to Lacan's kindness and tolerance (according to Miller), and then attacked Guattari for his apparent hypocrisy, of attacking "Lacan, Freud and psychoanalysis" while regularly sending in his dues to the *Ecole* (Roudinesco 1992, 34). See Guattari (1986a, 99–100) for his expression of revulsion for Jacques-Alain Miller who, with "his group from the rue d'Ulm [location of the *Ecole normale supérieure*], established a kind of monstrous symbiosis between Maoism and Lacanism" within the *Ecole freudienne.*

25. Among other texts, see Deleuze's "Letter to a Harsh Critic" (N, 7; P, 16), *Dialogues* (DEng, 16–17; DFr, 23–24), another conversation with Claire Parnet, "Les intercesseurs" [The Mediators] (N, 125; P, 171), and an interview with Robert Maggiori following the 1991 publication of *Qu'est-ce que la philosophie?* in which Deleuze notes: "What struck me most was that since his background wasn't in philosophy, he would therefore be much more cautious about philosophical matters, and that he was nearly more philosophical than if he had been formally trained in philosophy, so he incarnated philosophy in its creative state" (Maggiori 1991, 17–18). Deleuze also refers to Guattari on numerous occasions in *ABC 1996* (see "F comme Fidélité" [L as in Loyalty]; Stivale 1997c). See also Oury (1992), Virilio (1992), Negri (1993), Laruelle (1993), Pozzi (1993), Aronowitz (1993), Pelias (1993), and Wolfe (1993).

26. A sketch of but a few of the political and other activities (besides those mentioned above) to which Guattari devoted his energies in the 1960s and 1970s includes: founding the FGERI (Federation of Institutional Study and Research Groups); developing a collective for interdisciplinary discussion; helping found the OG (*Opposition gauche* [Left Opposition]); participating in the fundraising operation "A Billion for Vietnam"; founding OSARLA (Solidarity Organization for the Latin-American Revolution); participating in the occupation of the Odéon theater during May 1968; purchasing the abbey of Gourgas (Cevennes) as a location for

group activities, including his CERFI (Center for Institutional Training Study and Research) that undertook investigations into new city spaces by linking architecture to medicine, psychology, and community planning; and founding CINEL (Initiative Committee for New Spaces of Freedom), which supported diverse European leftist movements. See Guattari's "La Borde: A Clinic Unlike Any Other" (in Guattari 1995, 187–208), and Marongiu, Ragon, Perrignon, and Hennion (1992, 33).

27. Deleuze and Toni Negri best describe the experience of working with Guattari. First, Deleuze:

> Few people have given me the impression as he did of moving at each moment; not changing, but moving in his entirety with the aid of a gesture he was making, of a word which he was saying, of a vocal sound, like a kaleidoscope forming a new combination every time. Always the same Félix, yet one whose proper name denoted something which was happening, and not a subject. (DEng, 16; DFr, 23)

Then, Negri:

> What was reality for Félix? I would then accept to follow him in his realistic delirium: bifurcations and *ritournelles,* between production of subjectivity and machinic heterogeneity, in his chaosmosis universe. . . . I've never experienced such a full immersion in the real as when I gave myself over to Félix's neologistmatic madness. (1993, 156)

Guattari's own response to a question about his "difficult vocabulary" was:

> Personally, I myself would tend to say that I had to forge my own language in order to confront certain questions, and to forge a language means to invent words, key terms, carrying-case terms. . . . I am aware of trying to forge a certain kind of—and here, of course, I am going to use my own jargon—"concrete machine" that traverses different domains . . . capable not of integrating, but of articulating singularities of the field under consideration to join absolutely heterogeneous components. . . . I am interested in an "intradisciplinarity" that is capable of traversing heterogeneous fields and carrying the strongest charges of "transversality." (1986a, 152, 155; 1995, 37, 40)

Guattari also developed a "Glossary" of schizoanalytical terms (MR, 288–290; 1996, 287–295). Deleuze discussed the importance for philosophy of forging "barbarous words" in *ABC 1996* ("A comme Animal" [A as in Animal]; see Stivale 1997c).

28. It would be a mistake to understand the subsequent collaboration as though Guattari brought to it mainly a political element that Deleuze somehow lacked. Guattari insists that if he tossed Deleuze into the "stew" of post-1968 activities (specifically the CERFI), Deleuze was already quite involved on his own, e.g., with Foucault in the *Groupe d'Information sur les Prisons* (1986, 82; 1995, 28). See the conversation between Deleuze and Foucault, "Les intellectuels et le pouvoir" [Intellectuals and Power] (Foucault 1994, 2:306–315 [1977, 205–217].

29. Guattari discusses the importance of his activity with Oury in a number of texts; see 1986, 106–107 and 223–228, and 1992, 99–104 [1995, 69–74].

30. Recent translations of Guattari's works include *Chaosmosis* (1995),

Chaosophy (1995), *Soft Subversions* (1996), and *The Guattari Reader* (Genosko 1996). An initial obstacle that *Molecular Revolution* presents to readers is its overall division into three thematic sections: "1. Institutional Psychotherapy"; "2. Towards a New Vocabulary"; "3. Politics and Desire," a seemingly concise, thematic classification of Guattari's writing that is entirely arbitrary. For example, "Transversality," in Section 1, certainly constitutes a search for "New Vocabulary"; "Towards a Micro-Politics of Desire," again, in Section 1, clearly applies to "Politics and Desire." Despite footnotes provided to situate each essay chronologically, the reader attempting to understand the relationship between Guattari's psychoanalytical practice and his political engagement is forced to shuffle back and forth throughout the volume in order to reconstitute the influence of each domain of activity on the other. An even more serious objection is that this classification obscures the reader's understanding of Guattari's concurrent psychoanalytical and political development from the mid-1950s to the early 1980s.

31. Readers should be attentive to various discrepancies between the Penguin translation (*Molecular Revolution*) and terminology chosen in other translations, particularly in the Hurley, Seem, and Lane translation of *Anti-Oedipus*. For example, the important pair, *groupes assujettis* and *groupes-sujets* are translated in *Anti-Oedipus* as "subjugated groups" and "subject-groups," whereas they are rendered inconsistently in *Molecular Revolution* both as "dependent groups" and "independent groups" and as "subjugated groups" and "subject groups" (as in the "Glossary," MR, 288–290). Patton (1981) provides a discussion of terminological difficulties in early translations of Deleuze and Guattari, and the translators' Prefaces to subsequent translations of works by Deleuze and Guattari develop these problems.

32. Guattari continued his work on "transversality" in other essays. For example, in "The Group and the Person" (1966; in PT, 151–172; MR, 24–44), he aggressively defines a militant therapeutic approach as an alternative to Communist, bureaucratic (State), and psychoanalytical totalization. In "Causality, Subjectivity, and History" (1966–1967; in PT, 173–209; MR, 175–207) and "Students, the Mad, and 'Delinquents'" (1969; PT, 230–239; MR, 208–216), he proposes explicitly political readings of two historical periods, an analysis of "signifying breakthroughs" (*coupures signifiantes*) from Lenin to Vietnam in the former, an examination of the "institutional revolution of May 1968" in the latter.

33. The essay "D'un signe à l'autre" [1966; From one sign to the other] is both a response to the prevailing Lacanian psychoanalytical heterodoxy (specifically to Lacan's analysis of "The Purloined Letter") and a first sketch of the semiotic theory that Guattari develops subsequently (see Guattari 1977a, 1979a, and 1989a).

34. In referring parenthetically at this point to Lacan's "object small a," Guattari implies quite elliptically that while the subject is henceforth locked into alternate relations of conjunction and disjunction vis-à-vis the machinic production (MR, 113; PT, 242), he/she only obliquely has access to an opening to this other or to the other's understanding (see Guattari, "Transference," in Genosko 1996, 64–68; PT, 52–58).

Chapter 2

1. For Deleuze and Guattari's situation in relation to the mainstream Freudian psychoanalytic field, see Turkle (1978, 146–154). An array of critical responses greeted the publication of *Anti-Oedipus*. For the French reaction, see Domenach (1972), Donzelot (1972), Furtos and Rousillon (1972), Girard (1972), Lyotard (1972), Pierssens (1973), Stephane (1972), and the collection edited by Chassaguet-Smirgel (1974). In the United States, few writers took note of *Anti-Oedipus*, but Mehlman (1972) does consider Deleuze's Preface to Louis Wolfson's *Le schizo et les langues* (Deleuze 1970c), and Pierssens (1975) provides an introduction (in French) to a semiotic Deleuze circa *Logique du sens* (1969).

2. While it may be futile to enter into this seemingly irreconcilable debate, let me recall and resituate one celebrated statement in *Anti-Oedipus*: "It should therefore be said that one can never go far enough in the direction of deterritorialization" (AOEng, 321; AOFr, 384). To my mind, the key word in this quote is "therefore" since Deleuze and Guattari use the statement to conclude their preceding consideration of how the destructive task of schizoanalysis might be understood in terms of psychiatry, and also of antipsychiatric praxis. That is, in undoing the process that transforms madness into mental illness, and in opposing the perverted and psychotic reterritorializations effected by psychoanalysis, "one can never go far enough." See Land (1993b) for another view, and Chapter 3 below for a more extended discussion. See also Flieger (1997) on Oedipus in *Anti-Oedipus* and on *A Thousand Plateaus*.

3. Among other literary juxtapositions with *Anti-Oedipus*, see Andrews (1993), Colombat (1990), Holland (1993), Lecercle (1985), Noyes (1989), and Sawhney (1997). On cinema, see Potter (1992); on art, see Williams (1997).

4. Technically, their first jointly authored text was "La synthèse disjonctive" (Deleuze and Guattari 1970), an excerpt from *Anti-Oedipus*. As I noted in Chapter 1, Guattari's "Machine and Structure" (in Guattari 1972) owes much to Deleuze's *Logique du sens* and might be considered a protocollaboration.

5. The schizoanalysis of desiring and social production joins the destructive and twin positive tasks in the four theses of schizoanalysis presented in the final section of *Anti-Oedipus*: First, "every investment is social, and in any case bears upon a sociohistorical field" (AOEng, 342; AOFr, 409). Second, "within the social investments we will distinguish the unconscious libidinal investment of groups or desire, and the preconscious investment of class or interest" (AOEng, 343; AOFr, 411). The third thesis "posits the primacy of the libidinal investments of the social field over the familial investment. . . . The relation to the nonfamilial is always primary: in the form of sexuality of the field in social production, and the nonhuman sex in desiring-production" (AOEng, 356; AOFr, 427). The fourth and final thesis (introduced above) makes "the distinction between two poles of social libidinal investment: the paranoiac, reactionary, and fascisizing pole, and the schizoid revolutionary pole" (AOEng, 366; AOFr, 439).

6. For critical analyses of *Hearts of Darkness*, see Sussman (1992) and Worthy (1992).

7. While I had originally intended to bring Conrad's text into this juxtaposition, I limit myself to the cinematic and autobiographical intersections, given the

considerable work already developed on the Conrad–Coppola connection. See Bloom (1989), Cahir (1992), Dorall (1980), During (1987), Gillespie (1985), Greiff (1992), Hagen (1981, 1983), Jacobs (1981), Kinder (1979–1980), Miller (1985), Pinsker (1981), Stewart (1981), Sundelson (1981), and Watson (1981).

8. See Lewis (1995, 41–54) for a thorough discussion of the financing of *Apocalypse Now,* and its situation in the socioeconomic context of the Hollywood system.

9. For studies on Vietnam "at the movies," see Adair (1989), Anderegg (1991), Auster and Quart (1988), Desser (1991), Dittmar and Michaud (1990), Fernandez (1986), and Fuchs (1991).

10. This designation of the nomadic subject as residuum and the footnote that links the Real to the "two poles" in "Lacan's admirable theory of desire"— " 'the object small a' as a desiring-machine" and "the 'great Other' " [*grand Autre*] as a signifier which reintroduces a certain notion of lack)—are references recalling the "empty square" of Deleuze's "How Do We Recognize Structuralism?" (see Appendix) and Guattari's own development of bipolarity in "Machine and Structure" (see above, Chapter 1). This intersection becomes even clearer as Chapter 1 of *Anti-Oedipus* continues for Guattari's experience at La Borde clearly informs both the statement "Social production is purely and simply desiring-production itself under determinate conditions" (AOEng, 29; AOFr, 36), and his direct assertion that "fantasy is never individual: it is group fantasy—as institutional analysis has successfully demonstrated" (AOEng, 26-27; AOFr, 34). To give proper credit for this insight, I refer to the *Anti-Oedipus* translators' long footnote (AOEng, 30) explaining Guattari's reference to "institutional analysis" in which they cite not only Guattari's work with Jean Oury, but also Deleuze's Introduction to Guattari's *Pyschanalyse et transversalité* (Deleuze 1972) and Jacques Donzelot's essay on *Anti-Oedipus* (Donzelot 1972). On the body without organs, see Buchanan (1997c), Doel (1995), and McCarthy (1992).

11. Besides Deleuze's earlier work on Proust (1964a), see Lotringer (1980) for a similar treatment of Proust's fiction. See also Shaviro (1988; 1993, 67–80), for reflections on Proust in a discussion of "Deleuze and Guattari's Theory of Sexuality."

12. For Klossowski's works, see Deleuze and Guattari (1972b).

13. See Carrouges (1954) for a fascinating example of "bachelor machines" in art and literature, predating *L'Anti-OEdipe* by eighteen years in the original edition.

14. For a perceptive engagement with the molar–molecular distinction for a literary critical framework, see Jameson (1979).

15. For the reader unfamiliar with nineteenth-century French literature, these statements might appear inexplicable, at the very least. However, Deleuze and Guattari here employ expressions from Arthur Rimbaud's prose text, "Mauvais Sang," in *Une saison en enfer*: "Oui j'ai les yeux fermés à votre lumière. Je suis une bête, un nègre" (Yes, my eyes are closed to your light. I am a beast, a black) (1972, 97). The importance of Rimbaud's work for Deleuze and Guattari cannot be underestimated. See their discussion of the problematics of the "I" and of death as "a new departure" (AOEng, 331; AOFr, 395-396). See also Colombat's consid-

eration of the "Rimaldian project" in their work (1990, 264–270), and Deleuze's meditation on Rimbaud (1993, 42–45 [1997, 29–31]).

16. According to other actors, improvisation was used extensively by Coppola throughout the shooting; see the different interpretations of this process in *Hearts of Darkness* by Sam Bottoms (Lance), Frederic Forrest (Chef), and Albert Hall (the Chief).

17. On the critical reception of *Apocalypse Now*, see Dempsey (1979–1980) and Lewis (1995, 48–52). Many of the critics already listed in Note 7 provide ample critique of Coppola's Kurtz.

18. On the use of mythology in *Apocalypse Now*, see Bloom (1989), Bogue (1981), Dempsey (1979–1980), Hellman (1991), Pym (1979–1980), Riley (1979), Sharrett (1985–1986), Shichtman (1984), and Tomasulo (1990). For a summary of the four versions of the film's finale, see Lewis (1995, 51).

19. Frazer writes: "If the course of nature [for primitive peoples] is dependent on the man-god's life, what catastrophes may not be expected from the gradual enfeeblement of his powers and their final extinction in death? There is only one way of averting these dangers. The man-god must be killed as soon as he shows symptoms that his powers are beginning to fail, and his soul must be transferred to a vigorous successor before it has been seriously impaired by the threatened decay. . . . The mystic kings of Fire and Water in Cambodia are not allowed to die a natural death" (1922 [1960], 309–310). Jesse Weston (1920) studies Arthurian legend, from the Fisher King to Sir Gawain. See Gillespie (1985) for a careful study of these mythological links.

20. On the narration in *Apocalypse Now*, see Sharrett (1985–1986).

21. While I employ "Jerry" from the name addressed to him at the table by the General, the cast roster lists this character simply as "Civilian," played by Jerry Ziesmer, who also is the film's assistant director.

22. See Greiff (1992) for a study and contrast of the main and secondary characters.

23. On this Hau Phat scene and the images of women it presents, see Jeffords (1985).

24. As with much of this version of the screenplay, Coppola follows Conrad's text quite closely. For example, as in the final scene, Willard visits Kurtz's wife just as Marlow visited Kurtz's "Intended." Both Willard and Marlow lie to her about Kurtz's final words. The wife asks Willard, " 'Tell me what he said in the end.' Kurtz (*voiceover*): 'The horror, the horror.' Willard: 'He spoke of you, ma'am.' " The final shot of this draft is of the PBR boat floating down the river: "Kurtz's body; an exhausted, half-dead Colby. And holding Kurtz, Willard. We hear the Doors' 'The End' as we present the end titles. Fade out" (Coppola 1975).

25. For this critique, see Best and Kellner (1991), Bogue (1989), Callinicos (1982), D'Amico (1978), Holland (1987), Jameson (1997), and Lingis (1994b).

26. Deleuze and Guattari carefully trace these distinctions both in relation to anthropological and ethnographical studies, and in contradistinction to Oedipal repression (AOEng, 154–184; AOFr, 181, 217).

27. Deleuze and Guattari observe:

Perhaps that is what incites the anger of certain linguists against Lacan, no less than the enthusiasm of his followers: the vigor and the serenity with which Lacan accompanies the signifier back to its source, to its veritable origin, the despotic age, and erects an infernal machine that welds desire to the Law, because, everything considered—so Lacan thinks—this is indeed the form in which the signifier is in agreement with the unconscious, and the form in which it produces effects of the signified in the unconscious. (AOEng, 209; AOFr, 247).

28. See Louis Hjelmslev (1968). On Deleuze and Guattari's linguistic "seam," see Grisham (1991).

29. Deleuze and Guattari go on to criticize Lyotard for

continually arresting the process, and steering the schizzes toward shores [Lyotard] has so recently left behind: toward coded or overcoded territories, spaces, and structures. . . . The explanation is that, despite his attempt at linking desire to a fundamental *yes*, Lyotard reintroduces lack and absence into desire; maintains desire under the law of castration, at the risk of restoring the entire signifier along with the law; and discovers the matrix of the figure in fantasy, the simple fantasy that comes to veil desiring-production, the whole of desire as effective production. (AOEng, 244; AOFr, 290)

30. In the interview with Greil Marcus, Coppola says, "From the [Do Lung] bridge on, I started moving back in time, because I wanted to imply that the issues and the themes were timeless . . . and when you get to Kurtz's compound, you're at the beginning of time" (1979, 56).

31. Lewis (1995, 41–44) explains the shrewd, though risky financing by Coppola that ultimately made United Artists look "stupid while Coppola reaped the benefits of the film's box office success" (44).

32. See Deleuze and Guattari (1972b, 1973a), interviews in the *Anti-Oedipus* issue of *Semiotext(e)* (1977), Guattari (1974a, 1977a, 1979b, 1995), and Genosko (1996).

33. To this, Goulimari suggests an additional insight: "Kafka's minor literature achieves a double line of flight between the German of Prague and Yiddish theatre. In this double line of flight of an intensified gesture of the voice and an intensified gesture of the body, Kafka's literature is neither majoritarian nor minoritarian, but accomplishes a becoming minoritarian of identities large and small that belongs to everyone" (1993, 22–23). On *Kafka . . .* , see also Bensmaïa (1994) and Bhabha (1997).

Chapter 3

1. As this is but one approach to "rhizomatics of cyberspace," I refer the reader to a compilation by Mark Nunes of a pertinent discussion of this subject that took place on the Deleuze–Guattari discussion list in 1995. The first post is dated Wednesday, 31 May 1995 09:22:52 (EDT); the last post occurred on Saturday, 24 June 1995 03:17:41 -0700 (PDT). A second discussion took place in the winter of 1996. These are available, respectively, at http://www.dc.peach-net.edu/~mnunes/smooth.html and d2.html, and at the D&G List, archive:

http://jefferson.village.virginia.edu/~spoons/d-g_html/maind-g.html. See also Hamman (1996), Mullarkey (1997), Nunes (1998), and Shaviro (1995a, Chapter 12).

2. Robert Markley provides a less poetic but quite succinct definition of "cyberspace," "a consensual cliché, a dumping ground for repackaged philosophies about space, subjectivity, and culture" (1996a, 56).

3. With the elliptical reference to "life–death," I indicate the passing of two online interlocutors in 1993, Michael Current (who started the D&G List) and Mairi Maclean. Through archives established and maintained by the Spoon Collective, their texts remain accessible. For these archives, see gopher://jefferson.village.virginia.edu:70/11/pubs/listservs/spoons/deleuze-guattari.archive.

4. Notably, see the Dery collection (1994) on flame wars, the articles by Dibbell (1993a, 1993b) and Davis (1993, 1994), and Katz on "online gender bending" (1994). Since this discussion string occurred in mid-1994, an explosion of studies on "cyberspace" has appeared to extol or debunk the promise of the computer-mediated communication, for example, Stoll (1995), Turkle (1995), and David Wilson (1995), to limit myself to a strict minimum. I present further references in the context of "cyberpunk" fiction in Chapter 5. For studies specifically on rhizomatics and cyberspace, see Burnett (1993), Doyle (1994), Moulthrop (1994), Nunes (in press), and Saper (1991).

5. The Jake Baker case, in which a student was expelled from the University of Michigan and unsuccessfully prosecuted by the government after he posted a rape–murder scenario to a Usenet list in which he used a real woman student's name as victim, shows the willingness of institutions to become involved. Carnegie-Mellon University banned certain Usenet newsgroups because of their reputed sexual orientation (see Godwin 1995a, 1995b, 1995c).

6. Deleuze and Guattari present this same image of the "thinker" turning into "a sort of surfer as conceptual persona" in *What Is Philosophy?* (WIP, 71; Q, 70).

7. See Virilio (1996) for a perspective not dissimilar to Deleuze's. At the opposite end of the spectrum regarding "wariness," see Philippe Quéau (1993) and Pierre Lévy (1990, 1995a, 1995b).

8. See Verena Conley (1993) on "terminal humans" related to this "ecosophy."

9. For discussion following the second "Virtual Futures" conference in July 1995, see online exchange archived at gopher://jefferson.village.virginia.edu:70/11/pubs/listservs/spoons/deleuze-guattari.archive.

10. The "millerean Theweleit/MIWD knock-down" refers elliptically to two references in earlier discussions, to an essay by Miller (1993) and to volumes by Klaus Theweleit (1987, 1989).

11. Abou-Rihan suggests: "Ultimately, I think that this caution needs to be reworked in the context of a triadic schema: the molecular limit is defined not only in contradistinction to the full, as in fully organised, molar limit, but also in contradistinction to the emptiness of its own death (or silence, or madness) as well. And just like the molar and the molecular, this death is a formal limit; from the point of view of a molecular philosophy, it contaminates or infiltrates the other two constantly. The nomad is caught not only between the state and the war

machine, a rock and a hard place, but between those two and the abyss as a possible outcome of its irreversible/irrecuperable deterritorialization" (D&G List, 15 January 1995). Steve Shaviro proposes another trail for understanding the question of "caution" in *A Thousand Plateaus,* by considering the twenty-second "series," "Porcelain and Volcano," in *Logic of Sense.* Suggesting that "here Deleuze is asking, how can we unleash the creative power of the event, without falling into a nihilism of self-destruction?," Shaviro concludes, "I don't think Deleuze proposes any answer to this dilemma—the binary of either destroying oneself or just becoming the professor expounding on self-destruction—but only a kind of ungrounded hope, which he calls (ironically echoing Nietzsche) 'our own way of being pious.' But I think this helps give a sense of what he and Guattari are worrying about when they speak of caution, and of the dangers of empty or cancerous desires" (D&G List, 16 January 1995).

Chapter 4

1. Let us recall that Deleuze's earliest literary analysis was of Proust in *Proust et les signes* (1964a), and while the original edition understandably does not include the machinic concepts, the subsequent revisions (1970, 1971, 1976) progressively took account of perspectives developed in collaboration with Guattari.

2. In considering *A Thousand Plateaus* along the literary "seam," I realize certain procedural limitations in this approach. Notably, while this "seam" is readily discernible throughout Deleuze and Guattari's works, I am aware that in any discussion of a particular conceptual "plane of consistency," each one is bounded by and intersects other planes (e.g., the literary intersecting the psycho- and the sociopolitical, the semiotic, the aesthetic) in multidirectional break-flows that determine numerous and distinct juxtapositions between domains. For a treatment of Barthes's *S/Z* as protohypertext, see Landow (1994, 5–6, 52–53). See also Colombat (1997) on Deleuze's conception of "powers" of literature and philosophy.

3. Guattari calls Lyotard's conception of the "postmodern condition" "the paradigm of all submission and every sort of compromise with the existing status quo" and excoriates this view as not meriting "the name of philosophy, for it is only a prevalent state of mind, a 'condition' of public opinion that pulls its truths out of the air" (Genosko 1996, 110–112).

4. Although the association of Deleuze and Guattari with Barthes might appear unlikely, Barthes himself includes Deleuze among those to whom he owed a significant debt in writing *S/Z* (Barthes 1981, 78).

5. Taubin insists on "the way Tarantino lays bare the sadomasochistic dynamic between the film and the spectator" (1992, 4).

6. Deleuze and Guattari are quick to qualify this geographic specificity:

> At the same time, we are on the wrong track with all these geographical distributions. An impasse. So much the better. If it is a question of showing that rhizomes also have their own, even more rigid despotism, and hierarchy, then fine and good: for there is no dualism, no ontological dualism between here and there, no axiological dualism between good and bad, no blend or American synthesis. . . .

It is not a question of this or that place on earth, of a given moment in history, still less of this or that category of thought. It is a question of a model that is perpetually in construction or collapsing, and of a process that is perpetually prolonging itself, breaking off and starting again. (ATP, 20; MP, 30–31)

For a brilliant discussion of schizophrenia and literature written at the same time as *Anti-Oedipus,* see Vernon (1973).

7. Massumi (1992) provides a superb "user's guide" to *Capitalism and Schizophrenia* that shows these complex insertions and overlaps.

8. The image of the bursting head refers to *The Castle,* and the Stoker appears in Chapter 1 of *Amerika* (ATP, 525n19 and n20).

9. In a similar vein, Deleuze and Guattari argue:

If Kafka is the greatest theorist of bureaucracy, it is because he shows how, at a certain level (but which one? it is not localizable), the barriers between offices cease to be "a definite dividing line" and are immersed in a molecular medium [*milieu*] that dissolves them and simultaneously makes the office manager proliferate into microfigures impossible to recognize or identify, discernible only when they are centralizable: another regime, coexistent with the separation and totalization of the rigid segments. [The authors include a footnote reference to *The Castle,* "especially chapter XIV"]. (ATP, 214; MP, 261)

10. Other literary machinic assemblages operate in reference to Borges (ATP, 125; MP 157), Henry Miller (ATP, 129, 134, 138, 171; MP 161, 167, 172, 210), Pierre Klossowski (ATP, 131–132; MP 164), and Castaneda (ATP, 138–139; MP 173).

11. This connection between stammering and style will remain a constant throughout Deleuze's career; see "Balbutia-t-il" in Deleuze (1993), translated as "He Stuttered" in Boundas and Olkowski (1994, 23–29), and in Deleuze (1993 [1997], 107–114). See also Lambert (1997) on "stuttering" and other concepts in Deleuze's definition of literary practice.

12. E.g., on "becoming-intense (child, woman)," Virginia Woolf, D. H. Lawrence, Henry Miller, Proust, and Kafka (ATP, 276–277, 293–294; MP, 338–340; 360–361); on "becoming-animal," Virgina Woolf, H. P. Lovecraft, Hofmannsthal, Melville, Kafka, D. H. Lawrence, Slepian, Henry Miller, Faulkner, F. Scott Fitzgerald (ATP, 239–240, 243–246, 248, 252, 258–259, 303–306; MP 292–293, 297–300, 304, 308, 316–318, 373–376; on "becoming-imperceptible," Castaneda, H. P. Lovecraft, Slepian, Hofmannsthal, Proust, P. Moran, F. Scott Fitzgerald, Kerouac, Virginia Woolf, Kierkegaard, Michaux, Artaud, Henry Miller (ATP, 248–252, 273–274, 279–280, 281–286; MP 304–307, 336–337, 342–343, 345–350); on haecceities, Charlotte Bronte, D. H. Lawrence, Faulkner, Michel Tournier, Ray Bradbury, and Virginia Woolf (ATP, 260–263; MP, 318–321), and their relation to writing in Nathalie Sarraute, Artaud, Hölderin, Kleist, Nietzsche, and Proust (ATP, 267–269; MP, 327–333).

13. A related reflection concerns the philosopher as State functionary (Kant) in opposition to "outside thinkers" (e.g., Kierkegaard, Nietzsche, and Blanchot) (ATP, 376; MP 467), and the distinction between the "method" of a striated space (*cogitatio universalis*) as opposed to the exteriority of thought in smooth space, manifested in texts by Artaud and Kleist (ATP, 377; MP, 468). See *ABC 1996* ("K

comme Kant" [K as in Kant]) for Deleuze's reflections on his mixed feelings toward Kant's philosophy.

14. Tarantino says:

> The thing that I am truly proud of in the torture scene in *Dogs* with Mr. Blonde, Michael Madsen, is the fact that it's truly funny up until the point that he cuts the cop's ear off. . . . [Then] the cop's pain is not played like one big joke, it's for real. . . . That's why I think the scene caused such a sensation, because you don't know how you're supposed to feel when you see it. (Hopper and Tarantino 1994, 17)

15. For concrete examples of this practice, see work on rock 'n' roll by Lawrence Grossberg (1983–1984, 1984a, 1984b, 1984c, 1986a, 1988) and, more recently, on cultural studies (1992, 1993, 1997a, 1997b). See also Sande Cohen (1993) on these "lines" and the "luster of capital" in academe, and Alphonso Lingis (1994a) on the lines traversing the human body.

16. I complicate this title with the "of/for" in order to attempt to translate the ambiguously reflexive and reciprocal senses of the infinitive *se faire*, "to make of oneself," but also "to make *for* oneself." On the BwO, see Buchanan (1997c), Doel (1995), and McCarthy (1992).

17. This process of disarticulation sums up the key methodology of Deleuze and Guattari's project:

> Lodge yourself on a stratum, experiment with the opportunities it offers us, find an advantageous place on it, find potential movements of deterritorialization, possible lines of flight, experience them, produce flow conjunctions here and there, try out continuums of intensities segment by segment, have a small plot of new land at all times. It is through a meticulous relation with the strata that one succeeds in freeing lines of flight, causing conjugated flows to pass and escape and bringing forth continuous intensities for a BwO. Connect, conjugate, continue: a whole "diagram," as opposed to still signifying and subjective programs. We are in a social formation; first see how it is stratified for us and in us and at the place where we are; then descend from the strata to the more deeper assemblage within which we are held; gently tip the assemblage, making it pass over to the side of the plane of consistency. It is only there that the BwO reveals itself for what it is: connection of desires, conjunction of flows, continuum of intensities. You have constructed your own little machine, ready when needed to be plugged into other collective machines. (ATP, 161; MP, 197–198).

Suggestive means for deploying these strategies are presented in Abou-Rihan (1992), Bensmaïa (1995), Canning (1984), Dean and Massumi (1992), De Landa (1991), Dwyer (1997), Ecstavasia (1993), Gagnon (1991), Grant (1997), Griggers (1997), Land (1993a, 1993b, 1995), Mackay (1997), E. Martin (1996), Murphy (1997), Perez (1990), Plant (1997), Rodowick (1997), Saper (1991), Shaviro (1993, 1995b), and White (1995).

Chapter 5

1. See Haraway's reflections (1991a) on "The Cyborg Manifesto" in Penley and Ross (1991b). On Haraway and "cyborg-feminism," see also Blake (1993),

Braidotti (1994a, 102–110), Christie (1992), Dery (1996, 242–246), Ebert (1996, 105–117), Fraiberg (1993), and Plant (1997). Haraway (1997) extends her reflections on feminism and technoscience.

2. For an alternative reading of "highly genderized patterns of becomings" in SF texts, from the Deleuze–Guattarian perspective, see Braidotti (1997). I should note that, like Braidotti, I do not read Deleuze (and Guattari) as "narco-philosophers" or "cyberpunk thinkers," and agree with her that "Deleuze's thought . . . provides us with valuable inroads into the contemporary imagination, in its conceptual, political and aesthetic manifestations" (77).

3. The cyberpunk subgenre had already fallen into disrepute with its own authors by the late 1980s, some of whom refused even to pronounce the "Cyber-word"; see Dery (1996, 75–76), McCaffery (1991a), and Sterling (1989b, 18).

4. Markley offers a starkly dissenting view in his sharp critique of cyberspace:

> [Cyberspace] does not offer a breakthrough in human, or cyborgian, evolution, but merely (though admittedly) a seductive means to reinscribe fundamental tensions within Western concepts of identity and reality. . . . Rather than a consensual hallucination, it represents a contested and irrevocably political terrain that is unlikely to determine the future "elaboration of human culture." (1996a, 56)

Markley cites Benedikt (1991, 1). For commentary on cyberpunk as style, see Fitting (1991), Jameson (1991), McCaffery (1988, 1991a), and McHale (1992), and interviews with Greg Benford, William Gibson, and Bruce Sterling, in McCaffery (1990).

5. Given the profusion of texts on cyberspace and cyberpunk, a bibliography of related critical work swells rapidly, not unlike the growth of Internet and Web usage. Two useful bibliographies are in Gray (1995, 469–474) and McCaffery (1991b, 375–383); see also the "Notes" in Balsamo (1996, 165–211), and Turkle (1995, 271–320).

Volumes and special journal issues on these subjects include: Aronowitz, Martinsons, and Menser (1996), Benedikt (1991), Bukatman (1993), Cherny and Weise (1996), Dery (1994), Herring (1996), S. Jones (1995, 1997), Markley (1996b), Porter (1997), Shields (1996), and Strate et al. (1996); *Critique* 33, no. 3 (1992) (see Bukatman [1992], Csicsery-Ronay [1992], McCaffery [1992], and McHale [1992]); *Genders* 18 (1993) on "Cyberpunk: Technologies of Cultural Identity" (Foster [1993a]; see Cherniavsky [1993], Foster [1993b], Fuchs [1993], and Smith [1993]); *Journal of Computer-Mediated Communication* 1, no. 2 (1995) on "Play and Performance in Computer-Mediated Communication" (Danet [1995]); *Lusitania* 8 entitled *Being On Line. Net Subjectivity* (Sondheim [1996]); *Women and Performance* 17 on "Sexuality and Cyberspace: Toward a Prosthetic Feminism" (Senft [1996]); *Works and Days* 25–26 on "CyberSpaces: Pedagogy and Performance on the Electronic Frontier" (Stivale [1995]; in particular, see Haynes [1995], Joyce [1995b], Lang [1995], Nakamura [1995], and Pallez [1995]).

See also Blake (1993), Christie (1992), Clark (1995), Davis (1993), Dery (1996), Dibbell (1993a), Fisher (1997), Fitting (1991), Hayles (1993a, 1993b), Joyce (1995a), King (1994), McCarron (1995), Morton (1995), Pfeil (1990), Plant (1995), Porush (1994), Robins (1995), Ross (1990), Sponsler (1992, 1993), Tomas (1991/1992), and Wilbur (1997).

6. Bey indicates that "Net, Web, and counter-Net are all part of the same whole pattern-complex—they blur into each other at innumerable points. The terms are not meant to define areas but to suggest tendencies. In any case the answers to such questions are so complex that the TAZ tends to ignore them altogether and simply picks up what it can use" (1985/1991, 108–109).

7. On these distinctions, see Rosenthal (1991, 81–87), Gibson (1986c), and Ross (1991a; 1991c, 101–135).

8. Among other essays on relations of the "cyborg body" and prosthesis, see Balsamo (1995), Brothers (1997), Haraway (1989), Hayles (1997), Ito (1997), Landsberg (1995), Lupton (1995), Mason (1995), McRae (1997), Sobchack (1995), Stone (1992, 1995), Tomas (1995), Wills (1995, 66–91), and R. Wilson (1995).

9. On contagion and the viral in Deleuze, and in Deleuze and Guattari, see Ansell-Pearson (1997b), and O'Toole (1997).

10. See the critique from varying perspectives in the "Cyberpunk Forum/Symposium" (1988), Ross (1991b; 1991c, 137–167), Shirley et al. (1987), and Spinrad (1990, 109–121). On Shirley's trilogy, see Dery (1996, 101–103).

11. "Haecceity" is a term that Deleuze and Guattari utilize (borrowing *haecceitas*, "thisness," from Duns Scotus) to designate the heterogeneity, the positionality, speed, duration, and affects of individuated entities without subjectivation. For further discussion of this term, see Bogue (1989, 134–136).

12. Compare Rheingold's sound-bite prophetic speculation (1991) to his fearful and moralizing depiction of online sites in which incipient "teledildonics" already are in full swing (1993, 144–175). On "teledildonics" and "virtual lesbians," see Moore (1995).

13. Andrew Ross discusses this subgenre in even more chastening tones:

> Cyberpunk's idea of a counterpolitics—youthful male heroes with working-class chips on their shoulders and postmodern biochips in their brains—seems to have little to do with the burgeoning power of the great social movements of our day. . . . However rebellious its challenge to SF traditions, the wars, within the SF community, between the cyberpunks, the New Wave, and the New Humanists were all played out in boystown. (1991c, 152)

See also Balsamo (1996, 128–131), who states that "probably no collection so effectively betrays the masculinist values of the new cyberpunk writers as the science fiction anthology titled *Semiotext(e) SF*" (129), edited by Rucker, Wilson, and Wilson (1989). On these feminist issues, see also Counsil (1990), and Gordon (1990).

14. McCaffery here refers to Shirley's stated position in 1989a.

15. See also Haraway's discussion in "Situated Knowledges" (1988; 1991b, 183–201).

16. The concept "becoming-woman" has been the focus of particular debate among Deleuze–Guattarian readers and writers, especially from feminist perspectives. In attempting to come to terms with the challenging and diverse positions elaborated in this debate, I have gained immensely from insights provided by Braidotti (1994a, 1994b), Chauderlot (1996), Gatens (1996), Griggers (1997), Grosz (1994a, 1994b), and Probyn (1996). Grosz provides a suc-

cinct overview of the feminist critique as enunciated by Jardine (1985): "[Jardine's] anxieties seem related to the apparent bypassing or detour around the very issues with which feminist theory has tended to concern itself: 'identity,' otherness, gender, oppression, the binary divisions of male and female" (Grosz 1994a, 162). After providing details of certain feminist "reservations" about Deleuze–Guattarian rhizomatics (1994a, 162–164), Grosz concludes that "even if their procedures and methods do not actively affirm or support feminist struggles around women's autonomy and self-determination, their work may help to clear the ground of metaphysical oppositions and concepts so that women may be able to devise their own knowledges, accounts of themselves and the world" (1994a, 164). Furthermore, Grosz admits to feeling uncomfortable with Deleuze and Guattari's reference to "the man in the woman and the woman in the man" (ATP, 213; MP, 260), "which tends to obliterate the very real bodily differences and experiences of the two sexes" (1994a, 173). She nonetheless emphasizes the importance of "recogniz[ing] the micro-segmentarities we seize from or connect with in others which give us traits of 'masculinity' and 'femininity' whether we 'are' men or women" (173). While this may be dangerous political ground, says Grosz, "if we do not walk in dangerous places and different types of terrain, nothing new will be found, no explorations are possible, and things remain the same" (173). See her review of "becoming-woman" and reflections on "Deleuzian Feminism?" (1994a, 173–183) and her appreciation of Deleuze–Guattarian rhizomatics (1994b). For a critique of Grosz's position, see Ebert (1996, 180–182). See also Gatens's Spinozist reading of "becoming-woman" (1996, 174–176) that provides an alternative to the influential, but highly problematic version proposed by Jardine (1985, 208–223). Guattari reflects on "becoming-woman" in the interview in Chapter 8 (below) and in his interview with Stambolian (Guattari 1979b, 57–59; Genosko 1996, 205–206), and Deleuze discusses "becomings-woman" briefly in *ABC 1996* ("G comme Gauche" [L as in Left]).

17. See Counsil (1990) on this image.

18. On relations between the body and information, as flickering signifiers, see Hayles (1990, 1993b), and for different "boundary tales," see Stone (1991, 1995).

19. I return to the concept of "haecceity" in Chapter 7 from the perspective "spaces of affect" in the Cajun dance and music arena.

20. See Rucker (1989a, 76–77) on the "flicker cladding" that cloaks and transforms Willy at the novel's end.

21. See Jardine (1985, 178–201) for discussion of this inherent phallogocentrism.

22. For some of the SF discussion, see Hand (1991) and Tatsumi (1990). For feminist discussions, see Edwards (1990), Perry and Greber (1990), and Turkle and Papert (1990).

23. On other exemplary writers, see Armitt (1991), Donawerth (1990), Fitting (1989), Haraway (1989), Kaveney (1989), Lefanu (1988/1989), and Pfeil (1990).

24. See Fuss (1989) on further distinctions between these positions and Butler (1990) on the performance of gender.

25. See Mike Godwin's articles in *Internet World* and other journals for exceptionally clear analyses of these issues (e.g. 1995a, 1995c). See also the essays collected in Ludlow (1996). On "virtual community" and its myths, see Lockard (1997), Poster (1995, 1997), Rheingold (1993), Stivale (1997b), Stratton (1997), and Tabbi (1997).

26. For a list of possible "slipstream" writers, see also http://euro.net/mark-space/Slipstream.html.

27. On Hand's fiction, see Jurek (1991). On Cadigan's fiction (*Synners* in particular), see Balsamo (1996, 136–146), Dery (1996, 252–256), and G. Jones (1997). See also Kroker (1992), White (1995), and Shaviro's *Doom Patrols* (1995a) for speculation/reflection on all manner of becomings.

28. Surin concludes, "Indeed, 'cyberspaces' have striking affinities with 'the fold' that Deleuze takes to be the defining feature of the Baroque" (1997, 13). On these points in terms of the "globalization of culture," see Surin (1995). On "folds" and "multiplicities," see also T. Conley (1997).

Chapter 6

1. References to the English translation of Tournier's *Gilles et Jeanne* are presented in the text (abbreviated GJ) followed by page reference to the French original. Davis outlines how Tournier alters the historical texts and documents on the life and trial of Gilles de Rais (notably, Bataille's *Le procès de Gilles de Rais*) to his own literary ends, "to complete the story told in the historical texts" (1988, 130), or as Tournier himself puts it, to write "dans les blancs laissés par les textes sacrés et historiques" (*Gilles et Jeanne* 5; "in the blanks left by the sacred and historical texts"; my translation).

2. On the "return of the ogre" in *Gilles and Jeanne*, see among others Nettlebeck (1984) and Petit (1985).

3. This chapter has also gained immensely from analyses by Muecke (1984) and Patton (1984).

4. E.g., Garreau (1985).

5. See Foucault, "La pensée du dehors" (1966b; 1994, 1:518–539). Deleuze and Guattari also call this *pensée* a "nomadic thought" since nomads, exterior dwellers par excellence, invented and deployed war machines against and exterior to State apparatuses (MPEng, 417; MPFr 519). See also the Nietzschean connection in Deleuze's essay, "La pensée nomade" (1973a).

6. Regarding the war machine considered as a concept, Patton suggests that it "has no stable self-identity," but "is more like a conceptual 'heccéité,' a certain configuration of qualities that serve to make certain distinctions or to register certain oppositions, only to disperse upon closer examination into several determinations which make it up" (1984, 76).

7. "But as you are my sole heir, this fortune is also yours. You are very rich, my grandson. After my death you will be immensely rich. You will be master of Blaison, Chemillé, La Mothe-Achard, Ambrières, Saint-Aubin-de-Fosse-Louvain, *seigneuries* that come from your father. From your mother, you will have those of Briollay, Champtocé and Ingrandes, La Bénate, Le Loroux-Botereau, Sénéché,

Bourgneuf and La Voulte. Then, thanks to the marriage that I made for you with the Thouars heiress, you have Tiffauges, Pouzauges, Chabanais, Gonfolenc, Savenay, Lambert, Gretz-sur-Maine and Châteaumorant. Truly, my grandson, you are one of the wealthiest lords of your time" (GJ, 37; 47).

8. See Deleuze's study of Tournier's *Vendredi ou les limbes du Pacifique* in the appendix of *Logique du sens* (1969, LSEng, 1990).

9. Tournier's reinscription of tales into new contexts, like Tom Thumb, is a strategy for his "rappel au désordre" ("call to disorder") which, Davis argues, is "at the core of Tournier's creative urge" (1988, 203). See also Tournier's *Le vol du vampire* (1981, 32), and tales such as "Tristan Vox" and "La fugue du petit Poucet" ("Tom Thumb Runs Away") in *Le coq de bruyère* (1978).

10. Davis notes that Tournier "regards the possibility of describing mixed states ('faux sédentaire,' 'nomades sédentarisés,' 'voyageur sédentaire,' 'vagabond immobile') as a triumph of the intellect over binary oppositions. He attempts to overcome the limitations of the dichotomy by rejecting absolute barriers between opposites, and so the nomad in his texts is never entirely independent of the sedentary order" (1988, 196). On the transcendence of binarity in Tournier, see also Maclean (1987).

11. On the smooth/striated distinction, see Menser (1996), Nunes (in press), and Shaviro (1995a, Chapter 12).

12. The play of darkness and light and Prelati's praise of dissection recall another of Tournier's visionaries, the photographer Veronica in "Les suaires de Véronique" ("Veronica's Shrouds"), in *Le coq de bruyère* (1978).

13. Developing Michel Serres's insights, Deleuze and Guattari summarize the characteristics of the excentric, nomad science:

> (1) First of all, it uses a hydraulic model, rather than being a theory of solids treating fluids as a special case;.... (2) The model in question is one of becomings and heterogeneity, as opposed to the stable, the eternal, the identical, the constant. ... (3) One no longer goes from the straight line to its parallels, in a lamellar or laminar flow, but from a curvilinear declination to the formation of spirals and vortices on an inclined plane: the greatest slope for the smallest angle.... (4) Finally, the model is problematic, rather than theorematic: figures are considered only from the viewpoint of the affections that befall them: sections, ablations, adjunctions, projections. One does not go by specific differences from a genus to its species, or by deduction from a stable essence to the properties deriving from it, but rather from a problem to the accidents that condition and resolve it. (MPEng, 361–362; MPFr 447–448)

See also Serres (1977), and for more thorough studies of these dynamics, see Rosenberg (1993, 1994). On the "capture of space" as a literary concept, see Noyes (1989).

14. As Mireille Rosello suggests, Prelati serves as a "concurrent narrator," whose interpretation of Gilles's destiny "enlightens readers by unveiling for them what was previously hidden by the historical myth and by the 'facts,' " an interpretation based on "a theory having no relation to individual or social morality, one that helps him describe phenomena without judging in the name of Good and Evil" (1989, 89; my translation). See also Rosello (1990) for further analysis of Tournier's *Gilles et Jeanne* and other works.

15. See Foucault (1976, 27 [1978, 18]).

Chapter 7

1. On "dance arenas," see Hazzard-Gordon (1990), and on dance arenas and events in other traditions, see Keil and Keil (1992), J. L. Lewis (1992), Limón (1991), and Peña (1985).

2. See Hanna (1979, 17–49); see also Hanna (1983, 181–193) and S. Foster (1992)

3. By employing the term "structure of feeling" borrowed from Raymond Williams, I wish to evoke the useful distinction and tension he describes between a "produced past" and a "living presence" of "social experience which is still in progress" (1977, 128, 132).

4. One important and deliberate limitation to the scope of this examination concerns distinctions between Cajun music and zydeco. The latter designates the recent music of Louisianans of African-American and Caribbean origins. The term itself is derived from a regional pronunciation of "les haricots," particularly in the Clifton Chenier title, "Les Haricots Est Pas Salés" (The snapbeans aren't salted). While a thorough examination of zydeco music, dance forms, and arenas would no doubt require a separate study, scholars and folklorists already recognize the important influence of this musical form on Cajun music especially since much innovative Cajun music derives its energy as well as its instrumentation from a rich fusion with zydeco. See A. Savoy (1984, 302–306), Ancelet (1989), and Ancelet, Edwards, & Pitre (1991). For roots of the zydeco tradition, see *Louisiana Cajun and Creole Music, 1934: The Lomax Recordings* (1987), and for recent trends in zydeco, see the special issue of *Living Blues* (1991). See also *Hot Pepper* (1973) and *Zydeco* (1984).

5. See research by Ancelet (1984, 1989), Ancelet, Edwards, and Pitre (1991), *J'ai été au bal* (1989), A. Savoy (1984), and Severn (1991), as well as recent studies in folklore and performance by Keil and Keil (1992), J. L. Lewis (1992), Limón (1991), Lipsitz (1990), and Peña (1985).

6. See Bérubé (1994, 137–160), Nelson (1991), and Pfister (1992) for discussion of this conference and/or this volume. See also Pavel's (1992) critical assessment of this volume and of American "cultural studies." On the conference, Bérubé remarks, in contrast to the complaint made during the Illinois conference that "these counter-hegemonic proceedings were being recorded to produce a book—and upon publication, would therefore be forcibly inscribed into the dominant American imaginary," that "such gatherings do not sufficiently contribute to the commodification of critical discourse." He concludes that since "we do have potential readers, constituencies, and clients whom we haven't yet learned— or bothered—to address," it is incumbent upon the "Profession [to] revise [it]self" (1994, 171–172).

7. See Grossberg, Nelson, and Treichler's Introduction to this volume for a discussion of this elusive definition (1992, 1–16), and Grossberg's reflections on "cultural studies" as they relate to his critical project (1992, 16–27). See Buchanan (1997b) for a juxtaposition of Deleuze with Cultural Studies.

8. Acknowledging the term "Creole" as "slippery," Dormon uses it "to refer to individuals born in an American colonial possession of France or Spain, or to the families proceeding from the union of such individuals" (1983, 20).

9. See Brasseaux (1987, Chaps. 2–5) for a description of this emigration and resettlement.

10. This summary relies on Carl Brasseaux's oral history recounted in Severn (1991), as well as on Ancelet (1989). See also Brasseaux (1987; 1992), G. Conrad (1983) and Dormon (1983).

11. As a musical form, zydeco is distinct from Cajun music in emphasizing a jazz, blues, and R&B mix, usually with fundamental instrumentation of fiddle, piano or button accordion, rub board, and guitar, frequently enhanced through amplification and added instruments. As a dance form, zydeco inspires a more syncopated push–pull step than either the Cajun two-step or the jitterbug, and the many blues numbers inspire a close slow-dance shuffle not necessarily as stylized as the Cajun waltz. As noted earlier, the impact of zydeco and blues forms on Cajun music and on dance spaces is quite important. One could further complicate these already complex questions by considering them in terms of racial tensions that have existed and continue to exist in southern Louisiana, particularly as these relate to cultural expressions such as dance and music. Indeed, in terms of the tensions in Cajun culture regarding "authenticity," the proximity of zydeco dance and musical forms to the expressions of Cajun music and dance often contributes immeasurably to the perceived need to maintain strict boundaries around would-be "traditional" cultural forms. While these questions are beyond the scope of this chapter, limited to Cajun music of European origins and the dance spaces in which this music is performed, I develop in the chapter's final section the relations of different musical forms, including zydeco, in terms of the "global"/"local" dyad. See Blank and Strachwitz's *J'Ai Été au Bal* (1989) that develops quite clearly the link between Cajun music and zydeco.

12. This summary relies on Ancelet (1989), Ancelet, Edwards, and Pitre (1991), A. Savoy (1984), and the interview with Marc Savoy in *J'ai été au bal* (1989).

13. See the documentary tribute to Balfa, *Dewey Balfa: The Tribute Concert* (1993).

14. See Ancelet (1988) on teaching French in Louisiana.

15. While it would be impossible to acknowledge all those who have contributed to the Cajun cultural "renaissance" since the mid-1960s, two spokesmen, Revon Reed and Paul C. Tate, were honored at the 1993 Mamou (Louisiana) Cajun Music Festival. See Reed, Tate, and Bihm (1969) on "voice" in Cajun music as well as Reed's renowned *Lâche pas la patate* (1976, 119–123). See also *Cajun Country: Don't Drop the Potato* (1990) and *Louisiane francophone: Lâche pas la patate!* (n.d.).

16. A group that tends to straddle this divide is Steve Riley and the Mamou Playboys. Recording on the Rounder label, Grammy-nominated for their 1993 album *Trace of Time*, and touring extensively, the band still maintains a strong "traditional" sound, drawing from the stock repertoire of Cajun music, while also developing new and innovative compositions, enhanced by the virtuosity of Steve Riley (on accordion and fiddle) and David Greeley (on fiddle).

17. Vincent Canby's assessment is quite succinct: "Whoever 'fixed' *The Big Easy* has fixed it by making essential story points fuzzy, and by pouring soundtrack music over it under the mistaken impression that it was a hot fudge sunday. . . .

If one doesn't demand narrative coherence, it's possible to enjoy *The Big Easy* for the performances of [Dennis] Quaid . . . and [Ellen] Barkin" (1987, C6). Pauline Kael is more severe; summing up McSwain and Osborne's efforts to bring the guilty to justice, Kael jibes, "That should have included the scriptwriters. . . . The picture has an amateurish, fifties-B-movie droopiness" (1987, 100). See also Ansen (1987) and Schickel (1987) for more positive, albeit brief reviews.

18. See Ancelet (1990) for a precise explanation of these stereotypes.

19. On "spatial practices," see de Certeau (1984 [1990], li); on the "dance arena," see Hazzard-Gordon (1990). On dialogics, I adopt and adapt concepts suggested by Bakhtin (1981).

20. As Bogue notes, Deleuze and Guattari borrow the term "heccéités" from Duns Scotus (*haecceitas*) to designate "an 'atmosphere,' in the sense both of a particular meteorological configuration and of a given ambiance or affective milieu" (1989, 154). Massumi observes further that "the emphasis on the 'thisness' of things is not to draw attention to their solidity or objectness, but on the contrary to their transitoriness, the singularity of their unfolding in space–time (being as flux; metastability)" (1992, 183).

21. Turner discusses similar phenomena of "plural reflexivity" in terms of "liminal" or "framed spaces" (1977, 33–36). See also Turner (1982, 20–60).

22. Much rich visual documentation is available in Rhonda Case Severn's *Discovering Acadiana* (1991).

23. Both Buydens (1990) and Bogue (1991) develop the possibilities of *heccéités* in the musical form, and Buchanan (1997d) considers Deleuze's relation to popular music. Burnett (1993) and Saper (1991) approach *heccéités*, in different ways admittedly, for the hypertext computer environment. On Deleuze–Guattari and hypertext, see Moulthrop (1994) and Rosenberg (1994).

24. Traditional: Lawrence Walker. I transcribe all lyrics exactly as printed on the record jacket except two translations that I revise: the title (from "The Unlucky Waltz"); and in the second-to-last verse, from "That's the waltz I was playing when we were married."

25. See ATP, 310, Plateau 11, "1837: Of the Refrain."

26. The plaintive quality of voice and chant in Cajun music is an additional affective element of the music/dance arena (see Reed, Tate, and Bihm [1969]). Following Ross Chambers, the voice, chant, and cry in Cajun music would constitute the deterritorializing and nomadic force of Cajun French as a minor language, particularly expressing melancholy as an oppositional text: "As a social text, then, melancholy requires reading, not as the site of a personal unconscious, harboring individual 'anger,' but as the 'place'—a deterritorialized place criss-crossed by a nomadic subject—where a political unconscious becomes readable, in and as the tension of the self and the self-constituting other(s)" (1991, 107–109). In *ABC* 1996, Deleuze reflects on the relationship between "joy" and the spoken and sung "complaint" ("J comme Joie" [J as in Joy]). On relations of art and territory, see Bogue (1997).

27. For a more specific analysis of "flows," see Turner (1977; 1982, 55–58).

28. On the waltz conventions, see Plater, Speyrer, and Speyrer (1993, 35–36, 51–56).

29. Male/lead: (1) L forward (2) R together (3) L forward (4) R touches L, (1) R forward (2) L together (3) R forward (4) L touches R; female/partner: (1) R back (2) L together (3) R back (4) L touches R, (1) L back (2) R together (3) L back (4) R touches L (Plater, Speyrer, and Speyrer [1993, 57]).

30. Under the influence of country-music dance practices in the early 1990s, the reintroduction of line dances in the Cajun dance arena, usually to slow two-step numbers (formerly danced as the rock "freeze"), reintroduced a different form of territorialization that can effectively block all forward, two-step flow and also impede the dynamic jitterbug movement. Acceding to these diverse, and often conflicting tastes, the organizers of the 1993 Mamou Cajun Music Festival provided an open grassy space directly in front of the bandstand for line dancing, juxtaposed to but away from the wooden dance floor.

31. See Grossberg (1986b, 180–182) on the " 'hollow' or superficial" treatment of musical texts by rock 'n' roll fans.

32. One might define the constitution of "spaces of affect" in terms of frames of "play" or "games" that are simply boundaries between "inside" and "outside" (J. L. Lewis 1992, 191; see Goffman 1986; Bateson 1972) or that are more complex structures, e.g., embedded or "nested" frames that underlie play-forms in Western society (MacAloon 1984, 254–265; Turner 1977).

33. The "centrifugal"/"centripetal" dyad, and the terms' necessary overlap through the mixture of both orientations in most dance arenas, correspond to MacAloon's distinction that opposes the figurative "festival" (in which a joyous mood prevails) to a "spectacle" (generating a broad range of intense emotions, not necessarily joyous) (1984, 246; see J. L. Lewis 1992, 214). It is ironic, however, that the centripetal "spectacle" usually manifests itself quite precisely in festivals, usually those organized outside the local dance arenas of southern Louisiana. On the festival, in general, and its importance for Cajun self-representation, see Cantwell (1993, 199). On the festive and ludic versus the "solemn," see also Turner (1977).

34. See the examination of these re-presentations in Ancelet (1990).

35. See Stivale (1994) for an analysis of Les Blank's strategies of documentary re-presentation of Cajun music and culture.

36. Toups says:

> You add a little herbs and spices of rhythm and blues and a little bit of rock 'n roll—not out of line, there's a border that you can just go by, and you can't cross the border, 'cos then if you cross the border, you get away from your roots. So if you can just add little bits and pieces to it to keep the fresh feeling and the energy to give to the younger generation, but still keep that roots, tortured strong Cajun feeling in your heart, you can go a long ways. (1990, 160)

37. Thus, in some ways, these groups attempt to combine what Mark Slobin sees as distinct, even conflicting practices: on the one hand, these groups "band" with fans through an explicitly commercial relationship, but also attempt to "bond" with fans as forms of "affinity groups" that "serve as nuclei for the free-floating units of our social atmosphere, points of orientation for weary travelers looking for a cultural home" (1993, 98; see 99–108).

Chapter 8

1. The issue of *SubStance* in question (44–45, 1984), entitled "Gilles Deleuze," includes articles that discuss works by Deleuze and Guattari, particularly *A Thousand Plateaus*. The *Molecular Revolution* collection of essays (1984), discussed in Chapter 1, is a selection of Guattari's essays first published in *Psychanalyse et transversalité* (1972) and *La Révolution moléculaire* (1977a).

2. The translation by Michael Ryan, *Communists Like Us* (1990), includes an original "Postscript, 1990" by Toni Negri, yet omits Guattari's "Des libertés en Europe" (On freedoms in Europe) and Negri's "Lettre archéologique" (Archeological letter) to Guattari. Antonio Negri is an Italian intellectual who was accused of complicity in the Aldo Moro affair and of being the chief of the Red Brigade. Jailed under preventive detention in 1979, Negri was freed after four and one-half years in prison thanks to a vote by Italian electors. However, Negri's immunity was subsequently revoked by the Italian Congress, and at the time of the interview he was a fugitive living in exile. See "Italy: Autonomia" (1980) and Negri (1983).

3. Many of these essays are translated in Guattari (1995) and Genosko (1996). The "third collection" to which he refers is no doubt *Cartographies schizoanalytiques* (1989a).

4. For a discussion of the foundation of this Collège, see Ungar (1984).

5. Jean-Marie Le Pen is the leader of the French National Front Party.

6. The "Canaques" are the indigenous people of the French colony of New Caledonia who were seeking the independence promised by François Mitterand during his 1981 electoral campaign.

7. This reference to "Reagan's 'Chicago Boys' " appears in a slightly different form (as "the 'Chicago Boys' of Milton Friedman") in a footnote in Guattari and Eric Alliez's "Capitalistic Systems, Structures, and Processes" (1983; Guattari 1986a, 176; MR 278; Genosko 1996, 246).

8. See ATP, Chapter 13, "7000 B.C.–Apparatus of Capture," for further development of the concept of "capture." On "cartographies of subjectivity," see CS, 47–52; and "on the production of subjectivity," see *Chaosmose* (Guattari 1992, 11–52; 1995, 1–32).

9. Brother of Danny "The Red" Cohn-Bendit; see Brownmiller (1985).

10. Guattari was a member of the editorial group of this renewed version of the earlier journal *change International*.

11. Touted as a collection of memoirs "to do away with the master thinkers" (*pour en finir avec les maîtres à penser*), Aron's book contains several vicious attacks on various French intellectual figures.

12. However, only two months later, in May 1985, Guattari would present an address in homage of Foucault at a Milan conference. Published in *Les années d'hiver* as "Microphysique des pouvoirs, micropolitique des désirs" (1986b), the essay begins: "Having had the privilege of seeing Michel Foucault take up my suggestion—expressed somewhat provocatively—that concepts were after all nothing but tools and that theories are equivalent to the boxes that contained them (their power scarcely able to surpass the services that they rendered in circumscribed fields, that is, at the time of historical sequences that were inevitably

delimited), you ought not as a result be surprised in seeing me today rummaging through Foucault's conceptual tool shop so that I might borrow some of his own instruments and, if need be, alter them to suit my own purposes. Moreover, I am convinced that it was precisely in this manner that Foucault intended that we make use of his contribution" (1986b, 207–208; Genosko 1996, 173).

13. Deleuze and Guattari derive the concept of "plateau" from Bateson (1972, 113; see ATP, 21–22; MP, 32–33).

14. In other words, Guattari supported an experimental, Summerhill-like approach to education as opposed to the hierarchized, State-supported system in the lay (or *l'école libre*) domain.

15. See Guattari's own analysis of Kafka's works in Guattari (1986a, 264–271).

16. The terminological density of this "cartography" arises from Guattari's attempt to reconceptualize the unconscious and subjectivity without falling into the "topical petrifaction" of the Freudian and Lacanian psychic agencies. As he says in CS,

> We believe it necessary for reconstructing the analysis of formations of the Unconscious to minimize as much as reasonably possible the use of notions such as subjectivity, consciousness, meaning [*signifiance*] . . . understood as impermeable, transcendental entities for concrete situations. The most abstract and most radically a-corporal references are attached to the real; they cross into the most contingent Flows and Territories. . . . Thus, we have deliberately chosen to consider situations only from the perspective of intersections of Assemblages [*carrefours d'Agencements*], that secrete, up to a certain point, their own coordinates of metamodelization. An intersection can, of course, impose connections; but it does not constitute a fixed limit; it can be sidestepped; its linking power can decrease when certain of its components lose their consistency. (CS, 36; all translations my own)

17. In *L'inconscient machinique* (1979a), what Guattari there calls a "generative schizoanalysis" would correspond to the "concrete cartography," "whose objective is to bring to light new machinic senses/directions in situations where everything seems determined in advance" (IM, 192), i.e., molecular politics in action. What he designates as "transformational schizoanalysis" (IM, 193–196) and "three-dimensional schizoanalysis" (IM, 196–199) would correspond to the "speculative cartography." According to Guattari's schema, the "machinic kernels [*noyaux machiniques*] both detach assemblages from the rest of the world and connect them to the whole of the 'mecanosphere.' Each living being, each process of enunciation, each psychic instance, each social formation is necessarily connected to (mechanically subjugated by) a crossroad-point [*point-carrefour*]." These "synapses" operate "between, on the one hand, its particular position on the objective phylum of concrete machines," i.e., the "material flows," "and on the other hand, the hooking of its formula for existence onto the plane of consistency of abstract machines," i.e., the "ordologic." "It's up to the machinic kernels to hold together these two kinds of branching so that the most abstract machines are able to find their path to manifestation and so that the most material machines are able to find their path to metabolization and, eventually, to semiotization" (IM, 197–198).

During our discussion, Guattari traced out a schema of this speculative cartography, the terms of which he would later develop in CS, there abandoning the starkly binary cardologic/ordologic distinction. I have nonetheless maintained the terms of the 1985 schema while attempting to enhance the schema based on Guattari's answers to later questions.

18. An example of this analysis appears in Guattari's "Les rêves de Kafka" (1985a). See also in "Les ritournelles de l'Etre et du Sens (l'analyse du rêve d'A. D.)" (CS, 235–249).

19. To translate these terms, I follow the translation by Paul Bains and Julian Pefanis of Guattari's final work, *Chaosmose* (1992; *Chaosmosis* 1995), particularly Chapter 3 (pp. 59–76). In Figure 1 of CS, Guattari traces a square matrix at the angles of which are situated four categories of *foncteurs,* or "ontological functions." At bottom left are the "material and indicative fluxes [F.] (libido, capital, signifier, work)"; at top left, the "machinic Phylum [phi]"; at bottom right, "existential Territories [T.]"; at top right, "incorporal Universes [U.] (qualified as *conscientiels* [conscious-als]." Between each angle are connections of both vertical (phi-F.; U.-T.) and horizontal (phi-U.; F.-T.) form: the verticals are reciprocally linked (via a single unbroken line with arrows at both ends) and designated as (phi-F.) "processes of objective (content) deterritorialization—Expression" and (U.-T.) as "Processes of subjective (enunciation) deterritorialization"; the horizontals axes each contain two lines, a one-way unbroken line pointing from U. to phi and from T. to F., and a one-way broken line pointing from phi to U. and from F. to T. The upper lines (phi-U.) are designated as relations of "propositional Discursivity," the lower lines (F.-T.) as relations of "energetic Discursivity."

20. Guattari introduces Figure 1 in CS as follows:

> The category of deterritorialization should allow us to separate the problematic of consciousness—and consequently, of the unconscious—from the problematic of the representation of the I/ego (*Moi*) and of the unity of the person. The idea of a totalizing, indeed totalitarian, consciousness ("I am the master of my universe"), functions as a founding myth of capitalistic subjectivity. In fact, there only exist diversified processes of conscientialisation ["consciousness-becoming"], resulting from the deterritorialization of existential Territories, equally multiple and overlapping. But, in turn, these different instruments of catalysis of a *pour-soi* and of singularization modes of the relation to worlds of the *en-soi* and of alter egos, can only acquire the consistency of an existential monad to the extent that they [the instruments] succeed in affirming themselves in a second dimension of deterritorialization that I qualify as energetic discursivisation. (CS, 39)

21. This distinction roughly corresponds to the more elaborate development of an "apparatus of capture" by the State in ATP, Chapter 13. See Guattari and Alliez (1983/1986).

22. In *Psychanalyse et transversalité,* Guattari states that the institutional object (or "object-c") "complements the notion of 'part-object' in Freudian theory" (which Guattari associates with Lacan's "object-a") "and the notion of 'transitional object' in a manner derived from the definition given by D. W. Winnicott" (or the "object-b") (PT, 87–88). Laplanche and Pontalis define these latter "objects" as follows: the "part-object" is the "type of object towards which the component instincts are directed without this implying that a person as a whole is taken as love-object. In the main part-objects are parts of the body, real or fantasized (breast, faeces, penis), and their symbolic equivalents" (1973, 301); the "transi-

tional object" is a term "to designate a material object with a special value for the suckling and young child, particularly when it is on the point of falling asleep (e.g., the corner of a blanket or napkin that is sucked)" (1973, 464). Guattari argues that while " 'Je est un autre' " [I is an other] (Rimbaud's famous formula for the "I" 's alterity), "this other is not a subject. It's a signifying machine which predetermines what must be good or bad for me and my peers in a given area of consumption" (PT, 93), that is, a "group subjectivity" that unblocks the impasse of "repeated alterity" in which the grids of language capture the "object-a." This "object-c" is thus a fundamental principle of Guattari's clinical schizoanalytic practice. Whereas the "object-a" 's "individual phantasy represents this impossible sliding of planes," thereby anchoring "desire onto the body's surface," "the group phantasy" (or object-c) "superposes the planes, exchanges and substitutes them" (PT, 244–245), allowing a collective enunciation of group subjectivity that is "an absolute prerequisite for the emergence of any individual subjectivity" (PT, 90). See Guattari's essay "Machine and Structure" (PT, 240–248; MR, 111–119).

23. The second chapter of CS is entitled "Energetic Semiotics," which Guattari introduces as follows:

> Before developing my own conceptions on the topic of "schizoanalytic cartographies," I will briefly examine certain invalidating effects from the importation of thermodynamic notions into the human and social sciences. I will also evoke the stroke of genius, not to say stroke of madness, that led Freud to invent a semiotic energetics, of which the first theorizations, despite their naively scientistic character, were, in the final analysis, less reductionist than those that he was to develop subsequently, in the context of the institutionalization of psychoanalysis. (CS, 67)

The five subdivisions of this chapter are: "The Entropic Superego," "The Freudian Semiotic Energetics," "The Schizoanalytic Unconscious," "Non-separability, Separation, and Quantification," and "The Cartography of Assemblages" (CS, 67–92).

24. See Chapter 5, Note 16, regarding debate on the concept of "becoming-woman."

25. On the "Debussyst constellation of multiple Universes," see Guattari (1992, 75–77; 1995, 49–51).

Appendix

1. Although written in 1967, the essay appeared in 1973 (Deleuze 1973b). Other than this volume's status as the eighth of an eight-volume series, I have not been able to discover any reason for the six-year delay of publication. A recent supplementary issue of *Magazine littéraire* contains an essay by Toni Negri (1996) that situates Deleuze's structuralism essay as well as *Anti-Oedipus* in the context of the May 1968 cultural upheaval. On Deleuze's relationship (in *Difference and Repetition*) to the structuralism of Piaget, see Tim Clark (1997).

2. See Chap. 1, Note 19, for details on the different editions of Deleuze's study of Proust.

3. That Jacques Derrida does not appear in this list is not at all surprising: his initial trio of works—*La Voix et le phénomène* (1967a), *De la grammatologie*

(1967b), and *L'écriture et la différence* (1967c)—all appeared in the very year that Deleuze composed this essay. Deleuze was certainly familiar with Derrida's work: they both published review essays throughout the 1960s in *Critique,* shared the same editors for certain books (at PUF and Editions de Minuit), and in *Difference and Repetition* Deleuze cites Derrida's concept of *différance* from *Writing and Difference* (DREng, 318n28; DRFr, 164). However, Derrida did not participate in the founding phase of what one could "recognize" as structuralism to the same extent as the other authors that Deleuze cites. Moreover, Derrida also developed a critique of structuralism's premises and of many of these same cited authors, particularly Lévi-Strauss, Foucault, and Lacan. See Descombes (1979) for a succinct discussion (and comparison) of the concept of "difference" in Derrida and Deleuze, and Grosz (1995, 125–137) for possible intersections in terms of architecture.

4. See Guattari's severe critique of the "trinitarian religion of the Symbolic, the Real, and the Imaginary" (1986a, 211–213). See also Deleuze's comment in *Dialogues* about "the poverty of the imaginary and the symbolic, the real always being put off until tomorrow" (DEng, 51; DFr, 63). Thanks to Melissa McMahon for her insights on this and other points of this introduction.

5. Of the many works on Roland Barthes's development, see Bensmaïa (1987) and Ungar (1983). For a truly fascinating juxtaposition of critical positions on Proust's *A la recherche du temps perdu,* see the round table discussion between Deleuze, Roland Barthes, Gérard Genette, and Serge Doubrovsky in Bersani (1975).

6. Deleuze's above-cited comment to Cressole (in Chapter 1, p. 6) about the effect of reading Nietzsche—how Deleuze was henceforth opened to "multiplicities" and "intensities"—takes on new resonance here. To follow Deleuze's reworking of structuralism further, we can draw usefully from the more thorough development "Ideas and the Synthesis of Difference" (Chap. 4) in *Difference and Repetition.* Juxtaposing "the Idea" directly to "structure," Deleuze defines the three conditions for the Idea's emergence: the elements of the multiplicity not being "actually existent, but inseparable from a potential or a virtuality"; elements being determined by "reciprocal relations which allow no independence whatsoever to subsist"; and the actualization of a multiple ideal connection at once through "a differential relation . . . in diverse spatio-temporal relationships," and its elements "actually incarnated in a variety of terms and forms" (DREng, 183; DRFr, 237). Deleuze concludes: "This Idea is thus defined as a structure" that is "a 'complex theme,' an internal multiplicity—in other words, a system of multiple, non-localisable connections between differential elements which is incarnated in real relations and actual terms" (DREng, 183; DRFr, 237). And Deleuze insists that, "following Lautman and Vuillemin's work on mathematics, 'structuralism' seems to us the only means by which a genetic method can achieve its ambitions," understanding "genesis" in a particular way, that is, as taking place in time "between the virtual and actualisation" (DREng, 183; DRFr, 237-238). Deleuze describes this understanding: "In other words, [genesis] goes from the structure to its incarnation, from the conditions of a problem to the cases of solution, from the differential elements and their ideal connections to actual terms and diverse

real relations which constitute at each moment the actuality of time" (DREng, 183; DRFr, 238). See works by Lautman (1946) and Vuillemin (1938, 1960/1962).

7. The reference is to Proust's *Le temps retrouvé* (vol. 7 of *A la recherche du temps perdu*), 1954, 3:873. Deleuze discusses this in Chapter 5 of *Proust et les signes* (PSFr, 70–80; PSEng, 56–64). Michael Hardt notes:

> Deleuze asserts that it is essential that we conceive of the Bergsonian emanation of being, differentiation, as a relationship between the *virtual* and the *actual*, rather than as a relationship between the *possible* and the *real*. After setting up these two couples (virtual–actual and possible–real) [in *Bergsonism*], Deleuze proceeds to note that the transcendental term of each couple relates positively to the immanent term of the opposite couple. The possible is never real, even though it may be actual; however, while the virtual may not be actual, it is nonetheless real. In other words, there are several contemporary (actual) possibilities of which some may be realized in the future; in contrast, virtualities are always real (in the past, in memory) and may become actualized in the present. Deleuze invokes Proust for a definition of the states of virtuality: "real without being actual, ideal without being abstract" ([*Bergsonism*,] 96). The essential point here is that the virtual is real and the possible is not. This is Deleuze's basis for asserting that the movement of being must be understood in terms of the virtual–actual relationship rather than the possible–real relationship. (Hardt 1993, 16–17; see Deleuze 1966 [1988])

8. In *Difference and Repetition*, Deleuze develops this *t/c* distinction fully:

> Differentiation itself already has two aspects of its own, corresponding to the varieties of relations and to the singular points dependent upon the values of each variety. However, differenciation in turn has two aspects, one concerning the qualities or diverse species which actualise the varieties, the other concerning number or the distinct parts actualising the singular points. (DREng, 210; DRFr, 271).

9. We should note the derivation of this same term in both *Difference and Repetition* and *Logic of Sense*: having posited "organisation in series" as the foremost condition under which difference develops "this in-itself as a 'differenciator,' " Deleuze insists that "all sorts of consequences follow within the system. Something 'passes' between the borders, events explode, phenomena flash, like thunder and lightning" (DREng, 118; DRFr, 155). But he then asks, "What is this agent, this force which ensures communication? Thunderbolts explode between different intensities, but they are preceded by an invisible, imperceptible dark precursor [*précurseur sombre*], which determines their path in advance but in reverse, as though intagliated" (DREng, 119; DRFr, 156). In *Logic of Sense*, Deleuze states that this paradoxical element, the "differentiator" of heterogeneous series, derives from the principle of the emission of singularities: this "esoteric word and exoteric object . . . has the function of bringing about the distribution of singular points; of determining as signifying the series in which it appears in excess, and as signified, the series which it appears correlatively as lacking and, above all, of assuring the bestowal of sense in both signifying and signified series" (LSEng, 50–51; LSFr, 66). In the final section of Deleuze's *Abécédaire* (that is, in 1988), he describes the "dark precursor" as that which

puts different potentials into contact; once the dark precursor undertakes its course, potentials enter into a state of reaction from which emerges the visible event. So, there is the somber precursor and (*Deleuze gestures a Z in the air*) a lightning bolt, and that's how the world was born. There is always a somber precursor that no one sees and then the lightning bolt that illuminates. (ABC 1996, "Z comme Zigzag" [Z as in Zigzag])

For terms with similar resonance, see Agamben (1993, 1–2, 9–11, on "whatever" [*qualunque*], and 23–25, on "ease").

10. This is a conceptual trail that he will pursue with Guattari in *A Thousand Plateaus* as the "refrain" (*ritournelle*). Moreover, in *Difference and Repetition* (DREng, 121–123; DRFr, 159–161) and *Logic of Sense* (LSEng, 260–265; LSFr, 300–307), Deleuze links the movement of the "linguistic precursor" to "sense" as both "cosmos" and "chaos," a Joycean "chaosmos" that resonates directly with their collaborative works and with the title of Guattari's final theoretical work, *Chaosmose* (1992 [1995]).

11. Compare this to *Difference and Repetition*: after referring directly to the same passage in Lacan's analysis of the Poe tale (DREng, 102; DRFr, 135), Deleuze says,

given two heterogeneous series, two series of differences, the precursor plays the part of the differenciator of these differences. In this manner, by virtue of its own power, it puts them into immediate relation to one another: it is the in-itself of difference or the "differently different"—in other words, difference in the second degree, the self-different which relates different to different by itself. Because the path it traces is invisible and becomes visible only in reverse, to the extent that it is traveled over and covered by the phenomena it induces within the system, it has no place other than that from which it is "missing," no identity other than that which it lacks: it is precisely the object = x, the one which "is lacking in its place" as it lacks its own identity. (DREng, 119–120; DRFr, 156–157)

See also *Logic of Sense* (LSEng 40-41, LSFr 55-56).

12. The "Thirty-Second Series on the Different Kinds of Series" in *Logic of Sense* is crucial for studying Deleuze's detailed understanding of Lacan, the Oedipal complex, and the phallus as "object = x" (see LSEng, 227–230; LSFr, 265–268).

13. See Lacan (1966, 386–389), in "Réponse au commentaire de Jean Hyppolite sur la 'Verneinung' de Freud." Trans: This footnote and the following ones not preceded by "Trans:" are in the original essay by Deleuze.

14. Lacan no doubt has gone the furthest in the original *analysis* of the distinction between imaginary and symbolic. But this distinction itself, in its diverse forms, is found in all the structuralists.

15. Trans: On the concept of a pure, unextended *spatium*, see Deleuze (DRFr, 296–297; DREng, 229–231).

16. Trans: Althusser (1965a, 87–128; 1969, 89–127).

17. Trans: See Deleuze (LSFr, 88–89; LSEng, 71).

18. Trans: Althusser (1965a, 131–152; 1969, 131–151, "The 'Piccolo Teatro': Bertolazzi and Brecht").

19. Trans: The *coup de dés* metaphor is associated in French literature with Mallarmé's poem, "Un coup de dés jamais n'abolira le hasard ..." (1945,

455–477). Deleuze cites Nietzsche's *Zarathustra* in DRFr, 361–364, and DREng, 282–284. See also DRFr, 255–260, DREng, 197–202; NPFr, 29–31, NPEng, 25–27; LSFr, 74–82; LSEng, 58–65; FFr, 124–125, and FEng, 117. On the "tumbling dice" and repetition in Deleuze's works, see Conway (1997).

20. Trans: Deleuze draws this example from the work of Raymond Roussel. See DRFr, 159, and DREng, 121.

21. Trans: On the three types of determination, see DRFr, 221–224, and DREng, 170–173.

22. Trans: See DRFr, 237, and DREng, 183, for a definition of "structure" as multiplicity and the criteria following which an Idea emerges.

23. Trans: It is clear from this and later arguments (see the fourth criterion, p. 267) that Deleuze establishes one correspondence represented by the "differential relations-species-variables" triad, and another represented by the "singularities-organic parts-function" triad. Hence, our translation of "les uns . . . les autres" as "former" and "latter," rather than as "some species . . . others"; this translation, that is, as a random variation *between* species, would miss the "double aspect," only one side of which bears on species as such, the other side expressing itself as the distribution of parts *within* a species. On the distinction species/parts, see DRFr, 318–327, and DREng, 247–254 (in fact, most of Chap. 5 deals with this "organization" that happens at the moment of "actualization").

24. Althusser (1965b, 152–157; 1979, 177–180). Cf. also Balibar in Althusser (1965b, 205–211; 1979, 211–216). Trans: See Deleuze's reformulation: DRFr, 240–241, and DREng, 186–187.

25. Trans: This expression is drawn from Proust's *Le temps retrouvé* (1954 3:873; see PSFr, 71–73, and PSEng, 56–59). On the concept of virtuality, see DRFr, 269–276, DREng, 208–214. See also Note 7 above.

26. Althusser (1965b, 1:82 [1979, 64]; 1965b, 2:44 [1979, 97–98]).

27. Trans: On the distinction between differenciation and differentiation, see DRFr, 270–271, and DREng, 209–211. See also Note 8 above.

28. The book by Jules Vuillemin, *Philosophie de l'algèbre* [1960, 1962], proposes a determination of structures in mathematics. He insists on the importance in this regard of a theory of problems (following the mathematician Abel), and of principles of determination (reciprocal, complete, and progressive determination according to Galois). He shows how structures, in this sense, provide the only means of realizing the ambitions of a true genetic method.

29. Ortigues also marks the second difference between the imaginary and the symbolic: the "dual" or "specular" character of the imagination, in opposition to the Third, to the third term which belongs to the symbolic system.

30. Trans: See J.-A. Miller (1966, 49–51; 1977–78, 32–34).

31. Trans: Deleuze refers to Leclaire's analyses in discussing questions and problems as "living acts of the unconscious," in DRFr, 140–141, and DREng, 106–107, 316–317n17.

32. Trans: In a translator's note in WIP, Hugh Tomlinson and Graham Burchell remark: "In her translation of Sartre's *Being and Nothingness* (New York: Philosophical Library, 1956), Hazel Barnes translates *objectité*, which she glosses as 'the quality or state of being an object' (p. 632), as 'objectness' or, on occasion,

as 'object-state.' We have preferred 'objectality' in line with Massumi's translation of *visagéité* as 'faciality' in *A Thousand Plateaus*" (WIP, 3–4). On the question/problem as objective instances, see DRFr, 219–221, 359, and DREng, 169–170, 280–281.

33. Trans: On totemism and its structuralist interpretation, see MP, 288–289, and ATP, 236.

34. Trans: On serialization and its relation to Lacan's analysis, see LSFr, 51–55; LSEng, 37–40.

35. Trans: Deleuze says that Sollers's novel "takes as its motto a formula by Leibniz: 'Suppose, for example, that someone draws a number of points on the paper at random. . . . I say that it is possible to find a geometric line the notion of which is constant and uniform according to a certain rule such that this line passes through all the points . . . ,' " and adds: "The entire beginning of this book is constructed on the two formulae: 'Problem . . . ' and 'Missed. . . . ' Series are traced out in relation to the singular points of the body of the narrator, an ideal body which is 'thought rather than perceived' " (DRFr, 257; DREng, 326n16).

36. Trans: The allusion refers to Arthur Rimbaud's enigmatic prose poem "H" and to its final line, "trouvez Hortense" [find Hortense]. See Rimbaud (1972, 151).

37. Trans: On the refrain, see DRFr, 161, and DREng, 122–123.

38. Trans: See also DRFr, 157, and DREng, 199–120.

39. Trans: On the simultaneously relative and absolute status of movements (as characterizing the concept), see Q, 26–27, and WIP, 21–22.

40. Trans: See LSFr, 55–56, and LS, 40–41.

41. Trans: Deleuze cites Sollers and Faye in his discussion of the "blind spot" in DRFr 257, and DREng, 326.

42. Trans: See also LSFr, 63–64, and LS, 48–50.

43. Trans: See LSFr, 57–62, and LS, 44–47.

44. Trans: On the object = x and word = x, see DRFr 156–163, and DREng, 118–125.

45. Trans: See LSFr, 266–268, and LSEng, 228–230.

46. Trans: On the phallus as "object = x," see the thirty-second series in *Logic of Sense*.

47. See Macherey (1965, 242–252), in which Macherey analyzes the notion of value, showing that this notion is always staggered in relation to the exchange in which it appears.

48. Trans: On the status of different "orders" in relation to one another, see DRFr 236–242, and DREng, 182–186.

49. Trans: See DRFr, 251–266, and DREng, 195–206; LSFr, 67–73, and LSEng, 52–57.

50. Trans: See DRFr, 316–319, 354–357 (conclusion), and DREng, 246–248, 276–279.

51. Cf. the schema proposed by Leclaire (1958), following Lacan.

52. On the Marxist notions of "contradiction" and "tendency," see the analyses of Balibar in Althusser (1965b 2: 296–303 [1979, 283–293]).

53. Foucault (1966a, 230): structural mutation "[this profound breach in the expanse of continuities], though it must be analyzed, and minutely so, cannot be 'explained' or even summed up in a single word. It is a radical event that is

distributed across the entire visible surface of knowledge, and whose signs, shocks, and effects, it is possible to follow step by step" (1970, 217).

54. Trans: At the end of HDW, Deleuze provides a "summary bibliography" that contains several key references not included in the essay's footnotes: *Cahiers pour l'analyse* (1968), Jakobson (1963), Lévi-Strauss (1949), *Musique en jeu* (1971), Saussure (1915/1972), Todorov et. al. (1968), Troubetskoi (1939/1949).

REFERENCES

Considerable efforts have been made by scholars, myself among them, to develop complete bibliographical lists of works written by Deleuze and Guattari, and of the critical essays devoted to their work. As I do not attempt to offer complete bibliographies here, I recommend, for Deleuze, Séglard's brief bibliography in *Magazine littéraire* (1988) and Murphy's thorough bibliography in Patton 1996, 270–300; for Guattari, see Genosko 1996, 273–276; for critical references on Deleuze, see Boundas and Olkowski 1994, 305–336. For online references to Deleuze and Guattari, see Taylor 1997.

Abou-Rihan, Fadi. (1992). "Becoming-Gay, Becoming-Lesbian." *PRE/TEXT* 13. 3–4: 97–108.

Adair, Gilbert. (1989). *Hollywood's Vietnam: From "The Green Berets" to "Full Metal Jacket."* London: William Heinemann.

Agamben, Giorgio. (1993). *The Coming Community.* Trans. Michael Hardt. Minneapolis: University of Minnesota Press.

Agamben, Giorgio. (1995). "Sauf les hommes et les chiens." *Libération.* 7 Nov.: 37.

Alliez, Eric. (1993). *La Signature du Monde, ou qu'est-ce que la philosophie de Deleuze et Guattari?* Paris: Editions du Cerf.

Althusser, Louis. (1965a [1969]). *Pour Marx.* Paris: Maspero. *For Marx.* Trans. Ben Brewster. New York: Pantheon Books.

Althusser, Louis, et al. (1965b [1979]). *Lire le Capital.* Paris: Maspero. 2 vols. *Reading Capital.* Trans. Ben Brewster. New York: Verso.

Althusser, Louis. (1992 [1993]). *L'avenir dure longtemps, suivi de Les Faits.* Paris: Stock. *The Future Lasts Forever. A Memoir.* Trans. Richard Veasey. Eds. Olivier Corpet and Yann Moulier Boutang. New York: New Press.

Amiran, Eyal, and John Unsworth, eds. (1993). *Essays in Postmodern Culture.* New York: Oxford University Press.

Ancelet, Barry Jean. (1984). *The Makers of Cajun Music.* Austin: University of Texas Press.

Ancelet, Barry Jean. (1988). "A Perspective on Teaching the 'Problem Language' in Louisiana." *French Review* 61.3: 345–356.

Ancelet, Barry Jean. (1989). *Cajun Music. Its Origins and Development.* Lafayette: University of Southwestern Louisiana, Center for Louisiana Studies.

Ancelet, Barry Jean. (1990). "Drinking, Dancing, Brawling Gamblers Who Spend Most of Their Time in the Swamp." *The Times of Acadiana.* 20 June: 12–15.

Ancelet, Barry Jean. (1992). "Cultural Tourism in Cajun Country: Shotgun Wedding or Marriage Made in Heaven?" *Southern Folklore* 49: 256–266.

Ancelet, Barry Jean, Jay Edwards, and Glen Pitre. (1991). *Cajun Country.* Jackson: The University of Mississippi Press.

anderegg, Michael A., ed. (1991). *Inventing Vietnam: The War in Film and Television.* Philadelphia: Temple University Press.

andrews, Walter G. (1993). "Singing the Alienated 'I': Guattari, Deleuze and Lyrical Decodings of the Subject in Ottoman Divan Poetry." *Yale Journal of Criticism* 6.2: 191–219.

Anquetil, Gilles. (1984). "Dernier cri du prêt-à-penser: Les néolibéralisme." *Le Nouvel observateur.* 17 Aug: 22–23.

Ansell-Pearson, Keith. (1997a). "Deleuze Outside/Outside Deleuze: On the Difference Engineer." In Ansell-Pearson 1997c, 1–22.

Ansell-Pearson, Keith. (1997b). "Viroid Life: On Machines, Technics, and Evolution." In Ansell-Pearson 1997c, 180–210.

Ansell-Pearson, Keith, ed. (1997c). *Deleuze and Philosophy: The Difference Engineer.* New York: Routledge.

Ansen, David. (1987). "An August Heat Wave." *Newsweek.* 24 Aug: 60–61.

Anti-Oedipus. (1977). Special Issue of *Semiotext(e)* 2.3.

Apocalypse Now. (1979). Dir. Francis Ford Coppola. Zoetrope.

Armitt, Lucie, ed. (1991). *Where No Man Has Gone Before. Women and Science Fiction.* New York: Routledge.

Aron, Jean-Paul. (1984). *Les modernes.* Paris: Gallimard.

Aronowitz, Stanley. (1993). "On Félix Guattari." *Long News in the Short Century* 4: 172–179.

Aronowitz, Stanley, Barbara Martinsons, and Michael Menser, with Jennifer Rich, eds. (1996). *Technoscience and Cyberculture.* New York: Routledge.

Artaud, Antonin. (1976). "To Have Done With the Judgment of God." Trans. Helen Weaver. *Selected Writings of Antonin Artaud.* New York: Farrar, Straus and Giroux. 555–571. Rpt. *Semiotext(e)* 2.3: 61.

Artaud, Antonin. (1977). "The Body is the Body." Trans. Roger McKeon. *Semiotext(e)* 2.3: 59.

Asimov, Isaac. (1956). *I, Robot.* New York: Signet.

Auster, Albert, and Leonard Quart. (1988). *How the War was Remembered: Hollywood and Vietnam.* New York: Praeger.

Badiou, Alain. (1995). "Une lettre à Gilles (Juillet 1994)." *Libération.* 7 Nov.: 36.

Badiou, Alain. (1997). *Deleuze: "La clameur de l'Etre."* Paris: Hachette.

Bakhtin, M. M. (1981). *The Dialogic Imagination.* Ed. Michael Holquist. Austin: University of Texas Press.

Balsamo, Anne. (1995). "Forms of Technological Embodiment: Reading the Body in Contemporary Culture." *Body and Society* 1.3–4: 215–238.

Balsamo, Anne. (1996). *Technologies of the Gendered Body. Reading Cyborg Women.* Durham: Duke University Press.

Barthes, Roland. (1964 [1972]). *Essais critiques.* Paris: Seuil. *Critical Essays.* Trans. Richard Howard. Evanston, IL: Northwestern University Press.

Barthes, Roland. (1966; 1985 [1977]). "Introduction à l'analyse structurale des récits." In *L'aventure sémiologique*. Paris: Seuil. 167–206. Trans. Stephen Heath. In Barthes 1977, 79–124.

Barthes, Roland. (1970 [1974]). *S/Z*. Paris: Seuil. Trans. Richard Miller. New York: Hill and Wang.

Barthes, Roland. (1977). *Image-Music-Text*. Trans. Stephen Heath. New York: Hill and Wang.

Barthes, Roland. (1981). *Le grain de la voix*. Paris: Seuil.

Bateson, Gregory. (1972). *Steps to an Ecology of Mind*. New York: Ballantine.

Bear, Greg. (1985a). *Blood Music*. New York: Arbor House.

Bear, Greg. (1985b). *Eon*. New York: Tom Doherty Associates.

Bear, Greg. (1988). *Eternity*. New York: Popular Library.

Beausoleil. (1986). *Bayou Boogie*. Rounder Records 6015.

Beckett, Samuel. (1951 [1962]). *Malone Meurt*. Paris: Minuit. *Malone Dies*. Trans. Samuel Beckett. Middlesex, UK: Penguin.

Bellour, Raymond. (1988). "Gilles Deleuze. Un philosophe nomade." Introduction to special "Dossier" on Deleuze. *Magazine littéraire* 257: 14.

Benedikt, Michael, ed. (1991, 1992). *Cyberspace: First Steps*. Cambridge, MA: MIT Press.

Bennett, Tony. (1977). *Structuralism and Semiotics*. Berkeley: University of California Press.

Bensmaïa, Reda. (1987). *The Barthes Effect. The Essay as Reflective Text*. Minneapolis: University of Minnesota Press.

Bensmaïa, Reda. (1994). "On the Concept of Minor Literature: From Kafka to Kateb Yacine." In Boundas and Olkowski 1994, 213–228.

Bensmaïa, Reda. (1995). *The Year of Passages*. Trans. Tom Conley. Minneapolis: University of Minnesota Press.

Berland, Jody. (1992). "Angels Dancing: Cultural Technologies and the Production of Space." In Grossberg et al., 38–51.

Bersani, Jacques, ed. (1975). "Table ronde." In *Cahiers Marcel Proust* 7 (new series): 87–116. Paris: Gallimard.

Bérubé, Michael. (1994). *Public Access. Literary Theory and American Cultural Politics*. New York: Verso.

Best, Steven, and Douglas Kellner. (1991). *Postmodern Theory: Critical Interrogations*. New York: The Guilford Publications.

Bey, Hakim. (1985, 1991). *T.A.Z.: The Temporary Autonomous Zone, Ontological Anarchy, Poetic Terrorism*. New York: Autonomedia.

Bhabha, Homi. (1997). "Editor's Introduction: Minority Maneuvers and Unsettled Negotiations." *Critical Inquiry* 23.3: 431–459.

The Big Easy. (1987). Dir. Jim McBride. Kings Road Entertainment.

Blake, Charlie. (1993). "In the Shadow of Cybernetic Minorities: Life, Death, and Delirium in the Capitalist Imaginary." *Angelaki* 1.1: 125–139.

Blanchot, Maurice. (1969 [1993]). *L'entretien infini*. Paris: Gallimard. *The Infinite Conversation*. Trans. Susan Hanson. Minneapolis: University of Minnesota Press.

Blanchot, Maurice. (1971). *L'amitié*. Paris: Gallimard.

Bloom, Donald A. (1989). "Hero and Antihero in Conrad and Coppola." *West Virginia Philological Papers* 35: 52–64.

Bogue, Ronald. (1981). "The Heart of Darkness of *Apocalypse Now.*" *Georgia Review* 35.3: 611–626.

Bogue, Ronald. (1989). *Deleuze and Guattari.* New York: Routledge.

Bogue, Ronald. (1991). "Rhizomusicosmology." *SubStance* 66: 85–101.

Bogue, Ronald. (1997). "Art and Territory." *South Atlantic Quarterly* 96.3: 465–482.

Boundas, Constantin V. (1993a). "Editor's Introduction." In Boundas 1993b, 1–23.

Boundas, Constantin V., ed. (1993b). *The Deleuze Reader.* New York: Columbia University Press.

Boundas, Constantin V. (1994). "Deleuze: Serialization and Subject-Formation." In Boundas and Olkowski 1994, 99–116.

Boundas, Constantin V., and Dorothea Olkowski, eds. (1994). *Deleuze and the Theater of Philosophy.* New York: Routledge.

Bourdieu, Pierre. (1984 [1979]). *Distinction. A Social Critique of the Judgement of Taste.* Trans. Richard Nice. Cambridge, MA: Harvard University Press. *La distinction: Critique sociale du jugement.* Paris: Minuit.

Braidotti, Rosi. (1994a). *Nomadic Subjects.* New York: Columbia University Press.

Braidotti, Rosi. (1994b). "Toward a New Nomadism: Feminist Deleuzian Tracks; or, Metaphysics and Metabolism." In Boundas and Olkowski 1994, 157–186.

Braidotti, Rosi. (1997). "Meta(l)morphoses." *Theory, Culture, and Society* 14.2: 67–80.

Brasseaux, Carl. (1987). *The Founding of New Acadia: The Beginning of Acadian Life in Louisiana, 1765–1803.* Baton Rouge: Louisiana State University Press.

Brasseaux, Carl. (1991). "Oral History of Acadiana." In Severn, cassette 2.

Brasseaux, Carl. (1992). *Acadian to Cajun: Transformation of a People, 1803–1877.* Jackson: University Press of Mississippi.

Broadhurst, Joan, ed. (1992). Special Issue: "Deleuze and the Transcendental Unconscious." *Pli–Warwick Journal of Philosophy* 4.1–2.

Brothers, Robyn F. (1997). "Cyborg Identities and the Relational Web: Recasting 'Narrative Identity' in Moral and Political Theory." *Metaphilosophy* 28.3: 249–258.

Broven, John. (1987 [1983]). *South to Louisiana. The Music of the Cajun Bayous.* Gretna, LA: Pelican.

Brownmiller, Susan. (1985). "Danny the Red Is a Green." *The Village Voice.* 4 June: 1, 22.

Buchanan, Ian, ed. (1997a). Special Issue: "A Deleuzean Century?" *South Atlantic Quarterly* 96.3.

Buchanan, Ian. (1997b). "Deleuze and Cultural Studies." *South Atlantic Quarterly* 96.3: 483–497.

Buchanan, Ian. (1997c). "The Problem of the Body in Deleuze and Guattari, or, What Can a Body Do?" *Body and Society* 3.3: 73–91.

Buchanan, Ian. (1997d). "Deleuze and Popular Music, or, Why Is There So Much 80s Music on the Radio Today?" *Social Semiotics* 7.2: 175–188.

Bukatman, Scott. (1992). "Amidst These Fields of Data: Allegory, Rhetoric, and the Paraspace." *Critique* 33.3: 199–219.

Bukatman, Scott. (1993). *Terminal Identity. The Virtual Subject in Postmodern Science Fiction.* Durham, NC: Duke University Press.

Burchell, Graham. (1984). "Introduction to Deleuze." *Economy and Society* 13.1: 43–51.

Burke, James Lee. (1989). *Black Cherry Blues.* New York: Avon.

Burnett, Kathleen. (1993). "Toward a Theory of Hypertextual Design." *Postmodern Culture* 3.2. Online at http://muse.jhu.edu/journals/postmodern_culture/archive.html

Butler, Judith. (1990). *Gender Trouble: Feminism and Subversion of Identity.* New York: Routledge.

Buydens, Mireille. (1990). *Sahara: L'esthétique de Gilles Deleuze.* Paris: Vrin.

Cadigan, Pat. (1987). *Mindplayers.* New York: Bantam.

Cadigan, Pat. (1991). *Synners.* New York: Bantam.

Cadigan, Pat. (1992). *Fools.* New York: Bantam.

Cahiers pour l'analyse. (1969). Vol. 9.

Cahir, Linda. (1992). "Narratological Parallels in Joseph Conrad's *Heart of Darkness* and Francis Ford Coppola's *Apocalypse Now.*" *Literature/Film Quarterly* 20.3: 181-187.

Cajun Country: Don't Drop the Potato. (1990). Dir. Alan Lomax. Pacific Arts Video.

Callinicos, Alex. (1982). *Is There a Future for Marxism?* Atlantic Highlands, NJ: Humanities Press.

Canby, Vincent. (1987). "The Big Easy: Comedy About a Police Case." *The New York Times.* 21 Aug: C6.

Canning, Peter. (1984). "Fluidentity." *SubStance* 44-45: 35-45.

Canning, Peter. (1994). "The Crack of Time and the Ideal Game." In Boundas and Olkowski 1994, 73-98.

Cantwell, Robert. (1993). *Ethnomimesis: Folklife and the Representation of Culture.* Chapel Hill: The University of North Carolina Press.

Carrouges, Michel. (1954; 1976). *Les machines célibataires.* Paris: Chêne.

Castaneda, Carlos. (1968, 1974). *The Teachings of Don Juan: A Yaqui Way of Knowledge.* New York: Pocket Books.

Castaneda, Carlos. (1971). *A Separate Reality: Further Conversations with Don Juan.* New York: Pocket Books.

Castaneda, Carlos. (1972). *Journey to Ixtlan: The Lessons of Don Juan.* New York: Pocket Books.

Castaneda, Carlos. (1974). *Tales of Power.* New York: Pocket Books.

Chambers, Ross. (1991). *Room for Maneuver. Reading the Oppositional in Narrative.* Chicago: University of Chicago Press.

Chassaguet-Smirgel, Janine, ed. (1974). *Les Chemins de L'Anti-OEdipe.* Paris: Privat.

Chauderlot, Fabienne-Sophie. (1996, 29 Dec.). "Beyond *A Thousand Plateaus*: War or Negotiations?" Special Session on "After Deleuze and Guattari." MLA Convention, Washington, DC.

Cherniavsky, Eva. (1993). "(En)gendering Cyberspace in *Neuromancer*: Postmodern Subjectivity and Virtual Motherhood." *Genders* 18: 32-46.

Cherny, Lynn, and Elizabeth Reba Weise, eds. (1996). *Wired Women: Gender and New Realities in Cyberspace.* Seattle: Seal Press.

Christie, John R. R. (1992). "A Tragedy for Cyborgs." *Configurations* 1.1: 171-196.

Clark, Nigel. (1995). "Rear-View Mirrorshades: The Recursive Generation of the Cyberbody." *Body and Society* 1.3-4: 113-134.

Clark, Tim. (1997). "Deleuze and Structuralism: Towards a Geometry of Sufficient Reason." In Ansell-Pearson 1997c, 58-72.

Cohen, Sande. (1993). *Academia and the Luster of Capital.* Minneapolis: University of Minnesota Press.

Colombat, andre Pierre. (1990). *Deleuze et la littérature.* New York: Peter Lang.

Colombat, andre Pierre. (1996). "November 4, 1995: Deleuze's death as an event." *Man and Worlds* 29: 235–249.

Colombat, andre Pierre. (1997). "Deleuze and the Three Powers of Literature and Philosophy: To Demystify, To Experiment, to Create." *South Atlantic Quarterly* 96.3: 579–597.

Conley, Tom. (1997). "From Multiplicities to Folds: On Style and Form in Deleuze." *South Atlantic Quarterly* 96.3: 629–646.

Conley, Verena andermatt. (1993). "Eco-Subjects." In *Rethinking Technologies,* 77–91. Ed. Verena andermatt Conley. Minneapolis: University of Minnesota Press.

Conrad, Glenn R., ed. (1983). *The Cajuns: Essays on Their History and Culture.* Lafayette: University of Southwestern Louisiana, The Center for Louisiana Studies.

Conrad, Joseph. (1910; 1950). *Heart of Darkness.* New York: Signet.

Conway, Daniel W. (1997). "Tumbling Dice: Gilles Deleuze and the Economy of *Répétition.*" In Ansell-Pearson 1997c, 73–90.

Coppola, Eleanor. (1979). *Notes.* New York: Pocket Books.

Coppola, Francis Ford. (1975). "*Apocalypse Now: Draft.*" Online at http://www.geo-cities.com/Hollywood/9067/an_draft.html.

Counsil, Wendy. (1990). "The State of Feminism in SF: Talks with Pat Murphy, Lisa Goldstein, and Karen Joy Fowler." *Science Fiction Eye* 2.2: 21–31.

Critique. (1992). Vol. 33, No. 3.

Cressole, Michel. (1973). *Deleuze.* Paris: Editions Universitaires.

Csicsery-Ronay, Istvan. (1988). "Cyberpunk and Neuroromanticism." *Mississippi Review* 16.2–3: 267–278.

Csicsery-Ronay, Istvan. (1992). "The Sentimental Futurist: Cybernetics and Art in William Gibson's *Neuromancer.*" *Critique* 33.3: 221–240.

"Cyberpunk Forum/Symposium." (1988). *Mississippi Review* 16.2–3: 16–65.

Daigle, Pierre V. (1972, 1987). *Tears, Love and Laughter. The Story of the Cajuns and Their Music.* Ville Platte, LA: Swallow.

D'Amico, Robert. (1978). "Desire and the Commodity Form." *Telos* 35: 88–122.

Danet, Brenda, ed. (1995). "Play and Performance in Computer-Mediated Communication." Special issue of *Journal of Computer-Mediated Communication* 1.2. Online at http://shum.huji.ac.il/jcmc/vol1/issue2/vol1no2.html.

Davis, Colin. (1988). *Michel Tournier. Philosophy and Fiction.* Oxford: Clarendon Press.

Davis, Erik. (1992). "De Landa Destratified." *Mondo 2000* 8: 44–48.

Davis, Erik. (1993). "A Computer, A Universe. Mapping an Online Cosmology." *Voice Literary Supplement.* March: 10–11.

Davis, Erik. (1994). "It's a MUD, MUD, MUD, MUD World." *The Village Voice.* 22 Feb.: 42–44.

Dean, Kenneth, and Brian Massumi. (1992). *First and Last Emperors.* New York: Autonomedia.

De Certeau, Michel. (1984 [1980; 1990]). *The Practice of Everyday Life.* Trans. Steven

F. Rendall. Berkeley: University of California Press. Trans. of *L'invention du quotidien: Vol. 1: Arts de faire.* Paris: Gallimard/Folio.

De Landa, Manuel. (1991). *War in the Age of Intelligent Machines.* New York: Zone.

"Deleuze: A Symposium". (1996). Abstracts of conference, 7–9 Dec. Online at http://www.arts.uwa.edu.au/EnglishWWW/abstracts.html.

Deleuze, Gilles. (1953 [1991]). *Empirisme et subjectivité.* Paris: PUF. *Empiricism and Subjectivity: An Essay on Hume's Theory of Human Nature.* Trans. Constantin V. Boundas. New York: Columbia University Press.

Deleuze, Gilles. (1959). "Sens et valeurs." *Arguments* 15: 20–28.

Deleuze, Gilles. (1961). "De Sacher Masoch au masochisme." *Arguments* 21: 40–46.

Deleuze, Gilles. (1962 [1983]). *Nietzsche et la philosophie.* Paris: PUF. *Nietzsche and Philosophy.* Trans. Hugh Tomlinson. New York: Columbia University Press.

Deleuze, Gilles. (1963 [1984]). *La Philosophie critique de Kant.* Paris: PUF. *Kant's Critical Philosophy.* Trans. Hugh Tomlinson and Barbara Habberjam. Minneapolis: University of Minnesota Press.

Deleuze, Gilles. (1964a, 1970, 1971, 1976 [1972]). *Marcel Proust et les signes.* Paris: PUF. *Proust and Signs.* Trans. Richard Howard. New York: Braziller.

Deleuze, Gilles. (1964b). "Il a été mon maître." *Arts.* 18 Oct–3 Nov.: 8–9.

Deleuze, Gilles. (1965; 1974, 4th Ed.). *Nietzsche.* Paris: PUF, Collection SUP.

Deleuze, Gilles. (1966 [1988]). *Le Bergsonisme.* Paris: PUF. *Bergsonism.* Trans. Hugh Tomlinson and Barbara Habberjam. New York: Zone.

Deleuze, Gilles. (1968a [1990]). *Spinoza et le problème de l'expression.* Paris: Minuit. *Expressionism in Philosophy: Spinoza.* Trans. Martin Joughin. New York: Zone.

Deleuze, Gilles. (1968b [1994]). *Différence et répétition.* Paris: PUF. *Difference and Repetition.* Trans. Paul Patton. New York: Columbia University Press.

Deleuze, Gilles. (1969 [1990]). *Logique du sens.* Paris: Minuit. *Logic of Sense.* Trans. Mark Lester with Charles Stivale. Ed. Constantin V. Boundas. New York: Columbia University Press.

Deleuze, Gilles. (1970a). "Faille et feux locaux: Kostas Axelos." *Critique* 55: 344–351.

Deleuze, Gilles. (1970b, 1981 [1988]). *Spinoza: Philosophie pratique.* Paris: Minuit. *Spinoza: Practical Philosophy.* Trans. Robert Hurley. San Francisco: City Lights.

Deleuze, Gilles. (1970c). "Schizologie." Preface in Louis Wolfson. *Le Schizo et les langues,* 5–23. Paris: Gallimard.

Deleuze, Gilles. (1972 [1977]). "Trois problèmes de groupe." In Guattari 1972, i–xi. "Three Group-Problems." Trans. Mark Seem. *Semiotext(e).* 2.3: 99–109.

Deleuze, Gilles. (1973a [1977, 1977, 1985]). "La Pensée nomade." In *Nietzsche aujourd'hui,* 1: 159–174. Paris: UGE, 10/18. "Nomad Thought." Trans. Jacqueline Wallace. *Semiotext(e)* 3.1: 12–21. Trans. David B. Allison. In *The New Nietzsche,* 142–149. Ed. David B. Allison. New York: Dell, Rpt., *The New Nietzsche.* Cambridge, MA: MIT Press.

Deleuze, Gilles. (1973b). "A quoi reconnaît-on le structuralisme?" In *Histoire de la Philosophie, Vol. 8: Le XXe siècle,* 299–335. Ed. François Châtelet. Paris: Hachette.

Deleuze, Gilles. (1973c [1977]; 1990 [1995]). "Lettre à Michel Cressole." Appendix to Cressole 1973, 107–118. " 'I Have Nothing to Admit.' " Trans. Janis Forman. *Semiotext(e)* 2.3: 111–116. Rpt. in Deleuze 1990 (1995) translated as "Letter to a Harsh Critic."

Deleuze, Gilles. (1981). *Francis Bacon: Logique de la sensation.* Paris: Editions de la différence.

Deleuze, Gilles. (1983 [1986]). *Cinéma 1: L'image-mouvement.* Paris: Minuit. *Cinema 1: The Movement-Image.* Trans. Hugh Tomlinson and Barbara Habberjam. Minneapolis: University of Minnesota Press.

Deleuze, Gilles. (1984). "Michel Tournier and the World without Others." Trans. Graham Burchell. *Economy and Society* 13.1: 52–71.

Deleuze, Gilles. (1985 [1989]). *Cinéma 2: L'image-temps.* Paris: Minuit. *Cinema 2: The Time-Image.* Trans. Hugh Tomlinson and Robert Galeta. Minneapolis: University of Minnesota Press.

Deleuze, Gilles. (1986 [1988]). *Foucault.* Paris: Minuit. Trans. Seàn Hand. Minneapolis: University of Minnesota Press.

Deleuze, Gilles. (1988 [1993]). *Le pli: Leibniz et le baroque.* Paris: Minuit. *The Fold. Leibniz and the Baroque.* Trans. Tom Conley. Minneapolis: University of Minnesota Press.

Deleuze, Gilles. (1990 [1995]). *Pourparlers.* Paris: Minuit. *Negotiations.* Trans. Martin Joughin. New York: Columbia University Press.

Deleuze, Gilles. (1992 [1995]). "L'épuisé." In Samuel Beckett and Gilles Deleuze. *"Quad" et "Trio du fantôme."* Paris: Minuit. "The Exhausted." Trans. Anthony Uhlmann. *SubStance* 78: 3–28. Rpt. in Deleuze (1993 [1997], 152–174).

Deleuze, Gilles. (1993 [1997]). *Critique et clinique.* Paris: Minuit. *Essays Critical and Clinical.* Trans. Daniel W. Smith and Michael A. Greco. Minneapolis: University of Minnesota Press.

Deleuze, Gilles. (1994). "Désir et plaisir." *Magazine littéraire* 325: 59–65. "Desire and Pleasure." Trans. Melissa McMahon. *Globe* 5. Online at http://www.arts. monash.edu.au/visarts/globe/ghome.html.

Deleuze, Gilles. (1995). "Le 'je me souviens' de Gilles Deleuze." *Le Nouvel observateur.* 16–22 Nov. 114–115.

Deleuze, Gilles, and Carmelo Bene. (1979). *Superpositions.* Paris: Minuit.

Deleuze, Gilles, and andre Cresson. (1952). *David Hume: Sa vie, son oeuvre.* Paris: PUF.

Deleuze, Gilles, and Félix Guattari. (1970). "La synthèse disjonctive." *L'Arc* 43:54–62.

Deleuze, Gilles, and Félix Guattari. (1972a, 1975 [1977, 1983]). *L'Anti-OEdipe,* Vol. 1 of *Capitalisme et schizophrénie.* Paris: Minuit. *Anti-Oedipus,* Vol. 1 of *Capitalism and Schizophrenia.* Trans. Robert Hurley, Mark Seem, and Helen Lane. New York: Viking. Rpt., Minneapolis: University of Minnesota Press.

Deleuze, Gilles, and Félix Guattari. (1972b, 1990 [1995]). "Sur capitalisme et schizophrénie." *L'Arc* 49: 47–55. Rpt. in Deleuze 1990, 24–38 [1995: 13–24].

Deleuze, Gilles, and Félix Guattari. (1973a). "Gilles Deleuze, Félix Guattari." In *C'est demain la veille,* 137–161. Paris: Seuil.

Deleuze, Gilles, and Félix Guattari. (1973b [1977]). "Bilan-programme pour machines désirantes." *Minuit* 2: 1–25. Rpt. in Deleuze and Guattari 1972a, 1975. "Balance Sheet-Program for Desiring Machines." Trans. Robert Hurley. *Semiotext(e)* 2.3: 117–135.

Deleuze, Gilles, and Félix Guattari. (1973c [1977]). "14 Mai 1914: Un où plusieurs loups?" *Minuit* 5: 2–16. "May 14, 1914: One or Several Wolves?" Trans. Mark Seem. *Semiotext(e)* 2.3: 137–147.

Deleuze, Gilles, and Félix Guattari. (1975 [1986]). *Kafka: Pour une littérature mineure.* Paris: Minuit. *Kafka: Toward a Minor Literature.* Trans. Dana Polan. Minneapolis: University of Minnesota Press.

Deleuze, Gilles, and Félix Guattari. (1976 [1983]). *Rhizome: Introduction.* Paris: Minuit. Trans. John Johnston. In Deleuze and Guattari 1983, 1–65.

Deleuze, Gilles, and Félix Guattari. (1980 [1987]). *Mille plateaux,* Vol. 2 of *Capitalisme et schizophrénie.* Paris: Minuit. Trans. Brian Massumi. Minneapolis: University of Minnesota Press.

Deleuze, Gilles, and Félix Guattari. (1983). *On the Line.* New York: Semiotext(e).

Deleuze, Gilles, and Félix Guattari. (1991 [1994]). *Qu'est-ce que la philosophie?* Paris: Minuit. *What Is Philosophy?* Trans. Hugh Tomlinson and Graham Burchell. New York: Columbia University Press.

Deleuze, Gilles, and Claire Parnet. (1977 [1987]). *Dialogues.* Paris: Flammarion. Trans. Hugh Tomlinson and Barbara Habberjam. New York: Columbia University Press.

Deleuze, Gilles, with Claire Parnet. (1996 [1988]). *L'Abécédaire de Gilles Deleuze.* Dir. Pierre-andré Boutang. Video Editions Montparnasse.

Dempsey, Michael. (1979–80). "*Apocalypse Now.*" *Sight and Sound* 49.1: 5–9.

Derrida, Jacques. (1967a [1973]). *La voix et le phénomène. Introduction au problème du signe dans la phénoménologie de Husserl.* Paris: PUF. *Speech and Phenomena, and Other Essays on Husserl's Theory of Signs.* Trans. David B. Allison. Evanston, IL: Northwestern University Press.

Derrida, Jacques. (1967b [1976]). *De la grammatologie.* Paris: Minuit. *of Grammatology.* Trans. Gayatri Chakravorty Spivak. Baltimore: Johns Hopkins University Press.

Derrida, Jacques. (1967c [1978]). *L'écriture et la différence.* Paris: Seuil. *Writing and Difference.* Trans. Alan Bass. Chicago: University of Chicago Press.

Derrida, Jacques. (1995). "Il me faudra errer tout seul." *Libération.* 7 Nov.: 37–38.

Dery, Mark, ed. (1994). *Flame Wars: The Discourse of Cyberculture.* Durham, NC: Duke University Press.

Dery, Mark. (1996). *Escape Velocity: Cyberculture at the End of the Century.* New York: Grove/Atlantic.

Descombes, Vincent. (1979 [1980]). *Le même et l'autre.* Paris: Minuit. *Modern French Philosophy.* Trans. L. Scott-Fox and J. M. Harding. New York: Cambridge University Press.

Desser, David. (1991). " 'Charlie Don't Surf': Race and Culture in the Vietnam War Films." In anderegg 1991, 81–102.

Dewey Balfa: The Tribute Concert. (1993). [No director indicated] Hartford, CT: Motion Inc.

Dibbell, Julian. (1993a). "Let's Get Digital: Writer à la Modem." *Village Voice Literary Supplement.* March: 13–14.

Dibbell, Julian. (1993b). "A Rape in Cyberspace." *Village Voice.* 21 Dec.: 36–42. Rpt. in Dery 1994, 237–261.

Dittmar, Linda, and Gene Michaud, eds. (1990). *From Hanoi to Hollywood: The Vietnam War in American Film.* New Brunswick, NJ: Rutgers University Press.

Doel, Marcus. (1995). "Bodies without Organs: Schizoanalysis and Deconstruction." In *Mapping the Subject: Geographies of Cultural Transformation,* 226–240. Eds. Steve Pile and Nigel Thrift. New York: Routledge.

Doel, Marcus. (1996). "A Hundred Thousand Lines of Flight: A Machinic Introduction to the Nomad Thought and Scrumpled Geography of Gilles Deleuze and Félix Guattari." *Society and Space* 14.4: 421–439.

Domenach, Jean-Marie. (1972). "Oedipe à l'usine." *L'Esprit* 40.12: 856–865.

Donawerth, Jane. (1990). "Utopian Science: Contemporary Feminist Science Theory and Science Fiction by Women." *National Women's Studies Association Journal* 2.4: 535–557.

Donzelot, Jacques. (1972 [1977]). "Une anti-sociologie." *L'Esprit* 40.12: 835–855. "An Anti-Sociology." Trans. Mark Seem. *Semiotext(e)* 2.3: 27–44.

Dorall, E. N. (1980). "Conrad and Coppola: Different Centres of Darkness." *Southeast Asian Review of English* 1.1: 19–26.

Dormon, James H. (1983). *The People Called Cajuns.* Lafayette: University of Southwestern Louisiana, Center for Louisiana Studies.

Dosse, François. (1991–1992 [1997]). *Histoire du structuralisme. Vol. 1: Le champ du signe, 1945–1966. Vol. 2, Le chant du cygne, de 1967 à nos jours.* Paris: La Découverte. *History of Stucturalism.* Vol. 1, *The Rising Sign, 1945–1966.* Vol. 2. *The Sign Sets, 1967–Present.* Trans. Deborah Glassman. Minneapolis: University of Minnesota Press.

Doyle, Richard. (1994). "Dislocating Knowledge, Thinking out of Joint: Rhizomatics, *Caenorhabditis elegans* and the Importance of Being Multiple." *Configurations* 2.1: 47–58.

During, Simon. (1987). "Postmodernism or Post-Colonialism Today." *Textual Practice* 1.1: 32–47.

Dwyer, Tessa. (1997). "Straining to Hear (Deleuze)." *South Atlantic Quarterly* 96.3: 543–562.

Dyer, Robert, and R. A. Brinkley. (1977). ". . . returns home (Mythologies, Dialectics, Structures): Disruptions." *Semiotext(e)* 2.3: 159–172.

Ebert, Teresa L. (1996). *Ludic Feminism and After.* Ann Arbor: University of Michigan Press.

Ecstavasia, Audrey. (1993). "Fucking (with Theory) for Money: Toward an Interrogation of Escort Prostitution." In Amiran and Unsworth 1993, 173–198.

Edwards, Paul N. (1990). "The Army and the Microworld: Computers and the Politics of Gender Identity." *Signs* 16.1: 102–127.

Elmer-Dewitt, Philip. (1993). "Cyberpunk!" *Time.* 8 Feb: 58–65.

Evans, Martha Noel. (1979). "Introduction to Jacques Lacan's Lecture: The Neurotic's Individual Myth." *Psychoanalytic Quarterly* 48.3: 386–404.

Faye, Jean-Pierre. (1964). *Analogues.* Paris: Seuil.

Faye, Jean-Pierre. (1972). *Langages totalitaires.* Paris: Hermann.

Faye, Jean-Pierre. (1995). " 'J'étouffe, je te rappellerai.' " *Libération.* 7 Nov.: 38.

Featherstone, Mike, and Roger Burrows. (1995). "Cultures of Embodiment: An Introduction." *Body and Society* 1.3–4: 1–20.

Featherstone, Mike, and Roger Burrows, eds. (1996). *Cyberspace/Cyberbodies/Cyberpunk.* Thousand Oaks, CA: Sage.

Fernandez, Enrique. (1986). "Damned Yankees: How Hollywood Fights the Good Fight." *Village Voice.* 2 Dec.: 73–74, 78.

Fiedler, Leslie. (1968). *The Return of the Vanishing American.* New York: Stein and Day.

Fikes, Jay Courtney. (1993). *Carlos Castaneda, Academic Opportunism and the Psychedelic Sixties.* Victoria, Canada: Millenia Press.

Fisher, Jeffery. (1997). "The Postmodern Paradiso: Dante, Cyberpunk, and the Technosophy of Cyberspace." In Porter 1997, 111–128.

Fitting, Peter. (1989). "Recent Feminist Utopias: World Building and Strategies for Social Change." In Slusser and Rabkin 1993, 155–163.

Fitting, Peter. (1991). "The Lessons of Cyberpunk." In Penley and Ross 1991a, 295–315.

Fitzgerald, F. Scott. (1956). *The Crack Up.* New York: New Directions.

Fleutiaux, Pierrette. (1976). *Histoire du gouffre et de la lunette.* Paris: Julliard.

Flieger, Jerry Aline. (1997). "Overdetermined Oedipus: Mommy, Daddy, and Me as Desiring-Machine." *South Atlantic Quarterly* 96.3: 599–619.

Flynn, Laurie. (1994). " 'Spamming' on the Internet Brings Fame and Fortune." *New York Times.* 16 Oct.: Business, 9.

Foster, Susan Leigh. (1992). "Dancing Bodies." In *Incorporations* 6: 480–495. Eds. Jonathan Crary and Sanford Kwinter. New York: Zone.

Foster, Thomas. (1993a). "Incurably Informed: The Pleasures and Dangers of Cyberpunk." *Genders* 18: 1–10.

Foster, Thomas. (1993b). "Meat Puppets or Robopaths?: Cyberpunk and the Question of Embodiment." *Genders* 18: 11–31.

Foucault, Michel. (1963 [1986]). *Raymond Roussel.* Paris: Gallimard. *Death and the Labyrinth: The World of Raymond Roussel.* Trans. Charles Ruas. Garden City, NY: Doubleday.

Foucault, Michel. (1966a [1970]). *Les mots et les choses.* Paris: Gallimard. *The Order of Things.* [No translator attributed.] New York: Vintage.

Foucault, Michel. (1966b [1987]). "La pensée du dehors." *Critique* 229: 523–546. Rpt. in Foucault 1994, 1: 518–539. Trans. Brian Massumi. In *Foucault/Blanchot,* 7–58. New York: Zone Books.

Foucault, Michel. (1969 [1972]). *L'archéologie du savoir.* Paris: Gallimard. *The Archeology of Knowledge.* Trans. A. M. Sheridan Smith. New York: Harper and Row.

Foucault, Michel. (1976 [1978]). *La volonté de savoir.* Paris: Gallimard. *The History of Sexuality.* Trans. Robert Hurley. New York: Pantheon Books.

Foucault, Michel. (1977). *Language, Counter-Memory, Practice.* Trans. Donald F. Bouchard and Sherry Simon. Ithaca, NY: Cornell University Press.

Foucault, Michel. (1994). *Dits et écrits.* 4 vols. Paris: Gallimard.

Fraiberg, Allison. (1993). "of AIDS, Cyborgs, and Other Indiscretions: Resurfacing the Body in the Postmodern." In Amiran and Unsworth, 37–55.

Fraser, Miriam. (1997). "Feminism, Foucault and Deleuze." *Theory, Culture, and Society* 14.2: 23–37.

Frazer, James G. (1922 [1960]). *The Golden Bough.* New York: Macmillan.

Fuchs, Cynthia J. (1991). " 'All the Animals Come Out at Night': Vietnam Meets Noir in *Taxi Driver.*" In anderegg 1991, 33–55.

Fuchs, Cynthia J. (1993). " 'Death Is Irrelevant': Cyborgs, Reproduction, and the Future of Male Hysteria." *Genders* 18: 113–133.

Furtos, J., and R. Roussillon. (1972). "*L'Anti-OEdipe*: Essai d'explication." *L'Esprit* 40.12: 817–834.

Fuss, Diana. (1989). *Essentially Speaking: Feminism, Nature and Difference.* New York: Routledge.

Gagnon, Madeleine. (1991). *L'instance orpheline.* Laval, Quebec: Editions Trois.

Garreau, Joseph. (1985). "Réflexions sur Michel Tournier." *French Review* 58.5: 682–691.

Gatens, Moira. (1996). "Through a Spinozist Lens: Ethology, Difference, Power." In Special Issue: Patton 1996, 162–187.

Genders. (1993). "Cyberpunk: Technologies of Cultural Identity." Vol. 18.

Genosko, Gary, ed. (1996). *The Guattari Reader.* Cambridge, MA: Blackwell Publishers.

Gibson, William. (1984). *Neuromancer.* New York: Ace.

Gibson, William. (1986a). *Burning Chrome.* New York: Ace.

Gibson, William. (1986b, 1987). *Count Zero.* New York: Ace.

Gibson, William. (1986c, 1988). "The Gernsback Continuum." In Sterling 1986a, 1–11.

Gibson, William. (1988). *Mona Lisa Overdrive.* New York: Bantam.

Gibson, William. (1989). "High Tech High Life." Interview with Timothy Leary. *Mondo 2000* 7: 58–64.

Gillespie, Gerald. (1985). "Savage Places Revisited: Conrad's *Heart of Darkness* and Coppola's *Apocalypse Now.*" *Comparatist* 9: 69–88.

Girard, Rene. (1972). "Système du délire." *Critique* 306: 957–996.

Godwin, Mike. (1994). "Canning Spam." *Internet World* 5.7: 97–99.

Godwin, Mike. (1995a). "Artist or Criminal?" *Internet World* 6.9: 96–100.

Godwin, Mike. (1995b). "alt.sex.academic.freedom." *Wired* 3.02: 72.

Godwin, Mike. (1995c). "Running Scared." *Internet World* 6.4: 96–98.

Goffman, Erving. (1986 [1974]). *Frame Analysis.* Boston: Northeastern University Press.

Goodchild, Philip. (1996a). *Gilles Deleuze and the Question of Philosophy.* Cranbury, NJ: Associated University Press.

Goodchild, Philip. (1996b). *Deleuze and Guattari: An Introduction to the Politics of Desire.* Thousand Oaks, CA: Sage.

Goodchild, Philip. (1997a). "Gilles Deleuze: A Symposium. Introduction." *Theory, Culture, and Society* 14.2: 1–2.

Goodchild, Philip. (1997b). "Deleuzean Ethics." *Theory, Culture, and Society* 14.2: 39–50.

Gordon, Joan. (1990). "Yin and Yang Out." *Science Fiction Eye* 2.1: 37–40.

Goulimari, Pelagia. (1993). "On the Line of Flight: How to Be a Realist?" *Angelaki* 1.1: 11–27.

Grant, Ian Hamilton. (1997). " 'At the Mountains of Madness': The Demonology of the New Earth and the Politics of Becoming." In Ansell-Pearson 1997, 93–114.

Gray, Chris Hables, ed. (1995). *The Cyborg Handbook.* New York: Routledge.

Green, andre. (1966). "L'objet (a) de J. Lacan, sa logique, et la théorie freudienne." *Cahiers pour l'analyse* 3: 15–37.

Greiff, Louis K. (1992). "Conrad's Ethics and the Margins of *Apocalypse Now.*" *Literature/Film Quarterly* 20.3: 189–198.

Griggers, Camilla. (1997). *Becoming-Woman.* Minneapolis: University of Minnesota Press.

Grisham, Therese. (1991). "Linguistics as an Indiscipline: Deleuze and Guattari's Pragmatics." *SubStance* 66: 36–54.

Grisoni, D.-A. (1983). "La philosophie comme Enfer." *Magazine littéraire* 196: 78.

Grossberg, Lawrence. (1983–1984). "The Politics of Youth Culture: Some Observations on Rock 'n' Roll in American Culture." *Social Text* 8: 104–126.

Grossberg, Lawrence. (1984a). "Another Boring Day in Paradise: Rock and Roll and the Empowerment of Everyday Life." *Popular Music* 4: 225–228. Rpt. in Grossberg 1997b, 29–63.

Grossberg, Lawrence. (1984b). "The Social Meaning of Rock and Roll." *One Two Three Four* 1: 13–21.

Grossberg, Lawrence. (1984c). " 'I'd rather feel bad than not feel anything at all': Rock and Roll, Pleasure, and Power." *enclitic* 8: 94–110. Rpt. in Grossberg 1997b, 64–88.

Grossberg, Lawrence. (1986a). "Is There Rock After Punk?" *Critical Studies in Mass Communication* 3: 50–74.

Grossberg, Lawrence. (1986b). "Teaching the Popular." In *Theory in the Classroom* 177–200. Ed. Cary Nelson. Urbana and Chicago: University of Illinois Press.

Grossberg, Lawrence. (1988). "Postmodernity and Affect: All Dressed Up with No Place to Go." *Communication* 10: 271–293. Rpt. in Grossberg 1997b, 145–165.

Grossberg, Lawrence. (1992). *We Gotta Get Out of This Place: Popular Conservatism and Postmodern Culture.* New York: Routledge.

Grossberg, Lawrence. (1993). "Cultural Studies and/in New Worlds." *Critical Studies in Mass Communications* 10: 1–22. Rpt. in Grossberg 1997a, 343–373.

Grossberg, Lawrence. (1996). "The Space of Culture, the Power of Space." In *The Post-Colonial Question: Common Skies, Divided Horizon* 169–188. Eds. Iain Chambers and Lidia Curti. London: Routledge.

Grossberg, Lawrence. (1997a). *Bringing It All Back Home: Essays on Cultural Studies.* Durham, NC: Duke University Press.

Grossberg, Lawrence. (1997b). *Dancing In Spite of Myself: Essays on Popular Culture.* Durham, NC: Duke University Press.

Grossberg, Lawrence, Cary Nelson, and Paula Treichler, eds. (1992) *Cultural Studies.* New York: Routledge.

Grosz, Elizabeth. (1994a). *Volatile Bodies: Toward A Corporeal Feminism.* Bloomington: Indiana University Press.

Grosz, Elizabeth. (1994b). "A Thousand Tiny Sexes: Feminism and Rhizomatics." In Boundas and Olkowski 1994, 187–210.

Grosz, Elizabeth. (1995). *Space, Time, and Perversion.* New York: Routledge.

Guattari, Félix. (1972). *Psychanalyse et transversalité.* Paris: François Maspero.

Guattari, Félix. (1974a). "Interview/Félix Guattari." With Mark D. Seem. *diacritics* 4.3: 38–41.

Guattari, Félix. (1974b, 1977 [1977]). "Micro-politique du désir." In *Psychanalyse et Politique,* 42–56. Paris: Seuil. Rpt. as "Micropolitique du fascisme" in Guattari 1977a; "Everybody Wants to Be a Fascist." Trans. Suzanne Fletcher. *Semiotext(e)* 2.3: 87–98. Rpt. in Guattari 1995, 233–250.

Guattari, Félix. (1977a). *La révolution moléculaire.* Fontenay-sous-Bois, France: Editions recherches.

Guattari, Félix. (1977b [1981a]). "J'ai même rencontré des travelos heureux." In

Guattari 1977a, 189–191. "I Have Even Met Happy Travelos." Trans. Rachel McComas. *Semiotext(e)* 4.1: 80–81.

Guattari, Félix. (1977c [1981b]). "Devenir femme." In Guattari 1977a, 196–200. "Becoming-Woman." Trans. Rachel McComas and Stamos Metzidakis. *Semiotext(e)* 4.1: 86–88.

Guattari, Félix. (1977d [1977]). "Mary Barnes ou l'OEdipe anti-psychiatrique." In Guattari 1977a, 125–135. "Mary Barnes' 'Trip.' " Trans. Ruth Ohayon. *Semiotext(e)* 2.3: 63–71. Rpt. in Guattari 1984, 51–59, and in Genosko 1996, 46–54.

Guattari, Félix. (1977e). "Freudo-Marxism." Trans. Janis Forman. *Semiotext(e)* 2.3: 73–75.

Guattari, Félix. (1977f). "Psycho-Analysis and Schizo-Analysis." Trans. Janis Forman. *Semiotext(e)* 2.3: 77–85. Rpt. as "The Best Capitalist Drug." In Guattari 1995, 209–224.

Guattari, Félix. (1979a). *L'inconscient machinique: Essais de schizo-analyse*. Fontenay-sous-Bois, France: Editions recherches.

Guattari, Félix. (1979b). "A Liberation of Desire." In *Homosexualities and French Literature*, 56–69. Eds. George Stambolian and Elaine Marks. Ithaca, NY: Cornell University Press. Rpt. in Genosko 1996, 204–214.

Guattari, Félix. (1980a). "The Proliferation of Margins." Trans. Richard Gardner and Sybil Walker. *Semiotext(e)* 3.3: 108–111.

Guattari, Félix. (1980b). "Why Italy?" Trans. John Johnston. *Semiotext(e)* 3.3: 234–237.

Guattari, Félix. (1984). *Molecular Revolution: Psychiatry and Politics*. New York: Penguin Books.

Guattari, Félix. (1985a). "Les rêves de Kafka." *change International* 3: 33–43.

Guattari, Félix. (1985b). "Entretien 1985: Félix Guattari." In Jean Oury et al., *Pratique de l'institutionnel et politique*, 45–83. Vigneux, France: Matrice. "Institutional Practice and Politics." Trans. Lang Baker. In Genosko 1996, 121–138.

Guattari, Félix. (1986a). *Les années d'hiver, 1980–1986*. Paris: Barrault.

Guattari, Félix. (1986b). "1985–Microphysique des pouvoirs et micropolitiques des désirs." In Guattari 1986a, 207–232. "Microphysics of Power/Micropolitics of Desire." Trans. John Caruana. In Genosko 1996, 172–181.

Guattari, Félix. (1989a). *Cartographies schizoanalytiques*. Paris: Editions Galilée.

Guattari, Félix. (1989b [1989c]). *Les trois écologies*. Paris: Editions Galilée. *The Three Ecologies*. Trans. Chris Turner. *New Formations* 8: 131–147.

Guattari, Félix. (1990). "*Ritornellos* and Existential Affects." *Discourse* 12.2: 66–81.

Guattari, Félix. (1992 [1995]). *Chaosmose*. Paris: Editions Galilée. *Chaosmosis*. Trans. Paul Bains and Julian Pefanis. Bloomington: Indiana University Press.

Guattari, Félix. (1995). *Chaosophy*. Ed. Sylvère Lotringer. New York: Semiotext(e).

Guattari, Félix. (1996). *Soft Subversions*. Ed. Sylvère Lotringer. New York: Semiotext(e).

Guattari, Félix, and Eric Alliez. (1983, 1986 [1984, 1996]). "Systèmes, structures et processus capitalistiques." In Guattari 1986a, 167–192. "Capitalistic Systems, Structures, and Processes." Trans. Brian Darling. In Guattari 1984, 273–287, and in Genosko 1996, 233–247.

Guattari, Félix, and Jean Oury. (1984). "Créativité et Folie." *Créativité et Folie: Actes sud* 1: 34–50.

Guattari, Félix, and Toni Negri. (1985 [1990]). *Les nouveaux espaces de liberté.* Paris: Editions Dominique Bédou. *Communists like Us.* Trans. Michael Ryan. New York: Semiotext(e).

Hagen, William H. (1981). "*Heart of Darkness* and the Process of *Apocalypse Now.*" *Conradiana* 113.1: 45–54.

Hagen, William H. (1983). "*Apocalypse Now* (1979): Joseph Conrad and the Television War." In *Hollywood as Historian: American Film in a Cultural Context,* 230–245. Ed. Peter C. Rollins. Lexington: University Press of Kentucky.

Halberstam, Judith and Ira Livingston, eds. (1995). *Posthuman Bodies.* Bloomington: Indiana University Press, 1995.

Hamman, Robin B. (1996). "Rhizome@Internet." Online at http://www.socio.demon.co.uk/rhizome.html.

Hand, Elizabeth. (1990). *Winterlong.* New York: Bantam.

Hand, Elizabeth. (1991). "Distant Fingers: Women Visionaries for the Fin-de-Millenaire." *Science Fiction Eye* 8: 31–36.

Hand, Elizabeth. (1992). *Aestival Tide.* New York: Bantam.

Hand, Elizabeth. (1993). *Icarus Descending.* New York: Bantam.

Hanna, Judith Lynne. (1979, 1987). *To Dance is Human: A Theory of Nonverbal Communication.* Chicago and London: University of Chicago Press.

Hanna, Judith Lynne. (1983). *The Performer–Audience Connection: Emotion to Metaphor in Dance and Society.* Austin: University of Texas Press.

Haraway, Donna. (1988). "Situated Knowledges: The Science Question in Feminism and the Privilege of Partial Perspective." *Feminist Studies* 14.3: 575–599. Rpt. in Haraway 1991b, 183–201.

Haraway, Donna. (1989). "The Biopolitics of Postmodern Bodies: Constitutions of Self in Immune System Discourse." *differences* 1.1: 3–43. Rpt. in Haraway 1991b, 203–230.

Haraway, Donna. (1990). "A Manifesto for Cyborgs." In *Feminism/Postmodernism,* 190–233. Ed. Linda J. Nicholson. New York and London: Routledge. Rprt. in Haraway 1991b, 149–181.

Haraway, Donna J. (1991a). "The Actors Are Cyborg, Nature Is Coyote, and the Geography Is Elsewhere: Postscript to 'Cyborgs at Large.' " In Penley and Ross 1991a, 21–26.

Haraway, Donna J. (1991b). *Simians, Cyborgs and Women: The Reinvention of Nature.* New York: Routledge.

Haraway, Donna J. (1997). *Modest_Witness@Second_Millenium. Female Man©_Meets_ OncoMouse™.* New York: Routledge.

Hardt, Michael. (1993). *Gilles Deleuze: An Apprenticeship in Philosophy.* Minneapolis: University of Minnesota Press.

Harris, Kristina. (1994). "Dousing Flames." *Internet World* 5.8: 42–44.

Hayles, N. Katherine. (1990). "Postmodern Parataxis: Embodied Texts, Weightless Information." *American Literary History* 2.3: 394–421.

Hayles, N. Katherine. (1992). "The Materiality of Informatics." *Configurations* 1.1: 147–170.

Hayles, N. Katherine. (1993a). "The Seductions of Cyberspace." In *Rethinking Technologies*, 173–190. Ed. Verena andermatt Conley. Minneapolis: University of Minnesota Press.

Hayles, N. Katherine. (1993b). "Virtual Bodies and Flickering Signifiers." *October* 66: 69–91.

Hayles, N. Katherine. (1997). "The Posthuman Body: Inscription and Incorporation in *Galatea 2.2* and *Snow Crash*." *Configurations* 5.2: 241–266.

Haynes, Cynthia. (1995). "pathos@play.prosthetic.emotion." *Works and Days* 25–26: 261–276. Online at http://acorn.grove.iup.edu/en/workdays/wdhome.html.

Hazzard-Gordon, Katrina. (1990). *Jookin': The Rise of Social Dance Formations in African-American Culture*. Philadelphia: Temple University Press.

Hearts of Darkness: A Filmmaker's Apocalypse. (1991). Dir. Fax Bahr with George Hickenlooper. Documentary footage by Eleanor Coppola. Triton.

Hellman, John. (1991). "Vietnam and the Hollywood Genre Film: Inversions of American Mythology in *The Deer Hunter* and *Apocalypse Now*." In anderegg 1991, 56–80.

Herr, Michael. (1968; 1978). *Dispatches*. New York: Avon.

Herring, Susan, ed. (1996). *Computer-Mediated Communication: Linguistic, Social, and Cross-Cultural Perspectives*. Amsterdam and Philadelphia: John Benjamins.

Hjelmslev, Louis. (1968). *Prolégomènes à une théorie du langage*. Paris: Minuit.

Hjelmslev, Louis. (1971). *Essais linguistiques*. Paris: Minuit.

Hocquenghem, Guy. (1977). "Family, Capitalism, Anus." Trans. Caithin and Tamsen Manning. *Semiotext(e)* 2.3: 149–158.

Holland, Eugene. (1987). " 'Introduction to the Non-Fascist Life': Deleuze and Guattari's 'Revolutionary' Semiotics." *L'Esprit créateur* 27.2: 19–29.

Holland, Eugene. (1993). *Baudelaire and Schizoanalysis*. Cambridge: Cambridge University Press.

Hopper, Dennis, and Quentin Tarantino. (1994). "Blood Lust Snicker Snicker in Wide Screen." *Grand Street* 14: 10–22.

Hot Pepper: The Life and Music of Clifton Chenier. (1973). Dir. Les Blank. Flower Films.

Irigaray, Luce. (1977 [1985]). "Quand nos lèvres se parlent." In *Ce sexe qui n'en est pas un*, 203–217. Paris: Minuit. "When Our Lips Speak Together." Trans. Catherine Porter. In *This Sex Which Is Not One*, 205–218. Ithaca, NY: Cornell University Press.

"Italy: Autonomia." (1980). Special issue of *Semiotext(e)* 3.3.

Ito, Mizuko. (1997). "Virtually Embodied: The Reality of Fantasy in a Multi-User Dungeon." In Porter 1997, 87–110.

Jacobs, Diane. (1981). "Coppola Films Conrad in Vietnam." In *The English Novel and the Movies*, 211–217. Eds. Michael Klein and Gillian Parker. New York: Frederick Unger.

J'ai été au bal: I Went to the Dance. The Cajun and Zydeco Music of Louisiana. (1989). Dir. Les Blank and Chris Strachwitz. Ed. Maureen Gosling. Narr. Barry Jean Ancelet and Michael Doucet. Brazos Films.

Jakobson, Roman. (1960). "Concluding Statement: Linguistics and Poetics." In *Style in Language*, 350–377. Ed. Thomas A. Sebeok. Cambridge, MA: MIT Press.

Jakobson, Roman, and Morris Halle. (1963, 1970 [1956]). "Phonologie et phonétique."

In *Essais de linguistique générale*, 103–149. Paris: Minuit; Points. "Phonetics and Phonologie." In *Fundamentals of Language*, 3–51. The Hague: Mouton.

Jameson, Fredric. (1979). *Fables of Aggression: Wyndham Lewis, the Modernist as Fascist.* Berkeley and Los Angeles: University of California Press.

Jameson, Fredric. (1991). *Postmodernism, or, The Cultural Logic of Capitalism.* Durham, NC: Duke University Press.

Jameson, Fredric. (1992). *Signatures of the Visible.* New York: Routledge.

Jameson, Fredric. (1997). "Marxism and Dualism." *South Atlantic Quarterly* 96.3: 393–416.

JanMohamed, Abdul R., & David Lloyd, eds. (1990). *The Nature and Context of Minority Discourse.* Oxford: Oxford University Press.

Jardine, Alice. (1985). *Gynesis: Configurations of Woman and Modernity.* Ithaca, NY: Cornell University Press.

Jardine, Alice. (1987). "of Bodies and Technologies." In *Discussions in Contemporary Culture*, 151–158. Ed. Hal Foster. Seattle: Bay Press.

Jeffords, Susan. (1985). "Friendly Civilians: Images of Women and the Feminization of the Audience in Vietnam Films." *Wide Angle* 7.4: 13–22.

Jones, Gwyneth. (1997). "The Neuroscience of Cyberspace: New Metaphors for the Self and Its Boundaries." In *The Governance of Cyberspace*, 46–63. Ed. Brian D. Loader. New York: Routledge.

Jones, Steven G., ed. (1995). *Cybersociety: Computer-Mediated Communication and Community.* Thousand Oaks, CA: Sage.

Jones, Steven G., ed. (1997). *Virtual Culture: Identity and Communication in Cybersociety.* Thousand Oaks, CA: Sage.

Jouary, Jean-Paul. (1995). "Les vagues de Deleuze." Online at http://www.regards.fr/archives/95/9512/9512ide05.html.

Joughin, Martin. (1990). "Translators Preface." In Deleuze 1968a [1990]. 5–11.

Journal of Computer-Mediated Communication. (1995). "Play and Performance in Computer-mediated Communication." 1.2. Online at http://shum.huji.ac.il/jcmc/vol1/issue2/vol1no2.html.

Joyce, Michael. (1995a). *of Two Minds: Hypertext Pedagogy and Poetic.* Ann Arbor: University of Michigan Press.

Joyce, Michael. (1995b). "MOO or mistakeness." *Works*

Jurek, Thom. (1991). Review of *Winterlong* by Elizabeth Hand. *Science Fiction Eye* 8: 100–102.

Kael, Pauline. (1987). "*The Big Easy.*" *The New Yorker.* 7 Sept.: 100.

Katz, Alyssa. (1994). "Modem Butterfly." *Village Voice.* 15 March: 39–40.

Kaveney, Roz. (1989). "The Science Fictiveness of Women's Science Fiction." In *From My Guy to Sci-Fi: Genre and Women's Writing in the Postmodern World* 78–97. Ed. Helen Carr. London: Unwin Hyman/Pandora.

Keil, Charles, and Angeliki V. Keil. (1992). *Polka Happiness.* With photographs by Dick Blau. Philadelphia: Temple University Press.

Kinder, Marsha. (1979–1980). "The Power of Adaptation in *Apocalypse Now.*" *Film Quarterly* 33.2: 12–20.

King, Katie. (1994). "Feminism and Writing Technologies: Teaching Queerish Travels Through Maps, Territories, and Pattern." *Configurations* 2.1: 89–106.

Kroker, Arthur. (1992). *The Possessed Individual.* New York: St. Martin's Press.

Kuhn, Thomas. (1970). *The Structure of Scientific Revolutions,* 2nd Ed. Chicago: University of Chicago Press.

Lacan, Jacques. (1953 [1979]). *Le Mythe Individuel Du Nevrosé.* Paris: C.D.U. "The Neurotic's Individual Myth." Trans. Martha Noel Evans. *The Psychoanalytic Quarterly* 48: 405–425.

Lacan, Jacques. (1966 [1977]). *Ecrits.* Paris: Seuil. *Ecrits: A Selection.* Trans. Alan Sheridan. New York: W. W. Norton.

Lacan, Jacques. (1972). "Seminar On 'The Purloined Letter.' " Trans. Jeffrey Mehlman. *Yale French Studies* 48: 38–72.

Laclau, Ernesto, and Chantal Mouffe. (1985). *Hegemony and Socialist Strategy: Towards A Radical Democratic Politics.* New York: Verso.

Lambert, Gregg. (1997). "The Deleuzean Critique of Pure Fiction." *SubStance* 84: 128–152.

Land, Nick. (1993a). "Machinic Desire." *Textual Practice* 7.3: 471–482.

Land, Nick. (1993b). "Making It With Death: Remarks On Thanatos and Desiring-Production." *Journal of the British Society for Phenomenology* 24.1: 66–76.

Land, Nick. (1995). "Meat (or How to Kill Oedipus in Cyberspace)." *Body and Society* 1.3–4: 191–204.

Landow, George P. (1994). *Hypertext: The Convergence of Contemporary Critical Theory and Technology.* Baltimore: Johns Hopkins University Press.

Landsberg, Alison. (1995). "Prosthetic Memory: *Total Recall* and *Blade Runner.*" *Body and Society* 1.3–4: 175–189.

Lang, Candace. (1995). "Body Language: The Resurrection of The Corpus In Text-Based Vr." *Works and Days* 25–26: 245–260. Online At Http://Acorn. Grove.Iup.Edu/En/Workdays/Wdhome.Html.

Laplanche, J., and J.-B. Pontalis. (1973). *The Language of Psychoanalysis.* London: Hogarth Press.

Laruelle, François. (1993). "Fragments of An Anti-Guattari." Trans. Charles Wolfe. *Long News in the Short Century* 4: 158–164.

Laurel, Brenda. (1991, 1993). *Computers As Theater.* Reading, Ma: Addison-Wesley.

Lautman, Albert. (1946). *Le Problème Du Temps.* Paris: Hermann.

Lecercle, Jean-Jacques. (1985). *Philosophy through the Looking Glass.* Lasalle, Il: Open Court.

Lecercle, Jean-Jacques. (1996). "The Pedagogy of Philosophy." *Radical Philosophy* 75: 44–46.

Leclaire, Serge. (1956, 1971 [1980]). "La mort dans la vie de l'obsédé." *La Psychana-lyse* 2: 111–140. Rpt. as "Jérôme; ou, la mort dans la vie de l'obsédé." In *Démasquer le réel,* 121–146. Paris: Seuil. "Jérôme; or, Death in the Life of the Obsessional." In *Returning to Freud: Clinical Psychoanalysis in the School of Lacan,* 94–113. Ed. and trans. Stuart Schneiderman. New Haven: Yale University Press.

Leclaire, Serge. (1958). "A la recherche des principes d'une psychothérapie des psychoses." *Evolution Psychiatrique* 2: [Pp. Not Available].

Leclaire, Serge. (1967). "Compter avec la psychanalyse." *Cahiers pour l'analyse* 8: 91–113.

Lefanu, Sarah. (1988, 1989). *Feminism and Science Fiction*. Bloomington: Indiana University Press.

Lefebvre, Henri. (1974 [1991]). *La production de l'espace*. Paris: Anthropos. *The Production of Space*. Trans. Donald Nicholson-Smith. Oxford and Cambridge: Blackwell.

Lefort, Gerard. (1995). "A Vincennes, un éveilleur à l'oral." *Libération*. 6 Nov.: 10.

Lévi-Strauss, Claude. (1949, 1967 [1969]). *Structures élémentaires de la parenté*. Paris: PUF. *The Elementary Structures of Kinship*. Trans. James Harle Bell and John Richard von Sturmer. Ed. Rodney Needham. Boston: Beacon Press.

Lévi-Strauss, Claude. (1950). "Introduction à l'oeuvre de Marcel Mauss." In *Marcel Mauss: Sociologie et anthropologie*, ix–lii. Paris: Puf.

Lévi-Strauss, Claude. (1958 [1963]). *Anthropologie structurale*. 2 Vols. Paris: Plon. *Structural Anthropology*. Trans. Claire Jacobson and Brooke Grundfest Schoepf. New York: Basic Books.

Lévi-Strauss, Claude. (1962 [1963]). *Le totémisme aujourd'hui*. Paris: Puf. *Totemism*. Trans. Rodney Needham. Boston: Beacon Press.

Lévi-Strauss, Claude. (1963). "Réponses à quelques questions." *Esprit* 33.11: 628–653.

Lévi-Strauss, Claude. (1964–1972 [1964]). *Le cru et le cuit*. 4 Vols. Paris: Plon. *The Raw and the Cooked*. 4 Vols. Trans. John and Doreen Weightman. New York: Harper and Row.

Lévy, Pierre. (1990). *Les technologies de l'intelligence*. Paris: La DéCouverte.

Lévy, Pierre. (1995a). *Qu'est-ce que le virtuel?* Paris: La DéCouverte.

Lévy, Pierre. (1995b). *L'intelligence collective: Pour une anthropologie du cyberspace*. Paris: La Découverte.

Lewis, J. Lowell. (1992). *Ring of Liberation: Deceptive Discourse In Brazilian Capoeira*. Chicago: University of Chicago Press.

Lewis, Jon. (1995). *Whom God Wishes To Destroy. . . . Francis Coppola and The New Hollywood*. Durham, Nc: Duke University Press.

Limón, José E. (1991). "Dancing with the Devil: Society, Gender, and the Political Unconscious in Mexican-American South Texas." In *Criticism in the Borderlands: Studies in Chicano Literature, Culture, and Ideology*. Eds. Héctor Calderón and José David Salivar. Durham, NC: Duke University Press.

Lindroth, James R. (1983). "The Subjective Insert: Tradition and Memory in Two Contemporary Films." *Perspectives on Contemporary Literature* 9: 114–123.

Lingis, Alphonso. (1994a). *Foreign Bodies*. New York: Routledge.

Lingis, Alphonso. (1994b). "The Society of Dismembered Body Parts." In Boundas and Olkowski 1994, 289–303.

Lipsitz, George. (1990). *Time Passages: Collective Memory and American Popular Culture*. Minneapolis: University of Minnesota Press.

Living Blues. (1991). 22.4 (July–August).

Lockard, Joseph. (1997). "Progressive Politics, Electronic Individualism, and The Myth of Virtual Community." In Porter 1997, 219–231.

Lotringer, Sylvere. (1977a). "Libido Unbound: The Politics of 'Schizophrenia.' " *Semiotext(E)* 2.3: 5–10.

Lotringer, Sylvere. (1977b). "The Fiction of Analysis." *Semiotext(e)* 2.3: 173–189.

Lotringer, Sylvere. (1980). "Proust polymorphe." *Poétique* 42: 170–176.

Louisiana Cajun and Creole Music. 1934: The Lomax Recordings. (1987). Swallow LP-8003-2.

Louisiane francophone: Lache pas la patate! (N.D.). Pics/University of Iowa.

Ludlow, Peter, ed. (1996). *High Noon on the Electronic Frontier: Conceptual Issues in Cyberspace.* Cambridge: MIT Press.

Lupton, Deborah. (1995). "The Embodied Computer/User." *Body and Society* 1.3–4: 97–112.

Lusitania. (1996). Issue 8: *Being Online: Net Subjectivity.* New York: Lusitania Press.

Lyotard, Jean-François. (1971). *Discours, figure.* Paris: Klincksieck.

Lyotard, Jean-François. (1972 [1977]). "Capitalisme énergumène." *Critique* 306: 923–956. "Energumen Capitalism." Trans. James Leigh. *Semiotext(e)* 2.3: 11–26.

Lyotard, Jean-François. (1986 [1992]). *Le postmoderne expliqué aux enfants.* Paris: Galilée. *The Postmodern Explained.* Trans. Don Barry, Bernadette Maher, Julian Pefanis, Virginia Spate, and Morgan Thomas. Minneapolis: University of Minnesota Press.

Lyotard, Jean-François. (1995). "Il était la bibliothèque de babel." *Libération.* 7 Nov.: 37.

Macaloon, John J. (1984). "Olympic Games and the Theory of Spectacle in Modern Societies." In *Rite, Drama, Festival, Spectacle: Rehearsals Toward a Theory of Cultural Performance,* 241–280. Ed. John J. MacAloon. Philadelphia: ISHI.

Macherey, Pierre. (1965). "A propos du processus d'exposition du capital." In Althusser et al. 1965b, 213–256.

Mackay, Robin. (1997). "Capitalism and Schizophrenia: Wildstyle in Full Effect." In Ansell-Pearson 1997c, 247–269.

Maclean, Kirstine Mairi. (1987). "Une clé pour Michel Tournier: La transcendence de la polarité binaire et l'accession à un domaine supérieur." *Degré second* 11: 51–58.

Maggiori, Robert. (1991). "Deleuze–Guattari: Nous Deux." *Libération.* 12 Sept.: 17–19.

Maggiori, Robert. (1992). "Félix, la vie rhizome." *Libération.* 31 Aug.: 31–33.

Maggiori, Robert. (1995). "Un 'courant d'air' dans la pensée du siücle." *Libération.* 6 Nov.: 8–10.

Mallarmé, Stephané. (1945). *Oeuvres complétes.* Ed. Henri Mondor and G. Jean-Aubry. Paris: Gallimard/Pléiade.

Marcus, Greil. (1979). "Journey Up the River." *Rolling Stone.* 1 Nov: 51–57.

Markley, Robert. (1996a). "Boundaries: Mathematics, Alienation, and the Metaphysics of Cyberspace." In Markley 1996b, 55–77.

Markley, Robert, Ed. (1996b). *Virtual Reality and Their Discontents.* Baltimore: Johns Hopkins University Press.

Marongiu, Jean-Baptiste, Marc Ragon, Judith Perrignon, Christian Hennion. (1992). "Un militant tout-terrain." *Libération.* 31 Aug.: 33.

Martin, Emily. (1996). "Citadels, Rhizomes, and String Figures." In Aronowitz et al. 1996, 97–109.

Martin, Jean-Clet. (1993). *Variations: La philosophie de Gilles Deleuze.* Paris: Payot.

Marvin, Lee-Ellen. (1995). "Spoof, Spam, Lurk and Lag: The Aesthetics of Text-

Based Virtual Realities." In Danet 1995. Online at http://shum.huji.ac.il/jcmc/vol1/issue2/vol1no2.html.

Mason, Carol. (1995). "Terminating Bodies: Toward a Cyborg History of Abortion." In Halberstam and Livingston 1995, 225–243.

Massumi, Brian. (1987). "Translator's Forward: Pleasures of Philosophy." In Deleuze and Guattari 1980, 1987, ix–xv.

Massumi, Brian. (1992). *A User's Guide to Capitalism and Schizophrenia*. Cambridge: Mit Press.

Massumi, Brian. (1996). "Becoming-Deleuzian." *Society and Space* 14.4: 395–406.

May, Todd. (1994). *The Political Philosophy of Poststructuralist Anarchism*. University Park: Pennsylvania State University Press.

May, Todd. (1997). *Reconsidering Difference*. University Park: Pennsylvania State University Press.

McCaffery, Larry. (1988). "The Desert of the Real: The Cyberpunk Controversy." *Mississippi Review* 16.2–3: 7–15.

McCaffery, Larry, Ed. (1990). *Across The Wounded Galaxies: Interviews with Contemporary American Science Fiction Writers*. Urbana and Chicago: University of Illinois Press.

McCaffery, Larry. (1991a). "Introduction: The Desert of The Real." In McCaffery 1991b, 1–16.

McCaffery, Larry, Ed. (1991b). *Storming the Reality Studio: A Casebook of Cyberpunk and Postmodern Science Fiction*. Durham, Nc: Duke University Press.

McCaffery, Larry. (1992). "Skating across Cyberpunk's Brave New Worlds: An Interview with Lewis Shiner." *Critique* 33.3: 177–196.

McCarron, Kevin. (1995). "Corpses, Animals, Machines and Mannequins: The Body and Cyberpunk." *Body and Society* 1.3–4: 261–273.

McCarthy, Paul. (1992). "Postmodern Pleasure and Perversity: Scientism and Sadism." *Postmodern Culture* 2.3. Online at http://muse.jhu.edu/postmodern_culture/archive.html.

McHale, Brian. (1992). "Elements of a Poetics of Cyberpunk." *Critique* 33.3: 149–175.

McRrae, Shannon. (1997). "Flesh Made Word: Sex, Text and the Virtual Body." In Porter 1997, 73–86.

Mehlman, Jeffrey. (1972). "Portnoy in Paris." *diacritics* 2.4: 21–28.

Menser, Michael. (1996). "Becoming-Heterarch: On Technocultural Theory, Minor Science, and the Production of Space." In Aronowitz et al., 293–316.

Millard, William. (1995). " 'A Great Flame Follows a Little Spark': Metaflaming, Function of the 'Dis,' and Conditions of Closure in the Rhetoric of a Discussion List." *Works and Days* 25–26: 137–150. Online at http://acorn.grove.iup.edu/en/workdays/wdhome.html.

Millard, William. (1997). "I Flamed Freud: A Case Study in Teletextual Incendiarism." In Porter 1997, 145–159.

Miller, Christopher. (1993). "The Postidentitarian Predicament in the Footnotes of *A Thousand Plateaus*: Nomadology, Anthropology, and Authority." *diacritics* 23.3: 6–35.

Miller, J.-A. (1966 [1977–78]). "La suture (éléments de la logique du signifiant)."

Cahiers pour l'analyse 1-2: 39-51. "Suture (elements of the logic of the signifier)." Trans. Jacqueline Rose. *Screen* 18.4: 24-34.

Miller, J. Hillis. (1985). "*Heart of Darkness* Revisited." In *Conrad Revisited: Essays for the Eighties,* 31-50. Ed. Ross C. Murfin. University: University of Alabama Press.

Miller, Joseph D. (1989). "Neuroscience Fiction: The Roman à Synaptic Cleft." In Slusser and Rabkin 1989, 195-207.

Millett, Nick. (1997). "The Trick of Singularity." *Theory, Culture and Society* 14.2: 51-66.

Mohanty, Satya P. (1993). "The Epistemic Status of Cultural Identity: On Beloved and The Postcolonial Condition." *Cultural Critique* 24: 41-80.

Montesquieu. (1973 [1721]). *Persian Letters.* Trans. C. J. Betts. Baltimore: Penguin. Trans. of *Les lettres persanes.*

Moore, Lisa. (1995). "Teledildonics: Virtual Lesbians in the Ficton of Jeanette Winterson." In *Sexy Bodies,* 104-127. Eds. Elisabeth Grosz and Elspeth Probyn. New York: Routledge.

Morris, Meaghan. (1992). "*On the Beach.*" In Grossberg et al. 1992, 450-473.

Morris, Meaghan. (1996). "Crazy Talk Is Not Enough." *Society and Space* 14.4: 384-394.

Morton, Donald. (1995). "Birth of the Cyberqueer." *PMLA* 110.3: 369-381.

Moulthrop, Stuart. (1994). "Rhizome and Resistance: Hypertext and the Dreams of a New Culture." In Landow 1994, 299-319.

Muecke, Stephen. (1984). "The Discourse of Nomadology: Phylums in Flux." *Art and Text* 14: 24-40.

Mullarkey, John. (1997). "Deleuze and Materialism: One or Several Matters." *South Atlantic Quarterly* 96.3: 439-463.

Murphy, Timothy S. (1996). "Bibliography of the Works of Gilles Deleuze." In Patton 1996, 270-300.

Murphy, Timothy S. (1997). *Wising Up the Marks: The Amodern William Burroughs.* Berkeley: University of California Press.

Murray, David. (1981). "Anthropology, Fiction, and the Occult: The Case of Carlos Castaneda." In *Literature of the Occult,* 171-182. Ed. Peter B. Messent. Englewood Cliffs, Nj: Prentice-Hall.

Musique En Jeu 5. (1971).

Nakamura, Lisa. (1995). "Race In/For Cyberspace: Identity Tourism and Racial Passing on the Internet." *Works and Days* 25-26: 181-194. Online at http://acorn.grove.iup.edu/en/workdays/wdhome.html.

Nancy, Jean-Luc. (1995). "Du sens, dans tous les sens." *Libération.* 7 Nov.: 36.

Negri, Toni. (1983). "Un philosophe en permission." *change International* 1: 62-64.

Negri, Toni. (1993). "For Félix Guattari." Trans. Virgilio Rizzo. *Long News in the Short Century* 4: 156-157.

Negri, Toni. (1996). "1972. Deleuze, Guattari/*L'Anti-Oedipe*: La machine désirante." *1966-1996, la passion des idées: Magazine littéraire* (hors-série) 36-39.

Nelson, Cary. (1991). "Always Already Cultural Studies: Two Conferences and a Manifesto." *Journal of The Midwest Modern Language Association* 24.1: 24-38. Rpt. In Nelson 1997, 52-74.

Nelson, Cary. (1997). *Manifesto of a Tenured Radical.* New York: New York University Press.

Nettlebeck, Colin. (1984). "The Return of the Ogre: Michel Tournier's *Gilles et Jeanne.*" *Scripsi* 2.4: 43–50.

Noel, Daniel C. (1976). *Seeing Castaneda.* New York: Putnam's.

Noir, Michel. (1984). *1988: Le grand rendez-vous.* Paris: Lattès.

Noyes, John. (1989). "The Capture of Space: An Episode in a Colonial Story by Hans Grimm." *Pretexts* 1.1: 52–63.

Nunes, Mark. (in press). "Virtual Topographies: Smooth and Striated Space." In *Cyberspace Textuality.* Ed. Marie-Laure Ryan. Bloomington: Indiana University Press. Forthcoming.

Ortigues, Edmond. (1962). *Le discours et le symbole.* Paris: Aubier.

O'toole, Robert. (1997). "Contagium vivum philosophia: Schizophrenic Philosophy, Viral Empiricism, and Deleuze." In Ansell-Pearson 1997, 163–179.

Oury, Jean. (1992). "Jean Oury: 'Un chantier permanent.' " *Libération.* 31 Aug.: 35.

Pallez, Frederic. (1995). "Ordeal By Abandonment: Absence and Simulation in the Techno-Age." *Works and Days* 25–26: 287–305. Online at http://acorn. grove.iup.edu/en/workdays/wdhome.html.

Patton, Paul. (1981). "Notes For A Glossary." *I & C* 8: 41–48.

Patton, Paul. (1984). "Conceptual Politics and the War-Machine in *Mille Plateaux.*" *SubStance* 44–45: 61–80.

Patton, Paul. (1996). *Deleuze: A Critical Reader.* Cambridge, Ma: Blackwell Publishers.

Pavel, Thomas. (1992). "Les études culturelles: une nouvelle discipline?" *Critique* 545: 731–742.

Pelias, Michael. (1993). "In the Wake of Three Pillars." *Long News In The Short Century* 4: 180–183.

Peña, Manuel H. (1985). *The Texas–Mexican Conjunto: History of a Working-Class Music.* Austin: University of Texas Press.

Penley, Constance, and andrew Ross, Eds. (1991a). *Technoculture.* Minneapolis: University of Minnesota Press.

Penley, Constance, and Andrew Ross. (1991b). "Cyborgs at Large: Interview with Donna Haraway." In Penley and Ross 1991a, 1–20.

Perez, Rolando. (1990). *On An(archy) and Schizoanalysis.* New York: Autonomedia.

Perry, Ruth, and Lisa Greber. (1990). "Women and Computers: An Introduction." *Signs* 16.1: 74–101.

Petit, Susan. (1985). "*Gilles et Jeanne*: Tournier's *Le roi des Aulnes* Revisited." *Romanic Review* 76.3: 307–315.

Pfeil, Fred. (1990). "The Disintegrations I'm Looking Forward To: Science Fiction from New Wave to New Age." In *Another Tale to Tell: Politics and Narrative in Postmodern Culture.* 83–94. London and New York: Verso.

Pfister, Joel. (1992). "The Americanization of Cultural Studies." *Yale Journal of Criticism* 4.2: 199–229.

Pierssens, Michel. (1973). "L'appareil sériel." *Change* 16–17: 265–285.

Pierssens, Michel. (1975). "Gilles Deleuze: Diabolus in Semiotica." *Mln* 90.4: 497–503.

Pinsker, Sanford. (1981). "*Heart of Darkness* Through Contemporary Eyes; or, What's Wrong with *Apocalypse Now?*" *Conradiana* 13.1: 55–58.

Plant, Sadie. (1995). "The Future Looms: Weaving Women and Cybernetics." *Body and Society* 1.3–4: 45–64.

Plant, Sadie. (1997). *Zeros + Ones: Digital Women + the New Technoculture.* New York: Doubleday.

Plater, Ormonde, and Cynthia and Rand Speyrer. (1993). *Cajun Dancing.* Gretna, LA: Pelican Publishing.

Porter, David, Ed. (1997). *Internet Culture.* New York: Routledge.

Porush, David. (1994). "Hacking the Brainstem: Postmodern Metaphysics and Stephenson's *Snow Crash.*" *Configurations* 2.3: 537–571. Rpt. In Markley 1996a. 107–142.

Poster, Mark. (1989). *Critical Theory and Poststructuralism: In Search of a Context.* Ithaca, NY: Cornell University Press.

Poster, Mark. (1990). *The Mode of Information: Poststructuralism and Social Context.* Chicago: University of Chicago Press.

Poster, Mark. (1995). "Postmodern Virtualities." *Body and Society* 1.3–4: 79–95.

Poster, Mark. (1997). "Cyberdemocracy: Internet and the Public Sphere." In Porter 1997, 201–218.

Potter, Russel A. (1992). "Edward Schizohands: The Postmodern Gothic Body." *Postmodern Culture* 2.3. Online at http://muse.jhu.edu/journals/postmodern_culture/archive.html.

Pouillon, Jean. (1956). "L'oeuvre de Claude Lévi-Strauss." *Les temps modernes* 126: 150–173.

Pozzi, Lucio. (1993). "The Time Queen." *Long News in the Short Century* 4: 165–170.

Prigogine, Ilya, and Isabelle Stengers. (1979 [1984]). *La Nouvelle Alliance: Métamorphose de la science.* Paris: Gallimard. *Order Out of Chaos: Man's New Dialogue with Nature.* [Trans. not indicated.] New York: Bantam.

Probyn, Elspeth. (1992). "Technologizing the Self: A Future Anterior for Cultural Studies." In Grossberg et al. 1992, 501–511.

Probyn, Elspeth. (1996). *Outside Belongings.* New York: Routledge.

Proust, Marcel. (1954). *A la recherche du temps perdu.* 3 Vols. Paris: Gallimard/Pléiade.

Pym, John. (1979–80). "Apocalypse Now: An Errand Boy's Journey." *Sight and Sound* 49.1: 9–10.

Queau, Philippe. (1993). *Le virtuel: Vertus et vertiges.* Seyssel, France: Champ Vallon.

Rajchman, John. (1977). "Analysis in Power." *Semiotext(e)* 2.3: 45–58.

Rapaport, Herman. (1984). "Vietnam: The Thousand Plateaus." In *The Sixties without Apologies,* 137–147. Eds. Sohnya Sayres et al. Minneapolis: University of Minnesota Press.

Reed, Revon. (1976). *Lâche pas la patate: Portrait des Acadiens de la Louisiane.* Ottawa, Canada: Editions Parti Pris.

Reed, Revon, Paul Tate, and Kathy Bihm. (1969). "The Voice in the Soul of Cajun Music." *Louisiana Heritage* 1.4: 14–15.

Rheingold, Howard. (1991). *Virtual Reality.* New York: Simon and Schuster.

Rheingold, Howard. (1993). *The Virtual Community.* Reading, MA: Addison-Wesley.

Riley, Brooks. (1979). " 'Heart' Transplant." *Film Comment* 15.5: 26–27.

Riley, Steve, and the Mamou Playboys. (1993). *Trace of Time.* Rounder Records C-6053.

Rimbaud, Arthur. (1972). *Oeuvres complètes.* Paris: Gallimard.

Robins, Kevin. (1995). "Cyberspace and the World We Live In." *Body and Society* 1.3–4: 135–155.

Rodowick, D. N. (1997). *Gilles Deleuze's Time Machine*. Durham, NC: Duke University Press.

Rosello, Mireille. (1989). "Jésus, Gilles et Jeanne: 'Qui veut noyer son chien est bien content qu'il ait la rage.' " *Stanford French Review* 13.1: 81–95.

Rosello, Mireille. (1990). *L'in-différence chez Michel Tournier*. Paris: Corti.

Rosenberg, Martin E. (1993). "Dynamic and Thermodynamic Tropes of the Subject in Freud and in Deleuze and Guattari." *Postmodern Culture* 4.1. Online at http://muse.jhu.edu/journals/postmodern_culture/archive.html.

Rosenberg, Martin E. (1994). "Physics and Hypertext: Liberation and Complicity in Art and Pedagogy." In Landow 1994, 268–298.

Rosenthal, Pam. (1991). "Jacked In: Fordism, Cyberpunk, Marxism." *Socialist Review* 21.1: 79–103.

Ross, Andrew. (1990). "Hacking Away at the Counterculture." *Postmodern Culture* 1.1. Online at http://muse.jhu.edu/journals/postmodern_culture/archive.html. Rpt. In Penley & Ross 1991a. 107–134.

Ross, Andrew. (1991a). "Getting Out of the Gernsback Continuum." *Critical Inquiry* 17.2: 411–433.

Ross, Andrew. (1991b). "Getting the Future We Deserve." *Socialist Review* 21.1: 125–150.

Ross, Andrew. (1991c). *Strange Weather*. New York: Routledge.

Roudinesco, Elisabeth. (1992). "*Anti-Oedipe* chez les psy." *Libération*. 31 Aug.: 34.

Rucker, Rudy. (1982). *Software*. New York: Avon.

Rucker, Rudy. (1988). *Wetware*. New York: Avon.

Rucker, Rudy. (1989a). "Mutations in the 4th Dimension." Interview with Faustin Bray. *Mondo 2000* 7: 74–78.

Rucker, Rudy. (1997). *Freeware*. New York: Avon.

Rucker, Rudy, Peter Lamborn Wilson, and Robert Anton Wilson, eds. (1989). *"SF" Semiotext(e)* 5.2.

Saper, Craig. (1991). "Electronic Media Studies: From Video Art to Artificial Invention." *SubStance* 66: 114–134.

Saussure, Ferdinand de. (1915, 1972 [1966]). *Cours de linguistique générale*. Lausanne and Paris: Payot. *Course in General Linguistics*. Trans. Wade Baskin. New York: McGraw-Hill.

Savoy, Ann Allen. (1984). *Cajun Music: A Reflection of a People,* Vol. 1. Eunice, LA: Bluebird Press.

Savoy, Marc. (1988). "Maintaining Traditions." *Louisiana Folk Life* 12: 9–12.

Sawhney, Deepak Narang. (1997). "Palimpsest: Towards a Minor Literature in Monstrosity." In Ansell-Pearson 1997c, 130–146.

Schickel, Richard. (1987). "Deep City Blues in New Orleans." *Time*. 24 Aug.: 65.

Schwab, Gabriele. (1989). "Cyborgs and Cybernetic Intertexts: On Postmodern Phantasms of Body and Mind." In *Intertextuality and Contemporary American Fiction*, 191–213. Eds. Patrick O'Connell and Robert Con Davis. Baltimore: Johns Hopkins University Press.

Searle, John. (1969). *Speech Acts: An Essay in the Philosophy of Language*. Cambridge, UK: Cambridge University Press.

Searle, John. (1983). *Intentionality: An Essay in the Philosophy of Mind*. Cambridge, UK: Cambridge University Press.

Séglard, Dominique. (1988). "Bibliographie." *Magazine littéraire* 257: 64–65.

Senft, Theresa M. (1996). "Introduction: Performing the Digital Body: A Ghost Story." *Women and Performance* 17. Online at http://www.echonyc.com/~women/Issue17/introduction.html.

Serres, Michel. (1977). *La naissance de la physique dans le texte de Lucrèce. Fleuves et turbulences.* Paris: Minuit.

Severn, Rhonda Case. (1991). *Discovering Acadiana.* 2 Videocassettes.

Sharrett, Christopher. (1985–86). "Intertextuality and the Breakup of Codes: Coppola's *Apocalypse Now.*" *Sacred Heart University Review* 6: 20–39.

Shaviro, Steven. (1988). "A chacun ses sexes: Deleuze and Guattari's Theory of Sexuality." *Discours Social/Social Discourse* 1.3: 287–299.

Shaviro, Steven. (1993). *The Cinematic Body.* Minneapolis: University of Minnesota Press.

Shaviro, Steven. (1995a). *Doom Patrols.* Online at http://www.dhalgren.com/doom/index.html

Shaviro, Steven. (1995b). "Two Lessons from Bouroughs." In Halberstam and Livingston 1995, 38–54.

Shepard, Lucius. (1989). "Waiting for the Barbarians." *Journal Wired* (Winter): 107–118.

Shichtman, Martin B. (1984). "Hollywood's New Weston: The Grail Myth in Francis Ford Coppola's *Apocalypse Now* and John Boorman's *Excalibur.*" *Post Script* 4.1: 35–48.

Shields, Rob, Ed. (1996). *Cultures of Internet.* Thousand Oaks, Ca: Sage.

Shirley, John. (1985). *Eclipse.* New York: Popular Library.

Shirley, John. (1988a). *Eclipse Penumbra.* New York: Popular Library.

Shirley, John. (1988b). "Wolves of the Plateau." *Mississippi Review* 16.2–3: 136–150. Rpt. In *Heatseeker,* 346–364.

Shirley, John. (1989a). "Beyond Cyberpunk: The New SF Underground." *Science Fiction Eye* 1.5: 30–43.

Shirley, John. (1989b). "Call It . . . Revolutionary Parasitism." Interview with Judith Milhon. *Mondo 2000* 7: 88–92.

Shirley, John. (1990a). *Eclipse Corona.* New York: Popular Library.

Shirley, John. (1990b). *Heatseeker.* London: Grafton Books.

Shirley, John. (1996). "A Walk Through Beirut." In *The Exploded Heart,* 261–290. Asheville, NC: Eyeball Books.

Shirley, John, Jack Williamson, Norman Spinrad, and Gregory Benford. (1987). "Cyberpunk or Cyberjunk? Some Perspectives on Recent Trends in SF." *Science Fiction Eye* 1.1: 43–51.

Slobin, Mark. (1993). *Subcultural Sounds: Micromusics of the West.* Hanover, NH: Wesleyan University Press/University Press of New England.

Slusser, George E., and Eric S. Rabkin, eds. (1989). *Mindscapes: The Geographies of Imagined Worlds.* Carbondale and Edwardsville: Southern Illinois University Press.

Smith, Stephanie A. (1993). "Morphing, Materialism, and the Marketing of *Xenogenesis.*" *Genders* 18: 67–86.

Sobchack, Vivian. (1995). "Beating the Meat/Surviving the Text, or How to Get Out of This Century Alive." *Body and Society* 1.3–4: 205–214.

Sollers, Philippe. (1965). *Drame*. Paris: Seuil.

Sondheim, Alan, Ed. (1996). *Being On Line: Net Subjectivity. Lusitania* 8.

Spinrad, Norman. (1990). *Science Fiction in the Real World*. Carbondale and Edwardsville: Southern Illinois University Press.

Spivak, Gayatri Chakravorty. (1976). "Translator's Preface." In Derrida 1967b [1976]. ix–lxxxvii.

Sponsler, Claire. (1992). "Cyberpunk and the Dilemmas of Postmodern Narrative: The Example of William Gibson." *Contemporary Literature* 33.4: 625–644.

Sponsler, Claire. (1993). "Beyond the Ruins: The Geopolitics of Urban Decay and Cybernetic Play." *Science-Fiction Studies* 20: 251–265.

Stephane, Andre. (1972). "La fin d'un malentendu." *Contrepoint* 7–8: 239–250.

Sterling, Bruce. (1985). *Schismatrix*. New York: Arbor House.

Sterling, Bruce. (1986, 1988). "Preface." In Sterling 1988a. ix–xvi.

Sterling, Bruce. (1988b, 1989). *Islands in the Net*. New York: Ace.

Sterling, Bruce. (1989a). "Catscan: Slipstream." *Science Fiction Eye* 1.5: 77–80.

Sterling, Bruce. (1989b). "Coming In under the Radar." *Mondo 2000* 7: 98–101.

Sterling, Bruce, Ed. (1988a). *Mirrorshades: The Cyberpunk Anthology*. New York: Ace.

Stewart, Garrett. (1981). "Coppola's Conrad: The Repetitions of Complicity." *Critical Inquiry* 7.3: 455–474.

Stivale, Charles J. (1981). "Gilles Deleuze and Félix Guattari: Schizoanalysis and Literary Discourse." *Substance* 29: 46–57.

Stivale, Charles J. (1984a). "Introduction." *Substance* 44–45: 3–6.

Stivale, Charles J. (1984b). "The Literary Element in *Mille Plateaux*: The New Cartography of Deleuze and Guattari." *Substance* 44–45: 20–34.

Stivale, Charles J. (1984c). "The Machine at the Heart of Desire: FéLix Guattari's *Molecular Revolution*." *Works and Days* 4: 63–85. Online at http://jefferson.village.virginia.edu:80/spoons/d-g_html/d-gpapers.html.

Stivale, Charles J. (1991a). "Nomad-Love and the War-Machine: Michel Tournier's *Gilles et Jeanne*." *Substance* 66: 44–59.

Stivale, Charles J. (1991b). "Introduction: Actuality and Concepts." *SubStance* 66: 3–9.

Stivale, Charles J. (1991c). "Mille/Punks/Cyber/Plateaus: Science Fiction and Deleuzo–Guattarian 'Becomings.' " *Substance* 66: 66–84.

Stivale, Charles J. (1993). "Pragmatic/Machinic: Discussion with Félix Guattari (19 March 1985)." *Pre/Text* 14.3–4.: 215–250.

Stivale, Charles J. (1994). " 'Spaces of Affect': Versions and Visions of Cajun Cultural History." *South Central Review* 11.4: 15–25.

Stivale, Charles J. (1995). " 'This Funny Chemistry': Narrative Desire and Discourse In Text-Based Virtual Reality." *Works and Days* 25–26: 7–27. Online at http://acorn.grove.iup.edu/en/workdays/wdhome.html.

Stivale, Charles J. (1996a). "Cyber/Inter/Mind/Assemblage." In Sondheim 1996, 119–125.

Stivale, Charles J. (1996b, 1997a). " 'Spam': Heteroglossia and Harassment in Cyberspace." *Readerly/Writerly Texts* 3.2: 79–93. Rpt. in Porter 1997, 133–144.

Stivale, Charles J. (1997b). " 'Help Manners': Cyberdemocracy and Its Vicissitudes." *Enculturation* 1. Online at http://www.uta.edu/huma/enculturation.

Stivale, Charles J. (1997c). "L'Abécédaire de Gilles Deleuze, avec Claire

Parnet/Gilles Deleuze's ABC Primer—A Summary." Online at http://www. langlab.wayne.edu/romance/FreDdeleuze.Html.

Stoll, Clifford. (1995). *Silicon Snake Oil*. New York: Anchor/Doubleday.

Stone, Allucquère Roseanne. (1991). "Will the Real Body Please Stand Up?: Boundary Stories about Virtual Cultures." In Benedikt 1991, 81–118.

Stone, Allucquère Roseanne. (1992). "Virtual Systems." *Incorporations* 6: 609–621. Eds. Jonathan Crary and Sanford Kwinter. New York: Zone.

Stone, Allucquère Roseanne. (1995). *The War of Desire and Technology at the Close of the Mechanical Age*. Cambridge, MA: MIT Press.

Strate, Lance, et al., eds. (1996). *Communication and Cyberspace*. Creskill, NJ: Hampton Press.

Stratton, Jon. (1997). "Cyberspace and the Globalization of Culture." In Porter 1997, 253–275.

Sundelson, David. (1981). "Danse Macabre." *Conradiana* 13.1: 41–44.

Surin, Kenneth. (1995). "On Producing the Concept of a Global Culture." *South Atlantic Quarterly* 94.4: 1179–1199.

Surin, Kenneth. (1997). "The 'Epochality' of Deleuzean Thought." *Theory, Culture, and Society* 14.2: 9–22.

Sussman, Gerald. (1992). "Bulls in the (Indo)China Shop: Coppola's 'Vietnam' Revisited." *Journal of Popular Film and Television* 20.1: 24–28.

Tabbi, Joseph. (1997). "Reading, Writing, Hypertext: Democratic Politics in the Virtual Classroom." In Porter 1997, 233–252.

Tarantino, Quentin, dir. (1991). *Reservoir Dogs*. Miramax.

Tarantino, Quentin. (1994). *"Reservoir Dogs," "True Romance."* New York: Grove.

Tatsumi, Takayuki. (1990). "Eye to Eye with Connie Willis." *Science Fiction Eye* 2.2: 55–60.

Taubin, Amy. (1992). "The Men's Room." *Sight and Sound* 2.8: 2–4.

Taylor, Alan. (1997). "Deleuze and Guattari on the Web." Online at http://www.uta.edu/english/apt/d&g/d&gweb.html.

Theweleit, Klaus. (1987, 1989). *1. Male Fantasies: Women, Floods, Bodies, History. 2. Male Fantasies. Males Bodies: Psychoanalyzing the White Terror*. Minneapolis: University of Minnesota Press.

Thomas, Jean-Jacques. (1992). "Poststructuralism and the New Humanism." *Substance* 68: 61–76.

Todorov, Tzvetan, et al. (1968 [1981]). *Qu'est-ce que le structuralisme? Poétique*. Paris: Seuil. *Introduction to Poetics*. Trans. Richard Howard. Minneapolis: University of Minnesota Press.

Tomas, David. (1991, 1992). "Old Rituals for New Space: *Rites de Passage* and William Gibson's Cultural Model of Cyberspace." In Benedikt 1991, 1992, 31–47.

Tomas, David. (1995). "Feedback and Cybernetics: Reimaging the Body in the Age of Cybernetics." *Body and Society* 1.3–4: 21–44.

Tomasulo, Frank P. (1990). "The Politics of Ambivalence: *Apocalypse Now* as Prowar and Antiwar Film." In Dittmar and Michaud. 145–158.

Toups, Wayne, and Nathan Williams. (1990). "Interviews." *Caliban* 9: 160–177.

Tournier, Michel. (1970 [1972]). *Le roi des Aulnes*. Paris: Gallimard. *The Ogre*. Trans. Barbara Bray. Garden City, NY: Doubleday.

Tournier, Michel. (1977 [1988]). *Le vent paraclet.* Paris: Gallimard. *The Wind Spirit: An Autobiography.*Trans. Arthur Goldhammer. Boston: Beacon Press.

Tournier, Michel. (1978 [1984]). *Le coq de bruyère.* Paris: Gallimard/Folio. *The Fetishist.* Trans. Barbara Wright. Garden City, NY: Doubleday.

Tournier, Michel. (1981). *Le vol du vampire.* Paris: Mercure de France.

Tournier, Michel. (1983 [1987]). *Gilles et Jeanne.* Paris: Gallimard. *Gilles and Jeanne.* Trans. Alan Sheridan. London: Methuen.

Trubetskoi, Nikolai Sergeevich. (1939, 1949). *Principes de phonologie.* Paris: Klincksieck.

Turkle, Sherry. (1978; 1992). *Psychoanalytic Politics: Jacques Lacan and Freud's French Revolution.* New York: Basic Books. 2nd ed., New York: Guilford Press.

Turkle, Sherry. (1995). *Life on the Screen: Identity in the Age of the Internet.* New York: Simon and Schuster.

Turkle, Sherry, and Seymour Papert. (1990). "Epistemological Pluralism: Styles and Voices within the Computer Culture." *Signs* 16.1: 128–157.

Turner, Victor. (1977). "Frame, Flow and Reflection: Ritual and Drama as Public Liminality." In *Performance in Postmodern Culture,* 33–55. Eds. Michel Benamou and Charles Caramello. Madison, Wi: Coda Press.

Turner, Victor. (1982). *From Ritual to Theatre: The Human Seriousness of Play.* New York: PAJ.

Ungar, Steven. (1983). *Roland Barthes: The Professor of Desire.* Lincoln: University of Nebraska Press.

Ungar, Steven. (1984). "Philosophy after Philosophy: Debate and Reform in France Since 1968." *Enclitic* 8.1–2: 13–26.

Valleley, Jean. (1979). "Martin Sheen: Heart of Darkness, Heart of Gold." *Rolling Stone.* 1 Nov.: 46–50.

Vernon, John. (1973). *The Garden and the Map. Schizophrenia in Twentieth-Century Literary and Culture.* Urbana: University of Illinois Press.

Virilio, Paul. (1975). *L'insécurité du territoire.* Paris: Stock.

Virilio, Paul. (1992). "Un dîner, l'été dernier . . . " *Libération.* 31 Aug.: 35.

Virilio, Paul. (1996). *Cybermonde: La politique du pire.* Paris: Textuel.

Vuillemin, Jules. (1938). *Essai sur les notions de structure et d'existence en mathématiques.* Paris: Hermann.

Vuillemin, Jules. (1960, 1962). *La philosophie de l'algèbre.* Paris: PUF.

Watson, Wallace. (1981). "Willard as Narrator: A Critique and an Immodest Proposal." *Conradiana* 13.1: 35–40.

Welchman, Alistair. (1997). "Machinic Thinking." In Ansell-Pearson 1997c, 211–229.

Weston, Jesse L. (1920, 1957). *From Ritual to Romance.* New York: Doubleday.

White, Eric. (1995). " 'Once They Were Men, Now They're Land Crabs': Monstrous Becomings in Evolutionist Cinema." In Halberstam and Livingston 1995, 244–266.

Wilbur, Shawn P. (1997). "An Archaeology of Cyberspaces: Virtuality, Community, Identity." In Porter 1997, 5–22.

Willard. (1971). Dir. Daniel Mann. Bing Crosby Productions.

Williams, James. (1997). "Deleuze on J. M. W. Turner: Catastrophism in Philosophy?" Ansell-Pearson 1997c, 233–246.

Williams, Raymond. (1977). *Marxism and Literature.* New York: Oxford University Press.

Willis, Sharon. (1993–1994). "The Fathers Watch the Boys' Room." *Camera Obscura* 32: 40–73.

Wills, David. (1995). *Prosthesis.* Stanford, CA: Stanford University Press.

Wilson, David L. (1993). "Suit of Network Access." *Chronicle of Higher Education.* 24 Nov.: A16.

Wilson, David L. (1995). "Vigilantes Gain Quiet Approval on Networks." *Chronicle of Higher Education.* 13 Jan.: A17–19.

Wilson, Robert Rawdon. (1995). "Cyber(body)parts: Prosthetic Consciousness." *Body and Society* 1.3–4: 239–259.

Wittig, Monique. (1992). *The Straight Mind and Other Essays.* New York: Harvester Wheatsheaf.

Wolfe, Charles. (1993). "Hallucination Simplex." *Long News in the Short Century* 4: 184–190.

Women and Performance. (1996). Issue 17: "Sexuality and Cyberspace." Online at http://www.echonyc.com/~women/Issue17/index.html.

Works and Days. (1995). Issue 25–26: "Cyberspaces: Pedagogy and Performance on the Electronic Frontier. Online at http://acorn.grove.iup.edu/en/workdays/wdhome.html.

Worthy, Kim. (1992). "Hearts of Darkness: Making Art, Making History, Making Money, Making 'Vietnam.' " *Cineaste* 19.2–3: 24–27.

Zourabichvili, François. (1994). *Deleuze: Une philosophie de l'événement.* Paris: PUF.

Zydeco. (1984). Dir. Nicholas R. Spitzer. Flower Films.

INDEX

Note: The abbreviations GD, FG, and D&G refer, respectively, to Gilles Deleuze, Félix Guattari, and Deleuze and Guattari. References to titles of works by all authors are listed under the initial letter of the title.

FRAGMENT